THE
POWER
OF
PLACE

James A. Swan, Ph.D., is currently Associate Professor of Anthropology at the California Institute of Integral Studies and with his wife Roberta is co-producer of Spirit of Place symposia series. (He was one of the founding members of the Division of Environment and Population Psychology at the American Psychological Association.) Swan is author of *Sacred Places, Environmental Education,* and the forthcoming *Nature as Teacher and Healer.* He has published over 100 articles in magazines such as *Shaman's Drum, Audubon,* and *Environmental Health Digest.*

"The reason that some of the greatest works of art are linked to places, I think, like Florence, Venice, Jerusalem, the Four Corners, is that the making of place includes dance, theater, ritual, costumes, and architecture beautifully suited, all of which links to nature."

—Landscape architect, Lawrence Halprin

Cover art provided by FPG, International NY
Cover design by Carol W. Wells

Sacred Ground in Natural

THE POWER OF PLACE

& Human Environments

an anthology by

James A. Swan

*This publication made possible with
the assistance of the Kern Foundation*

QUEST BOOKS
The Theosophical Publishing House

Wheaton, Ill. U.S.A.
Madras, India/London, England

The Theosophical Publishing House
P.O. Box 270
Wheaton, IL 60189-0270

A publication of the Theosophical Publishing House,
a department of The Theosophical Society in America

Library of Congress Cataloging-in Publication Data

The Power of place : sacred ground in natural and human
  environments / compiled by James A. Swan.
      p. cm.
  "This publication is made possible with the assistance of the
Kern Foundation."
  Contains presentations made at the 1988 and 1989 Spirit of
Place Symposiums.
  Includes bibliographical references.
  ISBN 0-8356-0670-8 : $14.95
  1. Sacred space—Congresses.   I. Swan, James A.   II. Spirit
of Place Symposium (1988 : University of California, Davis)
III. Spirit of Place Symposium (1989 : Grace Cathedral
(San Francisco, Calif.))
BL580.P684 1991
133.3'33—dc20   90-50583
                                                                CIP

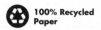

100% Recycled
Paper

This earth you stand on is your mother, whether you are red, white, black, brown, yellow, or blue. We must unite and help one another save our precious mother, for without Mother Earth to take care of and protect us we are a dead race.

Statement from the Navajo
Nation Historic Preservation
Dept. (delivered to the 1990
Spirit of Place symposium)

Contents

Acknowledgments

This anthology comes into being as the collective result of many, many people who have participated in the 1988 and 1989 Spirit of Place symposiums. Without the support of the Beldon Fund, the JRH Foundation, Joshua Mailman, Laurance Rockefeller, University Extension of U. C. Davis, and Grace Cathedral, the programs could never have happened. My wife, Roberta, co-produced the symposiums with great skill and patience.

Due to the requirements of space, we could only select a small number of presentations from the 130 given during these two programs. Many of the most stirring went beyond words, as they were songs, dances, costumes, rituals and symbolic shapes translated in wood carving, paintings, and photos. Hopefully someday a more pictorial presentation of the spirits of places can be done, giving credit to the images they draw up from the creative waters of the collective unconscious.

Shirley Nicholson, Senior Editor at Quest Books, deserves considerable credit for her eagerness to work with these presentations and bring them into a popular book format, as well as her editorial talents. Linda Allen, my literary agent, also deserves a special thanks for her skillful help in making this book become a reality.

At least 50% of the author's royalties from sales of this book go toward support for the Spirit of Place symposium and other programs and projects to identify, preserve and increase modern understanding and appreciation of sacred places.

(See pp. 361-62 for picture credits.)

Contributing Authors

Richard feather Anderson has a degree in architecture and thirteen years of experience in corporate architecture, urban design, and residential remodeling. Also a geomancer, he is director of the Westcoast Institute of Sacred Ecology in Berkeley, California. He is the former editor of the Berkeley Ecology Center newsletter and has published articles in the magazines *Design Spirit, Utne Reader,* and *Yoga Journal.*

James B. Beal is an aerospace engineer in the Advanced Quality Technology program at Martin Marietta Manned Space Systems in New Orleans. He studies the effects of low-level electromagnetic fields on health and creativity. Previously, he spent ten years with NASA at the Marshall Space Flight Center in Huntsville, Alabama, where he worked on the Saturn V Apollo Space Program.

William S. Becker is chairman of industrial design at the School of Art and Design at the University of Illinois in Chicago. Since working with Buckminster Fuller in the 1960s, he has been involved with the issues of renewable energy, sacred geometry, and the humanization of technology. He is currently working on a book about planetary issues and design with his wife Bethe Hagens.

Thomas Bender is an architect who lives on Neahkahnie Mountain in Nehalem, Oregon. He is one of the founders of the appropriate technology magazine *Rain* and is author of *The Environmental Design Primer,* as well as numerous articles in magazines including *Orion, East-West Journal,* and *Utne Reader.*

Edwin Bernbaum, Ph.D., is a research associate in comparative religion and mythology at the University of

California at Berkeley. He is a photographer and an experienced mountain climber. His articles and photographs have appeared in many magazines, including *Natural History, Shaman's Drum,* and *American Way.* He is the author of *The Way to Shambhala* and *Sacred Mountains of the World.*

Walter L. Brenneman, Jr., Ph.D., is a professor in the department of religion at the University of Vermont in Burlington. His books include *The Seeing Eye: Hermeneutical Phenomenology in the Study of Religion* and *Spirals: A Study in Symbol, Myth, and Ritual.*

Vine Deloria, Jr., J.D., is a Standing Rock Sioux. Former executive director of the National Congress of American Indians, he is a professor at the University of Colorado's Center for Studies of Ethnicity and Race in America at Boulder. His books include *Custer Died for Your Sins, We Talk, You Listen,* and *God Is Red.*

Rachel Fletcher is a designer and geometer who is artist-in-residence at Tufts University in Medford, Massachusetts. She was the cofounder and director of studies for KAIROS in London, which taught the principles of sacred geometry and architecture. Her articles on sacred geometry have appeared in *Parabola, Design Spirit, Via,* and *Building Design* magazines, and she is associate editor of *Design Spirit.*

Maelee Thomson Foster is a professional artist and associate professor of design in the department of architecture at the University of Florida, Gainesville. She has been studying megalithic sites of Europe since 1973 and received a commendation for her photography from the American Institute of Architects in 1989.

Elinor Gadon, Ph.D., is an associate professor at the California Institute of Integral Studies in San Francisco. Formerly, she taught in the graduate school of theology at Harvard University, and at The New School for Social Sciences, Tufts, and the University of California, Santa Barbara. She has traveled extensively throughout the East. She is author of *The Once and Future Goddess: A Symbol for Our Time.*

Bethe Hagens, Ph.D., is professor of anthropology and geography at Governor's State University, University Park, Illinois. She has published articles in magazines including *Creative Woman, Photovoltaics International,* and *Cultural Futures Research.*

Anna Halprin is a choreographer and dancer. She is director of the Tamalpa Institute in Kentfield, California, where she teaches dance, psychology, and spirituality to students from around the world. She has received numerous awards for her work in dance and theater, as well as for her applications of dance to healing. Her "Circle the Earth" dance ritual is performed in thirty countries. She is the author of *Movement Ritual* and the forthcoming *Circle the Earth: A Search for Living Myths Through Dance and Environment.*

Lawrence Halprin is a landscape architect. Among his best-known projects are the Levi-Strauss Plaza in San Francisco, Freeway Park in Seattle, the Franklin Delano Roosevelt Memorial in Washington, D.C., and the restoration of large areas of Jerusalem. He is the author of seven books, including *RSVP Cycles,* and two films, and the recipient of numerous awards, including the Gold Medal for Distinguished Achievement from the American Society of Landscape Architects.

Peter C. Hjersman has a degree in architecture from the University of California at Berkeley. He has worked in both the United States and Japan, synchronizing traditional spirit of place concepts with modern design. His projects have included toxic-free and allergy-free designs and geomantic energy designs, as well as houses, commercial buildings, and hospitals in Asia.

J. Donald Hughes, Ph.D., is president of the Colorado C. G. Jung Society and professor of history at the University of Colorado at Boulder and the University of Denver. He is former editor of *Environmental Review* and author of books including *American Indian Ecology* and *Ecology in Ancient Civilizations.*

Norris Brock Johnson, Ph.D., is an associate professor of anthropology at the University of North Carolina at Chapel Hill. His special interests include aesthetic anthropology and the symbolism and semiotics of space, place, and architectural form. As a senior fellow in landscape architecture at Dumbarton Oaks in Washington, D.C., he is working on a book on medieval period Japanese Zen Buddhist temples and temple gardens.

Stanley Krippner, Ph.D., a parapsychology researcher, is director of consciousness studies at the Saybrook Institute in San Francisco. The former president of the Association for Humanistic Psychology, he is author of many books including *Dreamworking, The Realms of Healing, Song of the Siren, Human Possibilities,* and *The Kirlian Aura.*

Bobby (Medicine Grizzlybear) Lake is a traditional Native healer and ceremonial leader. He is a professor at the Indian Education Evaluation and Resource Center at Gonzaga University, Spokane, Washington, where he provides technical assistance on Native cultures and education to school districts in Indian communities and on reservations. He is the author of *Chilula: People from the Ancient Redwoods* and the Quest book *Native Healer.*

Richard Leviton is a senior writer for *East-West Journal.* He is the former executive director of the Soyfoods Association of North America and former editor of *Soyfoods* magazine. He has published articles on mythology, the landscape and consciousness, and diet and the food industry. He is the author of *Tofu, Tempeh and Other Soy Delights.*

Kazuo Matsubayashi is a professor in the graduate school of architecture at the University of Utah in Salt Lake City. Born in Peru and raised in Japan, he has studied, practiced, and taught architecture in the United States and Japan. His special interests are architectural design and Japanese architecture.

David J. Nemeth, Ph.D., is assistant professor in the department of geography and planning at the University of Toledo in Toledo, Ohio. For many years he lived and worked in South Korea, beginning with Peace Corps service on Cheju Island in 1972. His recent work combines his interest in East Asia with environmental ethics.

Jay Hansford C. Vest, Ph.D., is assistant professor of liberal studies at the University of Washington, Tacoma. A Native American of Occaneechi-Monacan ancestry, he has researched and documented the sacred geography of Native peoples in Montana and Alberta. He has published articles in magazines including *Western Wildlands, The Trumpeter, Environmental Ethics,* and *Journal of Law and Religion.*

Sara Katherine Williams is an associate professor of landscape architecture at the University of Florida in Gainesville, and a landscape architect in private practice. Her special interests include historic preservation, park and recreation area design, and megalithic sites design processes.

Master Thomas Lin Yun is Grand Master of Black Sect Tantric Buddhism. An authority on Chinese Feng Shui geomancy, he has taught at Seton Hall University, South Orange, New Jersey; the University of California, Berkeley; and San Francisco State University. He has been a consultant to the United Nations, the Library of Congress, Pope John Paul II, the Dalai Lama, and the Bank of Hong Kong. He has established the Yun Lin Temple in Berkeley, California.

Elizabeth Rauscher, Ph.D., is the director of Tecnic Laboratories in Golden Valley, Nevada. She has worked as a research physicist at Lawrence Berkeley Laboratories and has taught at the University of California at Berkeley, Stanford University, and John F. Kennedy University in California. She has published four books, including a text on electromagnetism, and over one hundred articles, and has served as a consultant to the United Nations.

Daniel Stokols, Ph.D., is a professor and director of the Program in Social Ecology at the University of California, Irvine. He has published numerous articles in professional journals and anthologies, and, with Irwin Altman, co-authored *Handbook of Environmental Psychology.*

James A. Swan, Ph.D., is co-producer of The Spirit of Place symposiums, associate professor of anthropology at the California Institute of Integral Studies, and president of the Institute for the Study of Natural Systems, in Mill Valley, California. His books include *Environmental Education; Sacred Places: How the Living Earth Seeks Our Friendship;* and the forthcoming *Nature as Teacher and Healer.* He is also an actor, who has appeared on television in the series "Midnight Caller" and in the film *Tucker.*

Introduction

A fundamental element of religion is an intimate relationship with the land on which the religion is practiced.[1]
                                        Vine Deloria, Jr.[1]

The ancient Greeks sited a shrine at Delphi to honor the
earth Goddess Gaia. Their choice of location was not by
chance. At Delphi, Greek wisdom said that the "genus
loci" or spirit of place in that place made it most suitable
for honoring Gaia. The sages asserted among other things
that a mysterious substance called the "plenum" bubbled
up from the ground there in abundance, and that such
an abundance favored Gaia and the work of the priestess
oracle, Pithia, to prophesy—clearly establishing Delphi
as the touchstone place for planners and designers to visit
in pilgrimage to seek out their origin.

Pliny the Elder, the Greek naturalist and sage who lived
from 23 - 79 A.D., coined the term "geomancy" when he
met some Persian Magi who divined the right action for
each place, present and future, by tossing stones on the
ground and studying their configurations. The term was
new, but determining the right actions for each place was
not. The art and science of environmental planning and
architecture have been an integral part of human life since
even before King Solomon's temple. Geomancy is a parent
of the modern environmental design process. At the core
of geomantic wisdom everywhere is the assertion that not
all places are alike; some places have more power and
presence than others. We all know this when we walk into
a hallowed shrine like Chartres Cathedral, stand beside
Stonehenge's living stones, or ascend Mount Fuji with
thousands of other devout pilgrims.

Modern psychology and design have tossed aside such
ideas as places of power, but our bodies and minds still
hear their call and respond to them. Hundreds of thousands
of tourists flock to Delphi each year to witness the old
temples and shrines. Many, including the late mythologist

1

Joseph Campbell, have been moved to remark that the craggy hills of Delphi are one of the most inspirational places on earth. This is why Delphi is listed by the World Heritage Committee, a UNESCO organization, as one of the World Heritage sites of the world which have "exceptional and universal value" as a cultural or natural treasure.

Among those inspired by Delphi these days is a group of Greek governmental planners and industrialists who want to erect a new temple at Delphi: a massive aluminum smelter. The plant is to be sited seven and one-half miles to the southwest of Delphi in the tiny hilltop village of Aya Efthymia, upwind of the oracle's shrine, which has been there since 1400 B.C.

As in thousands of similar land-use conflict situations all around the world, the fate of Delphi is being decided in lengthy hearings where the proposed developmental plans are being weighed against the environmental and cultural heritage impacts. While modern science and technology enable more sophisticated analysis of all the variables involved than ever before possible, there is an important difference between modern design and planning and its parent, geomancy. Geomancers assert that there is a correct action for each place, which can best harmonize human actions with nature and the cosmos at that place. Perhaps symptomatic of our seduction by the reductionist Newtonian-Cartesian mode of scientific thinking, we try to weigh benefits and costs to determine right action. Geomancers, in contrast, say they ultimately consult with the "spirit" of the place to determine what is best done there. Missing from our modern practice of planning is the concept that there are forces beyond immediate secular forces and geological basics that bear on what is best done at each given site.

Linguists suggest that the most important words or concepts in a culture have the most minute variations of meanings, indicating an acute awareness of that dimension of reality. My dictionary lists twenty-one different meanings for "spirit." The majority refer to an ethereal life force possessing a spiritual quality that implies understanding a higher truth, which would seem to indicate that the concept of spirit is very important to us. To know the spirit of place then would seemingly be essential to the art of planning, designing and building sustainable societies. Yet a check of the massive library of the University of California system through 1989 reveals only two popular books with titles reflecting the spirit of place theme, both written by British diarists more than fifty years ago—Lawrence Durrell and Alyce Meynard—reflecting on their feelings about how the places they visit while traveling influence their writings.

Searching for a definition of "the spirit of place," I find no guidance in my dictionary. But another literary artist who was very aware of how place influenced his work, D. H. Lawrence, understood the spirit of place very well when he said in 1923:

> Every continent has its own great spirit of place. Every people is polarized in some particular locality, which is home, the homeland. Different places on the face of the earth have different vital effluence, different vibration, different chemical exhalation, different polarity with different stars: call it what you like, but the spirit of place is a great reality.[2]

As is so often the case in a technological society, artists have more license to speak freely about things of the spirit and their feelings than those in the fields of science and design, which have lost their early spiritual origins and forgotten their roots in the subjective experience of life. Hidden within Lawrence's statement is the implication that some special places may have extraordinary inspirational qualities, which is clearly a special secret to writers and anyone else who can gain the favor of a special place.

Ask yourself where in the world you think that you would feel most powerful. Nearly everyone, upon reflection, can name several special places of power. One exception is the gloomy Frederich Nietzsche, who felt that he spent most of his life being at the wrong place at the wrong time. However, all around the world there is a rich tradition of special places, the most significant of them almost always described in terms of their spiritual or sacred values. According to this wisdom, the power of the sacred places involves right action by human society, as the Chinese book of wisdom, the *I Ching*, advises: "Heaven and earth determine the places. The holy sages fulfill the possibilities of the places. Through the thoughts of men and the thoughts of spirits, the people are enabled to participate in the possibilities."[3]

"The spirit of place" or *genus loci* may be a nearly forgotten term in our modern vocabulary, but the magnetic pull of special places is seemingly growing more powerful than ever. Palenque, Lasceaux, Mount Fuji, Jerusalem, Stonehenge, Mount Kilimanjaro, Lourdes, the Great Pyramid, Machu Picchu—just to mention the names of sacred places is to stir fantasies and thoughts of travel. Tourism is fast becoming the world's largest industry, worth over $2 trillion in 1986, employing 65 million people and accounting for over 25% of the world's international trade in human services.[4] According to Lester Borley, Director of the National Trust of Scotland and an authority on world tourism, "perhaps the most powerful of all world tourism motives is the desire to visit special places which have a spiritual quality."[5]

One danger of our craving for sacred places is loving them to death. Stonehenge is now fenced off to protect it from millions of visitors. One proposal is to build a concrete replica nearby for tourists to visit—somehow assuming the experience of visiting the fabricated shrine would be the same as approaching the real one. At the Big Horn Medicine Wheel in Wyoming, an American Stonehenge, the Forest Service proposes an asphalt parking lot and interpretive program. This developmental plan is met by howls of protests from indigenous Indian tribes who see the stone astronomical observatory as their equivalent of Chartres Cathedral or Glastonbury. Northern Cheyenne medicine man Bill TallBull, leader of the Medicine Wheel Alliance, says his group wants the ancient stone circle to be preserved as a National Park, given the same respect as the Lincoln Monument.

On Mount Sinai, the holy mountain of Horeb where the Lord gave Moses the law, the Prophet Muhammad sought inspiration, and Saint Catherine had her visions, a large billboard today proclaims: "At this site will be 500 villas, a tourist village with 250 rooms, two hotels with 400 rooms, shopping center, school and hospital, supplied by all facilities."

Today some 30,000 visitors make a pilgrimage to Mt. Sinai every year to make the two-and-a-half mile hike up steps carved in rock in the sixth century by Byzantine monks. If this complex is built the Egyptian government projects some 565,000 tourists a year will visit Mt. Sinai, many taking the planned cable car ride to the summit where, according to one plan, they will find a restaurant and gambling casino.[6]

Jean Piaget made many important contributions to modern psychology, possibly because he was trained as a naturalist to observe objectively, to record his data and then to develop conclusions, rather than starting with a theory to explain how the world works. Among his insights is that at all times there is a "continuity of exchanges" going on between people and their environment.[7] I can find little in modern psychology to elaborate on Piaget's observation of how environments influence our lives. There is a slowly growing division of behavioral sciences called environmental psychology, but it has tended to avoid issues like sacred places in favor of handing out questionnaires to measure visitor satisfaction with the views tourists see driving through parks, or exploring how indoor environments affect mental health. This choice is probably largely due to funding being more readily available for conservative applications of psychology to immediate needs, although in any field basic questions are the most difficult to grasp effectively.

The issue of how nature influences consciousness is left almost exclusively to artists, poets and writers, even though the statistics on recreation show that we are drawn to special places to recreate, and our unconscious voices call us to visit special places even though we are not sure why.

Looking to the psychologies of traditional societies, one finds a wealth of information about the relationship between people and the environment. All around the world among indigenous peoples right relationship between place and people is seen as the core of mental health. Carl Jung agreed with this wisdom, incidentally, suggesting that the people of the United States would never find true peace until they come into harmony with the place where they live.

Have we as a species lost our need to be environmentally aware as we have become "civilized"? It seemed for a while that we no longer needed to listen to the gentle, soft voices of nature which come to us at special places. Guidance on right livelihood and creativity, we were taught, comes from books and media. The primal environmental awareness of place was set aside in favor of progress, development and growth in our land-planning vocabulary. But today our senses and our increasingly sensitive instruments are telling us we were heading toward a massive ecological catastrophe because we have lost our primary environmental understanding. Now we grope for answers, and as Jung suggested, many may lie in an objective understanding of our psychic roots.

The growing consensus among scientists, designers and even politicians is that we need to make the next few decades the years of the environment, or there will not be a future for our children. And if we do this seriously, our way of thinking and behaving will have to change, perhaps very dramatically, including recovering our forgotten sense of place. It is not that technology per se is evil and anti-ecological, but that the forces which shape it are un-connected to the natural intuitive wisdom which springs from place and nature. In the words of William Ruckelshaus, former Director of the U.S. Environmental Protection Agency (1970-73 and 1983-84):

> In creating the consciousness of advanced sustainability, we shall have to redefine our concepts of political and economic feasibility. These concepts are, after all, simply human constructs; they were different in the past, and they will surely change in the future. But the earth is real, and we are obliged by the fact of our utter dependence on it to listen more closely than we have to its messages.[8]

Following Ruckelshaus' guidance, we must learn to listen and be more aware of the voices of the earth and nature; rediscovering an art of survival which was known very well before the advent of modern science and technology. Unconsciously we still know that the spirit of place is important to us. Now we must understand why and what it can tell us as we rediscover how to perceive it.

The Spirit of Place Symposium Program

The spirit of place concept is not new, but its use in modern times has not been central or prominent. Here and there you find creative people, often world-renowned leaders in their fields, who understand the concept and apply it to their work. In most cases, however, they admit to not talking about such an idea much, for they do not even have a good language to describe it. After contacting people and places where ancient traditions are still honored and practiced, many people assert that they understand the spirit of place and how it works. But when faced with communicating why places are special to modern people, most representatives of traditional cultures report considerable frustration, for modern people have forgotten how to feel and dream. To create, or recreate, the art and science of knowing the spirit of each place, one strategy is to bring together those who do recognize the concept and explore the knowledge that already exists, seeking to build a critical mass of place consciousness which can bridge ancient wisdom with modern times.

In 1987 my wife and I began conducting the Spirit of Place symposiums by issuing a widely publicized call for papers, inviting people to submit proposals for presentations concerning the nature of place consciousness, its significance in traditional societies, and its potential value in modern times. We received over 100 proposals, from architects, landscape designers, scientists, artists, aerospace engineers, scholars, and members of traditional cultural groups from around the world. In September of 1988 70 people presented these papers at the University of California at Davis to an audience of 350, at a symposium which celebrated the spirit of place by a Paul Horn flute concert and an Anna Halprin dance concert.

We found that many people from all disciplines and many diverse cultural backgrounds had a strong desire to have place consciousness become a more important part of modern life. Indians and other indigenous peoples asserted that the spirit of place was a core concept for understanding their cultures. Some modern designers agreed on its importance. Sim Van der Ryn, former California state architect, went so far as to say, "I want to be a part of a culture where the spirit of place is part of everyone's language, experience and practice."

Representatives of six different Native American tribes attended this meeting as presenters, and there was clear agreement about their shared perception of the value of certain places. William Fields, a Cherokee and then Director of Indian Affairs for the U.S. National Park Service, stated that "sacred places in nature are the places where Indian people find health, beauty, balance, peace, meaning and love." Reading a special message from a Northern Cheyenne elders' council, Jose Lucero, a Tewa and member of the Santa Clara Pueblo, stated "Sacred sites are for the protection of all people for the four colors of man—black, yellow, red and white."

It also became clear that a serious psychology of place involved facing issues which modern psychology has not dealt with. Master Thomas Yun Lin, the Grand Master of Black Sect Tantric Buddhism and a world-renowed Feng-Shui geomancer, asserted that "we have over 100 senses to understand the places where we live and work." Architect Tom Bender made an important observation that there is a big difference between being a tourist and being a pilgrim, and that while people study tourism, almost no one studies making pilgrimages. Psychologist Robert Sommer, one of the original founders of environmental psychology, observed that some people seemed to "become voices for a place," such as John Muir for Yosemite or Henry David Thoreau for Walden Pond, and said that modern psychology could not explain why.

It was abundantly clear from this first program that the spirit of place is an extremely important concept to many people with applications to many areas of life. Consequently, in August of 1989 a second Spirit of Place symposium was held at Grace Cathedral in San Francisco, California, the largest religious building west of the Mississippi in the United States. The first session had substantiated the value of the concept of special places, and so this second program focused on exploration of sacred places and spaces. Following a similar procedure of issuing an open call for papers to address the general spirit of place theme, as well as the nature of sacred places and spaces and their value to human life, 60 proposals were selected. A crowd of some 350 people attended, and the program was celebrated in a special concert, "Celebration for Mother Earth," held in the massive nave of the church where 600 people listened. Then songs and dances of 12 different tribal groups were represented in a program based on an enactment of the Hopi creation myth, with the music of keyboard artist Steven Halpern and myself weaving together the fabric of the evening.

It became clear from this program that sacred places are seen around the world as touchstones of cultural identity, was well as inspirational points for health, creativity and religious worship. In modern times, we learned, churches have tended to use economic and political motives for siting their houses of worship, as opposed to geomantic wisdom. Religion, many people felt, had become a cultural mechanism to build community more than facilitating seeking spiritual communion. In contrast to this pattern, we found Grace Cathedral to be sited on an ancient Indian sacred place marked by two artesian springs. Chinese geomancers agreed with the significance of Grace's siting, declaring it "the eye of the dragon" of San Francisco. More than one person wondered aloud if this siting had helped build such a massive physical structure to communicate the human desire to express spiritual values and their importance in our life. There was a strong consensus that the most spiritual architecture tends to be built at special places which make them become amplifiers of the spirit of that place as well as design statements for religious traditions.

It also became clear that all around the world sacred places are in trouble. Developmental pressures threaten to turn them into roads, logging projects, parking lots, amusement parks, mines, electrical power generating plants and resorts. Part of the problem, it seems, is that modern society tends to see sacred places as belonging only to earlier civilizations, unless modern churches or cemeteries are built upon them. This makes it especially hard to establish sacred values of a place in a court case or planning board hearing. Many Indian people also asserted that this view makes it difficult to protect their ancestral burial grounds from being dug up, either in the name of research or for profiteering. And even those sites which are protected may be subject to vandalism, participants learned, after a delegation went to a Miwok fertility stone on top of Ring Mountain just north of San Francisco and found the ancient petroglyphs heavily scratched by modern graffiti and some malicious destruction for no understandable purpose.

Exploring how modern people might become more aware of the subtle significance of place, several scientists shared our growing understanding of how electromagnetic fields and unusual air, water and soil chemistry at certain places could help explain their uniqueness. A common finding among cultures all around the world, we found,

was that at sacred places there is more life force energy
which has both secular and sacred qualities. Our understanding of subtle fields and their influence on our lives
is just beginning to be understood, but a number of people
suggested that we can reinvent geomancy with the cooperation of modern science, if we are open-minded. Several
people noted that acupuncture was widely scorned in the
medical community until objective studies documented
its therapeutic values. Today acupuncture is licensed in
most states, even though modern science has yet to substantiate the existence of the life force energy *chi* which
acupuncture supposedly manipulates.

Reflecting on how architecture can shape our lives, many
people lamented about what Frank Lloyd Wright called
our modern "cash and carry" style of architecture and
design. Many people asserted this was partially due to
designers having lost touch with the psychological roots
of the design process in themselves as well as in contact
with nature. Reflecting on the potential for design to give
meaning to our lives, Standing Rock Sioux attorney-author
Vine Deloria, Jr., gave important guidance when he described
his own culture's architectural values and then said to
modern designers that a "building should tell you everything
about the society you live in; its history, its possibilities,
and its future."

We also found that one of the ways in which the power
of sacred sites are affirmed is by documenting special
experiences which people have at such places. These data
illustrate the power of place in human history, for nearly
all modern religions trace their origins to spiritual inspira-
tions received from pilgrimages to special places.[9]

From these two programs and 130 presentations, the
following selection of papers has been assembled to articulate
the spirit of place concept and its value to modern and
ancient times. Nearly all are original presentations, although
in one or two cases we have sought out special papers to
cover gaps in knowledge identified by the program participants. Their collective voice calls us to remember the
power of place. They urge us to learn again to listen to
the quiet voices of nature, to take this precious guidance
and turn it into a new earth wisdom which can be translated into an organic art, education, architecture, design
and planning, which result in an ecologically-sustainable
future.

Notes

1. Vine Deloria, Jr. *God Is Red.* New York, NY: Grosset and Dunlap, 1973, p. 296.
2. D. H. Lawrence. *Studies In Classical American Literature.* New York, NY: Thomas Seltzer and Sons, 1923, p. 8-9.
3. *The I Ching.* Richard Wilhelm trans. Princeton, NJ: Princeton University Press, 1967, p. 354.
4. "Ecotourism: Loving Nature on Its Own Terms." *Calypso Log,* June 1990, The Cousteau Society, pp. 16-17.
5. Lester Borley. Keynote address to the First World Congress on Cultural Parks, Mesa Verde, CO, September, 1984.
6. Lance Morrow. "Trashing Mount Sinai." *Time,* March 19, 1990, p. 92.
7. Jean Piaget. *The Child's Conception of the World.* New York, NY: Harcourt Brace and World, 1929.
8. William Ruckelshaus. "Toward A More Sustainable World." *Scientific American*, Vol. 261, No. 3, Sept. 1989, p. 168.
9. James Swan. *Sacred Places: How The Living Earth Seeks Our Friendship.* Santa Fe, NM: Bear and Co., 1990.

I
The Meaning of Place

At the 1988 Spirit of Place symposium, psychologist Robert Sommer reported on the damming of the Stanislaus River in California and showed slides of graffiti which people had painted on bridges in that area, expressing their outrage and grief about the loss of a wild river. At the end of his talk Sommer, reflecting on his presentation, said, "I am a spokesman for a place. I cannot say how or why I was chosen for this role, but it feels very right to me to do so."

Like a Freudian slip, when we disclose an underlying unconscious sentiment without conscious recognition that we are doing so, Sommer's remark reminds us that places call us to them and in some cases move us to become their voice. How many people would be happy to go just anywhere on a vacation? Few, I think. There is a deep voice inside us which understands nature and our own nature. In modern times the hectic pace of life tends to drown out this voice as we watch the clock, drive the freeway, catch the bus, read the newspaper, watch the news on television, prepare for an important meeting or rush to our next appointment. But an awareness of this voice is still there in the photos and paintings in our home and workplace, even in the ads on the billboards for beer, cigarettes and insurance. The voice calls out to us in popular music, too. "Chicago, Chicago," "Moon Over Miami," "Shenandoah," "The Erie Canal," "Galveston," "Grand Canyon Suite," "Sitting on the Dock on the Bay," "We Built This City on Rock and Roll" and a thousand other melodies speak of spirits of special places which are important to us, although we are not always quite sure why.

This nature wisdom also exists in many of the best of children's stories and popular movies. Winnie-the-Pooh has his "thinking place." Brer Rabbit has his "laughing place." Walt Disney's Fantasia features "A Night On Bald Mountain." Indiana Jones is always finding exciting adventures at sacred places of power. Is it simple coincidence that Steven Spielberg's Close Encounters of the Third Kind focused on Devil's Tower National Monument, the sacred place of the Lakota where the Sun Dance was once held? The arts gain their power from having an easier relationship with the unconscious than modern science has been able to establish. At their best, they remind us what it is to be fully human.

Recently T. George Harris, editor-in-chief of Psychology Today, asked my opinion as to why so many people were upset when the Rockefeller family sold Rockefeller Center to a Japanese corporation. Upon reflection, I responded that Americans do not have a strong place consciousness like other nations around the world, but that people need to have special places to feel grounded and bonded to the place where they live. Rockefeller Center, for many Americans, had become a sort of national symbol, perhaps even a special place of power.

In this first section, four papers help us remember just how important place is. Two of the four come from Native Americans because, unlike many countries around the world, the United States has attempted to deny and pave over the value of the earth wisdom of the indigenous people who understand the earth's quiet voices. We need to listen to what they say with great sincerity, to remember what we have forgotten about living in harmony with nature and the peace it can bring. My sense is that if we can listen to their wisdom, we will discover, as Bob Sommer reports, just how important place really is to us two-legged ones. As Freud and Jung counseled us, pay attention to those moments when the wisdom of the unconscious bubbles up into consciousness in dreams, feelings and voices and awakens our conscious mind to discrepancies that need to be corrected to restore harmony and balance in our lives. Learning to understand these quiet voices is a foundation for creating a new earth consciousness of ecological sustainability.

1

Spirit of Place in the Western World

J. DONALD HUGHES

Spirit of place is the power that is manifested in sacred space. People who enter the space, and are aware of the spirit, experience it in various ways: often as healing, meaning, transformation, strength, or connectedness with nature; though sometimes as threat, risk, or ordeal.

That some places are different from others in very special respects was evident to our earliest human ancestors; indeed, many of our non-human evolutionary progenitors sensed it, too. To understand how early humans responded to place, one can remember the deep cave chambers of Altamira and Lascaux, where Cro-Magnon hunters let the shapes of the walls suggest the sacred animal forms they painted there, or the earlier cave of Basua where Neanderthals found a zoomorphic stalagmite that became the body of a bear in their shamanic ceremonies.[1] A cave has numinosity; it resembles the womb of Mother Earth, and the space inside is sacred. Symbolically, what is placed as a seed within, whether it be an enactment of hunting, a call for healing, the transformative ritual of initiation, or the burial of a dead relative in the fetal position, will come to birth or rebirth in the outer world. A cave is a place of power, a place of spirit.

In the oldest surviving epic poem, which can be traced back to ancient Sumeria almost 5,000 years ago, we are told that the hero Gilgamesh and his companion approached the protective wall around a sacred park of cedar trees with the intention of cutting them down. Groves of trees, especially large, old ones, summon the presence of spirit as much as caves do. The grove that Gilgamesh threatened was probably like another described by the Roman poet

15

Ovid: "Here stands a silent grove black with the shade of oaks; at the sight of it, anyone could say, 'There is a spirit here!' "[2] There was a spirit in Gilgamesh's grove, too, but for him at least it took the form of a huge monster named Humbaba, and Humbaba understandably wanted to kill the intruders. This tells us a lot about how the ancients looked at sacred space. It had to be respected; it had to be approached in the right way, because depending on how one came to it, its power could be either vitalizing or very dangerous. Now Gilgamesh did break down the gate to the sacred grove, after a terrible fight killed Humbaba, cut down the cedar trees, and carried them back to his city to build a palace for himself. But he had made a big mistake. Disaster after disaster befell him: the goddess Ishtar sent the Bull of Heaven against him, his companion was killed, and he was driven to the end of the earth in a fruitless search for immortality, all because he had not respected the spirit of place.[3]

The ancient Egyptians were conscious of the power of place. Their tombs and temples were located and oriented according to the geometry of the Earth and heavenly bodies, particularly the sun. They practiced geomancy, the lore of establishing buildings in relationship to the forms and energies of the earth. When the pharaoh Akhenaton established a new capital for Egypt dedicated to his monotheistic sun god Aton, he selected a place where an opening in the eastern cliffs would cradle the rising sun on certain important days. The cliff opening and sun formed the hieroglyphic sign for "sunrise" or "the horizon of the Aton." The temples themselves were built with a succession of open courtyards, and their halls were forests of columns in semi-darkness, deliberately designed to enhance the awe of a spirit-filled place.

The sacred chambers of Egyptian temples were often used for a form of dream healing called incubation. After careful preparation, a person would sleep in a sanctuary, and would receive a dream that gave instructions or granted healing directly. Once a woman who wanted a child and had been unable to conceive slept overnight in a temple. Imhotep, the god of that place, appeared to her in a dream, showed her a plant, and told her to find it, make a tea of its leaves, and give it to her husband to drink. She did so, and that very night became pregnant by him.[4] The ability to grant significant dreams seems to be a virtually universal characteristic of sacred places, and the ancients recorded countless cases of this phenomenon. The pharaoh himself (or, sometimes, herself), sought and received messages in this way. Thothmes IV, before he became pharaoh, slept near the Great Sphinx and received instructions in a dream to clear the sand from that monument, which was considered to contain the god Harmakhis. After he did so and became king, he erected a carved stone stela that records the dream.

The ancients generally considered the experience of a great dream as a sign that the place where it came was inhabited by spirit. The Hebrew patriarch Jacob slept with his head on a stone and saw a dream of a great ladder reaching from Earth to Heaven, with angels ascending and descending, and Yahweh standing above it. He heard God say, "By you and your seed shall all the families of the Earth be blessed." When he woke up, Jacob exclaimed, "Surely Yahweh is in this place; and I did not know it." He felt fear, and continued, "How awesome is this place! This is none other than the house of God, and this is the gate of heaven."[5] He set up the stone as a pillar, and called the place Bethel, the House of God.

Mount Horeb, where Moses saw the burning bush, was declared to be a sacred place by the voice of Yahweh, which said, "Take your shoes off your feet, for the place on which you are standing is holy ground."[6] The Book of Exodus goes on to say it was no mortal who proclaimed that a particular location was sacred, but God's own voice. God also appeared to Moses on Mount Sinai. The existence of several holy places was an embarrassment in later Biblical times. From King Josiah on, the monarchy of Israel insisted that since God is One, God should have only one sanctuary, Mount Zion in Jerusalem. In most of the Bible, the words "holy place" refer to the Temple there. Bethel, Horeb, and Sinai, then, could not also be holy. Even though Mount Zion was undoubtedly a sacred place before it was consecrated for the Temple, the Jews believed that it was holy because it was sanctified by God's people at God's command, not because of any divine presence inherent in the spot. The dominant view in later Judaism was that God, the transcendent creator, should not be identified with his creation, even though it might serve as marvelous evidence of his power and benevolence.[7]

The Greeks and Romans, with their numerous gods,

were not troubled by such considerations. Their landscape was dotted with hundreds of places where spirit was manifested to them. Some of these had great antiquity. For example, mythology records that the site of Delphi was originally sacred to Mother Earth (*Ge* or *Gaia*), who gave dream oracles to people who came there and slept on the ground. Not surprisingly, Delphi was situated on the slopes of centrally located Mount Parnassos, the *omphalos*, or navel of the earth. It was also the lair of Python, Gaia's sacred snake. Afterwards, Apollo, the male god of the northern invaders, killed Python and took over the sanctuary. Then he began to give oracles of his own through the mouth of a priestess whom he possessed. Apollo's oracles were unclear and could often be interpreted in more than one way. But Mother Earth, by threatening to give clear prophetic dreams to everyone who slept on her breast anywhere, forced Apollo to compromise.[8] Apollo granted Gaia the right to have an altar in every one of his temples, and she agreed to hide the meaning of dreams in symbolism. This myth indicates that when the Greeks came to Greece in the years after 2000 B.C. and partially displaced the people of the land, they began to worship both their own gods and the gods of the local folk at places where the earlier inhabitants had already found the presence of spirits. The sacred structures of the local people were oriented with reference to land forms, which they usually perceived as body forms because of their feminine mounds and hollows and masculine promontories. What the landforms represented on a visible, symbolic level was the indwelling spirit of place.[9] Greek temple architecture fittingly represented the character of the locations chosen for it, its parts proportioned and related to express organic unity.

A sacred precinct, called *hieros temenos* in Greek and *templum* in Latin, was an area set aside and often walled to mark the boundary between holy and ordinary space. These usually contained groves of trees and springs or other water, though often mountaintops or other prominent features were so treated. Within them the environment was preserved in its natural state. The presence of spirit was often recognized in the quality of the environment itself, which called forth an inner response. As the Roman philosopher Seneca remarked, "If you come upon a grove of old trees that have lifted their crowns up above the common height and shut out the light of the sky by the darkness of their interlacing boughs, you feel that there is a spirit in the place, so lofty is the wood, so lone the spot, so wondrous the thick unbroken shade."[10] Of course, individual trees were inhabited by spirits called dryads, and naiads dwelt within streams, springs, and waterfalls. But it was always the place itself that was the temple, originally; the forest, not the structure erected to protect an image of the god. Worship was in the out-of-doors. It was illegal to disturb the place and the living things in it by hunting, fishing, polluting the water, tree-cutting, removing wood or leaves, plowing, sowing, pasturing domestic animals, setting fires, or erecting unauthorized buildings. Suppliants who sought protection in holy places were granted asylum and could not be killed. Punishments for violating these rules were severe and enforced by city governments.[11] However, the spirits themselves were thought to be perfectly capable of exacting their own revenge. When Erysichthon ignored the protests of a dryad and cut down her tree, he was stricken with hunger that could never be satisfied.[12] Hunger seems a particularly appropriate punishment for a crime against the land.

Some of the *temene* were therapeutic sanctuaries, where those suffering from illness would come to pray to Asclepius and other spirits of healing. Various forms of treatment, including dream incubation, were used to find cures.[13] Modern experts on environmental medicine who have studied ancient healing sites such as Epidaurus and Kos have remarked that their climate and exposure are conducive to the treatment of respiratory and other ailments. Hippocrates, the founder of medicine, recognized that some localities had healing properties, especially for certain diseases, while others had bad effects. He advised the founders of cities to take these factors into account.[14]

The philosophers also had something to say about place (*topos* in Greek). Theophrastus maintained that every living thing has an *oikeios topos* or "favorable place," where all the energies and conditions are suitable to its flourishing. Aristotle made a similar point in regard to animals. The Greek word used here to characterize a harmonious relationship between an organism and its environment is *oikeios*, which shares a root with the modern word "ecology."[15] Plato commented directly on the spirit

of place in his dialogue, the *Laws*. "Some localities have
a more marked tendency than others to produce better or
worse men, and we are not to legislate in the face of the
facts," he remarks, implying that *nomos*, human culture,
must be altered to accord with the natural environment in
a particular *topos*. "Some places, I conceive, owe their
propitious or ill-omened character to variations in wind
and sunshine, others to the waters, and yet others to the
products of the soil, which not only provide the body with
better or worse sustenance, but equally affect the mind
for good or ill." Plato continues, "Most markedly conspicuous
of all, again, will be localities which are the homes of some
supernatural influences, or the haunts of spirits who give
a gracious or ungracious reception to successive bodies
of settlers. A sagacious legislator will give these facts all
the considerations a person can, and do the best to adapt
legislation to them."[16] Here Plato has the beginnings of a
theory for geomancy. But he went even further. Following
Pythagoras, he extended the idea of a spirit inhabiting a
place to the entire universe, which he envisioned as a living
body inhabited by a world soul in vast organic unity. In
this view every place forms a meaningful part of the whole,
although some have more vital functions than others.
Plutarch adds that certain parts of the earth's surface (the
ones least inhabited by human beings) are essential to the
health and vitality of the rest.[17] Thus respected philosophers
would agree that proper relationship with spirit of place
is necessary to the well-being of the whole world.

The advent of Christianity as the dominant religion of
the Western world changed the way in which spirit of place
was conceived. Like Judaism, from which it sprang, Christianity was anxious that its followers not confuse creation
with the Creator. Paul the Apostle taught that the natural
world had fallen into sin along with mankind and needed
to be redeemed by the saving work of Christ.[18] John urged
Christians not "to love the world or the things in the world."[19]
By "world," he meant non-Christian society, but many in
the Church took it to mean the created earth. And if the
whole creation is fallen, what happens to spirit of place?
It is true that the New Testament does not teach that nature
is evil, but that even in its fallen state it exhibits the power
and deity of God. Within the first few centuries, however,
many Christians became convinced that the natural world

was the province of the devil. Although that idea is not really orthodox, since the sacraments show natural creation as a vehicle of the grace of God, the conception of the world in the power of darkness was an image that helped shape the imagination of medieval European Christianity. Bishop Synesius of Cyrene, for example, prayed to be released from "the demon of earth, the demon of matter, . . . who stands athwart the ascending path."[20]

In spite of this attitude, veneration of place emerged very soon in popular Christian piety. Jesus himself had loved nature, and had gone to special places to meditate and speak to his heavenly Father.[21] Once when the spirit of a place was violated, he became very angry, and drove the money-changers from the Temple that was intended to be a house of prayer for all people.[22] The places associated with his life became sacred and were occupied by churches and monasteries: Bethlehem, the place of his baptism in the Jordan, the Mount of the Beatitudes, the Mount of Transfiguration, the Mount of Olives, the Garden of Gethsemane, Golgotha or Calvary, the Holy Sepulcher. The actual locations had been forgotten, usually, so the places chosen for honor were ones recommended by their ambience. Actually, several of those just mentioned were located by Helena, the mother of the emperor Constantine, during her visit to the Holy Land at an advanced age in the early fourth century A.D. Most of them were founded on spots formerly occupied by classical sanctuaries.[23] In the Christian East, Byzantine architecture developed for churches was designed to present an inner space in which the worshipper was surrounded by sacred art and enveloped in a spiritual atmosphere.

As for those places where pre-Christian people had revered the spirit of place, they were to be destroyed. The oak of the god Thor at Geismar, cut down by St. Boniface,[24] and the Grove of Irminsul or Yggdrasil, the universal Tree, the most sacred place of the Saxons, leveled at the order of Charlemagne,[25] are well-known examples. The Christian Roman emperors of the late third and early fourth centuries A.D. commanded the destruction of all classical temples that had not already been adapted to other uses.[26] The same asylum for fugitives once offered in classical *temene* was later granted in churches. But it is also interesting that Christians considered it an act of merit to establish churches on the sites of classical sanctuaries. For church leaders, this was both a sign of Christian victory over evil powers and a way of attracting devotion away from paganism to the Church. Pope Gregory I (c. 601 A.D.) advised missionaries to select such sites for consecration, and also to Christianize the holidays and ceremonies that had been formerly celebrated in them.[27] For many people, such adaptation was a sign of continuity, since they could continue to visit the places where they had always found spirit, and conduct practices that were very much the same.

During Medieval times, numerous sacred sites were the scene of Christian devotion. Romanesque and Gothic architecture, which overwhelms the worshipper with visible evidence of the sacred, grew into forms that reflect the groves of trees that sheltered earlier sanctuaries. Cathedrals and abbeys were often built in places of great significance in pre-Christian antiquity. For example, the immense abbey church at Glastonbury in England was erected in a spot where there is evidence of there having been a center for Celtic religious ceremonies long before the first small monastery was established.[28] And the Arthurian legends that cluster around Glastonbury have pre-Christian elements in them that have resisted baptism into the Church. The sanctuaries of churches sometimes served as places for dream incubation in much the same way that classical temples had before them. Saints appeared to pious Christians in waking visions in these sanctuaries just as the old gods had done. Locations where visions were seen, healings occurred, or relics of the saints discovered became the goals of pilgrimages. Indeed, pilgrimages to sacred places became a major activity of the Middle Ages. Thousands made the journey to Santiago de Compostela in northern Spain, returning with scallop shells as a physical sign of their visit to the sacred spot.[29] The same customs were taken by colonists to the New World. El Santuario de Chimayo, a wonderful healing spot in New Mexico, is a Spanish church that occupies the sacred ground of a Native American medicine place, and uses the same soil for cures. This is only one example of thousands of Indian sacred places that were appropriated in the Americas.

Earlier, in the Mediterranean area, a series of terrible wars, the Crusades, were fought for possession of the eastern holy places and their relics. The conduct of the crusaders when they attained the objects of their military pilgrimages was hardly appropriate for sacred space. There was quarreling over relics, and a chronicler of the times says that during the capture of Jerusalem in 1099, the crusaders slaughtered their enemies in the holy city, and blood splashed up to the knees and bridles of their horses.[30]

Such brief desecrations of sacred space could be repaired, and the churches reconsecrated and sweetened with incense. The real danger to the concept of spirit of place in the dawn of the modern world lay in its denial by a series of worldviews that became extremely powerful. Protestantism affirmed spirit, but denied its connection with place, re-asserting God's transcendence in terms that separated spirit from all physical creation, and admitted the possibility of God's immanence only in the human soul, and for very strick theologians perhaps not even there. Pilgrimages and veneration of relics seemed Popish delusions. But Protestants could not deny their own experience of spirit of place. There were soon Protestant shrines, and they multiplied rapidly, as anyone who has visited Martin Luther's Erfurt and Wittenberg or John Wesley's Epworth and Oxford knows. And Protestants have located their own "Garden Tomb" in Jerusalem, which is visited regularly by tourists to the Holy Land, though its historicity is a matter for scholarly debate.[31] Still, visitors say there is a feeling in that place that is missing in some other sights on the tour.

The modern West generally has taken a different attitude. It does not deny place, but it denies that place has any spirit. Both capitalism and Marxism define land and what it contains as economic resources subject to use, and regard spirit as fantasy. In the modern world, nationalism places the claims of the state above those of the church, and has often demonstrated it by seizing church land, closing churches and monasteries, and effectively denying that sacred spaces as defined by the church are entitled to any respect other than that which the state may, for its own reasons, decide to give it. In America, the separation of church and state has shielded churches and synagogues to some extent, but eminent domain can easily turn a sanctuary into a freeway entrance. American Indian sacred places were officially denied protection until the American Indian Religious Freedom Act of 1978.[32] That law put

the rights of sacred land in the books, but the experience
of litigation has shown that it is ineffective in preventing
actual invasions and destruction of places where American
Indians find spirit manifest to them. The result is that the
destruction of Native American holy places, once done
openly and deliberately, now takes place through the
construction of dams, roads, and recreational areas. Of
course, nationalism has its own shrines. Every Soviet city
has its monuments to Lenin and the Great Patriotic War,
often designed to enhance the feeling of space set aside,
with walls and plantings and the eternal flame. We have our
Statue of Liberty portraying an ancient goddess, the Lincoln
Memorial and Supreme Court building recreating Roman
temples, and the National Archives where one approaches
the Constitution and Declaration of Independence as
holy relics. There is a spirit in these places, too, and though
the modern mind might hold that their location is arbitrary,
it is not. It is established by historical precedent and the
experience of the people who go there. When spirit grows
in a place, people love and honor that place. Still, it could
be said that it would take a very special person to go to
Washington to have dreams or experience healing.

On the other hand, there are places set aside by the state
to which we very well might want to go, to which a Native
American might want to go, for those purposes. These are
the national parks and wilderness areas. While no law
says they are sacred, they were created in natural areas
that often embody the spirit of place in particularly evident
ways. One can hardly look at Yosemite's soaring domes
and plunging waterfalls without feeling one is in a sacred
place, nor spend time among Yellowstone's geysers without
sensing the emergence of the chthonic spirit. Most of the
vocal exponents of conservation who succeeded in getting
the legislation passed to create the first public reservations
for nature protection had a sense of the spirit of place in
these special localities. John Muir certainly did. He spoke
of mountains and meadows as places of healing, renewal,
and worship. And when Hetch Hetchy—a valley like a
miniature of the more famous Yosemite, located in the same
national park and one of the places Muir honored most—
was threatened with flooding to become a reservoir for San
Francisco, he stated the principle of its sacredness un-
equivocally: "These temple destroyers, devotees of ravaging
commercialism, seem to have a perfect contempt for Nature,

and instead of lifting their eyes to the God of the mountains, lift them to the Almighty Dollar. Dam Hetch Hetchy! As well dam for water-tanks the people's cathedrals and churches, for no holier temple has ever been consecrated by the heart of man."[33] John Muir, George Catlin, Henry Thoreau, John Wesley Powell, Stephen Mather, Arthur Carhart, Aldo Leopold, Bob Marshall: none of these men who urged the preservation of special places in nature was conventionally religious, but they became the voices of a civic recognition of the spirit of place that saved from despoliation an unmatched series of temples made without hands. Every one of them, by the way, would have been hurt and angered to see the destructive fires that blackened the Yellowstone in the summer of 1988.[34] Wildfire is natural, but it is not ecological wisdom to put out every lightning fire for seventy years and then to expect uncontrolled fire to behave normally. But to return to our theme, we have in the parks and in the wilderness a last opportunity to experience the unalloyed spirit of place and to seek to know just what it is.

That is really what we are challenged to do today: to find the places where we connect with the larger cosmos, to keep them free of the impedimenta that would block access to the spirit, and to open ourselves to the values that come from those places. When place is respected and treated properly, spirit is never used up; on the contrary, it becomes stronger. And the more one studies the past experience of sacred place in human history, the more one is impressed by the variety of values that can emerge from it. It is as if this vast organism in which we live, Gaia, the biosphere and indeed the entirety of planet earth,[35] has a multitude of organs, of connections and nodes, no two exactly the same, and as we move among them, we give and receive, and subtract from her life or enhance it according to our attitude and our sensitivity.[36] The place where natural ecosystems are intact and functioning in the full spectrum of their beauty is the place where spirit is most manifest.

Notes

1. Paul Shepard and Barry Saunders. *The Sacred Paw: The Bear in Nature, Myth, and Literature.* New York: Viking, 1985, pp. 191-192.

2. Ovid. *Fasti* 3. 295-296.
3. N. K. Sandars, transl. *The Epic of Gilgamesh*. Harmondsworth, U.K.: Penguin Books, 1972.
4. G. Foucart, "Dreams and Sleep: Egyptian," in *Encyclopaedia of Religion and Ethics,* edited by James Hastings. New York: Charles Scribner's Sons, 1912, vol. 5, p. 35.
5. Genesis 28:11-22.
6. Exodus 2:5.
7. For more discussion of this point and others in this article, see J. Donald Hughes and Jim Swan. "How Much of the Earth is Sacred Space?" *Environmental Review* 10 (Winter, 1986): 247-259.
8. H. W. Parke and D. E. W. Wormell. *The Delphic Oracle.* Oxford: Basil Blackwell, 1956, pp. 4-5.
9. See Vincent Scully. *The Earth, the Temple and the Gods.* New York: Frederick A. Praeger, 1969.
10. Seneca. *Epistles* 4. 12. 3.
11. See J. Donald Hughes. "Sacred Groves: The Gods, Forest Protection, and Sustained Yield in the Ancient World," in *History of Sustained-Yield Forestry: A Symposium,* edited by Harold K. Steen. Durham, NC: Forest History Society, 1984, pp. 331-343.
12. Ovid. *Metamorphoses* 8. 738-878.
13. C. A. Meier. *Ancient Incubation and Modern Psychotherapy,* Evanston, IL: Northwestern University Press, 1967.
14. Hippocrates. *Airs, Waters, Places.*
15. See J. Donald Hughes. "Theophrastus as Ecologist," *Environmental Review* 9 (Winter, 1985): 296-306.
16. Plato. *Laws* 5. 747D-E.
17. Plutarch. "Concerning the Face Which Appears in the Orb of the Moon," *Moralia* 938D-E.
18. Romans 8:19-23.
19. I John 2:15.
20. Synesius of Cyrene. *The Essays and Hymns of Synesius of Cyrene,* translated by A. Fitzgerald, vol. 1 (Oxford, 1930), Hymn IV, pp. 240 ff.
21. Mark 6:46.
22. Mark 11:15-17; Matthew 20:12-13.
23. A. H. M. Jones. *Constantine and the Conversion of Europe.* New York: Collier Books, 1962, pp. 177-178.
24. Willibald. "Life of St. Boniface," in *The Anglo-Saxon Missionaries in Germany,* edited by C. H. Talbot. New York: Sheed and Ward, 1954, pp. 45-46.
25. Friedrich Heer. *Charlemagne and His World.* New York: Macmillan, 1975, p. 123.
26. John Bagnell Bury. *History of the Later Roman Empire from the Death of Theodosius I to the Death of Justinian.* London: Macmillan, 1923, vol. 1, pp. 369-377.

27. Bede. *A History of the English Church and People* 1. 30. Harmondsworth, UK: Penguin Books, 1955, pp. 86-87.
28. Geoffrey Ashe. *King Arthur's Avalon: The Story of Glastonbury.* New York: Dutton, 1958, pp. 13-41.
29. Horton Davies. *Holy Days and Holidays: The Medieval Pilgrimage to Compostela.* Lewisburg, PA: Bucknell University Press, 1982, pp. 219-221. The site of Compostela was hallowed as a pagan family tomb in pre-Christian times: see Marilyn Stokstad *Santiago de Compostela in the Age of Great Pilgrimages.* Norman, OK: University of Oklahoma Press, 1978, p. 6.
30. So says Raymond D'Aguilers, who was there, in his *Historia Francorum qui Ceperunt Iherusalem.* See August Charles Krey. *The First Crusade: The Accounts of Eyewitnesses and Participants.* Princeton, NJ: Princeton University Press, 1921, p. 261. Fulcher of Chartres says "If you had been there, your feet would have been stained to the ankles in the blood of the slain." Foucher de Chartres, *Chronicle of the First Crusade*, translated by Martha Evelyn McGinty. Philadelphia: University of Pennsylvania Press, 1941, p. 122.
31. Jack Finegan. *Light from the Ancient Past: The Archeological Background of the Hebrew-Christian Religion.* Princeton, NJ: Princeton University Press, 1969, vol. 2, p. 319.
32. Public Law 95-341, Senate Joint Resolution 102, 42 U. S. C. par. 1996, August 11, 1978. See Robert S. Michaelsen, "The Significance of the American Indian Religious Freedom Act of 1978," *Journal of the American Academy of Religion* 52 (No. 1, 1984): 93-115.
33. Edwin Way Teale, ed. *The Wilderness World of John Muir.* Boston: Houghton Mifflin, 1954, p. 320.
34. Michael Milstein. "The Long, Hot Summer," *National Parks* 62 (November/December 1988): 26-27, 50.
35. James E. Lovelock. *Gaia: A New Look at Life on Earth.* Oxford: Oxford University Press, 1979.
36. See Gary Snyder. "Good, Wild, Sacred," *The CoEvolution Quarterly* (Fall, 1983): 8-17.

2

Reflection and Revelation:
Knowing Land, Places and Ourselves

VINE DELORIA, JR.

The increasing interest in land, ecology, the living earth, and our responsibility toward other forms of life comes none too soon, considering the conditions we find developing on our planet. The end of organic life is now clearly possible, if present trends of exploitation and pollution continue. Therefore it behooves us to find in our history and ourselves some ways to reverse ecological destruction and bring environmental stability to the places in which we live.

When the nearly terminal condition of the planet is discussed, many people say that American Indian religious traditions offer a good understanding of land and life and may provide the larger society with conceptual tools to rescue itself from its own destruction. American Indians have thus become one of the previously neglected peoples to whom others will listen—albeit for the moment—to find the answers they seek. But what exactly is it that non-Indians want from Indians? Here the situation is not clear, and until Indians can get some kind of guidance about what non-Indians seek, we cannot offer much help.

Non-Indian interest seems to focus on the sacredness of land, the perception that Indians understand land much more profoundly than other peoples, and on the possibility of adopting or transferring that kind of relationship to the larger social whole. I believe there is some truth in this perception. However, I also believe that this assertion is being made by people who do not really think deeply about what land and sacredness are, and by people who would be content to receive the simple poetic admonitions and aphorisms that pass as knowledge in the American intellectual cafeteria.

Intellectually, tribal wisdom is not much different from insights a person with some degree of sensitivity and awareness about the world could discover upon serious reflection. But there is a nuance here that bears examination. Tribal wisdom is the distilled experiences of the community, and not the aesthetic conclusions of sensitive individuals or the poetic conclusions of personal preferences. Tribal insights have been subjected to the erosions of time; they have been tested by uncounted generations, and they have been applied in a bewildering variety of settings in which they have proven reliable. That is to say, tribal wisdom is *communal* wisdom; it is part of the tribal definition of what it is to be a human being in a social setting. Therefore, tribal wisdom differs considerably from the slogans and beliefs of the networks of concerned people that pass for communities in the modern world.

Within tribal traditions there is a real apprehension of and appreciation for the sacredness of land, and more specifically, for the sacred nature of places; the two ideas are but different expressions of the underlying relationship of humans with the world around them. It is possible to dissect this knowledge for the purpose of discussion, but the discussion should follow a particular sequence. It should not rely wholly on the goodwill of the listener. We can analyze what constitutes sacredness, but we must also recognize that some of what we say can be understood only by experience. Our task is to live in such a way that the information we receive through analysis becomes— over the passage of time and through grace and good fortune—our experience also.

The sacredness of land is first and foremost an emotional experience. It is that feeling of unity with a place that is complete, whatever specific feelings it may engender in an individual. There are two fundamental categories of emotional responses to sacred places: reflective and revelatory. The vast number of experiences we have with land, and in particular with places, are of a reflective kind. We experience the uniqueness of places and survey the majesty of lands. There we begin to meditate on who we are, what our society is, where we came from, quite possibly where we are going, and what it all means. Lands somehow call forth from us these questions and give us a feeling of being within something larger and more powerful than ourselves. We are able to reflect upon what we know, and in reflection we see a different arrangement, perhaps a different interpretation, of what life can mean. A wise person might be able to discern the intellectual content of these reflective experiences by intense thought, but his or her conclusion would be only a logical proposition and would lack the intensity of the emotion which lands and places evoke. Land has the ability to short-circuit logical processes; it enables us to apprehend underlying unities we did not suspect.

Revelatory experiences are another thing altogether. They tell us things we cannot possibly know in any other way. Moses approaches the burning bush, is told that it is a holy place, learns the name of God, and is given a vocational task to perform on behalf of his community. With this information come directions through which a new future is possible. Encountering a holy place always involves the manifestation of a personal spirit of immense and unmeasured power, a real spirit of place with which our species must have communion thereafter. Holy places exist in all countries and form the sacred configuration of the land. These places speak of the ultimate holiness of creation. They give a meaningful context to the reflective locations.

This distinction between reflective and revelatory places is not intended to downgrade the validity of reflective experiences of lands. It is the ability to reflect that creates the awareness and sensitivity of peoples to the qualitative intensity of revelatory places. But the distinction is necessary because revelatory places are known only through the experience of prolonged occupation of land, and they cannot be set aside because of the aesthetic or emotional appeal of particular places.

The most common experience of Indian tribes today is that of reflective places. One must suspect that common knowledge of lands among Indians always featured a high percentage of reflective places throughout Indian occupation of this continent. Tribal histories, for the most part, are land-centered. That is to say, every feature of a landscape has stories attached to it. If a tribal group is very large or has lived on a particular piece of land for many generations, some natural features will have many stories attached to them. I know some places in the Dakotas about which at least a dozen stories are told. These stories relate both secular events such as tales of hunting and warfare and sacred events such as personal or tribal religious experiences.

Each family within a tribe has its own tradition of stories about tribal ancestral lands. In theory it would be possible to gather from the people of the tribe all the stories that relate to every feature of the landscape. If these stories were then arranged chronologically, the result would be a history of the people somewhat similar to what whites mean by history. But the history would be considered artificial by most Indians because the intensity of the original experience—which was a function of the place and important in explaining the incident or event—would have been abandoned in favor of the chronology.

When non-Indians admire or try to emulate the Indian love of the land, they generally think of the reflective emotions that Indians have about lands and places. Unfortunately, most whites lack the historical perspective of places simply because they have not lived on the land long enough. In addition, few whites preserve stories about the land, and very little is passed down which helps people identify the special aspect of places.

A popular old story makes this point eloquently. A Crow chief, told that the government owned his land, said that they could not own it because the first several feet down consisted of the bones of his ancestors and the dust of the previous generations of Crow people. If the government wanted to claim anything, the chief continued, it would have to begin where the Crow people's contribution ended. This feeling of unity with the land can only come through the prolonged intimacy of living on the land.

Now, there is no question in my mind that a good many non-Indians have some of the same emotional attachment to land that most Indians do. For example, the land has impressed itself upon rural whites in Appalachia, the South, parts of the Great Plains, and other isolated areas, and made indelible changes in the way the people perceive themselves. One could not read *The Grapes of Wrath* or *Raintree County* without encountering such deep feelings.

And critical to the recognition of this attachment is the family, the community, as functioning parts of the landscape. It is not too much to argue that without the *group* of people sharing a sense of history on the land, there can be nothing more for the individual than a tourist's aesthetic feeling of beauty, which is but a temporary reflection of the deeper emotion to be gained from the land.

The first dimension of Indian feeling about the land is therefore an admission that we are part and parcel of it physically. However, our physical contribution makes sense only because our memory of land is a memory of ourselves and our deeds and experiences. These memories and experiences are always particular. One thinks of Gettysburg and President Lincoln's magnificent speech recognizing that the sacrifice of so many lives hallowed the ground beyond our power to add or detract. When asked where his lands were, Crazy Horse replied that his lands were where his dead lay buried. He was not thinking of the general contribution of flesh made by generations of Sioux to the Great Plains, but of the immediate past deeds of his generation. These had imprinted on the land new stories and experiences that gave the Sioux a moral title to the lands. Luther Standing Bear once remarked that a people had to be born, reborn, and reborn again on a piece of land before beginning to come to grips with its rhythms. Thus, in addition to the general contribution of long occupation, comes the coincident requirement that people must have freely given of themselves to the land at specific places in order to understand it.

One major difficulty which non-Indians face in trying to make an imprint on the North American continent is the absence of any real or lasting communities. Non-Indian Americans, not the Indians, are the real nomads. White Americans are rarely buried in the places they were born, and most of them migrate freely during their lifetimes, living in as many as a dozen places and having roots in and accepting responsibility for none of these locations. There is, consequently, no continuing community to which they can pass along stories and memories. Without a continuing community one comes from and returns to, land does not become personalized. The only feeling that can be generated is an aesthetic one. Few non-Indians find satisfaction in walking along a riverbank or on a bluff and realizing that their great-great-grandfathers once walked that very spot and had certain experiences. The feeling is one of lack of community and continuity.

When non-Indians live on a specific piece of land for a number of generations, they also begin to come into this reflective kind of relationship. The danger, however, is that non-Indian society as it is presently constituted encourages the abandonment of land and community. Further, it fails to provide a human context within which appreciation for and understanding of land can take place. A good deal of what constitutes present-day love of and appreciation for land is aesthetic, a momentary warm feeling that is invoked by the uniqueness of the place. This warmth does inspire the individual, but it does not sustain communities, and therefore a prolonged relationship with the land is forfeited.

When we discuss revelatory experiences we enter an entirely different realm of discourse. Holy places connected with revelation are exceedingly rare. If we carefully analyze Indian stories about religious experiences, we discover that many things we believed at first to be revelations are in fact reflections of or experiences directed by religious training and supervision. What then are revelatory experiences? Their first characteristic is that the old categories of space and time vanish. New realities take their places and suggest dimensions of life far beyond what we are normally able to discern and understand. Suddenly the everyday world does not exist because it is, in a fundamental sense, a predictable world which we can control. But in revelatory experience we find that we are objects within a place and no longer acting subjects capable of directing events. Some of the medicine men and women describe their feelings as intense dread and foreboding.

This feeling of dread cannot be emphasized too much, because it is this emotion that distinguishes reflection from revelation. A major error made today by people interested in Indian religion, and by Indians who purport to teach traditional ways, is the absence or avoidance of this dimension of the religious experience. The truly great medicine men and women who understood the nature of revelation did everything in their power to avoid the experience. They fully understood that giving up their lives might be required, and that whatever happened, the experience would radically change every measure they used to gauge normal life. Because the experience was so fearful, the great medicine men and women would use the holy places very seldom. They preferred almost any other method to solve their problems, and it was only in times of extreme crisis that they returned to the sources of their own personal vocational revelation for guidance.

Knowledge of the holy places in a tribe's past was a closely guarded secret. Probably only one or two people in any generation actually knew these locations. Knowledge of the holy place was specific to individuals and families, and this produced some strange combinations of information. For example, a family might know a specific holy place but would not know what ceremonies were to be performed there. A medicine man or woman, in a time of tribal crisis, might be told during a ceremony to perform another ceremony at a specific location. He or she might be instructed to obtain directions to the holy place from a secular person. With such specific information spread widely through the tribal community, the tribe could not possibly develop an ecclesiastical hierarchy or priesthood that would dominate the community. Tribes that did have priesthoods were almost always sedentary groups that had long since made their peace with the surrounding lands. In these cases knowledge of the holy places was widespread, but only a few priests knew what ceremonies to use and what occasions necessitated their use.

Indians who know about these things find it extremely difficult to describe what they know. There seems to be an abiding spirit of place that inhibits anyone from trying to explain what has been experienced there. I have visited some of these places, and quite frankly found them terrifying to the casual visitor—and anyone is casual who does not have a specific purpose for coming there. The most prevalent phenomenon is sudden awareness that one is being watched and should not be there. I suggest that a place that has been the site of a revelatory experience always retains something of the intensity of that experience. It is very easy to find oneself disoriented as to direction and time in these places. Consequently Indians have always acted with the utmost respect when they realized they were in such a place.

Another phenomenon attached to holy places is that the more information an individual has about the location, the more likely he or she is to encounter unique emotions and experiences there. Information heightens awareness by providing a context within which experiences can be understood. The intensity of dread is partially defused by a framework to make the experience comprehensible.

We have reports of religious experiences similar to those of American Indians from mystics of other religious and philosophical traditions. Common themes in these traditions are the disappearance or transformation of familiar apprehensions of time and space, and the appearance of a reality undergirding or transcending physical reality. These traditions do not, as a rule, rely on specific locations as does the American Indian tradition. There can be no denying that the European continent has a multitude of sacred places, and it is no accident that, as different religions have come and gone, the same locations appear as sacred and receive adoration, even though the language and religious context continues to change. One can project, then, that sacred places in North America may yet see a series of transformations in which new peoples using new languages rely on them for spiritual sustenance.

Quite frequently the result of a revelatory experience is the creation of a new ceremony, but not all ceremonies arise in this manner. So we cannot say that the creation of a ceremony is one criterion by which we judge whether a place has sufficient holiness to provide new ways of relating to higher spiritual powers. Since the primary content of most revelations within the Indian traditions is the definition of individual vocations that will serve the people in the immediate future, it is exceedingly difficult to classify most locations by a precise description of their primary content. Historically Indians believed that they lived between the physical and spiritual worlds, and consequently there was not much effort to make the kinds of distinctions that non-Indians find useful in understanding topics. Ceremonies were supposed to help keep the people attuned to the rhythms of the spiritual world, and therefore what was important was whether they fulfilled that function.

The most important aspect of sacred places, and in particular the holy places of which we have knowledge, is that they mark the location and circumstances of an event in which the holy became an objective fact of existence. Christians have the same idea in the doctrine of the Incarnation, except that they restrict holiness to the human species. Indians understand that there is holiness in everything, and that human beings are simply a part of the larger whole which must be shaped and informed by the holy. We can see some of the mystery of these things in Black Elk's vision when he meets the Six Grandfathers, and also later when as an old man he stands on Harney Peak and invokes them to help him and take pity on him. The complaint of many traditional Indians against the white man's understanding of things sacred is the tendency to reduce the holy to a subjective category of experience, and to fail to come to grips with the meaning of the objectification of the holy. Indians and New Agers part company at the point where New Agers argue that it is possible to create one's own reality—that belief is an avoidance of sacred experiences, and hence detaches one from real relationship with the land.

If we recognize the two kinds of sacred lands and admit the objectification of the holy as a particular event at a specific place, the question arises as to whether one can have the sacred experience of relationship to land. Is this experience restricted to American Indians, or is it possible for any devout and sincere individual seeking a higher spiritual reality? We can only discuss theoretical possibilities since it would be presumptuous to argue that fundamental experiences are limited to American Indians. But there are certain preconditions that make it unlikely that non-Indians would have these kinds of experiences, and these conditions also make it probable that it will be increasingly difficult for most American Indians to enter into or maintain such relationships with places.

Civilized life precludes most of the fundamental experiences that our species once had in relating to lands and the natural order. Today we rely entirely too much upon the artificial universe that we have created, the world of machines and electricity. In most respects we have been trained to merge our emotions and beliefs so that they mesh with the machines and institutions of the civilized world. Thus many things that were a matter of belief for the old people have become objects of scorn and ridicule for modern people. We have great difficulty in understanding simple things because we have been trained to deal with extremely complicated things, and we respond that way almost instantaneously. The old traditional Indians were in tune with the rhythms of life. They were accustomed to bringing in and relating to a whole picture of the land, the plants, and the animals around them. They responded to things as a part of a larger whole which was a subjective reality to them. We could say the traditional Indian stood in the center of a circle and brought everything together in that circle. Today we stand at the end of a line and work our way along that line, discarding or avoiding everything on either side of us.

In our electronic/electric, mechanical world, we rely on instruments of our own construction to enable us to relate to the rest of the world. The world becomes an object of our actions in an entirely new way, for we are able to overcome certain aspects of the natural world such as time and space that had always stood as barriers to us. But our mechanical instruments cannot help us relate to the rest of life except by reducing it to an object also. Consequently any apprehension of the sacredness of land must be filtered through our mechanical devices, and consequently we attribute to landscape only the aesthetic and not the sacred perspective.

Land, for traditional peoples, includes the other forms of life that share places with us. Thus some places were perceived by Indians as sacred because they were inhabited by certain kinds of birds and animals. The Black Hills, for example, was regarded as a sanctuary for the animals, and human beings were not supposed to dominate the hills or make their presence an inhibiting factor in the animals' use of the area. We might even say that the sacredness of lands extends to and is apprehended by other forms of life. Without their presence the land would lack an important dimension.

Not only is the presence of other forms of life necessary for the land, it is sometimes the determining factor in identifying sacred locations. There are many stories among the tribes regarding the role of guardianship played by birds and animals in protecting sacred places. Within the last several years we have experienced events in which Indians going to perform vision quests were prevented from entering certain locations by birds, animals, and reptiles who seemingly had intuited that the humans did not have the proper attitude. Such a situation may seem impossible or simply superstition, but there is a high level of predictability in these things. Within the traditional context, certain individuals being blocked was predicted prior to their efforts to enter a sacred location.

We thus move from simple appreciation of land to an apprehension of its sacredness and to the discovery that our analysis must include proper relationship with animals. But if these other forms of life can inhibit or even prohibit human beings from using lands, what is our status within the natural world? Unlike the religions of the Near East which see humanity as the supreme production of creation, traditional religions see our species as existing about halfway up the scale of life, when such a scale is based on relative strength, wisdom, and talents. Each bird, animal, or reptile is thought to possess major potentials which make it what it is. Thus the eagle can fly highest, the hawk see farthest, the owl see deepest, the meadowlark hear keenest, and so forth. Human beings have some talents, but not developed beyond those of any one of the other forms of life. The special human ability is to communicate with other forms of life, learn from them all, and act as a focal point for things they wish to express. In any sacred location, therefore, humans become the instrument by which all of creation is able to interact and express its totality of satisfaction.

The sacred place and the myriad forms of life which inhabit the land require specific forms of communication and interaction. These forms are the particular ceremonies which are performed at the sacred places. It is believed that birds and animals give up their lives and bodies so that human beings can perform the proper ceremonies by which every creature is blessed. The ceremony is a form of exchange of gifts and responsibilities. As gifts are given and responsibilities accepted, the world as we know it is able to move forward to completion of its possibilities. When we understand this demand for taking mature responsibility for the land and its places, we can understand the ceremonies which require human mutilations. Unless humans are prepared to offer their own bodies also, the circle cannot be completed.

The necessity of some form of sacrifice in the ceremony is a major stumbling block for non-Indians. Christianity teaches that Jesus made the one supreme sacrifice, and that following the Crucifixion no other sacrifices are necessary. But the rest of creation is involved in the Crucifixion only by logical extension and does not participate in the same way that Indian ceremonies involve it. Many non-Indians, when told that the relationship with land involves ceremonies and sacrifices, seem to feel self-conscious. They experience a sense of inadequacy because they have been trained by Western religions to feel that sacrifice is necessary because of their sinful nature. Traditional Indians do not see that sacrifice necessarily involves a sinful nature; rather it is the only way that humans can match the contribution of other forms of life. Without a commitment at this level of being, the relationship with the land remains only aesthetic, because one has remained detached from participation in the ceremonial event.

Although we rarely experience it, there must be times when non-human forms of life perform ceremonies without the presence of human beings. Traditional people granted this possibility, and as a result set aside certain specific locations where they would refuse to go in order to let other forms of life conduct their own ceremonial life. This possibility is the ultimate boundary of human apprehension of the natural world. In recent years we have seen good faith efforts by Congress and state legislatures to set aside areas of land as "wild rivers" or "wilderness areas." These lands are to be protected from commercial exploitation and are to be used by human beings only under rigid rules of behavior. But this effort does not go far enough. It is a mere balancing of possible human uses of land; it does not credit the land and non-human forms of life with an existence in and of themselves.

Tribes accorded each other respect when it came to using the land. Several tribes might share an area with different motives in mind, one tribe using the place for hunting and winter camp purposes, another using it primarily for religious purposes. Thus sacred lands frequently intersected, the sacred mountains and lakes of one tribe being the secular lands of another. It was commonly admitted that each tribal people had its own destiny to complete. Consequently, lands that had a powerful spirit frequently carried with them a form of sanctuary, so that people could come and go without having to deal with secular considerations. The Sioux and Cheyenne, for example, shared Bear Butte in western South Dakota. Each tribe had a different religious story that made the butte significant, and each tribe had tribal-specific ceremonies to perform with respect to that location. The

Pipestone Quarry in southwestern Minnesota was shared by a great number of tribes, since it provided the stone for the sacred pipes.

Over a long period of time tribes developed a general knowledge which linked together the most prominent sacred places. Some of these linkages evolved into ceremonial calendar years, instructing people when and where to hold ceremonies. Other combinations described hunting and fishing cycles and migrations. The Great Serpent Mound in Ohio is said to represent a Hopi migration, and some of the Hopi knowledge of the land is said to be comparable to ley line and geomancy knowledge which the early inhabitants of the British Isles and the Chinese possessed. In general, Indians would not radically change the contours or features of the land, and they tried to blend in changes to mark locations with existing features.

It is apparent that the Indian relationship with the land is one brought about by prolonged occupation of certain places. Non-Indians can work toward this condition, but it cannot be brought about by energetic action or sincerity alone. Nor can mere continued occupation create an attitude of respect, since the basic premise—that the universe and each thing in it is alive and has personality—is an attitude of experience and not an intellectual presupposition or logical conclusion. Yet we see in the present best efforts of groups of non-Indians an honest desire to become truly indigenous in the sense of living properly with the land. Thus we cannot help but applaud the interest non-Indians are now demonstrating in the areas of conservation and ecological restoration. The future looks far more hopeful than previously.

3

The Living Earth and Shamanic Traditions

STANLEY KRIPPNER

The 8th century Greek poet Hesiod described how in the beginning there was darkness, personified by the god Chaos. Then appeared Gaia, the deep-breasted earth; Africa, Asia, and Europe were named after other manifestations of this earth goddess. Among the ancient Slavic tribes, Mati-Syra-Zemlya ("Moist Mother Earth") was worshipped as a supreme being. Peasants would dig into the ground with their fingers, place an ear to the hole, and listen to what Mother Earth was telling them.

In ancient Egypt, Geb was the earth god. All the world's vegetation sprouted from Geb's back as he was lying on his stomach, prone. The Algonquin Indians worshiped Nokomis, the Earth Mother, and believed that all living things fed from her bosom. Balkan peasants considered the earth a person's parent and spouse, dressing the corpse for a wedding before burying it. Indeed, the first people who developed skills in the healing arts held a special reverence for the earth deities, whether they were male, female, or both.

The Healing Earth and Treatment Practices

The concept of the healing earth has entered into treatment procedures used by native healers and other magico-religious practitioners since prehistoric times. For example, the central element in the Navaho healing ceremony is the sand painting. This painting represents, simultaneously, the spiritual and physical landscape in which the patients and their transgressions exist, as well as the etiology of the disease and the mythic meaning of the procedure that

41

has been chosen for its cure. Stones, plants, and sacred objects often are placed inside the painting. Mythological relationships among the elements are represented in colored sand. The sand figures may be clouds or snakes or whatever is needed to portray the path of the disease as it proceeds through time and space. Dangers and diseases have their place in this matrix as well; if they have been the cause of illness or misfortune, they alone can correct it. Chanting, drumming, and a vigil bring the elements together. Patients become aware of the pattern of their sickness and their life, and how both are joined in the cosmos. Usually patients are surrounded by their friends, neighbors, and relatives who sing and pray to that purpose (Grossinger, 1982, pp. 105-106; Sander, 1979).

A variation of the sand painting is the ground painting constructed by the Southern California Diegueno Indians during the puberty ritual of young men in the tribe. They convey the design of their world by representing the horizon as a circle. Also included are the world's edge, various heavenly bodies, power animals (especially the crow, coyote, snake, and wolf), and the mortar and pestle used to grind up the mind-altering plants used in these ceremonies (Halifax, 1982, p. 66).

The Mesa and Its Use in Healing

In northern Peru, shamans often prepare a *mesa* (table) for purposes of healing. Both natural and human-made objects are set before the shaman on the ground (or on a cloth covering the ground), arranged in a rectangular form. The mesa is often thought of as a representation of the earth, and can be divided into various zones. In one formulation, a particular side of the mesa is identified with evil and dark magic; the items placed here by the practitioner may include a triton shell, a deer foot, or various stones. The other side represents divine justice and contains a rattle, religious artifacts, holy water, etc. A middle zone contains articles in which the forces of good and evil are evenly balanced, e.g., a bronze sunburst, a stone symbolizing the sea and winds, a piece of crystal. It is in the middle field that shamans exert their greatest effort to establish the balance between the powers necessary for healing (Sharon, 1978).

An example of a contemporary Peruvian shaman-healer who prepares a mesa during his healing ceremonies is don Eduardo Calderon Palomino who frequently creates an elaborate mesa in the style of an altar to represent the traditional cosmology. Its zones represent a synthesis of the masculine and feminine aspects of creation as well as Middle Earth, the Upper World, and the Lower World (Villoldo & Krippner, 1987). His mesa also includes a container which holds San Pedro cactus juice, a powerful mind-altering substance (Halifax, 1982, p. 67).

The Use of Mesas by North American Practitioners

I have seen mesas prepared by two Native American practitioners, don Jose Rios, a Huichol shaman-healer from the Mexican sierras, and Rolling Thunder, an inter-tribal medicine man from eastern Nevada. Both were featured speakers at an international conference on shamanism and folk healing held in the Austrian Alps during the summer of 1982. Asked to prepare the conference's final ritual, don Jose spread a large, colorful cloth before him, inviting members of the audience to place on it personal objects that were meaningful to them. In this way, he would create a mesa on the basis of what was made available spontaneously.

When over one hundred items had been placed on the cloth, don Jose and his associate, Brandt Secunda, began to sing, chant, and beat their drums. As they continued, I could see frustration reflected on don Jose's face. He muttered a few words in Huichol to Secunda that I later discovered to be, "The table will not rise." The chanting became louder and the drumming became more intense. Finally, don Jose seemed satisfied that his objectives had been met and concluded the ceremony.

A few days later, Rolling Thunder performed the mesa ceremony for a smaller group of people near Cologne, West Germany. He gave similar instructions, but requested that people not place weapons or money on the cloth, although both had been placed on don Jose's mesa. Rolling Thunder and his associates began to sing, chant, and drum. In this instance, the table purportedly "rose" quite easily, endowing "power" to the objects on the cloth.

Sand and ground paintings and the mesa ceremony are not the only ways in which the earth is ceremonially presented by shamans. In 1987, in a museum in Helsinki, Finland, I found a Lapp shaman's drum that had been painted to portray Middle Earth and its relationship to the Upper and Lower Worlds. It was decorated with images of some of the spirits who are said to inhabit these three realms. The Salish Indians of the Pacific Northwest design a staff for "spirit dancers" depicting a similar world. It is adorned with paddles representing water, eagle feathers representing the sky, deer hooves representing animal life, and cedar bark standing for plant life (Jilek, 1982, p. 137). These and other shamanic representations of the earth rest on the assumption that the planet is a living organism capable of great healing powers.

All Nature as Kin

The shamanic worldview acknowledges kinship among all aspects of nature. In most American Indian societies, plants, animals, rivers, and storms are considered demanding but generous beings in a world that responds to prayer and supplication. In addition to the Living (or Healing) Earth, other common primordial ancestors among native Americans are Grandfather Fire, Grandmother Moon, Mother Sea, and Father Sun. Different cultures will assign different names and genders to nature; Australian aborigines speak of the Sun-Woman Wiriupranali, and the Moon-Man Alinda.

The shaman is convinced that tremendous power rests in each aspect of nature because a net of power animates the cosmos. Because shamans specialize in the mastery of power, they are able to utilize the forces of nature to help members of their tribe. For the shaman, nature is personalized. Rocks, flowers, trees, and bodies of water are animate and have personal identities. The cosmos in all its parts as well as in its totality is felt to possess aware-ness, feeling, rationality, and volition. The shaman believes that the world of the human and the world of nature are essentially reflections of each other.

Native American shamans have always encouraged a basic respect for nature. In their healing ceremonies, they fre-quently speak of "the four-legged creatures and the two-legged creatures" as well as "the creatures that crawl on the ground, swim in the sea, and fly in the air." In this manner, human beings are seen as part of the natural order, not separate from it.

This concern is expressed in the mythology of the Yanomami Indians of the Amazon. For centuries, they have carefully regulated the waste materials that they have burned, taking the position that noxious fumes could burn a hole in the sky. This practice bears a remarkable similarity to the current concern over the destruction of the ozone layer due to humankind's disregard for harmful chemicals introduced into the atmosphere.

The Nature of Sacred Places

Some locations on Middle Earth are held to be more sacred than others. Shamans frequently locate "power spots" and use them in their healing ceremonies. These are the areas that are said to contain more "energy" and "vital force" than surrounding geographical locations.

As a child in his Pueblo village, Alfonso Ortiz's vision was directed to the mountaintop, the place where the paths of the living and the dead were said to converge. Ortiz recalled:

> A wise elder among my people, the Tewa, frequently . . . smiled and said, "Whatever life's challenges you may face, remember always to look to the mountaintop; in so doing you look to greatness. Remember this, and let no problem, however great it may seem, discourage you. . . ." Although he knew I was too young to understand, he also knew there was not much time left to impart this message to me and, perhaps, to others like me. In accordance with our beliefs, the ancestors were waiting for him at the edge of the village the day he died, waiting to take him on a final four-day journey to the four sacred mountains of the Tewa world. A Tewa must either be a medicine man in a state of purity or he must be dead before he can safely ascend the sacred mountain. (Halifax, 1982, p. 30)

Ortiz's statement implies that the shaman can utilize sacred geographical spots such as the mountaintop. These spots are also the places where tribal "ancestors" can be found by the shaman and consulted in time of need. Swan (1985, p. 110) has reviewed more than 100 case histories about power spots, observing that the most common experiences reported from them were feelings of ecstasy, unification with nature, interspecies communication, waking visions, profound dreams, the ability to influence the weather, feeling unusual "energies," and hearing words, voices, music, and songs.

One explanation of the nature of sacred places can be found in a Hopi creation myth. In the beginning, it is told, Tiowa, the Creator, saw a need to assign a guardian for the earth, and he gave the position to a wise woman named Spider Grandmother. Descending to earth, Spider Grandmother saw that she would need help with her task as a steward. She reached down, picked up two handfuls of earth, and spit into them. From each hand sprang a young man. The three sat quietly in meditation for a time, attuning their minds to that of Tiowa. Then Spider Grandmother sent one young man, Poqanghoya, to the North Pole to work his magic of giving form and structure to the earth, holding the planet together. The other, Palongwhoya, was given a drum and sent to the South Pole. When he reached the South Pole, Palongwhoya sat in meditation, then began to beat the drum to achieve harmony with Tiowa. Life energies were directed downward into the earth by the drumming, bringing the earth to life. These life energies are supposed to be strongest at the sacred places that contain more of the drum's vibrations than other spots (Swan, 1985).

The Exploitation of Mother Earth

During his apprenticeship, the medicine man Sun Bear had to learn how to sense earth energies by training his observations and perceptions. Sun Bear claims that he was then able to use this information to help him determine proper places to conduct ceremonies and healing sessions (Swan, 1985, p. 115). Sun Bear and other Native American shaman-healers take the position that human beings do not have the right to degrade Mother Earth. They feel that humans must remain in harmony with nature, or the ensuing disharmony will react against them.

Sometimes humans claim that their needs permit them to ravish the earth. The Black Hills of South Dakota have long been considered sacred by a number of American Indian tribes. Yet because large deposits of uranium ore may be found there, a number of mining companies want to initiate operations. In the Four Corners of the American

Southwest, heavily dotted with places sacred to the Hopi and Navaho, coal and uranium abound. Developers are eager to ravish these areas as well (Swan, 1985, p. 109).

A venerable American Indian, Chief Smohalla, foresaw this desecration, warning, "It is a sin to wound or to cut, to tear or scratch our common mother. . . . Am I to take a knife and plunge it into the breast of my mother? . . . Then, when I die, she will not gather me again into her bosom" (Walker, 1983, p. 264). This worldview can be ridiculed today, yet some version of it may be necessary to preserve as well as to heal the fragile planet which has for so long been our home.

References

Grossinger, R. (1982). *Planet medicine: From Stone Age shamanism to post-industrial healing* (rev. ed.). Boulder, CO: Shambhala.

Halifax, J. (1982). *Shaman: The wounded healer.* New York: Crossroads.

Sandner, D. (1979). *Navaho symbols of healing.* New York: Harvest/Harcourt Brace Jovanovitch.

Sharon, D. (1978). *Wizard of the four winds: A shaman's story.* New York: Free Press.

Swan, J. (1985). "Sacred places in nature: Is there a significant difference?" *Psi Research, 4* (1), 108-117.

Villoldo, A., & Krippner, S. (1987). *Healing states.* New York: Fireside/Simon & Schuster.

Walker, B. G. (1983). *The woman's encyclopedia of myths and secrets.* San Francisco: Harper & Row.

This paper was originally given at the Third International Conference on the Study of Shamanism, San Rafael, California, 1986, and published in the proceedings of that conference.

4

Power Centers

MEDICINE GRIZZLYBEAR LAKE

From the very beginning of creation there have been "power centers." Our elders teach us that the Great Creator made such places for a reason and purpose. Ancient myths and stories teach us that power centers are sacred places where the spirits and alleged "gods" reside, while some religious doctrines reveal that specific power centers are where one goes to make a direct contact with the Great Spirit which flows through all life, seen and unseen. Such places are sacred and holy, hence they should be respected, protected, preserved, and used properly.

The best-known power centers in a global sense are Mount Sinai, the Great Pyramids of Egypt, Stonehenge, Machu Picchu, the Mayan Temples, Mount Fuji, and the Himalayan Mountains (just to reference a few popular sites). On the continent of the United States, however, the more notable sites include (but are not limited to) Mount Shasta, Dawn Blue Lake, the San Francisco Peaks/Four Corners area, the Black Hills, Chief Mountain, Allegheny Mountains, Niagara Falls, the Cascades, Grandfather Mountain/Smokey Mountains/Chimney Rock, Lake Tahoe, Crater Lake, Upper Priest Lake, Flathead Lake, Mount Rainier, Doctor Rock/Chimney Rock in northwestern California, the Marble Mountains, the Trinity Alps, the ancient redwood forests, and Mount Chuchama/Tecate near San Diego. (Refer to Evans-Wentz, 1981, *Chuchama and the Sacred Mountains,* for a better understanding and more comprehensive list of power centers worldwide.)

What I would like to share with you here is my own spiritual

This article appeared in *The Quest* magazine, Winter, 1989.

Trididad, California, (known in Yurok as Tsurai-wa*) is a sacred place and power center. Native shamans, including Bobby and Tela Lake, trained here.*

viewpoint and explanation of the power centers as I have come to understand them over thirty-plus years of shamanistic training in such places by over sixteen medicine elders from different tribes.

In "One Step Beyond" (*Shaman's Drum,* Summer, 1986) I shared in detail one of my own spiritual experiences concerning a very sacred and powerful mountain used by the Native American people in northwestern California. This site has been controversial for over two decades due to the conflict over its ownership and legal use between the U.S. Forest Service and the Native tribes. The Sierra Club and Audubon Society have sided with the Native people in this dispute (refer to *Indian Historian,* 1974; *Akwesasne Notes,* 1978; U.S. Forest Service Environmental Impact Statement: G-O Road, 1978, *et al*). But there are other power centers on our Turtle Island, both small and large, low and high, dry and wet, whose power is positive or negative, or both, or neutral.

Shamanism in Northern America (Park, 1936) and *Shamanic Voices* (Halifax, 1979) offer a variety of examples on how the different kinds of power centers are used by different kinds of shamans from different geographical regions. The more classic and detailed examples, however, can be found in the works of Kroeber (1927) as in the example of Fanny Flounder; or DuBois (1932), Eliade (1964), Waters (1966), Bean (1976), and Buckley (1980, 1982). This literature can provide a serious base of study for those who are searching for ways in which Native American people actually pursued, acquired, and applied varying degrees of power from specific kinds of power centers, which include mountains, alpine lakes, caves, waterfalls, forests, prairie mounds, plateaus, rivers, and ocean sites.

The Power Center as a Real Source of Power

It is important to study this material because one can learn not only the significance and meaning of the power center but also how to approach and utilize the power center in a spiritual and proper manner, instead of trespassing upon it as many people are doing today. For example, some of the larger mountains such as Mount Shasta and Mount Saint Helens were not used for vision quests and power training by the indigenous people—not because the Indians lacked sophisticated mountain climbing skills, but because they "knew" exactly what kind of power was there and the reason it was there. Ella Clark (1953) explains that Native people recognized certain mountains not as the home of spirits and gods, but as giant spirits in the hierarchy of earth spirits. My elders have taught me that such places are where the Great Creator resides from time to time. Thus, people are not supposed to trespass upon this kind of power center because it is too powerful, too holy. Most humans are not pure enough to qualify to go there and meet the Great Creator directly, in his abode.

Our elders also teach that when such places are violated, the power reacts, first as a warning, then as penalty. One contemporary example is in the case of Mount Saint Helens, although Westerners might disagree with this contention. I suspect that the Western scientist would attempt to explain the power center, as in the case of Mount Saint Helens, in terms of thermodynamics, energy magnitude, mineral composition, and geological laws of cause and effect. But this does not explain *why* the power center is powerful per se, physically or psychically, or if the physical and spiritual laws are any different. Perhaps it is just a problem of semantics, and for this reason warrants clarification and explanation from the traditional Native understanding.

Medicine men/women, shamans from other countries, and spiritual/psychic leaders such as lamas and gurus can make the right connection with a power center and cause lightning, thunder, rain, and even snow on a clear day/night. This has been documented in a number of works ranging from Park (1936) to Eliade (1964) and Niehardt (1961), and including more recent examples as provided in Boyd (1974) on Rolling Thunder, and Wabun (1988) on Sun Bear. Goodman (1978) defines this phenomenon as a form of "biorelativity." He attempts to explain the power center's electrical potential in relation to mineral alloys and composition, plus atmospheric conditions. Contemporary medicine men such as Wallace Black Elk (Sioux), Charlie Thom (Karuk), Archie Fire Lamedeer (Lakota), or Thomas Banayca (Hopi) explain the process and connection in spiritual knowledge, while medicine women such as Flora Jones (Wintun), and Tela Starhawk Lake (Yurok-Karuk-Hupa), speaking from a female perspective, concur. In either case, it would behoove us to realize that there is, indeed, something very special about the power centers, and something incredible about the shamans who know how to connect with the power and apply it to weather control, healing, ceremony, ritual, agriculture, survival, or protection. No matter how many people in Western society scoff at the idea, such shamans have been using power centers to invoke rain, wind, snow, and ward off droughts for thousands of years; and some still do it.

This "something special" I am talking about is the knowledge and experience which the medicine man/woman/shaman has of the power center and his/her innate ability to connect with and utilize this power while other humans cannot. Perhaps the viewpoint expressed here will gain credibility as conditions continue to get worse in nature with each passing year (just read any daily newspaper for examples). But I hope it won't require physical evidence of natural disasters before Western society begins to realize the significance of these power centers, because by then it might be too late to preserve and protect the sites, or appreciate the people who still know how to use the power centers for the sake of humanity.

Most people in Western society recognize the worth of a

power center in monetary terms, meaning the value of minerals such as gold; or the natural resource it can provide as timber, gas, water, wind, and real estate type "energy." There are exceptions to this view, however, by those who seem to realize the aesthetic and natural beauty of power centers. Such a minority from Western society should be commended for their efforts to preserve the power centers as natural and historic resources, either tribal or national. But I would like to carry such people a step further and help them to realize the true spiritual value of the power centers for what they really are: a source of power. This essentially means a natural place which has physical, mental, emotional, and spiritual power (energy) beyond economic value.

Power Centers are the Home of Spirits and Spirits Have Laws

Let me try to explain this philosophical point by using certain analogies, comparisons, and examples. Some power centers are the residence of a special spirit being who is high in status in the hierarchy. Other power centers are the home of a particular family of spirits. Such entities have been placed on this earth from the very beginning of Creation for a purpose and a reason. They have a specific job to perform for the Great Creator. As a result, these spirits either serve to create that source of power and energy, or they guard, maintain, perpetuate, and use that power center as the basis for their purpose and function.

The spirits who reside within or comprise that power center adhere to and are governed by a system of natural laws. The laws are both spiritual and physical. These "spirits" or entities are both physical and spiritual. Their existence, the earth's existence, and our existence are dependent upon maintaining the "natural laws" in a harmonious state of balance. A law of physics, for example, states that for every action there is a reaction. This same concept applies to both the physical and spiritual dimensions (or if you cannot relate to this analogy, think of it in terms of matter and energy). Traditional Native ideology on the concept provides us with a warning: "Anytime human beings interfere with, violate, or alter the power center, they are causing a serious imbalance; hence a negative and detrimental reaction can occur" (interview with Grandpa David Monongye, 1972; Calvin Rube, 1978).

. Native people or shamans from other parts of the world who intend to approach and utilize a specific power center therefore prepare themselves properly (Park, 1936; Eliade, 1964; Brown and Black Elk, 1971; Evans-Wentz, 1980; Buckley, 1980; Lake, 1986). They demonstrate respect and protocol by purifying their body, mind, and soul of all negative influences and/or energies by use of ritual cleansing, fasting, and prayer. For example, the practitioner might bathe in herbs such as sage or angelica root, steam him/herself with Douglas fir boughs in an open pit, or use the sacred sweatlodge, a hot spring, a waterfall, or some kind of ceremonial lodge depending upon cultural background and belief. In traditional Native cultures, the practitioner normally uses the sweatlodge as a means to prepare. While in the lodge, he/she makes an invocation to the Great Creator, the spirit of the power center to be visited, and asks for permission to quest at the power center. He/she abstains from sex, drugs, alcohol, and any possible blood contamination via women's menses, fresh meats, injured people, or deceased people. He/she waits for a sign or omen. If none is received then he/she will not visit the power center, or will postpone the visit until a later date. The preparation ritual normally lasts four days, during which he/she fasts and stays clean, and continues for another three to four days after the practitioner leaves the power center. Why?

The period of abstaining afterwards is for protection. The practitioner believes the spirit from the mountain will follow him/her home and answer prayers, and so does not want to break the connection. In other situations, the practitioner might be infused with power and energy. It takes time for the human body to adjust mentally, emotionally, physically, and spiritually to the new power, to study a dream, or interpret a vision. The practitioner believes that power flows both ways, and does not want to break this connection.

There is another variable here worth noting, and it has to do with "energy vibrations." When a person receives power from a power center it raises his or her vibratory level. It takes time for the human mind/body/soul complex to adjust to the new vibratory level. If this vibratory process is interfered with or contaminated, the practitioner could become seriously injured or ill. I have personally doctored some people who became crippled from the experience because they did not follow the natural laws while "spiritually training" during a power quest.

The Role of Power Centers as a Life Force to the Earth

Another view I would like to share with you here is the role power centers serve in relation to the Mother Earth. This earth is a living organism (someday Western scientists will discover that reality). The power centers are hence vital to the life force of the earth, and as analogy, some power centers might be compared to psychic centers, or the endocrine glands found in the human body (Pelletier, 1977). They therefore serve as chakras, or vital glands in purpose and function comparable to the major glands found in the human body, in both the physiological and spiritual aspects (Kaplan, 1978).

The smaller power centers might be compared to other parts of the body such as organs, nerve centers, muscles, joints, arteries, and even cells for that matter (Pearce, 1977). So I ask, what happens to your power, your health, your function, and balance of the mind/body/soul complex when any part becomes disturbed, polluted, violated, or exploited without proper permission, preparation, or application? What if your pineal gland were suddenly removed, or your thyroid gland poisoned? Can you imagine the effect this would have upon your entire endocrine system? Obviously there would be some kind of physical and spiritual, mental and emotional reaction.

By the same token, are you aware of the fact that certain parts of your body also have power centers, and these power centers are highly protected by physical and spiritual forces? An example is cells and cellular energies. The purpose and function of the human power centers are to keep the human organism alive and functioning well, *i.e.,* to keep it in balance. What would happen to your well-being if one of the body's power centers were interfered with, altered, damaged, or destroyed? And how many of your power centers are irreplaceable? How important are natural minerals, water, air, and energy to the proper functioning of your body's organism and life force? And what effect do positive and negative energy have upon various parts of your own psychic centers? Get the point?

I don't mean to get off on a tangent here. I am simply trying to find a more humanistic way to help you understand just how vital power centers are to this earth, to all species which are a part of this earth, and to all living things (both seen and unseen) which are dependent upon this earth for survival. And I hope to call your attention to the fact that this Mother Earth is also dependent upon us for her survival.

Thus there are power centers upon the earth where one makes a pilgrimage to give, not just to take. Certain holy places are used as a specific place for us, as humans, to return the power. It is a reciprocal relationship and responsibility. One makes a pilgrimage to pray for the earth; to give it positive, loving, creative, and nourishing energy. This kind of energy is needed in order to replenish her psychic centers. As a living organism, the earth needs recharging because it can occasionally become drained. So whether you realize it or not, you are part of this earth, and you draw your vital energies from the earth. This energy flow must be recycled to keep up the life force, to keep it flowing harmoniously. Energy going one way causes a drain, then eventually a serious depletion.

The ancient, primordial, and contemporary sacred ceremonies and pilgrimages also provide a positive and natural return of the power and energy. That is why we, as medicine people, go to certain power centers to pray and give thanks. Our songs, prayers, tobacco, herbs, offerings, cleanliness, fasting, and sacrificing all serve as means to help keep creation alive. Such ritualistic pilgrimages to the power centers are a spiritual form of recharging and recycling energy back to its original source. And that is why we stay "clean" when we go to a power center. A contaminated or negative transmission can harm the power center; it can also cause a harmful backlash.

There are other power centers such as caves and rock outcroppings, or designated mounds, that are used for seeking a vision, to acquire power, or to channel and redirect the power into a person, ceremony, ritual, or sacred dance. Charlie Thom, a Karuk medicine man (interview, August, 1982) for example, explains it this way:

A medicine man must go to the mountain or some other power center to pray for his people. That is his job. I connect with the power and shoot it straight down from the mountaintop into the sacred dance. It is like a beam of light, or electricity. It will make the healing more powerful. It strengthens the dancers. And I ask the spirits from the mountain to come down and dance with us in the ceremony; as our ancestors originally did in the beginning.

In 17 Matthew in the New Testament, we learn that Jesus did the same thing for his people as a means to gain stronger healing power for his patients. The original teachings of Jesus as found in the Essenes provides an interesting view about this subject, which is similar to Native beliefs about the earth, powers, and power centers.

There have been many times during my own healing sessions when I felt the power weakening. I was being drained, or the case required stronger power and medicine. In such situations I had to go up on the mountain, into a cave, inside an ancient redwood tree, visit a sacred waterfall, or use the sweatlodge in order to receive support from the spirits, Mother Earth, and the Great Creator. I prayed and asked for guidance to help my patient. I pleaded for the spirit and the Great Creator to let the healing power/ energy flow stronger through me so I could channel it into the patient. Over the years as I have been taught and trained, I have learned that different sicknesses, injuries, and people require different sources of power, energy, and medicine in order to be cured. During the power quest I could feel the power surge through my entire body, the vibration some-times knocking me unconscious. I could feel the connection to the power in the same way an electrical current flows from the outlet into a television set, x-ray machine, CAT scan, ultrasound, or whatever. Fasting and abstaining from sex and water, drugs and alcohol, and even certain foods at that time made the current stronger and the con-nection last longer. So in addition to places which provide a religious experience there are, indeed, specific places upon this earth which definitely provide a natural source of healing energy that can be tapped and transmitted to the self and/or patient.

Degrees of Power

Certain power centers have different purposes and sources of power, and different degrees of power. For example, there are "good luck rocks" where our Native American people go to pray for good luck in gambling (Spott and Kroeber, 1942; Lake, 1982). There are power centers which Native people have traditionally used to bring rain, such as Rain Rock, or Thunder Rock (Harrington, 1938). And there are power centers where Native people have quested in order to become warriors, athletes, fortune tellers, seers, basket-makers, canoe-makers, hunters, or doctors (Park, 1936; Buckley, 1980; Lake, 1982). The questor contacts the power by dreaming, by finding a power object, or by making contact with a ghost that becomes his or her spirit ally. Sometimes the power is manifested through an animal, bird, fish, snake, or herb. And lastly, there are power centers that are used only by women for visions and spiritual knowledge. Such places are used as a source of power to cope with life crisis during puberty, menses, childbirth, menopause, or loss of a spouse (Lake, 1982). In all the above examples one can use the power center as a holy place, meaning a quiet and spiritual site where one can pray in privacy to the Great Creator, Mother Earth, the spirits, and nature.

Conclusion

In conclusion, power centers have been established upon this earth from the beginning of creation. Many of the sites are still active and are being used today by Native American people in various parts of the country, and by esoteric practitioners in other countries around the world. The power centers have a specific purpose and function. The power centers are located in specific geographical places for a specific reason and purpose. Some power centers serve as vital energy sources of Mother Earth. Various power centers are used for vision quests, ceremonies, rituals, healing, power acquisition, and pilgrimages. While this may seem like a far-fetched metaphysical statement, some of our traditional Native people believe that certain power centers are actually doorways to other dimensions (Krippner and Villoldo, 1978) or UFO bases for extraterrestrial beings (David Monongye, 1970; Thomas Banyaca, 1974; Beeman Logan, 1976; Medicine Grizzlybear Lake, 1984). And some of the power centers are negative sources of power, being the residences of bad spirits, forces, and energies (Vallory, 1972; Buckley, 1980; Lake, 1982).

All of the power centers, regardless of their purpose and function, should be respected. Power centers used by Native tribal groups and individuals should not be interfered with, violated, damaged, destroyed, or confiscated by those in Western society who see only the economic value of the land. The continued economic exploitation of the earth's vital power centers is causing a very serious imbalance worldwide which can no longer be ignored (*Time*, January, 1989). We are seeing the result of the law of physics in this regard: for every action there is a reaction. Weird weather patterns, volcanic eruptions, increased earthquake activity, record-breaking snowstorms, floods, droughts, pestilence, and new diseases are all reactions. Such phenomena are evidence that the power centers are being violated. Mother Earth is not only becoming polluted but it is also becoming weak and very sick. Her psychic centers are seriously damaged and need healing. In order to be healed, power sites must be protected and preserved. If she dies, we all die. It is as simple as that. Thus, what I have tried to present here is not a metaphysical and romantic notion but a different form of truth and reality.

References

Akwesasne Notes. "G-O Road, Sacred High Country Controversy." Mohawk Nation/Roosevelttown: New York, 1978.

Angulo, de Jaime. *Indian Tales.* New York: Ballantine Books, 1953.

Bean, Lowell. "Power and Its Application in Native California." In Bean and Blackburn, Thomas (eds), *Native Californians.* Romano: Ballena Press.

Black Elk, and Neihardt, J. G., *Black Elk Speaks*, Lincoln: University of Nebraska Press, 1961.

Boyd, Doug. *Rolling Thunder.* New York: Random House, 1974.

Brown, J. E. "The Native Contributions to Science: Engineering and Medicine." *Science,* 38-40, 1975.

Buckley, Thomas. "Monsters and the Quest for Balance in Native Northwest California." In Halpin, M., and Ames, M. (eds.) *Manlike Monsters on Trial; Early Records and Modern Evidence.* Vancouver: University of British Columbia Press, 1980.

Clark, Ella. *Indian Legends of the Pacific Northwest.* Berkeley: U.C. Berkeley Press, 1953.

Dixon, R. "Some Shamans of Northern California." Berkeley: *Journal of American Folklore*, 1904.

DuBois, Cora. "Wintun Ethnography." *American Archaeology,* 1953.

Evans-Wentz, W. Y. *Chuchama and Sacred Mountains,* Waters, Frank, and Adams, Charles L., (eds.) Chicago: Swallow Press, 1981.

Eliade, Mircea. *Shamanism.* Pantheon Books: New York, 1964.

Eliade, Mircea. *Myths, Rites, Symbols,* Beane, W., and Doty, W. San Francisco: Harper and Row Publishers, 1975.

Goodman, Jeffrey. *We Are the Earthquake Generation.* New York: Berkeley Books, 1978.

Halifax, Joan. *Shamanic Voices.* New York: E. P. Dutton, 1978.

Harrington, J. P. "Tobacco Among the Karok Indians," *American Archaeology and Ethnology.* Berkeley: U.C. Berkeley, 1938.

Kroeber, A. L. *Handbook of the Indians of California.* Washington, D.C.: Bureau of Ethnology (78), 1927.

Krippner, Stanley and Villoldo, Alberto. *The Realms of Healing.* Millbrae: Celestial Arts, 1976.

Lake, Robert. *Chilula: People from the Ancient Redwoods.* Lanham: University Press of America, 1982.

Lake, Medicine Grizzlybear. "One Step Beyond, A Native Vision Quest Experience." *Shaman's Drum,* vol. 5, Summer, 1986.

Park, Willard Z. *Shamanism in Western North America.* New York: Banta Publishing Company, 1938.

Pearce, Joseph. *The Magical Child.* New York: E. P. Dutton, 1977.

Pelletier, Kenneth. *Mind As Healer, Mind As Slayer.* New York: Dell Publishing Company, 1977.

Time Magazine. "Planet of the Year: Earth." New York, January, 1989.

Wabun, and Sun Bear. *The Path of Power.* Spokane: Bear Tribe Publishing Company, 1988.

Valory, Keith. "Yurok Doctors and Devils: A Study in Identity, Anxiety, and Deviance." Unpublished Ph.D. dissertation. Berkeley: U.C. Berkeley, 1970.

II

Traditional Views of Place

Bringing a special message from a Northern Cheyenne elder's council to the 1988 Spirit of Place program, Jose Lucero, a member of the Santa Clara Pueblo and a trusted messenger for many Indian tribes, stated on behalf of the elders: "Sacred sites are for the protection of all people, for the four colors of man, black, yellow, white and red."

Lucero's message met with widespread agreement among the other tribal representatives assembled at that session, and has been echoed by others at each subsequent Spirit of Place program. Another message Lucero delivered in 1989 came from Grandfather David Monongye, respected Hopi elder who has since passed on to the next world. This message included the assertion, "The Hopi describe the earth as a spotted fawn. Each spot has a certain power."

In our modern art and music we celebrate the specialness of place, but traditional cultural spokespeople say there is more to the power of place. Places have a spirit, which is both the overall ambience of the place and the spiritual presence there, they say. Kenneth Cooper, a warm-hearted grizzly bear of a man who is a cultural specialist of the Lummi tribe of western Washington, has sung powerful chants and played hauntingly beautiful flute music at each Spirit of Place program. Cooper says that his music comes "on the wind" to him when he is alone praying at one of the sacred stands of old-growth cedar trees beside a rushing glacial stream on the side of snow-capped Mount Baker, which overlooks Puget Sound where Salmon Woman lives. "When we walk in the mountains among the wise old trees, anything you want to know you can find there," Cooper says. The trick to gaining this knowledge is to learn to "listen with your third ear, your heart."

In this section, we see that all around the world cultures seek to cultivate the power of place through right actions, which include rituals. Sometimes the rituals become shrines; a good work of architecture is really a ritual which honors the power of place. Perhaps this is one reason why shrines like those at Stonehenge, Palenque, Delphi, Chartres, Lourdes and the astrologically-aligned circle of stones on Medicine Mountain near Sheridan, Wyoming, have such an attractive power for so many people. And this power, which makes us become more fully who we are, also makes us more humble, for as Mircea Eliade points out in his classic work The Sacred and the Profane, *"Men are not free to choose the sacred site, . . . they only seek for it and find it by the help of mysterious signs."*[1]

Accepting the basic premises presented in this chapter, one is led to the idea that perhaps in Canada and the United States we need a new land use category, the Sacred Site. In Asia, the Middle East, Africa, and Australia, recognized sacred places are maintained and interpreted by priests or special sites rangers who represent the indigenous peoples of that area. One wonders what a national network of such shrines might do to encourage an ecological conscience and preserve pride in Indian culture.

Notes

1. Mircea Eliade, *The Sacred and the Profane.* Harcourt, Brace and Jovanovich, 1959, p. 28.

5

The Spots of the Fawn:
Native American Sacred Sites, Cultural Values and Management Issues

JAMES A. SWAN

Introduction

"Draw not nigh hither," says the Lord to Moses, "put off thy shoes from off thy feet, for the place whereon thou standest is holy ground," declares the Bible in Exodus 3:5. "The idea of a sacred [place] where the walls and laws of the temporal world dissolve to reveal wonder," according to mythologist Joseph Campbell, "is apparently as old as the human race."[1] The names of many of these special places are familiar to us—Delphi, Palenque, Lasceaux, Lourdes, Mount Fuji, Mount Sinai, Mecca, Jerusalem, Mt. Omei, Tai-Shan, the Ganges River and Stonehenge are just a few of the more famous places of numinous power which dot the surface of the earth, and to which people assign the term "sacred."

"Man becomes aware of the sacred because it manifests itself, shows itself, as something wholly different from the profane"—according to Mircea Eliade, who calls the act of manifestation of the sacred a "hierophany" or an appearance of nonordinary reality.[2]

As we seek to create a new environmental conscience and consciousness from which to approach environmental problems and build a sustainable society, we need to understand just what a consciousness of ecological sustainability is, for clearly modern society does not have such a mindset. Throughout history all sustainable societies have had an acute awareness of certain places being sacred. Normally these places have been the central focus of cultural values and meaning, as well as the physical anchors for myths, legends, ceremonies and rituals.

63

If we look to the land use concepts and policies of the nations of the world, the startling fact arises that the United States of America and Canada do not have a well-established legacy of sacred places. There are places of historical significance—battlegrounds, old homes and churches, cemeteries, archeological remains of earlier times, special monuments—but none of these by themselves are said to be places of sacred *power* which manifests as a result of nature alone, and not simply a product of human work and design. There also are numerous parks, monuments, reserves and wild areas which are set aside. The rationale for the preservation of these islands of pristine natural features is usually explained in terms of unusual flora and fauna and perhaps natural scenery. At no time do we use the term "sacred" to describe the significance of a place as a justification for its preservation. This is in sharp contrast to the American Indian culture, which sees the landscape as being dotted with special places of spiritual value and power, a view which is in keeping with nearly all other nations around the world which still have a strong connection to the cultures of their ancestry.

For the last decade I have been engaged in a study of sacred places of American Indian peoples.[3] The purpose of this work has been twofold: 1) to better understand place consciousness through the senses of a more environmentally sensitive culture; and 2) to seek to understand just how the earth wisdom of American Indian peoples can be helpful to modern society for us to learn to live in better harmony with nature. In this chapter I will summarize what I have found and briefly discuss the implications for modern society, as well as for heritage preservation.

What Is a Sacred Place?

Just what is a sacred place? A thing or a place becomes sacred ultimately to us when it is perceived as somehow able to energize within us those feelings and concepts we associate with the spiritual dimensions of life. Sacred places fall into three general categories. One type is the interior of a religious building like a church, temple, shrine or mosque. These interior spaces aren't necessarily associated with any other greater sacred site, although some are, such as the great cathedrals of Europe which are built over old pagan worship sites, with the original spring still bubbling in their basements. One of the greatest differences between ancient and modern sacred architecture is that modern sacred architecture tends to be placed without serious consideration of the spiritual significance of the ground on which it is built. In our modern secular world, the siting of sacred buildings tends to have a more political origin than a spiritual one.

A second category of sacred place involves a specific site which is called into harmony with the greater whole through sacred design, a "microcosm of the macrocosm" as Joseph Campbell put it.[4] Examples of such sites would be the solar-lunar observatory on Fajada Butte at Chaco Canyon, the "Woodenhenge" circle of poles at Cahokia near St. Louis, Missouri, or the medicine wheel stone circle in the Big Horn Mountains of Wyoming.

A third type of sacred place may be marked by some human structures or art work, but derives its sacred identity from nature itself. For many traditional cultures which are threatened by developmental pressures from modern society, places of this latter category are the most difficult to defend, as their identity is based on a perceptual reality which goes beyond what contemporary society believes is possible. In this paper, I focus primarily on sites within this latter category, especially those held as sacred to American Indian peoples—Alaskan Eskimos, Aleuts,

Big Horn Medicine Wheel, Wyoming

American Indians and Polynesians—because these kinds of sites are least understood by modern secular society, and the establishment of such places in the long run may have the greatest impact on helping shape a modern consciousness of ecological sustainability.

Sacred Places in the Native American Culture

Working among the Navaho for many years, Franz Newcomb and Gladys Reichard relate:

> . . .locality is of the greatest importance to the Navaho. Names of people, of animals, of dangers, names of arrows, of lightnings and plants, have power when known and properly used. Even so the names of places are charms. As the modern writer or dramatist gives his work setting, so also does the Navaho myth. Whenever a protagonist meets someone who is more powerful, the first question he must answer is 'where are you from?'[5]

Every culture has its organizing and energizing symbols which are translated into mythic themes to regulate and direct daily life. The landscape to Native Americans is a rich tapestry of myth, magic and meaning, as Native Americans tend to anchor their myths through associations to specific places. Mount Taylor in New Mexico is a special place where mortals can more easily access the spiritual realms, according to Hopi and Navaho tribes, much like Mount Fuji in Japan and Mount Olympus in Greece. The windswept rocky brown hills which stretch out into the Pacific Ocean just west of Santa Barbara, California, today called "Point Conception," is to the Chumash Indians the "Western Gate"—a place where human souls enter and exit from the earth plane. In Hawaii, the *mo'o*, two women who can change their shapes into lizards, are the guardians of Kaiwainui Marsh. At the Shark and Turtle Rock near the village of Vaitogi in American Samoa, it is said that if the children of the village come out and chant a special chant, a shark and a turtle will surface offshore and swim in a circle for several minutes, acknowledging an ancient legend about self-sacrifice in times of food shortage. Living in a world with such mythic anchoring makes myths come to life and serve as constant reminders of the cultural agreements which create the standards of the day. The two realities, the temporal one and the mythic realm, become less distinct, and more and more the living landscape becomes a place of magical spiritual power.

Of all the mythic tales of the American Indians, one of the most beautiful is the Hopi Indian creation myth, which also offers an explanation of sacred places. In the beginning, it is told, Tiowa, the Creator, saw a need to have a guardian for the earth, and so he assigned the task to Spider Grandmother. Descending to the earth's surface, Spider Grandmother saw she would need help, and so she reached down and picked up two handfuls of earth. She spit into her hands, and instantly two handsome young men appeared, one named Poqanghoya and the other named Palongwhoya, who became her helpers.

Spider Grandmother and the twins sat in meditation for a time to link their minds, and then Poqanghoya journeyed north to the North Pole, where he began to work his special magic, the power which gives structure and form to life. Then Palongwhoya went to the South Pole. He made his prayers, and in the stillness he heard a distant, slow rhythm, which he began to beat out on his magical drum. The distant sound was the heartbeat of Tiowa, and when the two beats were in perfect harmony, a surge of life force energy came shooting down to the earth. It struck the navel of the earth, the South Pole, and went on down and down until it came to the crystal at the very center of the earth. Striking this crystal, the energy then shot out in all directions, channeled by the structural magic of Poqanghoya. The reflected life energy then popped from the earth's crust, bringing the planet to life. At some places this life energy is more abundant, sacred places, the Hopi say. They call them the "spots of the fawn."[6]

According to the Hopi and other Indian peoples, sacred places enable humans to stay in closer touch with various spiritual realms, which are the roots of health, healing, meaning, creativity and the basis for personal power, for true power in the Indian reality, is a manifestation of spiritual attunement.

Just how does one know that such and such a place is one of these sacred vibratory centers? Two of the most common ways to identify sacred places, according to Indians I have interviewed, are personal experiences in dreams and waking states, and animal behavior. Sacred places have more energy, *Skan* in Sioux, and this energy tends to influence your mind as well as whatever else goes on outwardly.

Animals are especially good indicators, for they aren't encumbered by our modern system of beliefs and attitudes. In the Indian cosmology, everything is connected to everything else and each person and family have a special set of kinship ties to nature which are shown through unusual associations with animals. For a raven, an eagle, an owl or an osprey to appear at a certain time, especially when one is making a pilgrimage to a special place, is seen as an act of communication with the Creator, the animals serving as special messengers for the higher force. Indians and other traditional peoples see animals, in addition to their biological values, as affirmations of themselves and the spirits, which perhaps is one reason why few animal species have been driven to extinction by the actions of Indian people.[7]

In general sacred places have the ability to help people become more closely linked with spiritual realms and to be more energized and inspired. The churches of modern society differ in shape and design, but the artifacts within call to mind a unity of experience which is common among all such buildings of the same faith. In the Indian mindset, all sacred places are vessels to make contact with the Creator, even though the actual form and nature of the places themselves vary considerably. The following is a list of categories of Native American sacred places which I have become acquainted with over the last ten years through interviews with Indian people all across the United States. The categories have been developed according to the kind of sacred function or quality they are seen as manifesting.

Categories of Sacred Sites

1. *Burial Grounds and Graves.* The deceased have a continuing relationship with the living, according to Native Americans. Grave sites represent tangible linkages between the two worlds, and are sacred. The location of such sites is determined through a variety of divining techniques, and they range from locations distant from any habitation to special places in yards, which is where Samoans bury their dead. The sites themselves range from simple pit graves and stone cairns to elaborate mounds, such as those found by the thousands throughout the Eastern half of the United States.

2. *Purification Sites.* Purity of mind, body and spirit is seen as essential to taking on power arising from alignment with spiritual realms. Methods of purification include bathing in special springs and rivers, fasting, prayer, rituals, sweatlodges and isolation in wild places. In all tribes that I know, there are special places where such purification rites are undertaken.

3. *Healing Sites.* Health in the Native American view results from living a life of continual alignment with the many realms of the cosmos. In Indian culture to "walk in harmony and balance on the Earth Mother" is a commonly used phrase to describe following one's intuition to maintain or regain health. Illness occurs in the Indian view when we fall out of harmony with nature and the Creator, who works through nature. Healing then requires restoration of intuitiveness, as well as removing any physical and mental symptoms of illness. The following are some of the most common types of healing sites:

   a. Springs or other bodies of water, such as Coso Hot Springs in California or Indian Hot Springs in west Texas. Here muds, mosses and rocks, as well as waters, may be used to heal.

   b. Ceremonial sites. These are places said to be especially suited for performing healings, and often may be associated with unusual landforms, such as Navaho sand painters use in their designs.

   c. Meditational sites, typically isolated locations where people go to pray and fast. By being in such places they may experience healing. At Chimayo in New Mexico a simple Catholic church marks the place where Indians for centuries have come to be healed. The power in part is said to arise from the earth there. To preserve this tradition, some floor boards have been removed to allow people to take away some sacred earth.

4. *Special Flora and Fauna Sites.* Certain herbs and animals are said to have special powers. Groves of virgin red cedar in the Pacific Northwest are said to have special powers which go beyond utilitarian uses of the trees for building materials, musical instruments and traditional clothing. The peyote cactus, the Jimson weed and various mushrooms having hallucinogenic properties all have sacred values. In a similar fashion sage and sweet grass taken from special places are used to make smoke smudges

for purification. Deer, elk, wolverine, buffalo, moose, eagle and other animals also have special powers, and the places where they live and are taken have special meaning. Often, Indians say, an animal seems to act as a guardian of a special place, and such an animal is special and sacred. At an ancient rock altar in the Sierras, which I visit from time to time, a marmot family has lived as long as the Forest Service rangers and I can recall. The marmot sits proudly on the stone outcropping like a watchman, announcing his work with loud cries to all who approach, like a watchdog.

5. *Quarries.* Certain stones, gems, crystals and minerals have special powers. They bring with them a harmonic linkage to their place of origin and spiritual realms beyond. The deep red catlinite sandstone bowls of medicine pipes, which come from Pipestone National Monument in Minnesota, are an example of sacred stones from a special place.

6. *Vision Questing and Dreaming Places.* In dreams and visions, the voice of the Creator speaks most clearly, Indian culture asserts. Bear Butte in the Black Hills of South Dakota is a famous vision questing place for Plains tribes. The hills above Santa Barbara, California, have hundreds of caves once used by Chumash Indians to seek visions, some of which have been recorded in extraordinary rock art paintings and carvings.

7. *Mythic and Legendary Sites.* The association of certain places with various myths and legends helps us recall the meaning and value of myths, much as we use photos and paintings to remind us of important events. The giant Sleeping Bear sand dune on the eastern shore of Lake Michigan in Michigan is an example of such a site. It supposedly marks a mother bear waiting for her cubs to swim ashore.

8. *Temples and Shrines.* Human-made structures marking sacred places are found throughout the United States, ranging from simple circles of stones in the Great Plains to the thousands of mounds found throughout the South and East. Perhaps the most striking is the quarter-mile-long Serpent Mound earth effigy in southern Ohio, which is the largest serpent earth effigy in the world. It is important to understand that sacred structures mark sacred places, or as Hawaiian kahuna Momi Lum says, "The land isn't sacred because the temple is here; the temple is here because the land is sacred."[8]

9. *Spiritual Renewal.* Harney Peak in the Black Hills of South Dakota, like Mount McKinley or Denali in Alaska and Mount Katahdin in Maine, are examples of places of special inspirational value which can be traced back far before modern recreation uses. Just as Christians have Jerusalem and Muslims have Mecca, Indian people have special places which seem to be touchstones of renewal.

10. *Astronomical Observatories.* The Bighorn Medicine Wheel stone circle which sits on the shoulder of Medicine Mountain near Sheridan, Wyoming, the solar-lunar observatory on top of Fajada Butte at the mouth of Chaco Canyon, and the circle of wooden poles found at Monk's Mound just across the river from St. Louis, Missouri, are all examples of ancient astronomical sites. In earlier times, science and spirit were woven together into a whole rather than being arbitrarily separated. Observatories provide a structuring rhythm to organize the year's activities, as well as determine the best times to hold certain ceremonies.

11. *Historical Sites.* Places which are associated with historical events and structures enable us to feel a closer affinity with the past, such as the events and cliff dwellings at Mesa Verde. What took place in the past has an influence on the sacredness of places today.

12. *Sunrise Sites.* Certain places which afford an unobstructed view of the rising sun are used as ceremonial places by many tribes, to pay tribute to Grandfather Sun who comes from the east and his influence in our lives. Often such sites may be marked by petroglyphs or other ceremonial structures.

13. *Fertility Sites.* On Ring Mountain in Tiburon, California, there is a large serpentine boulder with numerous petroglyphs, most of which are circular with two hemispheres in opposition, etched into its dark green surface. It is said that the Coastal Miwok tribe originally made these markings as part of fertility rites, in which couples walked up to the rock and carved figures symbolizing the female genital organs in the soft stone. Then they would rub the fine green powdered rock on their skin to enhance fertility and healthy childbirth.

14. *Baptismal Sites.* At several places in Hawaii there are volcanic stones with bowl-shaped impressions on the top. History has it that these shallow basins are traditionally used to bathe young children as they are being given names or otherwise being blessed. In a related type of site the

placenta from a child's birth is buried in the ground or hung in a special tree.

Weaving Together Culture, Consciousness and Place

The Salish tribe of the Pacific Northwest has a term *skalalitude*, which refers to a sacred state of mind when all things are in balance and the spiritual dimension of life seems to predominate consciousness, which results in "magic and beauty being everywhere." A Jungian analyst might use the term "numinous" to describe the same state of mind. Skalalitude results from multiple contact with different sacred sites, each of which has a special purpose associated with its unique powers. Collectively, proper alignment with all the various kinds of sacred places results in an affirmation of self, just as all the colors of the rainbow come together to form white light when focused in a crystal prism. This concept is similar to the belief of the ancient Chinese Taoist sages that right relationship with the five sacred mountains of China would result in awakening the true inner self or "Great Man."

The idea of right consciousness arising from multiple contacts with sacred places is found throughout Indian culture. The Hopis of the Southwest conduct major ceremonies in their annual cycle to invite the kachina spirits, which live in the San Francisco Peaks, to join in the life of the villages for a few months of the year. In this agricultural tribe, the ceremonies help to establish the ties to the sacred mountains for most, although special spiritual leaders visit other sacred places in the area to conduct special non-public ceremonies.

In contrast to the stationary life-style of the Hopis, the Lakota or Sioux of the Great Plains once moved in an annual migrational pattern between Wyoming and South Dakota, following the buffalo and the spiritual forces. In the winter they rested in the winter camps of Wyoming. In the spring, they journeyed to Harney Peak, *Hinhan Kaka Paha,* the highest place in the Black Hills, to conduct the "welcoming back the thunders" ceremony associated with spring rains. Then they journeyed to the sacred meadow, *Pe Sla*, in the heart of the *Paha Sapa* or Black Hills, to conduct the "welcoming back all people in peace" ceremony. From there in late summer they traveled to *Mato Tipila* or Devil's

Tower in Wyoming to conduct the Sun Dance. Each of these ceremonies was tied to a special place whose spirits favored the success of the ceremony at a special time. Each of the ceremonies was in turn conducted by a special family or clan whose special medicine made that ceremony most successful. This pattern of migration also followed the path of the annual buffalo herd migrations. It is an extraordinary example of people and nature living in harmony together, aided by appropriate spiritual practices tied to place.[9] Similar annual patterns of ceremonies and rituals linked to special places can be found throughout the Indian peoples of North America. Place for them is not just a physical location, but a psychic touchstone from which to better understand the cosmos without and the self within. To assume that in a few generations the human species could evolve into not needing special places to affirm self-identity implies an evolutionary leap of unprecedented dimensions in human history.

Sacred Places and the Law

Many of the early treaties between whites and Native Americans included provisions calling for the protection of the rights of Native Americans to access and/or live upon certain sacred places, such as the Lakota retaining rights to the Black Hills of South Dakota. As time passed and conditions changed, such as the discovery of gold and other precious metals in the 1800s, many Indian treaties were broken, a point which continues to be argued in the courts today. Many of the initial treaties called for peaceful co-existence, but in reality this principle led to government actions to "civilize" the tribes and then assimilate them into mainstream culture. These policies were officially stopped on July 8, 1970, by President Richard Nixon, who delivered a message to Congress declaring that the policy of "termination" for Indian tribes had failed miserably, and that the new policy should be one that encouraged "tribal self-determination." Since this historic act, government programs have sought to preserve Indian tribes, reversing nearly a century of programs which sought to suppress or eradicate the existence of Indian cultures in contemporary times.

If we look specifically at federal acts concerning the

preservation of sacred sites, there are at least two critical
questions to pose. One is to ask what has been done to
preserve sacred sites for cultural heritage reasons. The
second is to ask what has been done to preserve sacred
places for contemporary use by American Indians, as
well as for heritage preservation. It should be noted here
that it is of no value to try to distinguish between American
Indian culture and American Indian religion, because the
two are inseparably connected.

1. Preserving Sacred Sites as Part of Overall Cultural
Heritage Preservation: The Antiquities Act of 1906 is an
early legislative cornerstone in establishing a policy of
seeking to preserve cultural heritage sites as part of the
nation's system of parks and monuments. Prior to this,
certain specific sites, such as the Serpent Mound Effigy
in Ohio, had been given specific protection, but the
Antiquities Act moved farther by adding additional protection for existing sites on federal properties as well as
empowering the President to set aside national monuments
from the public domain.

The Historic Sites Act of 1935 calls for the National
Park Service to initiate a National Register of Historic
Sites, including the establishment of National Historic
Landmarks. Section six of the Historic Sites Act calls for
protecting "Archeological sites that have produced information of major scientific importance by revealing new cultures
or by shedding light upon periods of occupation over large
areas of the United States." The National Historic Preservation Act of 1966 extends this policy to include recognition
for cultural heritage sites on private as well as public lands.

The Archeological Resources Protection Act of 1979
takes this direction one step farther, stating that "existing
Federal laws do not provide adequate protection to prevent
the loss and destruction of . . . archeological resources and
sites resulting from uncontrolled excavations and pillage."
The act calls for securing protection for archeological
resources for present and future generations, as they are
an ". . . irreplaceable part of the Nation's heritage." It also
encourages cooperation and exchange of information
between governmental authorities, the professional community, and private individuals.

These acts demonstrate progressive commitment to
protecting cultural heritage resources. Their focus, however,

deals only with some sacred sites, especially those with artifacts over 100 years old. While some sites can be identified in this manner, others may have no artifacts but still be seen as very sacred, for their "power" to Indians comes from the spirit of place and not the remains of the past found there. It is also important that these acts tend to focus on sites which have historic value rather than those which may be still used by Indian tribes practicing their traditional religion. These acts collectively are seen by some Indians as depriving them of their religion, by taking away the bones of their ancestors and the artifacts of the past which still have tremendous value in the ongoing practice of their spiritual traditions.

2. Preserving Sacred Sites for Ongoing Use: The First Amendment to the Constitution of the United States provides for protection of religious beliefs. The implementation of the First Amendment, however, is open to interpretation. A recent decision in the *Thomas vs. Review Board* (1981) case represents an important precedent concerning the American Indian religion, in that the court's opinion found that "religious beliefs need not be acceptable, logical, consistent, or comprehensible to others in order to merit First Amendment protection."[10] While any single decision cannot be transferred to all similar cases, this decision seems to imply that if a religious system can be demonstrated to exist, regardless of whether it is consistent with the religious beliefs of the majority of people, it should be given consideration for protection under the First Amendment.

One of the most important steps forward in terms of establishing the legitimacy and nature of the American Indian religion is the American Indian Religious Freedom Act of 1978. The main thrust of the act is:

> . . . that henceforth it shall be the policy of the United States to protect and preserve for American Indians their inherent right to freedom to believe, express, and exercise the traditional religions of the American Indian, Eskimo, Aleut, and Native Hawaiians, including, but not limited to, access to sites, use and possession of sacred objects, and the freedom to worship through ceremonials and traditional rights. (P. L. 95-341, August 11, 1978)

The key phrase in terms of sacred sites is "access to sacred sites." Implementation of the American Indian Religious

Freedom Act immediately called for the Federal Government to undertake a study of just how this act effects policies and programs. Completed within a year's time following the passage of this act, this study found two general kinds of problems associated with sacred places. One concerns guaranteed access, and the other concerns defining just what is a legitimate sacred site.

The American Indian Religious Freedom Act seeks to resolve these problems by having land managers consult with "native traditional religious leaders" to determine which sites on federal lands are sacred and how they are used. In many cases this is being done. At the 1990 Spirit of Place symposium, we learned from several National Park Superintendents in the Southwest that they regularly consult with Indian spiritual leaders before building trails and developing interpretive programs which involve known sacred sites. A difficulty with this approach is determining just who is a legitimate traditional religious leader. In many cases, several different groups assert that they are the "real" spokespeople for a tribe or band, claiming others to be invalid. In many traditions, popular voting is unknown, and the position of "spiritual leader" is gained through gradual recognition by the community rather than any formal ordination process.

The problem is further complicated by the sensitive nature of the information requested. Some religious leaders do not wish their religion to be made public, as the Indian religion is more personal and secretive than modern religions are. When they do talk about what is sacred, leaders may want their statements kept confidential. So it is difficult for other tribal members or the public to determine just which places have been declared to be sacred and why.

An additional complication is the difficulty of determining who is a legitimate Indian. Some Indians refuse to register with the Bureau of Indian Affairs. Some tribes don't recognize Indians born off the reservation as being legal members of the tribe. There are few full-blooded Indians in any tribes, and simple physical inheritance doesn't necessarily mean that a person is a legal Indian. Just what amount of "blood" is necessary to make a person a legitimate spokesperson varies from agency to agency. In Texas, people with 5 percent or more Indian blood may legally possess peyote for ceremonies. Someone such as myself, with Canadian Indian ancestry, could not be considered a legal Indian in the United States, even if you are a full-blooded Indian.

These complications in determining who is a legal Indian and what is the real Indian religion can complicate preserving sacred places. At Pipestone National Monument in Minnesota, site of the sacred quarry where the blood red stone for bowls of sacred medicine pipes is quarried from a thin layer of special sandstone, one group of Lakota insists that no rock from the quarry should be made into artifacts to be sold, as this is sacrilegious. Another group of Lakota feels just the opposite, and make their living by selling artifacts they carve from the soft red stone. The Park Service, which manages the site, is left with trying to arbitrate these disputes.

Even with these problems, many government agencies are taking steps to preserve sacred sites associated with Native American religions. The U.S. Navy grants Native Hawaiians access to certain sites on governmental lands to perform ceremonies. In a similar fashion the Shoshone and other tribes, who have long used the Coso Hot Springs for healing, may do so on a permit basis, even though the springs are located in the middle of the China Lake Naval Weapons Center. Bear Butte, in the northeast corner of the Black Hills of South Dakota, is a vision quest site used today by many Indians, as well as being a South Dakota state park. Park authorites have tried to make a number of policies to insure that vision questing can continue, although at times controversy has flared up about restricting access to both Indians and tourists.

To balance these positive steps, a 1988 U.S. Supreme Court decision concerning the opposition of Native Americans in northern California to the construction of a logging road near a sacred site, Doctor Rock in Del Norte County, could not support the Indians' claims that the road should not be built. Writing for the five to three majority opinion, Justice Sandra Day O'Connor said, "Even if we assume [the road] will virtually destroy the Indians' ability to practice their religion, the Constitution simply does not provide a principle that could justify upholding their [legal] claims."

One of the central reasons there is so much difficulty in modern courts recognizing Indian sacred places stems from modern religions being "commemorative" religions. They honor a historically important person, like Gautama Buddha, Jesus Christ or Muhammad, and the places this person frequented, as well as the symbols he left us. Such religions act like museums, preserving artifacts and the sentiments associated with the special spiritual leader who gave us these symbols and the rituals based upon them. Native American spirituality, in contrast, is based on the ongoing personal experience of the spirit, with special places being recognized as touchstones which enable such experiences to happen more easily and frequently because of their spiritual power.

Many sacred places do not lie on federal lands, meaning that the future of such places will be determined by the states and by private individuals. One of the most effective state bodies concerened with sacred sites is the California Native Heritage Commission.

California Native Heritage Commission

So often it seems that sacred places are not recognized until someone proposes to develop them. In an effort to establish a more comprehensive approach to the preservation of the Native American religion and its sacred places, in 1976 the State of California enacted AB-4239, creating a new governmental agency solely responsible for safeguarding the religious and heritage rights of California Native Americans. This California Native American Heritage Commission is composed of nine members appointed by the Governor, five or more of whom are to be elders, traditional people, or spiritual leaders of tribes or Indian organizations located in the state. These are nominated by Native American organizations, tribes or groups within the state.

One of the primary duties of this commission to date has been to "identify and catalog places of special religious or social significance to Native Americans, and known graves and cemeteries of Native Americans on private lands." Based on this survey, two important actions may be undertaken to preserve and protect sacred sites and Native American access to them. Private landowners on whose property graves and cemeteries are located will be notified, and they will be given the identity of those Native

Americans descended from the deceased. The second provision concerns Native American sacred places and places with cultural significance for Native Americans that are located on private lands and inaccessible to Native Americans. In such cases recommendations are to be made to the state legislature relative to the state or other public agencies acquiring these lands or easements on them for the purpose of facilitating access to them. This is in addition to providing for safeguarding those sites located on existing state or federal lands.

Values of Sacred Places to All: The Need for Research

The concept of sacred places in nature dates back to the earliest of human times. For most cultures down through the ages, these special places of spirituality have been the cornerstones of consciousness and culture. My own research suggests that when modern people can set aside the cognitive restraints of contemporary culture, they too step into situations where the natural power of places manifests in their lives.

Each cultural group tends to focus on developing certain aspects of consciousness and potentiality, while repressing others. In contrast to tribal psychologies, which see the interaction between people and nature as the root of health, healing and meaning in life, our modern behavioral sciences have little to say about how the mind and nature interact. Survival needs have encouraged American Indians and other indigenous peoples to develop perceptual sensitivities to place. We deny that these sensitivities exist or have value, and yet research shows that we share them and that in owning them may lie important links to health and creativity. Recent research on migratory behavior in birds, fish and insects suggests that a good deal of their orientation is in response to subtle environmental fields of the earth.[11] A growing body of data asserts that people also possess similar orientation abilities, but seldom are consciously aware of them. Other research shows that at least some sacred places possess unusual soil, geological formations, air ionization and water chemistry.[12] From these data, it seems very possible that the special ambience we sense at some sacred places is at least partially attributable to environmental conditions, which in turn are capable of influencing our lives. Acute burn treatment wards in some hospitals are now immersing patients in special environments with high negative ion content and strong positive electromagnetic fields, which are exactly the field conditions found at certain sacred places, such as sacred "breathing mountains" of the Hopi, according to physicist Elizabeth Rauscher. Aerospace engineer James B. Beal informs me that he has been consulting with Japanese firms on creating optimum environmental fields in special stress reduction centers in Japan, and that the fields have many of the same characteristics as those found at natural sacred places. (See chapters by Rauscher and Beal for details.)

Another approach to studying the significance of place is to look at case histories of unusual experiences which people report having at special places. This is especially valuable with people who have not previously used any hallucinogenic substances and have had no expectation of sacred power in the place. In the last decade I have gathered over 200 reports of these experiences. They clearly point toward some places having the ability to trigger altered states of awareness in some people.[13] Carl Jung called this "psychic localization," a concept which deserves far more serious attention in behavioral scientific research in these times of ecological crisis when we search for better ways to harmonize our lives with nature.[14] There is a gaping hole in modern psychology, the void in our understanding of how the mind and nature interact. The sacred places within us, in many ways, are as unknown to many modern people as sacred places in the world around us. Denial of these regions of ourselves can lead to mental imbalance, just as denial of the pollution of the oceans and the destruction of the tropical rain forests can disrupt global ecology.

Recently novelist Tom Robbins remarked in an interview that "it's getting harder to go anyplace in the world that has its own identity."[15] Though global society now exists, it is the uniqueness of each spirit of place that can diversify us, if we are willing to pay attention to its gentle voice. These voices need especially to be heard in our North American culture, which is a melting pot of traditions searching for a way to create a new and better life. Place is a power which works on and through people to make them unique and give them identity in communities. North

America has a legacy of sacred places in nature. We must come to appreciate them and learn from them what the spots of the fawn have to teach us.

Notes

1. Joseph Campbell. *The Mythic Image.* Princeton, New Jersey: Princeton University Press, 1974.
2. Mircea Eliade. *The Sacred and the Profane.* New York, New York: Harper and Row, Inc., 1961. Also see W. Y. Evans-Wentz. *Chuchama and Sacred Mountains.* Chicago, Illinois: Swallow Press, 1981; and C. Grant. *The Rock Paintings of the Chumash.* Berkeley: University of California Press, 1965.
3. James A. Swan. *Sacred Places In Nature: How The Living Earth Seeks Our Friendship.* Santa Fe, New Mexico: Bear and Co., 1990.
4. Campbell, *Op. Cit.*
5. Franc J. Newcomb and Gladys Reichard. *Sandpaintings of the Navajo Shooting Chant.* New York: Dover Publications Inc., 1975.
6. Frank Waters. *Book of the Hopi.* New York: Viking Press, 1965.
7. J. Donald Hughes. *American Indian Ecology.* El Paso, TX: Texas Western Press, 1983.
8. Sue Lanci. "Mo'okini Luakini Heiau," *Spirit of Aloha,* November-December 1988, pp. 22-27.
9. Ronald Goodman and Stanley Red Bird. "Lakota Star Knowledge and The Black Hills," paper presented at the First International Ethnoastronomy Conference sponsored by the Smithsonian Institute, September 1983, Washington, D.C. See also Anthony F. Aveni. *Native American Astronomy.* Austin, TX: University of Texas Press, 1977; Peter Mattheissen. *In The Spirit of Crazy Horse.* New York: Viking Press, 1983; P. Matthiessen. *Indian Country.* New York: Viking Press, 1984.
10. Ellen Sewell. "The American Indian Religious Freedom Act," *Arizona Law Review,* Vol. 25, No. 1, pp. 429-453, 1983.
11. Robert Becker and Gary Selden. *The Body Electric: Electromagnetism and The Foundation of Life.* New York: Quill-Wm. Morrow, 1985. See also William Corliss. *Handbook of Unusual Natural Phenomena.* Glen Arm, MD: The Sourcebook Project, 1977; A. S. Presman. *Electromagnetic Fields and Life.* New York: Plenum Press, 1970.
12. P. E. Taylor. *Border Healing Woman: The Story of Jewell Babb.* Austin, TX: University of Texas Press, 1981.
13. Swan, Op. Cit.
14. Carl G. Jung. *Civilization In Transition.* Princeton: Princeton University Press, 1964.
15. "Tom Robbins: if only Africa had sushi. . . ." *Marin Independent Journal,* April 30, 1990.

6

Sacred Places of India: The Body of the Goddess

ELINOR W. GADON

The whole of the subcontinent of India is sacred land, sacred to the goddess. Wherever people worship the Mother Goddess, they revere the earth as her body. Hindus refer to their country as *Bharat Mata*, Mother India. A sacred place is called *tirtha*, literally "crossing over," like fording a river, crossing from the profane to the liminal space of the sacred. Pilgrimages to such places are a popular expression of awe and reverence for the sacred geography of India. Mountains, hills, rivers and caves are often said to possess sacred powers, and these are places where one makes contact with the divine.

The crossing over often implies a physical crossing as well as a site with sacred power. Rivers are often *tirthas*. *Tirthas* are seen as portals from the human to the divine, from this world to the other. Often sacred sites are associated with the major gods and goddesses of the Hindu tradition, whose elaborate mythologies are told in the *puranas*, the "old tales" that are sacred scripture. Others are places where local deities manifest. But in either case, the sacred object is the site itself. The power comes from the place, not so much from the deity associated with it.

The inherent power of many sacred sites in India is very persuasive, due in part to the long continuity of associated religious practice. Archeological evidence recovered from a typical site often reveals multiple layers of ritual use. For example, in one place I visited in North India, one that is identified with the narrative of the historical Gautama Buddha, the earliest foundation was from the third century BCE. It was the remains of a monolithic sandstone pillar on which the Emperor Ashoka had inscribed the Buddha's teachings. The site was layered sequentially: the ruins of the Buddhist monument, a Hindu temple, an Islamic mosque, the tomb of an Islamic saint and on top of that another Hindu temple. This great mound, now twelve feet high, was sacred in its own right, a veritable document of the religious history of that area. It told of conversion and conquest, of the gradual dominance of Hinduism over Buddhism in the first millennium, of the suppression of Hinduism by invading Muslims and of the eventual return of Hindu worship in that place.

This site at Sankisa near the Nepalese border was the spot where the Buddha is said to have returned to earth after visiting his mother in heaven to inform her in person of the good news of his enlightenment. I journeyed to this long-forsaken village, off the path of any but the most intrepid researcher, on a photography assignment to document all of the places associated with the historical Buddha. It was the monsoon season, and I arrived in the late afternoon in a drenching downpour. Today Sankisa is a primitive village with no electricity; at sunset one retires for the evening meal in darkness and then sleeps.

Waking up to the first light of day, grateful that the rains were over and I could get on with the task at hand, I walked eagerly to the site of the pillar. At the foot of a huge grass-covered mound was an endearing life-size pink-beige sandstone sculpture of a baby elephant that once crowned the monumental pillar but was now housed in a protective iron cage. The elephant is one of the sacred animal emblems of early Buddhism. All around the grass-covered, overgrown ruins, on the sloping sides and top of the mound, were peacocks, their majestic iridescent tails spread out in the bright, warm sunlight.

Fully present in the moment, I had been privileged to witness the celebration of nature, the interconnection of all life, just as the Buddha had once taught.

It is often difficult to determine how a specific sacred site became special. It seems clear that reverence for the geographic place itself was crucial in distinguishing certain places. Arduous pilgrimages to remote sites—where the appropriate rite is to bathe in the icy waters of a pool or a river, to enter a cave or view a mountain peak—indicate that the great attraction of many sacred places is tied to the geography of that place. Sometimes a temple is there as well, but it is obvious that the environment, not the temple, is the source of the numinous. The temple simply serves to mark or specify the sacrality of the local geography.

Underlying the extraordinary number of sacred sites associated with geographical places in India is the intuition that the land, the earth itself, is an immense repository of sacred power. The sacrality of the land rather than a unified political tradition has given Hindus the strong sense of Mother India. Significant in the Indian Independence Movement was their commitment to India as a homeland because of the land itself and the myths and rituals associated with it. The many different linguistic, ethnic and sectarian traditions were often divisive forces, sometimes explosively so.

> The whole of India's sacred geography with its many *tirthas*, those inherent in the natural landscape and those sanctified by the deeds of the gods and the footsteps of the heroes, is a living geography and as such it has been central to the shaping of the Indian sense of regional and national unity. The recognition of India as a sacred landscape, woven together north and south and east and west by the paths of the pilgrims, has created a powerful sense of India as *Bharat Mata*—Mother India (Eck, 1981:336).

This is the theme of the Indian national anthem, based on a poem by the Indian poet-philosopher Robinda Natsogur.

> The fundamental conviction that the earth itself, or the Indian subcontinent itself, is a goddess, indeed, that she is one's mother, pervades the modern cult of *Bharat Mata* (Mother India) in which all Indians are called sons or children of India and are expected to protect their mother without regard for personal hardship and sacrifice.
> ... Kali's appearance—naked, disheveled, and in disarray—becomes a symbol of the present condition of the motherland: a place of sickness, death, poverty and exploitation (Kinsley 1986:181).

The most ancient expression in the Hindu tradition of the sense of the earth being sacred is found in the *Rig Veda* hymns, several of which praise the goddess Prithvi.

> ... It is clear that the hymns to Prithvi are grounded in reverence for the awesome stability of the earth itself

and the apparently inexhaustible fecundity possessed
by the earth. Prithvi is the earth in a literal sense as
much as she is a goddess with anthropomorphic characteristics (Kinsley, 1986:178).

The Vedic material goes back to the second millennium
BCE but is based on a concept that we in the modern West
are just beginning to understand as the Gaia hypothesis.

"The idea of the earth as a personified goddess and the
idea that the cosmos as a whole is a living being persist
and are central in later Hindu mythology" (Kinsley,
1986:178). A common iconography of the Gupta dynasty,
3rd to 5th centuries A.D., shows the god Vishnu whose
special role is to preserve the universe, rescuing the earth
goddess Bhudevi, who has been held prisoner at the bottom
of the sea by a demon. Vishnu in the form of a giant cosmic
boar dives down and picks up the goddess on one of his
tusks. The Guptas identified with Vishnu and saw themselves as protecting the earth, "a mythological model that
expressed their understanding of their political role"
(Kinsley, 1986:181).

Texts extol her as Mahadevi, the Great Goddess. She
is one, though manifest in many forms. As *prakriti*, she is
the primordial essence of nature, the very stuff of creation,
the basic matter of the cosmos. "As the spider weaves her
web, the Devi creates the universe out of her own body"
(Kinsley 1986:179). In the *Devi-bhagavata-purana*, parts
of the universe are identified with her body—the earth,
her loins; the oceans, her bowels; the mountains, her bones;
the trees, her hair; the rivers, her veins. The sun and the
moon are her eyes. The underworld is said to be her hips,
her legs and her feet (Kinsley, 1986:179).

According to the mythology and cult of the Shakta *pithas,*
the whole of the subcontinent is seen as various parts of
the body of the goddess. When incarnate as Sati, wife of
the god Shiva, outraged and humiliated because of her
father Daksha's insults to her husband, she throws herself
into the sacrificial fire. Shiva, inconsolable, wanders the
earth with her dead body, until Vishnu, in order to avert
cosmic disruption, following the grieving god around,
gradually cuts up Sati's body until nothing remains. Every
place where a part of the goddess's body was dropped is
sacred, a place of pilgrimage and a site for a temple to the
goddess. The most sacred of all, at Kamarupa in Assam,

is the site where her yoni, her vulva, fell. Today a great temple documents worship at the site. Documentation of worship at the site goes back to the fourth century.

Every village has its own goddess, sacred to that place, with her own name and her own story. Her numinous precinct is often marked by a humble stone or a tree stained with the red color of the goddess. Her devotees come there with petitions and offerings. Although her powers are specific to that locality, she is linked to the greater pan-Indian Great Mother.

The river goddesses Ganga and Jumna take their places at either side of the threshold of the inner shrine of the Hindu temple, the place of crossing over from the sacred to the profane. Ganga is said to have descended from the heavens at a time of great drought. Worried that her descent onto the plains of North India would cause destructive flooding, she asked Shiva to catch her waters in his matted hair. So we often find the small figure of the goddess in his hair, and she became one of his wives. Known as Mother Ganga, her river is the most holy, its waters purifying. The most sacred place on the river is the major pilgrimage center in North India, Varanasi (Benares). It is said that if you die by the river you will have instant *moksha*, liberation, saved from the endless cycle of reincarnation.

The stories of the river change, but the river lives on. The Ganges is described as the soul of India. Personified as the goddess, it is also imaged as a way to cross the sea of *samsara*, a crossing over from this world to the next. In the Krishna tradition the devotee never wants to get to the other side, but wants to spend all eternity bathing with the god in the waters of the sacred Jumna. Bathing is a sexual metaphor for the union of the soul with god.

Another way of understanding the relationship of the goddess to the land is the iconography of Lakshmi, who represents abundance. In a life-size sculpture from the second century, carved from warm pink-beige sandstone, her body celebrates its procreative capacities. One hand cups her firm round breast, the other points to her vulva, the threshold out of which all life emerges. She stands on two large lotus buds rising from a pot of water. Growing up her back, one with her human form, is a magnificent over-sized lotus plant. In the lotus blossoms are two peacocks, symbols of passion. The meaning of this devotional image from the second century is the interconnection of all of life, with the lotus symbolizing the emergence of life from the waters.

Other personifications of the abundance of the land—tree spirits, *yakshas* and *yakshis*, worshipped in the pre-Buddhist nature cults—were incorporated into Buddhist iconography, taking their place on the towering gateways of Buddhist stupas. There the *yakshi* is shown with her arms and legs entwined in the branches of a tree. The woman-and-tree motif is long-standing in Indian culture, going back 5,000 years to the earliest Indian civilization in the Indus Valley.

Alas, though Indians have the concept that the earth is alive and the land is sacred, there appears to be little concern for the quality of the environment. Modern Indians are very poor caretakers of their natural resources, poor conservators. I don't know what lessons are to be learned from this paradox, but apparently a living mythology is not enough.

Bibliography

Diana L. Eck. "India's *Tirthas:* 'Crossings' in Sacred Geography." *History of Religions* 20, no. 4 (May 1981):323-344.

David Kinsley. *Hindu Goddesses: Visions of the Divine Feminine in the Hindu Religious Tradition.* Berkeley: Univ. of California, 1986.

7

Ancient Theatres as Sacred Spaces

RACHEL FLETCHER

Introduction to the Theatres

With few exceptions, modern theatre is a self-contained and indoor experience, far removed from vast realities of the larger world. Today's audiences are familiar with thrust stages and arenas, black boxes, and open-air playhouses, but for the most part, dramatic events take place within a secluded proscenium setting. Participants are isolated from one another by darkness and from the world beyond by theatre walls. A square proscenium frame separates actor and audience, while also drawing viewer focus to the smaller immediate world of the play.

In contrast, the great theatres of classical Greece were magnificently orchestrated environments, open to the air, the elements, and the wide arc of the horizon that echoed their spacious circular form. Performances unfolded under the gaze of a rising and setting sun, before audiences nestled deep in the earth and exposed to vast expanses of sky. Typically, the playhouse was oriented to the nearby temple dedicated to the theatre's patron deity, Dionysus. Both the temple and the later playhouse were situated to complement the natural sanctuary of the far mountains and valleys. Indeed, as religious events and observances, dramatic productions bore testimony to gods as well as humans.

We know through historical studies that plays were produced with the consent and support of the entire civic community. Theatre was an instrument of *polis* and proportioned to it. Every free member of society was expected to contribute to festival productions, either as performer, chorist, producer, or simply as audience participant. The seating arrangement in the auditorium bowl permitted the attending community to meet across inevitable social barriers, in full sight and knowledge of one another. In fact, according to legend, when Aristophanes remarked about Socrates' ugly appearance during a performance of *The Clouds,* the philosopher rose from his seat in the audience to display his face before his countrymen (Bieber, 1961, p. 44). At the theatre, one's very presence was part of the dramatic setting.

Proportion in Nature

In a sense we can say that Greek dramas, whose stories and histories addressed essential life values, were enacted in the collective presence of man, nature, and the gods. In turn, theatre design followed principles that govern all forms of life and mediate human, natural, and cosmic realms.

Each level of Greek theatre, from the local arrangement of interior parts to the vast organization of the global landscape, resonated and reflected the others in a totality of interdependent elements. Playhouses were designed according to a symmetry characterized by harmony and proportion. While today we think of symmetry as characterized only by equality—that bilateral arrangement of parts in which the whole is divided into identical mirror images and distributed uniformly on either side of an axis— we are ignorant of the classical sense of symmetry as proportional, as integrating diverse elements by relating parts and whole.

For ancient architects, symmetry reflected a principle of unity in keeping with a belief in an integrally living world. In geometric terms, the timeless perfection of unity is represented by the circle or sphere, the eternal round. Circles convey vast fields with unlimited potential for pattern and form, but they can also render order and orientation in the world. The circle's central point brings focus to its surroundings, inviting a sense of place and belonging in the world. The center and circumference together express the relation of local affairs to the global, the near to the far.

Some traditional mathematical philosophies held that this entire spherical universe is organized harmonically according to geomerically graduated intervals of growth. For example, Plato believed the world to be ordered by divine intelligence according to laws of symmetry and the proportions of simple geometric forms. The universe, he says in the *Timaeus*, is "a single visible living being, . . . a whole of complete parts, . . . a single complete whole, consisting of parts that are wholes." (30d, 33a). Plato's view, which recurs today in Lovelock's Gaia principle and modern holistic thought, associates proportion with the natural logic that orders the entire universe and joins together all forms of natural, human, and cosmic "life."

Geometry's elementary shapes—the square, the triangle, and the pentagon—are ideally suited as patterns of living forms. This is because they derive from the incommensurable values $\sqrt{2}$, $\sqrt{3}$, and ϕ (*Phi*)[1] which replicate through endless divisions in space, even as the identical ratio remains present in the relationship of one level of subdivision to the next. This unique quality of continuity implies that every level of form, from the micro- to macrocosmic, can be united through proportion and measure.

The square, triangle, and pentagon demonstrate the classical definition of symmetry in which diverse parts relate proportionally to every other and to the greater whole. They are a mathematical means of addressing fundamental questions about the composition of our world. Incommensurable symmetries appear in nature, with examples from plant, animal, and human life. The nautilus shell (see Figure 1) for example, is structured mathematically on Golden Mean proportions. A rectangle of 1 x $\sqrt{\phi}$ encloses the shell as a whole, while the nautilus spiral proceeds along equally spaced axes whose lengths progress in 1 : $\sqrt{\phi}$ ratio (Fletcher, 1988, pp. 42-45).

Proportion offers a natural basis for aesthetics, creating harmony in composition and the visual effect of wholeness

---

1. Incommensurables cannot be expressed in finite whole numbers. The quantity $\sqrt{2}$ is stated as 1.4142135 . . . $\sqrt{3}$ is equal to 1.7320508 . . . and ϕ or ($\sqrt{5}$ + 1) /2 is 1.618034. . . . The absolute value of these quantities, however, can be displayed in geometric form. The relationship between the side of a perfect square and its diagonal is precisely in the ratio of 1 : $\sqrt{2}$. The relationship between the half-side of an equilateral triangle and its altitude is in the ratio of 1 : $\sqrt{3}$. The relationship between the side of a regular pentagon and its diagonal is in the ratio of 1 : ϕ or 1 : ($\sqrt{5}$ + 1) /2. Because of its truly unique mathematical properties, the ratio 1 : ϕ is also called the Golden Mean or the Golden Section.

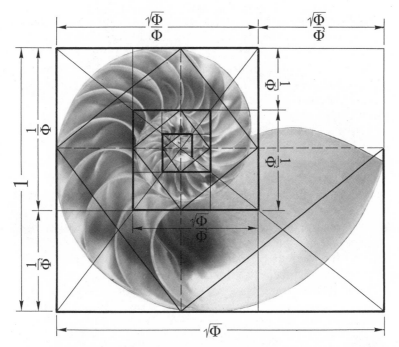

Figure 1. Proportional study of a nautilus shell

or gestalt. The mutual support of parts and whole lends structural strength and integrity. Philosophically, the notion of proportion addresses the fundamental paradox of the unity of God and the diversity of the created world.

Proportion in Ancient Theatres

As Greek theatre departed from its ritual origins in dithyramb (choric hymn) and circular dance to develop a complex interior form comprised of stage or scene building (*skene*), auditorium (*theatron*), and central dancing ground (*orchestra*), the total theatre experience remained holistic, environmental, and participatory.[2] The ritual altar of early

2. Scholars generally agree that the oldest part of the ancient theatre was the round orchestra, a central performance area that probably derived from pretheatrical circular dancing grounds, accommodating contemporary dithyramb and dramatic forms of choral song and dance.

   Simon (1982, p. 3) presumes that ring dances were originally performed on the circular orchestra, basing this conclusion on the derivation of the word "orchestra" from ὀρχέομαι (*orcheomai*, "to dance"), which means literally a "dancing place." The term "orchestra" may also relate with ὄρχος

times retained its place at the center of the theatre's orchestra, spatially mediating choral, acting, and viewing areas. As a pebble creates a symmetry of rings when dropped into water, this central altar focused the ever-widening spheres of the natural world and cosmos, from the near orb of the auditorium bowl, dug deep into the surrounding hillside, to the faraway orbits of planets and stars.

In the human sphere, the altar at the center focused the immediate round of choral activity and the wider concentric arcs of auditorium seating.[3] Imagine this massive stone altar attracting, as a lodestone, the diverse attentions of theatre audiences into its central vortex. In marking the orchestra center physically with an altar, what might have been regarded as a purely abstract and geometric conception of center became a tangible and visceral convergence.

As the nucleus determines the energetic state of an atom, the theatre's orchestra focused the playhouse round and, further, the great spherical world beyond.[4] This global sphere, however, was not precisely the same as a geometrically perfect sphere. Strictly speaking, mathematical spheres have no intrinsic locations for "up," "down," "left," or

---

(*orchos*), a "row of vines" and ὄρχις (*orchis*), meaning "testicles" or "ovaries," associations that further link the orchestra's shape and function to earlier forms of cthonic Dionysian worship.

Aristotle tells us that tragedy flowered directly from the circular chorus of dithyramb, proceeding through stages that included a chorus leader, and later a separate actor. Eventually there developed a number of actors representing unique and specific characters engaged in dialogue (Aristotle, *Poetics* 4:11-14). A rectilinear stage space or *skene* used by actors developed independent from the area of the chorus.

3. The theatron's plan of concentric arcs resembles R. E. Wycherley's (1976, p. 5) description of Athens' total spatial layout: "We can imagine the city as expanding in continually widening circles around the acropolis, or more often on one side of it. The lower city of Athens, Thucydides tells us . . . was on the south side originally; in classical times it had spread all round, forming a 'wheel-shaped' city . . . with the Acropolis as hub." Since the theatre of Dionysus was built into the south slope of the Acropolis, possibly the center or "hub" of Thucydides' " 'wheel-shaped' city" was located in the vicinity of the theatre, even perhaps at the orchestra-center itself.

4. Greek audiences were likely to experience their environment spherically, given the concave depression of the playhouse theatron and the spherical nature of the sky above, perceived as such because of the apparent curvilinear path of the planets and sun. From the time of Anaximander in the seventh century B.C., the Greeks were accustomed to visualizing the earth at the center of a universe of concentric spheres, each containing an orbit of the sun, the moon, one of the planets, or the fixed stars (Aristotle, *Metaphysics* 12, VIII:1073b-1074a; Guthrie, 1962, pp. 93-99).

"right." The pure sphere is completely without direction, except as oriented to its own center. In contrast, the Greek theatre was perceptually the center of a physically real-world sphere with directions of its own. The precise location for the pole-star was known to the Greeks as part of their cosmological science and geography (Allen, 1963, p. 453; Vitruvius, *The Ten Books on Architecture*, 9, I:2). When oriented to the "great circle" of the horizon, the pole-star fixed the cardinal "horizon-tal" axes of north-south and, at right angles, east-west.[5] A presumed vertical axis stretched directly above and below the horizon, with zenith at the top of the heavenly dome and nadir at the bottom of the earth's bowl.

While the altar at the orchestra's center did not create the world's cardinal axes, these global directions were not realities for theatre audiences without a local point of reference. In providing the world with a center, the altar enabled audiences to experience the world spherically and to assume a centralized place within. As Eliade (1959) says, ritually created centers possess the power of the world's Great Navel. By establishing a central point of reference in an otherwise formless expanse, "a universe comes to birth" (*ibid.*, p. 44). Order is made out of chaos. The world is " 'found' " (*ibid.*, p. 23).

Sacred Place

With the orchestra resolving the polarity of near and far, that is, the local quality of the center and the more distant global boundary, it became possible to address the deities believed to be present in the landscape. Assuming that Greek theatre evolved from ancient sacrificial rites, then possibly the theatre and its orchestra center acted like the temple and altar of the Archaic[6] Greek *temenos*, or sacred precinct. According to Bergquist (1967), these districts were situated intentionally to relate altar sacrifices

---

5. This does not mean that the cardinal directions derived primarily from the significance associated with north. Traditionally, the orientation of the directions was based on the importance of east (hence, the term "orient" for east) and the position of the rising sun. The use of the pole-star was later devised to standardize locations for the cardinal points (Bergquist, 1967, pp. 112-114).

6. "Archaic" refers to the period of early Greek culture dating approximately from 700 to 480 B.C. (Bergquist, 1967, p. 6).

to the landscape through cosmic or astronomical phenomena. In the majority of examples studied, the temple
was oriented to the cardinal points, "the longitudinal axis
being exactly, or only with an insignificant deviation,
east-west or north-south" (*ibid.*, p. 68). To Bergquist, siting
the temple entryway to the east was of special significance
because it enabled the worshipper to have simultaneous
visual contact with god as statue—image, near the altar—
and god as sun—image appearing naturally in the sky
at dawn.

This organic relationship between temple design and
setting suggests that the Archaic Greek people approached
divinities through the natural and cosmic landscape,
even though they were not, strictly speaking, a culture
of nature-worshippers. Possibly, given the open-air context
of Greek theatre, the chorus leader and orchestra center
were like priest and altar, mediating playhouse "congregants"
with the gods as they manifested in the landscape. Under
these conditions, while painted appearances and illusions
contributed to the skene's scenic background (Pickard-
Cambridge, 1946, pp. 122-127), the major scenic emphasis
would not have been the painted world of the stage and
skene. Audiences would have experienced drama taking
place primarily against a living, breathing natural landscape.

This bond between humans and their wider surroundings
required that the theatre be placed appropriately with
respect to its natural setting. Early classical theatres were
often located near pre-existing temples or temenoi, themselves probably site-specific. For example, the theatre
of Dionysus Eleuthereus, situated on the south slope of
the ancient Acropolis in Athens, lay very near the temple
of its patron deity.

Ancient Greek theatres expressed an intimacy and
continuity with the immediate physical site unparalleled
in Western theatre. Scully (1969, pp. 204-206) explains
how architects sited the Hellenistic playhouse at Epidaurus
near the major shrine of the healer Asclepius. Noting a
similarity between the theatron's shape and the "horns"
of the mountains, he says, "Here the tentative curves of
the hills are made definite and sure in the curves of the
theatre, and the whole visible universe of men and nature
comes together in a single quiet order, healed" (*Ibid*, p.
206). In drawing our attention to the common linguistic

origin of "heal" and "whole," Scully gives the reason for the theatre's healing properties. In articulating the forms implicit in the surrounding environment, the playhouse achieves wholeness and becomes simultaneously a place for healing.

Theatre was connected to its setting through siting techniques which emphasized unique and spectacular qualities in the immediate physical landscape. At Taormina in Sicily, the theatre auditorium faces the great volcanic mountain of Etna as it descends to the sea below, binding the elements—earth, air, fire, and water—in a single view. With the passage of time and the built surfaces of theatres now eroded, it is difficult to tell where Greek theatre ends and the natural landscape begins. As the theatre of Delphi first appears to one approaching, the line of sight continues straight up from the auditorium's central aisle through the natural cleft in the mountainous rock.

The Sacred Calendar

Greek theatre served not only to situate citizens in their community, their heritage, and their locale; it also placed them in the natural course of time. Dramatic festivals were tied to an annual round of seasonal celebrations and calendrical rites based on agricultural cycles and celestial periods of the sun and moon (Harrison, 1963; Hunningher, 1961, pp. 21-41; and Pickard-Cambridge, 1927, pp. 126-129). Festival dates were fixed by a complex lunar calendar, with dramatic competitions probably coinciding with the period of the full moon (Pickard-Cambridge, 1953, pp. 65-66; Neugebauer, 1969, p. 106).

Greek dramas were often written to highlight moments in the seasonal round or daily cycle. Literary references to cosmic phenomena might be timed in performance to coincide with natural events. The *Agamemnon* of Aeschylus, for example, begins when a beacon of firelight signals the warriors' safe return from the Trojan War. For ancient audiences, the beacon's appearance must have symbolized the daily emergence of the sun-spirit from the dark of night, for the Watchman says, "I salute you, torch of the night whose light is like the day" (11. 23-24).

Very likely, the Watchman's torch was produced theatrically by the early morning rise of the actual sun over the eastern horizon. At the theatre of Dionysus, where classical performances began at dawn (Pickard-Cambridge, 1953, pp. 67 and 272, n.1) and where the auditorium was south-facing, the sun's ascent and journey from east to west was clearly visible to theatre audiences looking beyond and above the orchestra and stage. The physical triumph of Greece over Troy, thus associated with the cosmic victory of light over darkness, was witnessed concretely by theatre audiences.

Possibly, this beacon also symbolized the new solar year springing forth from the barren cold of winter, for the Watchman awaits its arrival "to release me from this watch a year's length now" (11. 1-2). In fact, the *Agamemnon* was produced for the Great Dionysia festival in Athens at the theatre of Dionysus, a competition coinciding with our month of March and the birth of spring and the new year in the Archaic Greek calendar.

Some modern scholars have speculated on the link between theatre and cosmic events of greater scope and duration than the cycles of the day or year. Alwyn Scott (1981) locates the origins of ancient drama and theatre architecture in rituals of calendar-fixing based on long-term solar and lunar periods. He suggests that the theatre of Dionysus in Athens was designed from the outset to function like an astronomical clock, in much the same way that Stonehenge in prehistoric Britain is known today to have been a solar and lunar observatory.

Scott has identified key positions and alignments among Dionysus' archaeological remains which correspond precisely to declinations for the rising and setting of the sun and moon, relative to the solstices and equinoxes. Theatre architecture at Dionysus may have also included certain counting devices for determining the years between important eclipses of the sun and moon, as well as the metonic cycle of 18.61 years when lunar and solar calendars coincide most perfectly. Speculative as his thesis may be, Scott raises important considerations concerning the possible scope of the Greek understanding of cosmic patterns and their expression in art, science, and religion.

Geometric Proportions in Ancient Theatres

To further impart a sense of harmony in the theatres, architects may have recorded geometric proportions in the actual measurements of theatre buildings, expressing

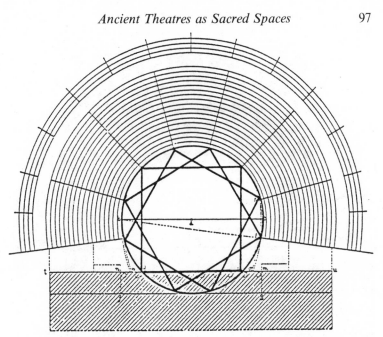

Figure 2. The ancient Greek theatre according to Vitruvius. Adapted from Dörpfeld and Reisch, 1896, p. 163.

the Greek understanding of cosmic and natural order in the living world. In the late first century B.C., Vitruvius connected theatre design with cosmic pattern, reporting that Greek and Roman theatres were typically arranged according to twelvefold patterns of symmetry that incorporated a geometry either of triangles or of squares. The plans were drawn, he says, "as the astrologers do in a figure of the twelve signs of the zodiac, when they are making computations from the musical harmony of the stars" (*The Ten Books on Architecture*, 5, VI:1).

According to Vitruvius (*ibid*, 5, VII:1), Greek theatre plans were typically drawn by taking a circle whose center and circumference matched the position and size of the playhouse orchestra (see Figure 2). Like the circle of the zodiac, the perimeter divided into twelve equal arcs. These, in turn, defined the apexes of three inscribed squares.

One of the squares had two sides parallel with the skene, one of which cut a segment of the circle at the precise location of the *proskenion* limit.[7] A line drawn parallel to

7. Although Vitruvius mentions a proskenion, or decorative surface applied to the skene front, probably one did not exist until Hellenistic times, when it also provided a supporting wall for a raised stage (Pickard-Cambridge, 1946, p. 159-160).

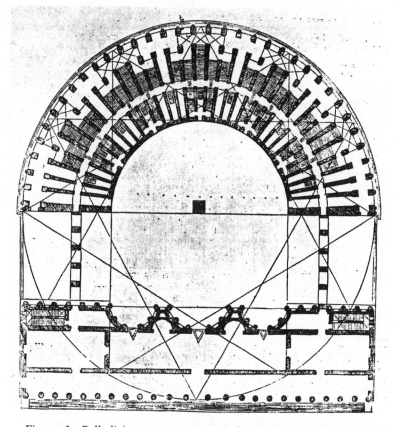

Figure 3. Palladio's reconstruction of the ancient Roman theatre according to Vitruvius. From Barbaro, 1556, in Zorzi, 1969, Pl. 452.

the proskenion and tangent to the original circle corresponded to the skene front. Eight of the twelve apexes
or angles fixed the extent of the theatron wrapping around
the orchestra center. The arc of the four remaining, when
cut away from the orchestra circle, made way for the stage.

Vitruvius (*ibid.*, 5, VI:1-2) says that Roman theatres
followed a twelvefold arrangement similar to the Greek
(see Figure 3). Again, the orchestra perimeter was divided
into twelve equal arcs,[8] but these noted positions for

---

8. It is unclear whether Vitruvius intended the initial circle of his geometric
model to match the perimeter of the orchestra or the arc of the auditorium.
Based partly on the evidence of extant Roman ruins, the modern interpretation is that Vitruvius meant the primary circle to correspond to the
orchestra (Oosting, 1981, pp. 31-32).

Palladio's study for the Barbaro edition of Vitruvius, however, is based inscribed triangles, rather than squares. The triangles, in turn, corresponded to key locations on the scene building, *scaena* (Greek, *skene*), and auditorium, *cavea* (Greek, *theatron*).

One triangle had an apex pointing toward the cavea center and a base coinciding with the front line of the scaena, or *scaenae frons*. A line drawn parallel to the scaena that also bisected the circle divided the stage from the orchestra and cavea. Compared to the Greek, the triangular geometry of Roman theatres allowed for a larger scaena, but smaller orchestra and auditorium. Opposite the stage along the perimeter of the half-circle were seven apexes designating stairways in the lowest auditorium level. The five remaining apexes corresponded to key positions in the scaena. One marked the central entry way in the scaenae frons. Two on either side pointed toward additional doors on the right and left. The outermost apexes located passages into the wings.

The Theatre of Dionysus

Variations on the Vitruvian formula appear in the record of actual theatre buildings. For example, the ancient theatre of Dionysus in Athens represents a composite of at least five different phases of construction taking place over a minimum of six centuries.[9] Too little survives the early classical periods to make an evaluation, but remains from the Roman era support the Vitruvian account (see

---

on a circle conforming to the overall size of the playhouse (see Figure 3). A design result of the Palladio-Barbaro interpretation is that the outermost stage doors do not correspond precisely to their designated triangle points, but the Vitruvian model otherwise remains intact.

9. The sequence of phases includes: an early orchestra, terrace, and Older Temple of Dionysus dating at least to the sixth century, B.C., of which only a fragment remains; the Periclean phase in the latter half of the fifth century, B.C., which was contemporary with the Odeum of Pericles and the Later Temple of Dionysus and which featured temporary wooden seats and stage buildings (the orchestra circle was also moved to the north); the reconstruction in stone of the skene and auditorium under Lycurgos, completed in 330 B.C. (the orchestra was moved to the north once again); the Hellenistic theatre dating about the mid-second century B.C. and possibly featuring a raised stage above a permanent stone proskenion; and, finally, the Roman reconstruction of the scaena about the first century A.D., featuring a new two-storied and decorated scaenae frons, a five-foot-high stage, and a smaller orchestra relaid in marble with a large rhombus design (Pickard-Cambridge, 1946, pp. 265-271).

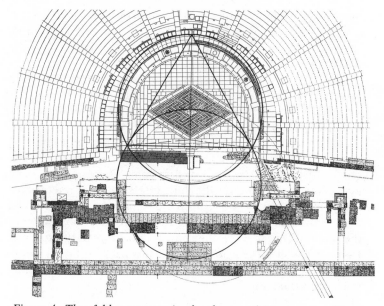

Figure 4. Threefold symmetry in the theatre of Dionysus in Athens. Author's proportional study based on the archaeological ground-plans of Dörpfeld and Reisch, 1896, Pl. 3.

Figure 4). The base of an equilateral triangle inscribing a circle that generally coincides with the orchestra severs the circle roughly at the eventual stage line. A large ornamental rhombus set in tile within the Roman orchestra circle has acute angles intersecting the triangle's two remaining edges.

Further analysis of the Roman orchestra at the theatre of Dionysus, however, suggests the application of more sophisticated and elaborate geometric techniques than the simple Vitruvian models. For example, details of the ornamental rhombus set in tile derive from a complex geometry that combines the *vesica piscis*[10] with twelvefold symmetry (see Figure 5).

The Theatre of Epidaurus

Unlike the theatre of Dionysus, in which each new playhouse phase was adapted from earlier periods, the Hellenistic theatre of Epidaurus was a complete and

10. In geometry, a *vesica piscis* is the area of overlap obtained by drawing two circles of equal radius such that the center of one circle lies on the circumference of the other.

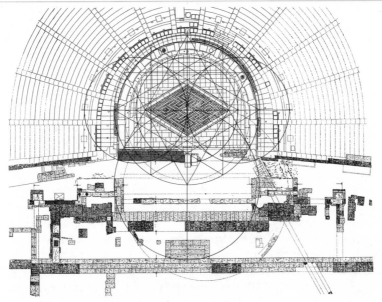

Figure 5. The vesica piscis and twelvefold symmetry in the theatre of Dionysus. Author's proportional study based on the archaeological ground-plans of Dörpfeld and Reisch, 1896, Pl. 3.

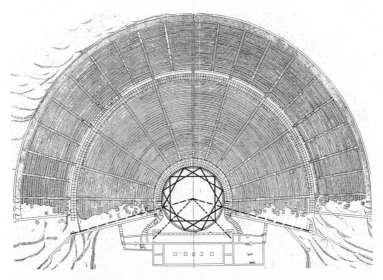

Figure 6. Fourfold symmetry and the theatre of Epidaurus. Author's proportional study based on the archaeological ground-plans of von Gerkan and Müller-Wiener, 1961, Pl. 1.

singular conception whose original orchestra and theatron remain intact today. The theatre plan supports Vitruvius' depiction of ancient Greek playhouses (see Figure 6). The orchestra perimeter is divided into twelve equal arcs. These in turn determine the apexes for a pattern of inscribed squares. Eight of the twelve apexes roughly define the boundaries of the theatron, although the geometry isn't precise until axes taken from the center through the first and eighth apexes meet the outer edge of the lowest auditorium level. The remaining four points define the size of the skene, in the sense that axes taken from the center through the first and fourth apexes mark the inner edges of the *paraskenia* (side buildings).

However, the theatre of Epidaurus also expresses threefold symmetry, since the base of an equilateral triangle inscribing the orchestra circle marks the boundaries of the theatron at its innermost edge (see Figure 7). Furthermore, geometric studies performed by the German scholars von Gerkan and Müller-Wiener (1961, Pl. 3) show that the front edges of the skene derive from a perfect pentagon. A circle that inscribes the pentagon coincides with the inner edge of the orchestra perimeter, while a circle that circumscribes the pentagon corresponds to the inner limits of the theatron.

The two levels of the Epidaurus theatron relate proportionally according to the Golden Section or 1 : ϕ. If the width of the higher level equals the side of a regular

Figure 7. Threefold symmetry and the theatre of Epidaurus. Author's proportional study based on the archaeological ground-plans of von Gerkan and Müller-Wiener, 1961, Pl. 1.

pentagon, then the width of the lower is the same pentagon's diagonal. The number of rows in each auditorium level totals 21 and 34, respectively. These numbers belong to the Fibonacci number series (1, 1, 2, 3, 5, 8, 13, 21, 34, 55, 89, 144 . . .), a progression that approximates the characteristics of a true Golden Mean progression in finite whole numbers.

Palladio's Olympic Theatre

During the Renaissance, classical techniques of architecture and theatre practice were revived by Alberti, Serlio, Palladio, and others. Palladio's Olympic theatre, completed posthumously in 1585 for the Olympic Academy in Vicenza, adapts the Vitruvian model for Roman theatres within an interior setting. Owing to a uniquely configured rectangular site, the auditorium and orchestra are not classically circular, but ellipse-like. Within this context, however, the proportional relationships among the orchestra, cavea, and scaena become apparent by means of a twelve-fold arrangement of triangles (see Figure 8A).

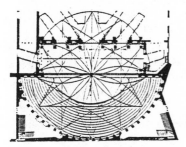

Fig. 8A

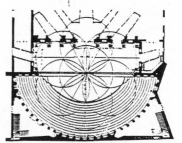

Fig. 8B

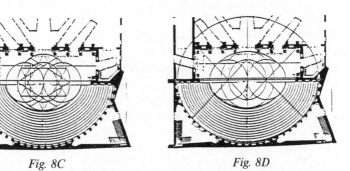

Fig. 8C   *Fig. 8D*

Figures 8A-8D. Palladio's Teatro Olimpico. Author's proportional study developed from studies and measured drawings of Scamozzi, 1776.

In fact, the theatre's ellipse-like proportions follow a combination of twelvefold symmetry and vesica piscis geometry comparable to that of the Roman theatre orchestra at Dionysus.[11] In Figure 8B, six identical circles are drawn about the circumference of a seventh circle of equal radius, producing twelve axes of symmetry. The various arcs establish the orchestra and proscenium opening, as well as passages into the scaena.

In Figure 8C, four equally spaced triangles are inscribed within the central circle. A smaller concentric circle is drawn about their points of intersection. Two additional circles of equal radius are drawn such that their centers lie on the circumference of the smaller central circle. A geometric matrix thus established, the ellipse-like arcs of the cavea and orchestra are derived in Figure 8D.

Although the Olympic Theatre did not enjoy active theatrical use, becoming instead a showcase for civic events and ceremonies, it is nevertheless an important example of Italian Renaissance academic theatre, a living illustration of the period's indebtedness to ancient principles of harmony and proportion in playhouse design.

Theatre as Microcosm

In contrast to the Greek and Roman theatres, Palladio's Olympic Theatre was an indoor playhouse that utilized artificial light. The application of mathematical proportions to its measured plans, however, revived a classical technique designed to connect the theatre to the larger world and cosmos.

Classical theatres expressed a sense of symmetry and harmony in which each element of the playhouse complex united proportionally, resulting in a chain of relationships that included ever-widening spheres in the natural and cosmic realms. Greek theatres were microcosms containing the elements of a complete cosmic order: sun and moon; *omphalos* and *axis mundi*; zodiac and cardinal axes; and temporal cycles of days, months, seasons, and years.

The plays themselves make countless references to natural and cosmic phenomena. In the *Agamemnon*, Clytaemnestra relates how word of the Argive victory

---

11. The author's analysis is developed from studies and measured drawings by O. B. Scamozzi (1776).

over Troy has been conveyed by torch relay. As one locale after another is illuminated, we sense the capacity of nature's living spirit to generate the fire's motion:

Hephaestus, launching a fine flame from Ida,
Beacon forwarding beacon, despatch-riders of fire,
Ida relayed to Hermes' cliff in Lemnos
And the great glow from the island was taken over third
By the height of Athos that belongs to Zeus,
And towering then to straddle over the sea
The might of the running torch joyfully tossed
The gold gleam forward like another sun,
Herald of light to the heights of Mount Macistus . . .

(11. 281-289)

Here in the modern West, where we have only begun to rediscover the living ways of nature, we do not fully know the Greek experience of a sacred and animated landscape. We can only guess how participants existed at the center of a world in which humanity, nature, and cosmos were inextricably bound by a common life force.

Today, these classical theatres are models for holism, examples of architecture as the ground for the inseparability of spiritual wholeness and ecological health. For ancient audiences, the world might be confined to the locality of the playhouse proper, but it could also expand to embrace the entire globe. Performances were occasions to rejoice in the embrace of human community within the theatre's auditorium and to experience humanity as held in the wider embrace of earth-mother-goddess-nature in the womb of the earth below and sky-father-god-cosmos in the vast heavenly arc up and over the playhouse bowl. In Greek theatre, the boundaries between "theatre-as-world" and "world-as-theatre" remained perpetually open and fluid. Polarities of center and periphery, near and far, and local and global were ever expressed and resolved anew.

Selected Bibliography

Aeschylus. *Agamemnon.* Trans. L. MacNeice. In *Ten Greek plays in contemporary translations,* edited by L. R. Lind. Boston: Houghton Mifflin Company, 1957.

Allen, R. H. 1963. *Star names: Their lore and meaning.* New York: Dover Publications, Inc.

Aristotle. *Metaphysics.* Trans. R. Hope. Ann Arbor: The Univ. of Michigan Press, 1960.

_____. *Poetics.* Trans. S. H. Butcher. New York: Hill and Wang, 1961.

Bergquist, B. 1967. *The Archaic Greek temenos: A study of structure and function.* Trans. E. Hornfelt and K. Schaar. Lund, Sweden: C. W. K. Gleerup.

Bieber, M. 1961. *The history of the Greek and Roman theater.* Princeton: Princeton Univ. Press.

Dörpfeld, W., E. Reisch. 1896. *Das Griechische theater.* Athens: Barth & von Hirst.

Eliade, M. 1959. *The sacred and the profane.* New York: Harcourt, Brace & World, Inc.

Fletcher, R. 1988. Proportion and the living world. *Parabola* 13 (1): 36-51.

Gerkan, A. von, and W. Müller-Wiener. 1961. *Das theater von Epidauros.* Stuttgart: W. Kohlhammer.

Guthrie, W. K. C. 1962. *A history of Greek philosophy.* Vol. 1, *The earlier Presocratics and the Pythagoreans.* Cambridge: Cambridge Univ. Press.

Harrison, J. E. 1963. *Themis: A study of the social origins of Greek religion.* London: The Merlin Press Ltd.

Hunningher, B. 1961. *The origin of the theater.* New York: Hill and Wang.

Oosting, J. T. 1981. *Andrea Palladio's Teatro Olimpico.* Ann Arbor: UMI Research Press.

Pickard-Cambridge, A. W. 1946. *The theatre of Dionysus in Athens.* London: Oxford University Press.

————. 1953. *The dramatic festivals of Athens.* London: Oxford University Press.

————. 1927. *Dithyramb, tragedy and comedy.* London: Oxford University Press.

Plato. *Timaeus and Critias.* (D. Lee, Trans.). Middlesex, England: Penguin Books, 1971.

Scamozzi, O. B. 1776. *The buildings and the designs of Andrea Palladio.* Trans. H. Burns. Trent: La Roccia, 1976.

————. 1776. *Le fabbriche e i disegni di Andrea Palladio.* Facs. ed. Trento: La Roccia, 1976.

Scott, A. P. H. 1981. *A speculative study to search for the genesis of the architectural form of the ancient Greek theatre to indicate a possible origin of Greek drama in calendar-fixing.* Ann Arbor: University Microfilms International.

Scully, V. 1969. *The earth, the temple and the gods.* Rev. ed. New York: Frederick A. Praeger, Publishers.

Simon, E. 1982. *The ancient theatre.* Trans. C. E. Vafopoulou-Richardson. New York: Methuen.

Vitruvius. *The ten books on architecture.* Trans. M. H. Morgan. New York: Dover Publications, Inc., 1960.

Wycherley, R. E. 1976. *How the Greeks built cities.* New York: W. W. Norton & Company.

Zorzi, G. 1969. *Le ville e i teatri di Andrea Palladio.* Venezia: Neri Pozza Editore.

8

The Himalayas, Realm of the Sacred

EDWIN BERNBAUM

Most people know the Himalayas as the highest mountains on earth. What is not so well known is that they are supremely sacred to more than half a billion people in South Asia and Central Asia, which makes them extremely important as sacred sites.

The whole range is viewed as a sacred place. Lying to the north of India, it is embodied in a deity known as Himalaya, or King of the Mountains. A famous quote from the Puranas, ancient texts of Hindu mythology, says of Himalaya and the value of contemplating it: "In the space of a hundred ages of the gods I could not describe to you the glories of Himachal [another word for Himalaya]; as the dew is dried up by the morning sun, so are the sins of mankind by the sight of Himachal." It goes on to say that just by thinking of these mountains this occurs. The sense of the sacred and the reality that it reveals liberates us from what has been translated here as "sins."

The word "Himalaya" means "the abode of snow," and one reason the mountains are venerated is that their snows are the source of the life-giving waters, of the holy rivers which course down through India and other parts of Asia. These rivers emerge from glaciers and run down through forests. The sacred has two aspects, the divine and the demonic. The mountains are not only beautiful and exalted; they are eerie and mysterious. In a picture I took I saw the claw and the cap of the yeti, or abominable snowman, which exemplifies the demonic element.

Beyond the Himalayas to the north there is almost no rainfall. What allows people to live in a very delicate and beautiful harmony with their environment are the snows

107

and the glaciers. Remote villages in Ladakh in northwest India are watered by streams coming down from glaciers in these desert mountains. People are an important part of the sacred in the Himalayas. They live all over. If you go walking in the Himalayas, it is not like walking in the Sierras and the Colorado Rockies with designated wilderness areas. You walk where people are living. The paths are the equivalent of interstate highways, but without the vehicles.

The Himalayas are also interwoven with many pilgrimage and carriage routes, which often coincide. On these roads you may see traders with caravans fingering beads as they walk, praying with every step as they pass sacred places, combining business with religion. Many pilgrimage routes follow trade routes and vice versa.

There are numerous shrines throughout these mountains to invoke the local deities and spirits of the area. Crossing a pass you will find cairns of rocks and prayer flags. A monk at the top of a pass may give an exuberant yell as he puts a stone on a cairn. His cry is translated as, "May the gods be victorious!" The gods and deities protect the people, watch over the land and ultimately protect the practice of religion.

As you go to higher passes and emerge from the clouds, you experience a strong sense of transcendence. The sacred brings you in touch with another reality that not only transcends the ordinary world but also infuses it. It is easy to experience the sacred in such places. For that reason many monasteries are built high up in the mountains. One of the most spectacularly situated monasteries in the Himalayas is in Bhutan. It is built on a sacred site. Sacredness in a place arises not only from the physical form, but from the holy people who have meditated there. In this case one of the main figures who brought Buddhism into Tibet from India is supposed to have flown there on a tiger and meditated in a cave. Therefore the monastery is named "Tiger's Nest." It was built for meditation and for conducting rituals which benefit people in the area.

Monasteries also serve as centers of learning, sacred learning which is mixed with the secular. Monks not only study and perform rituals; they also meditate. Many of the great monasteries were destroyed by the Chinese occupation, and religion is now practiced under limited circumstances.

Taktsang, The Tiger's Nest, monastery in the Himalayas of Bhutan

To attain the ultimate vision of reality, or to transcend that reality and achieve enlightenment, many people go up beyond the monasteries to meditation huts.

The Himalayas have a sacred role in the West as a symbol of the ultimate, the ultimate challenge. This can be materialistic, but it also has a spiritual dimension. A book along these lines got me interested in the Himalayas as a teenager. It was an account of the first expedition to climb one of the highest mountains of the world, one of the so-called 8,000 meter peaks. The name of the book is *Annapurna*, which is the name of the mountain which was climbed in 1950. What sets this book apart from almost all other expedition books is that as the leader of this expedition approached the summit, he had an experience of the sacred, a very profound experience. He writes about it in a simple way, relating it to both Eastern and Western experience. (As an aside, I got this book when I was thirteen or fourteen when my sister took it out of the library thinking it was a Nancy Drew mystery. When she found it was about an expedition, she threw it out, and I came upon it and was entranced. As it turns out, the book is about a woman, but in a higher order of existence.)

Maurice Herzog, who wrote the book, tells about his experience as he was approaching the summit of Annapurna at 26,000 feet above sea level:

> I felt as though I were plunging into something new and quite abnormal. I had the strangest and most vivid impressions such as I had never before known in the mountains. There was something abnormal about the way I saw Lachenal [his companion] and everything around us. I smiled to myself at the paltriness of our efforts, for I could stand apart and watch myself making these efforts. But all sense of exertion was gone, as though there were no longer any gravity. This diaphanous landscape, this quintessence of purity, these were not the mountains that I knew, these were the mountains of my dreams.
>
> The snow, sprinkled over every rock and gleaming in the sun, was of a radiant beauty that touched me to the heart. I had never seen such complete transparency, and I was living in a world of crystal. Sounds were indistinct. The atmosphere like cotton wool. An astonishing happiness welled up in me, but I could not define it. Everything was so new, so utterly unprecedented. It was not in the least like anything that I had known in the Alps, where one feels bouyed up by the presence of others. By people of

whom one is vaguely aware or even by the dwellings one
can see in the far distance. This was quite different. An
enormous gulf was between me and the world. This was
a different universe: withered, lifeless, a fantastic universe
where the presence of man was not foreseen, perhaps not
desired. We were braving an interdict, overstepping a
boundary, and yet we had no fears, we continued upward.
I thought of the famous ladder of Saint Teresa of Avila,
something clutched at my heart.

Herzog is describing an experience of transcendence,
but many traditions would describe it as immanence, not
something apart and other but right here. In both cases
there is a sense of the unknown, of mystery. In a sense,
the ultimate mystery is ourselves, that which we are closest to.

This experience was not a pleasant one for Herzog. He
forgot where he was, and on the summit he dropped his
mittens and didn't bother to pick them up or put on others
because of his state of mind. He came down the mountain
to the high camp with his hands bare. The rest of the account
is a very moving description of the suffering he went through,
which led to the amputation of almost all of his fingers
and toes. The sacred makes great demands. It is not just
a place to go for holidays.

The Himalayas run between Tibet and Nepal, stretching
1000 to 1500 miles, basically from Ladakh near Pakistan
all the way to the northeast frontier agency in India above
Assam and east of Bhutan. The most famous mountain for
the outside world is Everest, the highest mountain on earth.
Everest has an aura of sanctity in the West because of its
symbolism of something ultimate. It also is sacred to the
Sherpas on the south side and the Tibetans who live on
the north side, who are very closely linked. According
to their beliefs, the deity of the mountain is Miyolangsangma.
She is one of the five sister goddesses of long life who reside
along mountains and high lakes along the borders of Nepal,
Tibet and Sikkim. The Tibetan name of Everest is "Jomo-
langma." It is usually mistranslated as "goddess mother
of the world," indicating the Western need to see it as a
supreme sacred mountain. It is actually a fairly minor
sacred mountain for the local people. The name comes
from one of two names which translate as "the lady goddess
which is the benefactress of bulls" or else "the immovable,
unshakable good mind."

From the south Mt. Everest has a Nepalese name,

"Sagarmatha," which means literally "the top or the fore-head of the sky," but it is close to a Sanskrit word which means "the churning stick of the ocean." The person who concocted this name, probably in the first half of the first century, perhaps had in mind a myth from Hindu mythology pertaining to the churning of the ocean. In this tale the devas or gods and the demons or titans wrap a snake around a mythical mountain named "Mandara." Using this mountain as a churning stick, they churn up everything out of the ocean, trying to extract the nectar of immortality, while getting poison and milk and all sorts of other things along the way.

The mountain Mandara appears in the ancient epics, such as the *Mahabharata*, in which one of the main heroes, a prince named Arjuna, goes up into the Himalayas to perform austerities to get powers from the gods to defeat his enemies. He practices on the slopes of Mt. Mandara, and as he leaves he addresses the mountain. In Hinduism the mountains are not only the seat of the gods; they become gods themselves. Arjuna says:

> Mountain, thou art always the refuge to the good who practice the law, the dharma. The hermits of holy deeds who seek out the road that leads to heaven. It is by thy grace, mountain, that Brahmins, warriors, and commoners attain to heaven and devoid of pain walk with the gods. King of mountains, great peak, refuge of hermits, treasury of sacred places, I must go, farewell.

Mount Everest from Rongbuk Monastery in Tibet

In this brief farewell are many of the ways in which people view the Himalayas, ways which enshrine and reinforce their experience of the sacred in these mountains.

Very close to Mt. Everest is a mountain 10,000 feet lower. Everest is 29,000 feet in height and this is 19,000 feet. It is called Khumbila and is much more sacred for the people on the south side of Everest, the Sherpa people. They live in sight of both mountains, but Khumbila is right in the center of their territory. As such, it is the seat of the country god of the area, the one who watches over them, is involved in their everyday lives, provides them with food and water and punishes them if they go against the decrees of religion or offend the deity. The Sherpas will not let anyone climb Khumbila, whereas they will help people climb Mt. Everest. They fear that if someone does try to climb Khumbila, the mountain god will send down the yeti, the abominable snowman.

The first time I was out there I trekked through the mountains with the head lama, the Abbot or Rimpoche of the main monastery on the south side of Everest. As we were walking along the trail, he told me a story about a yeti. The story concerns a mani wall, consisting of stones with mantras or prayers carved into them. A good Buddhist passes one of these walls with right shoulder toward it.

The story was about a lama who was called to visit a sick person. It was late in the day and snow was on the ground. As the lama came to one of these mani walls, he walked past with his right shoulder toward it. The wall was higher than his head. When he got beyond it he found the fresh tracks of a yeti that had been walking the other way on the opposite side of the wall. Since he had walked around the wall correctly, he avoided the yeti and was not killed. The moral, of course, is obvious.

There are scores of sacred mountains throughout the Himalayas and into Tibet. They are all extremely important to the local people but do not have universal significance. More widely recognized are four great mountains of Tibet, that are the guardians of the country. They are situated at the four points of the compass around central Tibet. The northern one is called Nyenchen Thanglha, and it is next to the northern Tibetan plateau. It is particularly important because the god of this mountain, who also *is* the mountain, is a warrior-god, like Khumbila. He is both warrior and a king and protects the people, and in particular the hill of the Potala, the palace where the Dalai Lama lived, the heart of Tibet.

Another important mountain of these four is called "Yarlha Shampo." The sky god is said to have descended to that mountain on a sky rope to become the first king of the Tibetan people. This is the valley where the tombs of the ancient kings can be found, including the tomb of the first historical king of Tibet, Songsten Gampo, and the most important. He lived in the seventh century A.D.

The ultimate sacred mountain of Tibet is Kailas. It is the supreme example of the mountain identified with the axis mundi, the cosmic axis of the universe. Unlike Everest, which is surrounded by many other mountains, Kailas stands by itself. It is near the source of several major sacred rivers including the Indus and the Brahmaputra, and is not far from the source of the Ganges. It is sacred to both Hindus and Buddhists. "Kailas" is a Sanskrit word. Tibetans know it as *Kang Rinpoche*, the precious One of Glacier Snows.

For the Buddhists, Kailas is the seat of a Buddhist tutelary deity of the highest class of deities, call Chakrasamvara, or Demchok in Tibet. He is said to reside on the summit in a mandala. He and his consort embracing symbolize the union of compassion and wisdom, one masculine and one feminine. Their sexual embrace releases the great bliss that leads to enlightenment and the ability to help others attain it, the ultimate goal of Buddhism.

Not only is the deity often portrayed in a mandala, but the entire region around Mt. Kailas is viewed as a mandala. Smaller mountains around Kailas are portrayed in this mandala in supportive roles. This mandala is commonly seen with eight spokes of a wheel terminating in lotus blossoms. Meditators identify themselves with the deity in order to see the space around them transformed into a sacred space in which they can attain the ultimate goal of awakening.

This same pattern is behind the scheme of the universe, with the cosmic axis. In Hinduism and Buddhism Kailas is not always identified with the mythic mountain at the center of the universe. That mountain is Mt. Meru or Sumeru. A painting of it in Bhutan looks strangely like a model of the solar system or an atom. The universe can be depicted according to the Wheel of Time system, and right in the center is the cosmic mountain, Mt. Sumeru, rising some

80,000 miles above and 80,000 miles below, linking heaven to hell and all the realms of existence. Surrounded by oceans are floating continents, the southernmost of which is our continent. What look like swirling electrons are the months of the year. So swirling around the sacred mountain is not only sacred space, but sacred time. Time and space come together here.

A more common depiction of Mt. Meru is with the palace of Indra, the King of the Gods, on the top. Above him lie spaces of meditation and trance. The continents also lie around the mountain, topped by mountains. The shape of Mt. Meru is often compared to a flower, opening up. The dome-like shape of Kailas suggests temples and Buddhist stupas or reliquary mounds.

Kailas is also sacred to the Tibetans because of a very famous mountain-climbing contest, which took place in the eleventh or twelfth century, between Tibet's most famous yogi, Milarepa, and a priest of the indigenous Bon tradition of Tibet. This mountain was a center of the older religion. Milarepa came to Kailas, and the Bon priest told him he could stay only if he converted to the Bon religion. Milarepa said no, that his tradition was more powerful. They had a series of contests to see which tradition was more powerful, culminating in a climb up Mt. Kailas. The Bon priest started riding up on his sacred drum, but Milarepa made a mudra (gesture), and the Bon priest stopped at a certain height and could only fly circles around the mountain. Milarepa then snapped his fingers, and with the first ray of the sun went immediately to the summit. The Bon priest was so astounded he fell off the drum, and he and the drum rolled down the mountain together. There is a gulley on the mountain which is said to be the track of the drum as it went bouncing down.

Kailas is considered the ultimate place for pilgrimage for both Hindus and Buddhists. The number of people who actually go there is very restricted because of politics today, but this always has been so because it is an extremely difficult pilgrimage to make. You have to cross high passes on the Tibetan plateau, and it is very cold. Only a few people have even seen Kailas, but the mountain does not have to be present to be sacred for people. There is something about the clarity, about the sense of space, at Kailas which is extraordinary.

One goes on pilgrimages here to acquire merit, for a

future rebirth or a better life this time or for the power of helping others achieve enlightenment. In order to acquire more merit, you make the pilgrimage more difficult. People sometimes make full-length body prostrations all around the mountain. It normally takes three days to walk around, going over an 18,000 foot pass. These people measure the distance with their bodies, going over streams and glaciers. Some do it barefoot.

The high point of the circumnavigation is Drolma La, the Pass of the Savioress. Drolma, the Savioress, is a very important deity in Tibetan Buddhism. Just before the pass is a narrow passageway in rocks which, it is said, those with bad karma are not able to pass through.

Kailas is venerated today for many reasons. One of the most important is that it is the dwelling place of Shiva, the great god of destruction, the archetypal yogi, and the Lord of the Dance. He is one of the three aspects of the Supreme Deity. He manifests himself as the god of destruction, but when Shiva dances and meditates on this mountain, he becomes the god of creation and preservation as well. Originally a celibate yogi, he was seduced by Parvati, the daughter of Himalaya, who is extremely important for a number of sacred mountains in the Himalayas.

Many pictures of Shiva show a woman's head on top of his. This is Ganga, the goddess of the Ganges. One of the most famous and important myths, which links mountains and rivers for the Hindus, is the descent of the Ganges from the heavens. The earth needed water. A sage whose sons had been destroyed for evil-doing needed water to put on their ashes to revive them. So he appealed to the supreme deity, who asked Ganga to descend from heaven. She did not want to because, she said, if she fell on the earth, she would smash it. So Shiva offered to let her fall into his hair as he sat on Kailas. She twisted down through his braids, and then came out of a glacier called the "cow's mouth," fifty to a hundred miles away.

Gharwal is a region in India with many sacred places where many sadhus or holy men wander about. They often are devotees of the god Shiva and are identified by a trident they hold, a symbol of Shiva. He is the ultimate model for a supreme yogi. He is known as Lord of the Mountains.

Shiva's wife, Parvati, is known as Daughter of the Mountain. As a manifestation of the sacred, she is both divine and demonic, benevolent and wrathful. Annapurna is the name of one of her forms. It means literally "She Who Is Filled With Food or Grain." She is the presiding goddess of Benares, the most holy city in India, on the banks of the Ganges. It is said that Parvati provides for the needs of people during their life by giving them food, while Shiva provides for the people upon death, giving them liberation. Tossing the ashes of the cremated dead in the holy Ganges liberates them.

Annapurna is also sacred to the local people around the mountain, as a number of deities reside there. Hidden within the Annapurna range is a valley with only one entrance, called the Annapurna Sanctuary, which is sacred to the local people. In former times they would not allow untouchables, meat, eggs or women into this valley, believing they would offend the local deities. When I went up into this valley, the old men of the village were grumbling about landslides across the trail, which they blamed on Western women trekking up and offending local deities. We stayed there about a month and got caught in an avalanche.

Next to the only route into this sacred valley is a very sacred peak called the Fish's Tail, which the Nepalese government has banned for climbing. As a sacred mountain, it acts as a magnet: the deity that is most important to the pilgrim is attracted to this mountain.

People in India are often given names of gods, such as Ram or Vishnu, which is more than just a name. The highest mountain in India is Nanda Devi, which means "the Goddess of Bliss." She is a form of Parvati, wife of Shiva. In order to reach into her inner sanctuary, you have to go through an extraordinarily difficult gorge, the Rishi Ganga or Ganges of the Sages, who are supposed to live in this area. The mountain is almost 26,000 feet high.

Many years ago one of the foremost climbers in the United States, Willi Unsoeld, came to this area and saw the mountain. He decided that if he ever had a daughter he would name her after the mountain. In the course of time he had a daughter and named her Nanda Devi Unsoeld. When she reached the age of about twenty-one, she decided to climb the mountain after which she had been named. So she and her father organized an expedition, which included some of the foremost American climbers. They got up to about 24,000 feet. One morning Devi, as she was called, sat up and said, "I am going to die." Fifteen minutes later she died in her father's arms.

Her father had been a Peace Corps Director in Nepal, and Devi had grown up part of her life there and spoke Nepalese. The local people had been impressed by her and her golden hair, because another name for Parvati is "the Golden One." The belief in the area today is that she did not really die but that when Willi named her Nanda Devi the goddess incarnated in her, and this was the goddess's way of going back home to her mountain.

The third highest mountain in the world is Kangchenjunga, 28,000 feet high. It is the most sacred of the highest peaks, especially to the people of Sikkim, and also Nepalese. The name means "the Five Treasures of Great Snow." These are the treasures of gold, silver, gems, grains and holy books; they are both material and spiritual treasures. For this reason, one of the deities associated with this mountain is the Buddhist god of wealth. In his hand is a mongoose which spits out jewels. The mountain is also a god, and it has played an important role in the history of Sikkim, a principality that was swallowed up by India just a few years ago. The story is that Sikkim was a legendary hidden country, and these are special sacred places that only the select few can reach. There they find an ideal atmosphere for practicing meditation, and everything to sustain life; therefore in this place they can quickly attain enlightenment. Many of these places are scattered along the border between India and Nepal. From time to time when things were turbulent in Tibet, people left their homes to follow a holy person said to be able to find one of the sacred valleys. This sort of movement happened as late as 1975. The result is that many of the valleys along the Tibetan-Indian-Nepalese border were settled by Tibetans looking for hidden valleys, much the way the Pilgrims came to America looking for the promised land.

A lama was prophesied to find a way to Sikkim, which in the old days was a sacred hidden valley. He got to the snow mountains and could go no further. So the god of Kangchenjunga took on the form of a goose and flew over the mountains, revealing to the lama the way into Sikkim. The lama came over the mountains and settled, and he appointed one member of his party as the ruler of the country, the *Chogyal*. That lineage has come straight down to the last one, who married an American named Hope Cook and was overthrown by Indira Gandhi.

In celebration of the power of Kangchenjunga and to give thanks to it, the lama created a number of sacred dances which are said to be capable of exorcising evil, enabling Buddhism to flourish.

In western Sikkim, there is a major mountain called Chomolhari, which means "The Divine Mountain of the Goddess." Since this is the most sacred mountain in western Bhutan, the people do not want it climbed. One Indian party got permission from the king of Bhutan, but this was opposed by the queen and the lamas. However, the king overruled them. Two of the climbers died on the mountain, and about three hundred yaks were killed. The local people said that after that there were enormous storms, because the goddess was offended.

When George Leigh Mallory was asked why he wanted to climb Mt. Everest, he replied, "Because it's there." He died on its slopes. What is it that is there? Just what did he and others seek in this place? It seems to me that at a sacred place, what is real to people is revealed. There is a reality there that transforms the person who contemplates it or interacts with it. This reality is embodied in a sacred mountain.

When I was visiting Mt. Everest for the first time, I saw it at its foot at sunset, and it was sublime. Then I slept out at about 17,000 feet. This was in 1968 when Tibet was completely closed to the outside world. As I lay there in my sleeping bag, I looked up at a ridge and imagined myself gliding up that ridge, right to the border of Tibet. It suddenly hit me that I was in an area where there were unknown, unexplored places. But then it came to me that the whole world is like that. There are places right here with valleys and mountains, places no one has described, labeled, fixed, or made ordinary. That thought took me back to a time when I was two or three years old, living in the mountains. My parents would drive me down in the early mornings to see airplanes taking off. Then the world was vast and fresh and endlessly fascinating. As I lay there on Mt. Everest, in my sleeping bag, the world felt that way to me again. Contact with the sacred opens us to that sense of wonder, that sense of a deeper, fuller life, which is expressed in the laughter and play of children.

9
Megalithic Sites Reexamined as Spatial Systems

MAELEE THOMSON FOSTER
SARA KATHERINE WILLIAMS

Understanding sense of place begins with a realization that we live not in a world of things, but of relationships in which psychological and physiological, tangible and intangible systems unite to form a synergistic whole, the whole being greater than the sum of its parts.

Drawing upon our diverse experiences as artists, landscape architects, and educators, we believe that particular sites have had significance to humankind before modifications, and that sense of place may be identified, analyzed, preserved, and enhanced by utilizing the Design Process—not as a tool leading to a product, but rather as a means of investigating the evolution and meaning of a site. Based upon research and carefully timed site visits to the British Isles, we believe that key site forces and design determinants commonly identified with the Design Process may be clues to understanding sites where the builders' culture is no longer active. At an ancient yet still used site in Hong Kong, we see the same forces at work in a living context. From these precultural insights of universal design modern designers should be able to learn determinants to create a contemporary sense of place that is both functional and meaningful.

The Design Process, a creative problem-solving approach, begins with a clearly defined statement of the problem based upon perception and investigation. It emphasizes inventory, then analysis of pertinent issues. The relationship of these issues to each other, pertaining to the site and to human needs, are expressed in a synthesis. Synthesis is not merely a coming together of parts, but rather a unique composite of interrelationships that have the power to generate concepts that respect both the integrity of the site and the needs of the users. From these concepts, the design evolves.

Throughout this process, psychological and functional requirements, available technology, and spiritual/intellectual needs define opportunities and constraints that lead to a holistic design solution. The myriad site forces that dictated the design of megalithic sites are the same design determinants currently utilized by environmental designers. Other forces may have been utilized by prehistoric designers, but for this study, we will concentrate upon issues and terminology emphasized by design professions. By reevaluating megalithic sites in the context of the Design Process, we present a unique approach towards a more holistic understanding of these powerful, elegant spatial systems and their relevance to design today.

Not mere stone constructions, megaliths are site oriented spatial systems. An estimated 40,000 to 50,000 megaliths (Daniel, 1963, 12), were erected by Neolithic and Early Bronze Age people of Western Europe between 5000 B.C. and 500 B.C. (Service and Bradbery, 1979, 15). These are now considered among the "earliest stone structures still standing anywhere in the world" (Renfrew, 1983, 153). Their importance lingers for many contemporary inhabitants in legends, societal structure, and customs.

Serious academic interpretations of megalithic sites focus upon the stones themselves, associated artifacts, human remains, and chronological data. However, our approach recognizes megaliths as structure, space, and site, totally integrated as complex organizations of visual and experiential spaces expressing multi-layered functional and spiritual levels. Megalithic sites celebrate not only the uniqueness of the particular place, but also encompass region, cosmos, and significant moments. They reflect the builders' cohesive efforts over time.

A chronological typology consists of standing stones, stone alignments, barrows,[1] chambered barrows,[2] stone circles, and henged stone rings (Daniel, 1980, 78-85). The primary design determinants identified for this study are: meaning, usage, scale and proportion, materials and technology, orientation, climate, water, circulation, and topography.

Meaning

Meaning is defined as an intense bond with the cyclic patterns of nature and the cosmos (Burl, 1983, 16-7) and the duality of real and spiritual worlds, life and death, literal and abstract, negative and positive, created complex spatial responses that are both functional and symbolic. Of special importance was the connection of one particular site or space to other physical and symbolic points in the region and cosmos. Placement of each individual stone and the spaces between were carefully considered to communicate the greatest meaning. Sites are still believed to possess healing and regenerative powers.

Usage

The chiefdom social structure took the megalithic site as both symbol and territorial organizer (Renfrew, 1973, 170). Outliers served as landmarks and organized surrounding support spaces, linking megalithic sites to other spaces, sites and circulation routes. The immediate space of the megalith was utilized as a gathering place for rituals, social market or trading center, an observatory providing calendric information; a place for ritual burials. Megaliths, designed and built by successive generations, brought order to their lives and environment. They were designed for people.

Scale and Proportion

Size of the megalith responded to the specific significance of the site itself and how it was to be used. For example, the Loupin' Stanes cannot hold a large crowd, but is instead scaled for a family. Its gentle stream valley, unusual in a region characterized by rugged crags and forests, is a rare place where even such a small, intimate gathering could be sheltered. Long Meg and her Daughters is at cathedral scale. The slight, almost bowl-shaped slope within this circle allows the individual to see the rest of the crowd, not just those individuals immediately adjacent, thus emphasizing his or her connection to the group. Long Meg, the tallest stone, richly carved with sun spirals, dominates the top of the slope. This site shows sophisticated manipulation of not only physical, but psychological scale.

Statistical analyses of surveys indicate use of a common module: the megalithic yard of 2.72 feet (Thom, 1979, 34-55), or according to other interpretations, a body fathom of 1.6 meters based upon human proportions (Burl, 1979, 97). The complexity of many stone circles' layouts indicates a remarkably advanced understanding of geometry, scale and proportion in both practical applications and aesthetic statement.

Materials and Technology

Available materials explain some differences between sites. Barrows are constant across the British Isles, but the proportion of stone to earth varies. Eastern Britain's rich soil resulted in large earthen mounds; to the west and north in the British Isles, soil becomes thinner, eventually resulting in freestanding stone dolmens.[3] Choice of stone did not respond merely to what was readily available; the builders would transport stones for hundreds of miles, evidently choosing them for specific qualities or properties. (Daniel, 1963, 18)

Technological advances altered megalithic designs. Circles originated as clearnings in forests. These were soon further defined with timbers similar to reconstructed crannogs.[4] Later modifications relied less upon natural forest enclosure and more upon man's manipulations and constructions. Timber structures were translated into stone, with Stonehenge showing the final transformation of wood technology (Daniel, 1980, 88-9).

Orientation

Orientation visually and spiritually linked people to site, region, and cosmos. Many earlier megaliths were lunar-oriented; later ones solar. Much of the variance between stone circles is the result of orientation to different cosmic events. Statistical and astronomical studies, such as those reported in Alexander Thom's *Megalithic Sites in Britain*, indicate that slight asymmetries in shape result from remarkably accurate observations of cosmic movements that are subsequently recorded within the design of the circle itself.

Earthen barrows were usually oriented on an east-west axis, but shifted to focus upon distant man-made or natural elements specific to the individual site (Grinsell, 1984, 9-10). Now restored, Newgrange chambered long barrow, one of three related barrows, displays a multi-functional concave entry with a small, carefully placed opening—a light scoop that channels the first rays of the Winter Solstice sunrise along a 62-foot passageway to energize the chamber within (Service and Bradbery, 1979, 221-4). The exterior concavity links chamber, forecourt, and the broad gathering space beyond. Enclosing Newgrange is an earlier stone circle— perhaps the oldest known (Burl, 1980, 208). It and the incised southeast outlier stone may have been used to chart sun angles prior to construction of the chambered barrow (Foster and Williams, 1988, 746). Because of its prominent siting on a bluff and the high reflectivity of the quartz surface, the complex was visible for a great distance, thus serving as orientation and landmark for the region.

Climate

During the megalithic period, the British Isles were blessed with sunny skies, calm seas, and ample but not excessive rainfall—a climate conducive to sea trade, cosmic observations and exterior gathering. About 1500 B.C., the cold, wet Sub-Atlantic period began. As the climate continued to change, megalith building ceased (Service and Bradbery, 1979, 18).

Water

Megaliths lacking surface water are near wells or under-ground streams. Dowsers—and engineers—have discovered three underground streams flowing beneath Stonehenge; they cross directly under the altar (Chippindale, 1983, 244). Water was used in ritual, for human needs, circulation, trade, and as a visual design force. If near a large body of water, the megalith often faced the reflective surface in which the cosmic event dictating orientation was cap-tured and intensified. Avenues often led to or originated at rivers. Large bodies of water act as backdrop to accent the megaliths, intensify light, and emphasize the contrast of form in space.

Circulation

Water and land approaches were carefully considered in site selection and design and in manipulation of spatial experiences. Trackways and sea routes provided a linkage of sites, the megalith itself serving as beacon and territorial symbol (Burl, 1976, 287).

Topography

Relationship of megalith to topography responded to spiritual, experiential, and functional goals. Symbolically, the horizon may represent the earth goddess impregnated or highlighted by cosmic bodies; sacred peaks were identified and brought into the space by defined sight lines (Ponting, 1984a, 50-2). Perceptually, character of the site and placement of the stones depended upon the interplay of vertical stones, dynamic horizon, and the spaces between, resulting in strong emotional responses. The topography of the region was incorporated into the approach, heightening the experience.

Topography influenced placement of megaliths as they related to viewers. Not the most obvious, but the most experientially exciting or meaningful placement was chosen. Barrows could be feminine (cradled in the embrace of the earth) or masculine (activating the skyline); however, masculine barrows were not on the very top of hills or ridges but slightly down the slope, thus becoming the horizon/summit for the people below (Burl, 1979, 233-4).

Modifications of the immediate terrain were necessary for adequate functioning. Relatively level, well-drained sites were necessary for dancing, processionals, ceremonies, and measurement of shadows. Henges—man-made rings of ditches and banks—create artificial horizons, further claim space, and emphasize sacred territory. Topography embraces the design determinants, and synergistically, these determinants come together to emphasize and reinforce meaning through experience.

The multi-planed valley of Swinside is punctuated by numerous prominent outliers and oblique passes, creating prolonged pilgrimage, fleeting views of the site and sudden sense of arrival. Approaches are manipulated so that the circle seems to suddenly appear on the gentle plain. Tightly-spaced stones and ridgelines create proportionately related concentric spaces. Structure, space, and site are experienced as a totality.

Neighboring Castlerigg is similar in size, age, and elevated position within a strongly defined viewshed, but is more obviously connected to larger systems and employs space and scale differently. The unique stone rectangle within the circle points east northeast to Mell Fell, on whose peak is a smaller earthen circle with a single gap pointing back to Castlerigg (Burl, 1980, 48). This line is but one of many sighting lines that identify cosmic events and important neighboring sites, yet these lines also create a highly sophisticated internal geometry (Thom, 1979, 145-151). The very name, "stone circles," is misleading, as none are true geometric circles. Professor Alexander Thom's numerous detailed surveys of Castlerigg and other sites clearly show an internal proportional geometry that relates to region and cosmos.

Whereas tightly-knit Swinside is intimate, celebrating the land in its repose upon a slight plateau within a tight bowl-shaped valley, extroverted Castlerigg is more connected to the sky. Through large voids between the stones, space pushes out into the open sky, then drops sharply from its high, flat plateau, to be contained eventually by far distant peaks. Dramatic play of clouds and light further connect participants to the sky.

Holistic View of Design Determinants: Synthesis

Analysis of isolated design determinants explain unique aspects of specific sites. These issues may be examined individually but cannot be fully understood or used effectively in the Design Process without building upon the *relationships* among these determinants. Reductionism—the inability to synthesize after separating components for individual study—is a common problem in design today. Consequently, in our urban areas, in our ecological relationships, and in site-specific designs, we often find merely an assemblage of parts that never come together in a comprehensible, fulfilling, healthy unity that we see so beautifully expressed in megalithic sites.

Through interpretive descriptions of three major complexes of the British Isles representing differing spatial
organizations—the Orkney Islands, Callanish, and Stonehenge—the megalith builders' ability to design holistically
employing multi-layered perceptions is revealed. The
ancient yet active Yan Yuen Shek in Hong Kong allows
us to glimpse meaning through examining the usage of
megalithic sites.

Megaliths densely populate the northern Orkney Islands
(Service and Bradbery, 1979, 188-201), where an impressive
group is organized as a linear system, connecting the
chambered tomb of Maes Howe in the east, with the Atlantic
Ocean and the well-preserved neolithic village of Skara
Brae in the northwest (Hadingham, 1977, 26). Between
two large henged circles, one solar-oriented, the other
lunar (Burl, 1976, 99-102), a narrow isthmus dynamically
separates yet connects their spatial territory. Axis and
processional path, spatially compressed by water and
punctuated by a single standing stone, pass by but not
through the circles; the massive Watch Stone of the isthmus
increasing yet controlling the spatial tension of land/water,
positive/negative. At the neolithic village of Skara Brae,

The Ring of Brogdar on the Orkney Islands, northern Scotland.
Cosmic events, important segments of the horizon, and connections
to adjacent sites are enhanced by the placement of the stones and the
spaces between.

the six-mile ceremonial path terminates in the midsummer sunset reflected in the sea. The designers' ability to consciously organize space is evident in what Professor Foster believes may be hand-held diagrammatic carvings of the village plan found at the site (Foster and Williams, 1988, 749).

Callanish, located in the remote Outer Hebrides, is a radial organization, reaching out to position and unify nineteen known megalithic sites, each visually unique yet with one common purpose—to observe the moon activate the forms of earth goddess and moon child as it travels along the ridgeline to the south (Ponting, 1984a, 9). This complex astronomical drama creates the focus for the cross-like alignment of Callanish and its megalithic system. Optimal viewing position is confined within a large diamond-shaped region (Ponting, 1984a, 50) formed by topography and water.

Callanish, like most megalithic sites, is rich in legends and folk memories; many may be understood through careful site analysis and utilization of the Design Process. Facing the loch to the southwest and positioned on a rising slope, the wide avenue of stones creates a nave-like space on a northeast-southwest axis. Continuing along this axis, at the northern limit of the flattened stone circle, the southwest-oriented axis bends and turns slightly to the south (Ponting, 1984b, 50). Continuing south southwest along the stone alignment, the axis, shot through space by the wedge-shaped rock outcrop, now connects earth and cosmos. With the reflective loch below and just above the ridge of mountains to the south, the axis designates a specific point in the sky. Here, the moon pauses once every 18.6 years (Ponting, 1984a, 45). When the moon is full on Midsummer's morn, it is a celebrated event, for standing within the ancient appointed nave, the tall stones appear to capture and embrace the moon, holding the "shining one" of legend (Ponting, 1984a, 30) to the earth until the first rays of dawn, when to the sound of the cuckoo's call, it wisps away.

Site selection for Stonehenge was determined by astronomical alignments that could best be observed at this site. Within the henge and the fifty-six Aubrey holes, forming a near-perfect rectangle, four Station Stones were placed to provide sight lines to these events (Chippindale, 1983, 220). This original activation of the site was the first of three major building phases that continued for 2000 years

(Hadingham, 1984, 44-5). Site significance remained the constant through many changes in megalithic forms (Gingerich, 1977, 64-73).

Numerous trackways leading from distant sites to Stonehenge reinforce our view of Stonehenge as a centralized spatial system—the highly activated node of a complex matrix of processional paths, trade routes, trackways, waterways, and ley lines (Michell, 1977, 84-5). Stonehenge is connected to other equally dense metropolitan-scaled nodes (Service and Bradbery, 1979, 231-48), including Avebury and Silbury Hill (the largest pre-industrial man-made mound in Europe, its use unknown) (Burl, 1979, 129-33). Conceived and initially constructed during the same period, Stonehenge bears a direct relationship to the mass of Silbury Hill—it appears to be the near dimensionally exact positive of the Stonehenge negative. Flipped upside down, its flattened conical top would fit into the spatial enclosure of the Sarsen Trilithon Ring (Foster, 1986, 16).

An introverted focus organizes territorial mounds and barrows around a clearly defined sequence of concentric circles and a circular spatial enclosure which captures thirty segments of encircling sky. The strong axis, generated by the River Avon (Atkinson, 1986, 66-7), midsummer solstice sunrise (Michell, 1977, 82-3) and midwinter solstice sunset determines the Avenue and orientation of the enclosure

Stonehenge, Winter Solstice, 1988. The spatial system is activated in a celebration of the relationships of the individual to humankind, the earth, and the cosmos.

to the northeast. Symbolically, the rising sun travels southwest on axis to pause within the gate-like space formed by the Heel Stone and its companion stone (now missing) (Hadingham, 1984, 44-5), then moves across the earth-defined concentric circles of the henge, through the portal (Burl, 1979, 268), and into the sacred circular enclosure, to be accepted by the womb-like space within. Now weakened by its thrust, the axis escapes upon a shaft of light from the tight centralized space through a narrow opening to point, to foretell, the Midwinter solstice sunset in the southwest. From this central space, additional sight lines fan out to other astronomical events along the east-west cross axis determined by the geometric placement of the four Station Stones. Due to changes in societal perceptions of appropriate behavior, Stonehenge is rarely activated in a manner that we believe reflects the original design meaning and usage—the celebration of the individual's relationship to the universe and to fellow humankind. Stonehenge was designed for people, and the full wonder and joy is lessened without human participation.

In the Wanchai district of Hong Kong may be found recent human traces that penetrate the mystical veil of the spirit world, offering insight into the sensual and emotional power of megaliths. At Yan Yuen Shek, a fertility site, sequential spatial nodes activate the processional path of a point-generated system. Now paved, the ancient pathway winds around the hillside. Near the gateway, a simple rock, with its waxy inheritance left by colorful candles, generates the first node. One stops, and casts a backward look to the known: all is hidden ahead. Fortune tellers sit along the much traveled route at specific days during the month.

Thirty meters below, the city and bay become visible with the first bend of the path. The water between Hong Kong's island shore and the Kowloon peninsula forms a reflective embracing crescent. Shrine stones, specific stopping places, grow in frequency and intensity of use on the upward climb. The goal is hidden for an exceedingly long ascent.

Colored papers, flickering in the breeze, announce arrival. Paved stairs redefine vertical movement to a womb-like cave, aglow with light falling upon multicolored mementos. Waves of heady incense issue forth from the recess. The path pulls away and continues its climb, punctuated with vivid patches of symbolic red. The curve of the hill, the natural rock, lush vegetation, all shield the menhir from view. Suddenly, sunlight catches the glittering stony presence as it penetrates the sky. Its axial tip points to both the Midsummer Solstice sunrise and the Midwinter Solstice sunset, caught in the notch of the hill. The negative space formed by hill and menhir frames the echoing vertical of the city's tallest building, due north of the megalith.

The Design Process allows us to intellectually infer function and possible meaning, but lacks the heightened sensitivity of experience. Yan Yuen Shek provides a rare sensual glimpse of the tangible and symbolic use of a megalithic site.

E. V. Walter, in his recent book *Placeways*, identifies the current Western approach of separating emotion from intellect, symbol from reason, as the impetus for the loss of sense of place. An integrated balance of common sense, feeling, intellect, and imagination is needed (Walter, 1988, 2). Any loss of this balance destroys the integrity of the place.

Often invoked in contemporary designs, but seldom brought to life, "sense of place" too often refers to superficial impressions cued by commonly recognized icons and images. Degraded now to mere cliché, "sense of place" no longer expresses an understanding or concern about site or people. Choice of specific forms, elements and their detailing must first build upon a holistic response to the site—its unique utilization of design determinants and the many forces working synergistically within the site. Prehistoric spatial concepts, re-examined, may serve as our model for the future. Sensing the significance of place, and innately utilizing the Design Process, the megalith builders enhanced that significance as they created meaningful, functional spatial systems.

Notes

There is considerable discrepancy in the terminology of megalithic sites, with even more variation between regions and countries. For this paper, we have used these very generalized definitions:

1. Barrow: A mound of earth which may take many configurations, including long, round, disk and bell.

2. Chambered barrow: An earthen mound with a well-defined chamber within.
3. Dolmen: Upright stones (orthostats) support a horizontal stone or series of stones (capstones), forming a chamber. Today, most are free-standing with little or no soil covering them.
4. Crannog: A Neolithic village constructed on wooden pilings set over lakes or marshes, circular in shape. The name derives from "crann" (tree) because of the large amounts of wood used. (O'Riordain, 1979, 88)

References

Atkinson, R. J. C. (1980). *The prehistoric temples of Stonehenge and Avebury*. London, England: Pitkin Pictorials Ltd.

Atkinson, R. J. C. (1986) *Stonehenge*. New York: Pelican Books.

Atkinson, R. J. C. (1978). *Stonehenge and neighboring monuments*. London, England: Her Majesty's Stationery Office, Government Bookshops.

Burl, Aubrey. (1983). *Prehistoric astronomy and ritual*. Aylesbury, Bucks, U.K.: Shire Publications.

Burl, Aubrey. (1979). *Prehistoric Avebury*. New Haven: Yale University Press.

Burl, Aubrey. (1983). *Prehistoric stone circles*. Aylesbury, Bucks, U.K.: Shire Publications.

Burl, Aubrey. (1980). *Rings of stone*. New Haven and New York: Ticknor & Fields.

Burl, Aubrey. (1979). *The stone circles of the British Isles*. New Haven: Yale University Press.

Chippindale, Christopher. (1983). *Stonehenge complete*. Ithaca, New York: Cornell University Press.

Daniel, Glyn. (1963). *The megalith builders of western Europe*. Baltimore: Pelican Books.

Daniel, Glyn. (1980). Megalithic monuments. *Scientific American, 243*. (1), 78-89.

Foster, Maelee Thomson. (1986). From megalithic architects, a spatial system at Stonehenge. *Florida Architect, 33*, (1), 14-18.

Foster, Maelee Thomson and Sara Katherine Williams, (1988). Site-oriented spatial systems: megaliths. In Margaret McAvin (Ed.), *Landscape and Architecture: Proceedings of the 1987 Annual Meeting of the Council of Educators in Landscape Architecture*. Washington, D.C., Council of Educators in Landscape Architecture.

Gingerich, Owen. (1977). The basic astronomy of Stonehenge. *Technology Review, 80*, (2), 64-73.

Grinsell, Leslie V. (1984). *Barrows in England and Wales*. Aylesbury, Bucks, U.K.: Shire Publications.

Hadingham, Evan. (1975). *Circles and standing stones*. New York: Walker and Company.

Hadingham, Evan. (1984). *Early man and the cosmos.* New York: Walker and Company.

O'Riordain, Sean P. (1979). *Antiquities of the Irish countryside.* London and New York: Methun.

Ponting, Gerald, and Margaret Ponting. (1984a). *New light on the stones of Callanish.* Isle of Lewis: G. & M. Ponting, 1984.

Ponting, Gerald, and Margaret Ponting. (1984b). *The stones around Callanish: A guide to the "minor" megalithic sites of the Callanish Area (II to XIX).* Callanish, Isle of Lewis: G. and M. Ponting.

Postins, M. W. (1982). *Stonehenge sun, moon, wandering stars.* Kenilworth, Warwickshire, England: B. J. T. Print Services Ltd.

Renfrew, Colin. (1973). *Before civilization: The radiocarbon revolution and prehistoric Europe.* Middlesex, England: Penguin Books.

Renfrew, Colin. (1983). The social archaeology of megalithic monuments. *Scientific American, 249* (5), 153-163.

Service, Alastair, and Jean Bradbery. (1979). *Megaliths and their mysteries: The standing stones of old Europe.* London: Weidenfeld and Nicolson.

Thom, Alexander. (1979). *Megalithic sites in Britain.* Oxford, U.K.: Oxford University Press.

Walter, E.V. (1988). *Placeways.* Chapel Hill, North Carolina: The University of North Carolina Press.

10
Holy Wells of Ireland

WALTER L. BRENNEMAN, JR.

Scholars interested in the study of religion and the religious have made use, at least since the turn of the century, of the notion of the sacred.[1] Incorporated in their understanding of the sacred have been ideas of transcendence, purity, otherness, power and the non-rational. More recently, the sacred has been associated with the notion of world or worldhood in a phenomenological sense.[2] Eliade also related the sacred to space, and his work is valuable in this regard. It is Eliade who suggests that sacred space is heterogeneous in essence; in other words, it provides us with breaks in space, otherness, in which the power of the sacred can manifest itself. For example, a single tree in an otherwise open meadow provides a break in the homogeneity of the openness that allows the sacred to break through. In fact, our field work in Ireland has led us to confirm this particular example over and over, as we so often found trees deemed as sacred that were left uncut within a farmer's meadow. In one case we found that a new two-lane road divided itself to allow a previously existing sacred tree to remain in place.

Sacred Space

We should like, in our use of sacred space, to emphasize a few other aspects that have either been overlooked or that in our opinion need more stress. To begin with, sacred space always rests upon a foundation of power. What differentiates sacred power from, let us say, electric power or political power is that the experience of power is so moving to the subject that its source is attributed to a

134

supernatural referrent. One of my favorite examples of this distinction occurred a few years ago to a neighbor of mine. A dairy farmer, he was drawing a load of manure down a busy road, about to make a left turn into his dooryard. Behind him was a large milk truck. Just as he was beginning the left turn, the truck began to pass and struck the tractor, splitting it in half and throwing my neighbor from his seat. Miraculously, he was unhurt. His response was encapsulated in his statement that "someone must have been riding with me that day." Now he could have said, "I can't believe how lucky I was!" and in so doing attributing his salvation to our secular notion of "luck." However, he chose to provide obliquely an unseen and thus supernatural rider who, he implied, was responsible for his present existence. We infer, in this New England Protestant context, that the rider was God.

When we apply this distinction to space, we find that the experience of power that occurs in a particular space is named, and that its supernatural nature is acknowledged. But there is a further distinction between secular and sacred power in space that must be emphasized. This distinction lies in the world-creating power of the sacred. We use the term "world" in a phenomenological sense, world as experienced by an individual or culture. Thus what is created in not simply the physical or spatial world, but also the idea of world or worldhood.

By this we mean that the world is saturated with and held together by the power of the sacred, so that all those within the precincts of that world assent to and acknowledge the symbol through which the sacred expresses itself. Further, they see this central symbol as responsible for the creation and presence of the world.

We find such a situation in the creation of the world of Christianity. The history and symbols present in the miraculous birth, life, death and rebirth of Jesus became the container of a sacred power that radiated out from that symbol, transforming many in its path, until in 383 A.D. the Emperor Theodosius declared Christianity to be the religion of the state. The Christian world was thus created, and within its boundaries most assented, regardless of social status, to the creative power of Jesus the Christ.

The boundaries of the world established by the sacred are limited by the horizon of its power. Beyond the boundary is the profane; within the boundary is the sacred, which is constituted by a series of geographical and social components, which, though different, are interrelated and interdependent due to their common experience of sacred power and their assent to and naming of that power.

In thinking of this sacred world-creating power, we are reminded of an old Sherwin Williams paint advertisement. It was a logo in which was an image of the world globe with an outline of the various continents. Above the globe was an arm, sleeves rolled up, pouring a can of red Sherwin Williams paint over the "world." That paint spread as far as it could and colored the entire area, creating its own "red world." The paint can and the paint are like the emergence of a particular symbol of the sacred, which spreads, like the paint, from a center, transforming all it covers into its way of being, thus creating a world. The ad read, "Sherwin Williams Covers the World."

The power of the sacred, then, is world-creating, and it brings with it a universalizing force that unifies the interrelated components of the world. Its power is explosive in nature and expands outward from its center to the outer limit or boundary. Its continued existence depends on uniformity of experience and expression within the boundaries, and those who threaten this uniformity must be expelled. For example, the Hindu world before the British was constituted by "Mother India," her sacred mountains and rivers, and by the four *varnas* or castes that reflected the cosmology of that world. Despite radical distinctions between the castes, they were all interdependent and necessary for the existence of the world, in the same sense that the rivers and mountains and plains were all contributors to and necessary for the wholeness of the physical and spatial world. But all of this was a result of a common experience of world creation, a common understanding of how the world was created and the nature of that creating and sacred power. This same description can be applied to the world of medieval Christendom. Here, the Muslim invasion was an instance of threat to the uniformity of experience of the sacred within the world.

Loric Power

The experience working with the holy wells of Ireland, however, presented my wife and me with a different sense of power that was manifest in and about the location of the wells themselves. The power that we experienced seemed to be the opposite of the sacred, though it too was manifest in space. What we felt when we were standing by a spring surrounded by a wooded grove, often in the shape of a bowl or vessel, was a power that was drawing us inward toward a center. It was implosive rather than explosive, and was connected exclusively to that place. This centering was the most outstanding sensation, an impression of being truly within that place and responding to its power and uniqueness. It was like no other place on earth, and it was precisely because of this uniqueness that it was powerful. The spring, the trees, the stone manifested something that was nothing more than it was. It did not point beyond itself, but was its own self in its own uniqueness that invited us within it; that absorbed and, in a sense, intoxicated us with its presence.

We have chosen to call this form of power of place "loric power," for this same sense of uniqueness and intimacy is present in all lore, by which we mean the unique particulars of a person or thing which set it apart. For example, the power of story-telling lies in the event of the telling and in the unique way that a particular teller tells it. The story is not meant to be repeated in a uniform way from teller to teller, as is a myth in the sacred tradition. At the same time, there is an otherness in loric power which is shared by the sacred. There was an element of mystery as we stood in that dark grove and drank from the spring in a cup marked "Drink me for eyes." The loric and sacred share a participation in the archetypal, repeating timeless and powerful themes. The difference is that the sacred derives its primary power from the eternal identical repetition of the archetype, whereas the loric derives its primary power from the differences manifested from repetition to repetition.

Further, the notion of place is central to an understanding of loric power. Whereas the sacred is world-creating, the loric is place-maintaining. In Ireland this power is expressed in her geography—her rivers, caves and hills. An understanding of the sense of intimacy that resides in such places provides a key to the understanding of the loric. As a power, intimacy is so self-contained that it is completely hidden to those who possess it. Intimacy is revealed only to those who chance to enter a place in which the possessors dwell.

When a stranger enters, he or she is immediately aware
of the otherness and the intimate nature of the•"place."
One senses the odors unique to the place—its sounds and
artifacts. One may feel extremely uncomfortable and wish
to flee, or be drawn inward into the vortex of the power.
It is this quality of intimacy, based on uniqueness, that
provides the possibility for placehood, which in turn is
the ground of the loric.

Some years ago, my wife and I were members of a tomato-
picking crew in southeastern Pennsylvania. We were the
only white members on the crew, and when we had occasion
to enter the home of another member, we were struck by
a rush of sensations that conveyed the intimacy of the
place, its inhabitants and thus its loric power. It was strangely
other to us as whites, and we were both afraid of and drawn
to what we experienced in that place. It is this same power
of the loric that establishes the ground of the holy wells
of Ireland in both Celtic and Christian times.

Pre-Christian Ireland

Before the coming of the Christians in the fourth and
fifth centuries A.D., it is safe to surmise that Ireland did
not understand herself as a world in the sense in which
we have been speaking. This is the case for several reasons.
First, though scholars disagree on dating, there was no
central government or high kingship that was effective in
unifying the country until the tenth century A.D. at the
earliest, and then for only a brief time. Rather, Ireland
consisted of a great many holdings called *tuaths* which
were organic, self-sufficient entities ruled by a local chieftain.
In other words, there existed a conglomerate of decentralized
"places" which were not bound together by political unity.
These places were defined by geography, by the land itself
and its particular configuration.

Thus, for example, a particular valley or glen would
establish itself as a tuath governed by the head of a prominent
clan or family that was attached to the place. In fact, the
word *tuath* translates from the Irish as both the place or
dwelling land and the people who live there. The people
come from the land and are attached to her throughout
their lives as to a mother. Because of this notion migration
was seldom, and even in warfare it was not possible to
"take" or occupy another's land permanently. Each "place"

St. Lassair's Well, Kilronan, County Roscommon

or tuath, then, had its unique identity, was self-regulated, and thus was imbued with loric power.

A second reason for evidence of the prominence of loric power is the lack of a unifying cosmogonic myth in Ireland. Recall that it is the world-creating myth that is assented to by all that evidences the presence of sacred power. In Ireland the myth of creation must be pieced together from various sources and myths, and further was compiled after the coming of the Christians by the monks themselves. It then contained allusions to Noah, which sheds doubt on its early dating.

Let us look more carefully at the structure of the tuath and its loric character. Previously we observed that no land could be taken or possessed by a clan outside of the tuath, and that the people of the tuath were thought to have originated from and belong to the land. Amplifying these notions is the mythic perception that the chieftain of the tuath is married to the "place," who is both his wife and his mother.[3] Thus it was not propitious to abide elsewhere than the tuath where one was born, or to betray her love by taking the land of another.

Though each tuath was self-maintaining and unique because of its geography, a common structure was found in each of them. This structure was comprised of a center from which the fecundating and nurturing power of the place originated. At the center was a large burial mound, often surrounded by an earthen wall called a "ring fort." We saw an excellent example of this structure at the provincial center of Ulster, located just outside the town of Armagh. Sometimes the mound was a natural hill upon which was perched a stone, rather than an earthen fort, such as is found at Grianan Aileach in County Derry. The mound contained the power of the ancestors, and was also the location of the Otherworld, a place of which we will speak in detail shortly. Other power objects were a sacred tree, symbolizing the clan as a whole; a sacred stone in which resided the power of the chief; and a sacred spring symbolizing the goddess herself and the object of the chief's marriage. Thus the spring or well was of paramount importance, and was the primary source of fecundity and life for the entire tuath, whose welfare was dependent upon the successful mating of the chieftain at the well.

The Goddess and the Otherworld

This mythic scenario is characteristic of many cosmic religious traditions. By cosmic tradition we mean those religions whose power source resides in the earth. Further, these religions are characterized by the prominence of goddess figures and the technology of horticulture; in the case of Ireland it is that of cereal grain cultivation. Because the source of divine power resides in the earth in such traditions, the earth itself is experienced as sacred, and is often imaged as a goddess. Sacred space, then, has to do with the shape and power intrinsic to the earth herself, and is not based upon some event that occurred there, such as we find in historical religions whose hierophany is located in the sky. In other words, the very configuration of the land, as we have earlier said, makes the earth powerful.

The cosmology of ancient Ireland further amplifies the cosmic nature of her attitude toward the supernatural. This cosmology sheds light upon the importance of the sacred spring within the tradition, and it points out some aspects of Irish tradition that are sacred rather than loric in character. From the perspective of Western and even most Eastern cosmologies and the worldviews deriving from them, the Celts have an inverted cosmos: the source of all power is not found in the sky but in the otherworld beneath the earth. The result is that power and wisdom radiate upward from below rather than downward from the sky. This positioning of power provides an experience of the sacred very different from that found in such historical religions as Christianity and Islam. The experience is one of intimacy with the sacred rather than of separation from it. To be sure, all power did not reside in the earth; for example, the sun did exude a divine force upon life. But such celestial forces and divinities were understood by the Irish Celts as powers secondary or complementary to the forces found in the otherworld and on the earth.[4]

The otherworld in Ireland is located in various places, which provides several complementary shades of meaning. The most common location of the otherworld is beneath the surface of the earth, and access to that world for the living is possible only at certain places on the earth's surface which are containers of loric power. We have already mentioned the most common of these access points, the burial mound, called a *sid*, that functions as a center of the tuath. The sid is hollow and opens of its own accord at certain critical times to allow movement both from the surface downward and vice versa. Upon the sid various rituals of kingship in Ireland took place, such as inauguration and periodic festivals and banquets of symbolic import. Access to the otherworld can also be gained through a lake, cave, or well.[5] As these examples indicate, the emphasis on geographical entrances provides a clue as to the importance and power of the holy well.

Another location of the otherworld is an island to the far west. In general the direction in its extremity is understood as being the otherworld. Originally in Celtic lore, Ireland herself was seen as the otherworld and a holy place, because of her western location vis-a-vis the then known world.[6] Another place in which the otherworld is found is beneath a lake or sea. This theme is present in several Celtic traditions, including the French, where the otherworld is depicted as a submerged city presided over by a magico-divine princess.[7] In Ireland the sea theme is present in a tale from the Leabhar na hUidre, where another magical princess escapes the flooding of a well to live beneath Lough Neagh.[8] Three hundred years later she is transformed into a salmon and returns in human form to the surface world. Her divine nature is confirmed when she is baptized as the goddess Murigen, or "born of the Sea."[9]

The otherworld in Irish myth is understood as the first form or archetype of all life and wisdom. The surface world is a reflection of that archetype and contains the same structural components, but it lacks the power present in the otherworld except at critical times and in particular places. The two worlds are like two electric circuits, one (the otherworld) alive, and the other (the surface world) dead until a contact wire links the two. This connection occurs at particular times and places when access is established between the two worlds.

The otherworld itself is generally described as a pleasant place, though there are some descriptions of certain otherworld islands which contain tormenting or horrible forms. Many descriptions suggest a feminine identity to the otherworld, thus one of its names is *Tir na mBan*—the Isle of Women. In the tales "The Adventures of Conle" and "The Adventures of Bran," one finds the otherworld described as a land of women ruled by a seductive queen. It is the queen who *is* the otherworld, possessing the occult or hidden wisdom of which the otherworld is the source.[10] The theme of most adventure tales in Irish literature and myth is that of the young warrior journeying to the otherworld to gain the affection of its irresistible queen, and thus to attain the hidden wisdom necessary to rule the surface world.[11] Still another otherworld theme is the queen as guardian of a sacred spring, which is the true source of wisdom. The queen is actually identified with the spring, and her marriage to the young warrior constitutes the archetype of the marriage of the king to Ireland, which is the world.[12]

The otherworld was also understood as the site of the cosmic *bruiden*, or banquet hall, in which the perpetual feast of the otherworld queen and her consort, the Lord of the Otherworld, was held. There were five bruiden in the otherworld, and these were reflected in the inauguration sites of each of the five provinces of Ireland.[13]

Let us briefly review the components of each site: a sid

or burial mound on which sat a bruiden or banquet hall where the chieftain lived; a sacred tree or *bile*, beneath which he was crowned; a holy well, symbol of the goddess with whom he mated; and a sacred stone symbolizing his power or, alternatively, functioning as a "bed" or throne on which he sat to preside over the tuath. These same elements were present in the otherworld, which contained the archetypes of these power-bearing forms, as well as several other magico-religious objects that were, in turn, reflected in the inauguration sites of the surface world. Taken together, these sacred objects were identified with Ireland because they conveyed sovereignty, and because Ireland, the goddess, *is* sovereignty. They were managed by the Lord of the Otherworld who is the sun of the otherworld, the divine smithy and the husband of the goddess, Ireland.

The otherworld, then, is the pre-barren birth state. She is the Great Mother, the voluptuous, mysterious, forbidden container of secrets. She is the Original Mother, and most essentially, the sacred spring, the otherworld well of Segais whose water creates the world and imbues it with wisdom. It is she who provides the power and models for the actualization of the surface world, and it is she who through this power sacralizes the world. Within this feminine "place" were located the five bruiden with their host, the Lord of the Otherworld, and the magical weapons forged by him. He was the husband of the hidden woman, and through his mating with her the world was born. When the Lady at the Well is raped by the Lord of the Bruiden, the well overflows and the world is reborn. It is this well that forms the model of the present holy wells of Ireland.

The Well of Segais

Now let us examine more closely the otherworld well of Segais in an effort to establish its symbolism. Thus we can understand more fully the sacrality of the surface wells which are modelled after it. Myths about this well tell us that it is identified with the magical, beautiful woman, who is often guardian and keeper of the well.[14] It is frequently visited by warrior chieftains seeking her favor, which takes the form of sexual intercourse, symbolically identical with drinking from the well and achieving wisdom.

Around the well are nine hazel trees, all in the tradition of the aforementioned bile, whose red berries drop into the well. These berries are magical and cause a mist to arise from the water, which is called in Irish *na bolcca immaiss*, or "bubbles of mystic inspiration."[15] Further, there are five salmon, also divine beings, who live in the well and consume the berries, thus known as *eo fis*, the salmon of wisdom.[16] As the well is the source of the holy rivers Shannon and Boyne on the surface world, the berries and salmon periodically flow into these rivers. Whoever eats the berries or is fortunate enough to catch and eat a salmon is endowed with wisdom and becomes an accomplished bard or *file*.[17]

The symbolic meaning of the Well of Segais is contained primarily in its identification with the Great Goddess, the central fecundator and power of Irish spirituality. More precisely, the well is the vagina of the goddess, which consumes the offering of the Lord of the Otherworld. He is finally transformed into the sacred salmon who lives in the belly or *yoni* of Ireland. Through the offering of the male to the female, the goddess overflows with power, thereby revivifying the world. Here we see that power is primarily manifest in the feminine mode, and as such is ambivalent. The goddess is both devouring mother, in the consumption of her husband/son, and nurturing mother, in her role as recreator of the world.

The salmon symbolizes the son, lover and husband, now full of divine wisdom through his death, offered to the goddess, within whom he dwells. Here again, however, one encounters ambivalence, for the salmon is a fish of two waters, the salt and the fresh, the feminine and the masculine. His boundary crossing, as with the mercurial Hermes of alchemy, brings the hidden power of the goddess to the surface, and thus encourages transformation in ordinary humans. The salmon symbolizes the male lord who has, like Jonah, been swallowed by the watery feminine, and through this intimate relationship has absorbed the healing quality associated with her. This meaning accounts for the male lord's ambivalence, and for the fact that the salmon is sometimes understood in this role as "anima," as a woman or girl.

The nine sacred hazel trees, or bile, stand by the well of Segais. The berries of these trees fecundate the well, producing the mist of wisdom or feeding the salmon of wisdom. The sacred tree in Irish myth plays a masculine role, symbolizing the ancient, timeless, ancestors, the Lords of the Otherworld who are sacrificed to the goddess/ well and cause her to overflow, bringing about the wisdom of a new creation or transformation. The wisdom is always a hidden wisdom, and so it manifests itself as a mist or cloud through which the world is seen in a shadowy form.

One final component of the well of the otherworld is the *lia fal*, the sacred stone and one of the primary power bearers of the otherworld. This stone was most probably situated near the well of Segais, although it is not perfectly clear in the text.[18] My interpretation is based on the fact that sacred stones are commonly in association with holy wells on the surface world prior to Christian times, and these surface wells are understood as reflections of the Well of Segais.

One of the best known of these sacred stones was the one located at Tara, primary inauguration site of the high kings of Ireland. Here, the stone played a role in the ritual of inauguration. The stone itself was commonly understood to be in the form of a pillar and was therefore interpreted to symbolize the power of the king as fecundator.[19] O'Rahilly amplifies this interpretation by associating the stone with the sun god and, consequently, the Lord of the Otherworld. The connection with the sun is made through the otherworld god's role as divine smithy. It is the smithy who manifests the lightning stroke of the sun in his forge and the voice of thunder on his anvil.[20] As the sun of the otherworld, the stone possesses the voice associated with it on the surface world, but is often in the shape of a circle and understood as a "circle of light," identified with the sun.[21] These linkages are further indication that the stone of Fal did, in fact, lay by the well of Segais in the otherworld.

The Otherworld and the Surface World

We must now reflect upon the relationship between the otherworld and the surface world, and how that relationship establishes a certain degree of sacrality into early Irish spirituality. We have seen that the relationship between overworlds and underworlds is that of a mirror reflecting its object of perception. In other words, the overworld has its gaze set upon the otherworld as its model, and thus reflects the same structure upon its surface, in the same way that a mirror reflects what lies before it. In terms of ontology, then, the otherworld is the primary source of being, while the overworld is but a reflection of that being. Thus we must conclude that in the Celtic perception the world of mist, intoxication and magical swords and salmon is of greater reality than the more prosaic world of day-to-day existence.

Because of the fact that the otherworld functions as a model or archetype for the overworld, and because it constitutes a series of interrelated and interdependent parts which extend outward from center to horizon, we conclude that we are dealing with the phenomenology of world, not of place. This same phenomenology is present through the symbolic identity of over- and underworlds on the surface of Ireland. Thus, through the imitation of the sacred archetypes, Ireland participates in world-hood and in the power of the sacred. Each provincial center, with its mound, bruiden, tree, stone and well, participates through imitation, and helps to establish a world on the surface of Ireland. In addition, there were certain deities that were present in the otherworld, and thus were deities of a universal nature and not limited to place. Such gods as Lug, the Dagda, Brigid and Morigan were connected with a place, but were known and recognized in varying degrees throughout Ireland.[22] This same archetypal and universal nature applied to the well of Segais, which was thus imitated by each holy well in each tuath of Ireland.

Recall that the power of the sacred distinguishes itself by its tendency to universalize those objects and rituals with which it comes into contact. In addition, it creates a uniformity throughout time; thus rituals imbued with sacred power are repeatable in exactly the same way at different points in time. For example, the Catholic mass is repeated by priests in exactly the same way throughout the world. The idea of the sacred is that it presents a power that is eternal and changeless, and this power manifests itself in the myths, symbols and rituals of any authentic religious tradition. Through this eternalizing and universalizing power, a world, characterized by its interdependence and uniformity, is created. Throughout the entire "world" the same symbols, myths and rituals are recognized, assented to and practiced.

The Sacred Worldhood of Ireland

Applying this understanding to the situation of pre-Christian Ireland, we can see that a certain amount of sacred power was present through the identity and reflection of the otherworld and the overworld. The ritual complex located at the center of each tuath and province was thus to a certain extent sacred, and understood itself as a part of a world which was sacred. This consciousness of worldhood and sacrality increased with time, and became especially evident after the establishment of an effective high king, who reigned from Tara in the present county of Meath. The sacred worldhood of Ireland was marked ritually every seven years by a major feast held by the high king at Tara, which was attended by the chieftains of all of the four provinces of Ireland, with Midi or Meath, in which Tara is located, representing the fifth. The space on which Tara was located was structured as a microcosm of Ireland, the sacred world. As such, on the hill of Tara were located the Central Hall or Bruiden, residence of the high king, surrounded by the Hall of Munster, the Hall of Leinster, the Banquet Hall of Connacht and the Assembly Hall of Ulster. This scheme was reduplicated on smaller scale within the Central Hall. "And he (Domnall) summoned the men of Ireland to this feast of Tara. A couch was prepared for Domnall in the midst of the royal palace at Tara and afterwards the host was seated. The men of Munster in the southern quarter of the house. The men of Connaught in the western part of the house. The men of Ulster in the northern. The men of Leinster in the eastern side of it." In the middle of the hall the five kings were seated around Domnall, recapitulating yet again the structure of the world. "The center of Ireland around Domnall in that house. Thus was the court made. The king of Leinster on the couch opposite in the east, the king of Munster on his right hand, the king of Connaught at his back, the king of Ulster on his left hand."[23]

Clearly, this structure reflects the power of sacred space and worldhood. It does so in a most beautiful and alluring way, the various levels of the world forming a spiral with ever-decreasing circles coming to rest at the couch of the high king, husband of the goddess Ireland and sacred center of the world.

Despite, however, this increasing evidence of sacred

space in Ireland, the power of the loric was the dominating force. It was manifest both through the importance of place and through the attitude of decentralization and attachment to place evident in the thought and action of the Irish people. Brian macCenneidigh (Kennedy), later known as Brian Boru, was perhaps the most successful of the early Irish high kings in unifying Ireland and establishing an Irish world. Of course, this was long after the introduction of Christianity to Ireland, as Brian was born in 941 A.D. Brian was successful in defeating the Danes, who were then disrupting the unity of Ireland, at the battle of Clontarf in 1014 A.D. But, characteristic of the Celtic attachment to the person of the leader, after Brian was killed in the battle, and despite the newly won possibility of unity in Ireland, "On the conclusion of the battle, the troops disbanded, each clan going to its own territory."[24] Ireland after Clontarf settled back into a period of disunity until well after the coming of the British in 1171 A.D.

In terms of the dialectic of sacred and loric power, we must conclude that the establishment of the power of sacred space in Ireland, and of a sense of worldhood, comes quite late. This is not to say, as we have tried to show, that some sense of sacred space was not present at such places as the ritual complexes of the provinces which contained holy springs. But what we are presented with in this era is a syncretism of sacred and loric, in which the loric is the dominant force, which ever and again compels the Irish to acknowledge their love for and wonder before the mystery of the place.

Patrick's Christianization of Ireland

With the coming of the Christian hermits in the late third century and, later, of St. Patrick in 432 A.D., Ireland became more and more influenced by the sky god Yahweh and by the world-creating power of the sacred. To be sure, as we have already indicated, the power of place and of region maintained itself for a long period, even within the structures of the monastic institutions that established themselves. But the transformation of the dialectic, once set into motion, was inevitable. The effect on the holy wells was a reversal, or inversion, of their power source.

The career of Patrick in Ireland summarizes this process.[25]

Perhaps the best known story about Patrick's Christianization of Ireland is that of his ascent up the sacred mountain on the Connemara, from where he cast out all the serpents of Ireland. That peak is now known as "Crough Patrick." To understand this tale as it relates to the wells and the power of place, bring to mind the fish/eel/serpent who dwells in the well. It is the presence of these serpentine, ambivalent creatures that sets into motion and makes manifest the creative power of the well. The fish in the well symbolizes the mating of the king to the goddess and his sacrifice to her, and makes possible the recreation of the king and the place. To stop this power, the king, now symbolic of the Lord of the Otherworld, must be separated from the goddess, and this evil practice put to an end. If the unification of the king and the queen is not possible, the regenerative power of the earth will be broken. Only the king will remain, but now the King of Heaven, a celibate Father, self-creating and in need of no feminine power.

The next task was the reinfusing of the wells with a new

St. Augustine's Well, Kilshanny, County Clare

power that was universal, derived from outside the earth, and whose source was the King of the Universe, who dwelled in the heavens and not under the earth. To this end, Patrick made the "great circuit of Ireland" in the manner of the ancestral kings, establishing God's world in each valley and glen as he could. He granted a holding to each chief, who in turn founded a center or monastery safe from the sacrifices of the druids without. In each monastery, Patrick blessed the well, infusing it through the authority of his rod with the power of the universal King of Heaven. Often this ritual involved an exorcism of the indigenous spirit of the well.

The final inversion or revisioning of the syncretism is symbolized in a tale concerning Patrick and the daughters of Loegaire, chief of the province of Connaught. This tale is recorded in the *Tripartite Life of St. Patrick*, a ninth-century text, which itself is a compilation of data taken from the *Book of Armagh*.[27]

In the tale, Patrick went to pray and read scriptures at the well of Clisbach, the holy well attached to the inauguration site of Connaught, Cruachan. He was accompanied by a few of his clerics dressed in white. Presently, there appeared the two daughters of King Loegaire of Connaught, Ethne the Fair and Fedelm the Ruddy, who came each morning to bathe in the sacred spring. The daughters inquired of Patrick as to whether he was of the elves or of the gods, as he and his clerics looked strange. Patrick replied that he was of the one God, and that it would be well if they were too. The maidens asked, "Who is your God and where is he? Is he in heaven or in earth, or under the earth, or on the earth? . . . Hath he sons and daughters? Is there gold and silver, is there abundance of every good thing in his kingdom?" Patrick, filled with the Holy Spirit, answered, "Our God is the God of all things, the God of high mountains and lowly valleys; the God over Heaven and in Heaven and under Heaven."[28]

Following this inspiring description, the maidens wished to be baptized by Patrick, and then they asked to see Christ face to face. "And Patrick said to them: 'Ye cannot see Christ unless ye first taste of death, and unless ye receive Christ's Body and Blood.' And the girls answered: 'Give us the sacrifice that we may be able to see the spouse.' Then they received the sacrifice and fell asleep in death;

and Patrick put them under one mantle in one bed; and their friends bewailed them greatly."[29]

Here is direct evidence of the inversion of power sources manifest in the same structure. In other words, the story maintains the loric context of the holy well, attached to a provincial inauguration site and containing its rock-tree-fish, and the ritual sacrifice to the well. But rather than sacrificing the sons to the goddess, who is mother, the daughters are sacrificed to the sky god, who is father. Power now comes from the top downward rather than from the bottom up, as in Celtic lore. The masculine sky-father now takes precedence over the feminine earth-mother. The center of the ritual remains the well, but a well in which the indigenous power of place is now dependent upon the extrinsic power of the sacred. The Christianity of St. Patrick succeeded in historicizing the holy well in just the same way that it historicized the Celtic vegetation rites appearing on the continent.

But what of the components of the well complex? The lia fal or sacred stone is transformed from a natural to a synthetic symbol and becomes a cross of stone.[31] The bile or sacred tree, symbolic of the ancestor gods of the tribe, becomes the tree of life situated in the garden. The fish dwelling in the well, symbol previously of the king who is son and lover of the goddess, becomes a Christian saint whose power is now manifest in the well. The face of the well itself is transformed from loric spring to sacred fount, a "place" for the absolution of the sin of humankind's original and universal curse.

The holy wells of Ireland, however, are still in use only because the power of the loric continues to be manifest through them. It is the quality of placehood and intimacy manifested through particular geographic configurations that makes this possible. By its very nature, the loric goes unnoticed by those who participate in its rituals, and thus, at the holy wells, it acts as a silent host for the sacred power of the Christian Church, which has been overlayed upon it. Nonetheless, in the holy wells of Ireland, one may dwell within their placehood enfolded in loric power, while simultaneously experiencing the Christian sense of sacred space. Sacred and loric power remain syncretized in and through the phenomenon of space, yet each retains its essential nature.

Notes

1. Emile Durkheim's use of the term in his book *The Elementary Forms of Religious Life*, 1915, was pivotal. Further development was made by Rudolph Otto with his 1923 study entitled *The Idea of the Holy*. Today's thinking is largely influenced by historian of religion Mircea Eliade in such works as *The Sacred and the Profane*, 1957.

2. See Walter Brenneman, Jr., and Stanley Yarian. *The Seeing Eye: Hermeneutical Phenomenology in the Study of Religion.* University Park: Pennsylvania University Press, 1982; and William Paden, *Religious Worlds*. Boston: Beacon Press, 1988.

3. c.f. Alwyn and Brimley Rees. *Celtic Heritage.* New York: Thames & Hudson, 1989, p. 146; and Proinsias ManCanna. *Celtic Mythology.* London: Hamlyn Publishing, 1970, p. 120.

4. See T. F. O'Rahilly. *Early Irish History and Mythology.* Dublin: Dublin Institute for Advanced Studies, 1964. O'Rahilly writes: "In Celtic belief the Otherworld was the source of all wisdom and especially of that occult wisdom to which humanity could not (except in a very limited degree) attain" (p. 318).

5. See Rees brothers, op. cit., pp. 3036, 6 for a discussion of the cave entry to the otherworld.

6. This point is implied in the cosmogonic myth of Cessair who, at the time of the flooding, is instructed to escape to the western islands which became Ireland. See M. D'Arbois de Jubainville. *The Irish Mythological Cycle.* Dublin: Hodges, Figgis & Co., 1903.

7. Jean Markale. *Les Celtes et la Civilization Celtique.* Paris: Payot, 1969, pp. 21-22.

8. *Leabhar na hVidre (The Book of the Dun Cow).* Dublin: Royal Irish Academy, ms. 23E25.

9. See Jean Markale, op. cit., p. 24.

10. The Rees brothers clarify the identity between the complex of women-wisdom-otherworld-fecundity. See Rees, op. cit., pp. 308ff.

11. See "The Wasting Sickness of Cuchulainn," in Myles Dillion, ed., *Serglige con Culainn.* Dublin: 1953, pp. 135-149.

12. Tales containing this theme are "Nera and the Otherworld," "The Thief of Carmun," and "The Phantom's Frenzy." The magical queen appears at a well on the surface world in "The Tale of the Drunkard and the Well." See Jean Markale, op. cit., Chap. 1.

13. T. F. O'Rahilly, op. cit., pp. 120-124.

14. The woman's guardianship of the well can be found in the following tales: "Nera and the Otherworld," "The Thief of Carmun," and "The Phantom's Frenzy," all Irish tales. The theme is also found in other Celtic cultures, for example, "Owein or the Lady of the Fountain," from Wales, and "The Tale of the Town of YS," from France. See Jean Markale, op. cit., chap. 1.

15. *Metrical Dindsherchas*, iii pp. 286-288, in Cecile O'Rahilly, ed. and trans., *The Book of Leinster*. Dublin: the Dublin Institute for Advanced Studies, 1967.

16. The salmon is an important Irish symbol identified with wisdom and the divine in general. Many gods, for example Fintan, the Dagda, Goll manCornag Cu Roi, and particularly the Lord of the Otherworld, often take the form of salmon. See T. F. O'Rahilly, *Early Irish History*, pp. 318-321.

17. T. F. O'Rahilly, ibid., p. 322.

18. Cecile O'Rahilly, *The Book of Leinster*, pp. 286-288.

19. This interpretation is suggested by A. and B. Rees, *Celtic Heritage*, p. 141. They compare *lia fal* to the lingam of Siva in Indian tradition.

20. See T. F. O'Rahilly, op. cit., pp. 58, 60, 110-111.

21. T. F. O'Rahilly makes this clear from the meaning of the Irish word *fa'l* and *fai'l*, which translates variously as hedge, fence, circlet for the arm, and in Cormac's glossary 598, as light. See *Early Irish History*, pp. 520-521.

22. See Marie-Louise Sjoestedt. *Gods and Heroes of the Celts*. New York: Gordon Press, 1976, for a thorough discussion of the character, symbolism and universal nature of these deities.

23. Quoted from *Celtic Heritage*, pp. 147-148 and taken from "A New Version of the Battle of Mag Rath," C. Morstrander, ed. and trans., *Eriu*, V, p. 233.

24. Seumas MacManus. *The Story of the Irish Race*. Old Greenwich: Devin-Adair, 1979, p. 282.

25. The Patrician material is based on the research of Mary G. Brenneman, 1979-1988.

26. See Whitley Stokes, ed. *The Tripartite Life of St. Patrick*. London: Eyre and Spottiswoode, 1887.

27. *The Book of Armagh* (Dublin, The Royal Irish Academy) dates approximately from the ninth century and is considered to be the most authentic source of material on St. Patrick.

28. *The Book of Armagh*, vol. 1, p. 101.

29. Ibid., p. 103.

30. See Sir James Frazer. *The Golden Bough*. New York: The Macmillan Co., pp. 316-319.

31. The high crosses of early Christian Ireland emerged either symbolically or literally from the unformed, natural symbol of the sacred stone by the well, especially in its form as standing stone. For a thorough discussion of the distinction between natural and synthetic symbols, see Walter L. Brenneman, Jr. *Spirals: A Study in Symbol, Myth and Ritual*. Washington, D.C.: University Press of America, 1979, pp. 36-37.

11

Sacred Geography of the Blackfeet

JAY HANSFORD C. VEST

In cautioning the planners of cities, Plato declared that particular locations possess ecological and spiritual qualities which markedly affect human character development.[1] This advice echoes through time with an essential wisdom for contemporary land use planners. Located in northwestern Montana along the eastern slopes of the Continental Divide, just south of Glacier National Park, the area known as the Badger-Two Medicine is a place deserving the sagacious consideration advised by Plato. In 1855 these wildlands were retained in reservation status via a treaty between the United States and the Blackfeet Indians;[2] however, an *Agreement* was subsequently negotiated in 1895 between the parties to the treaty ceding the Badger-Two Medicine wildlands to the United States.[3] In this *Agreement*, the Blackfeet reserved the rights "to go upon" these lands, to hunt and fish thereon, and to harvest timber therein for personal-domestic use.[4] The Badger-Two Medicine area later became a unit within the Lewis and Clark National Forest.

Affirming the powers of place described by Plato, traditional Blackfeet respect the Badger-Two Medicine area as sacred land; the entire province of wildlands is regarded as a holy place. It is a region of sacred geography wherein "nature is sacred because it reveals, or symbolizes, the Great Mystery."[5] Any disturbance of the area's natural integrity will desecrate its power and thereby diminish

Reprinted with permission from *Western Wildlands,* published by the Montana Forest and Conservation Experiment Station, University of Montana.

the central values of traditional Blackfeet religion; it is precisely in this context that controversy has arisen during the forest planning process. While the area is a de facto wilderness strategically located between Glacier National Park and the Bob Marshall Wilderness complex, the Forest Service (USDA) leased the lands for oil and gas exploration. Forest planners have declared that "the area is not available for wilderness classification because of rights retained by the Blackfeet Tribe in the Agreement of 1896." In supporting this claim, the agency further argues that "under the Agreement, the Blackfeet Tribe retains the right to cut and remove timber," and because of the reserved right the area cannot be designated wilderness. This claim seems hypocritical when one considers the earlier Forest Service decision to lease the area for oil and gas exploration, as if this activity *would not* interfere with Blackfeet reserved rights.[6]

The inconsistency manifest in the Forest Service plan reflects a policy designed to facilitate a comprehensive program of oil and gas development; the plan's implementation will violate traditional Blackfeet religious practice within the Badger-Two Medicine area. Consequently, practicing Blackfeet traditionalists have joined conservationists in appealing what appears to be a dishonest forest plan.[7] In light of this controversy, my purpose in this essay is to review the scholarly record and document the traditional claim to the area's sacredness.

The reason why the Badger-Two Medicine area needs to be wilderness can be confirmed through an understanding of the vision quest's role in traditional Blackfeet religious practice. Professor Joseph Epes Brown has declared the vision quest to be the foundation of Native American religions. The vision quest, he explains, is "the most profound spiritual dimension at the heart of these cultures." In retreat, "the individual opened himself in the most direct manner to contact with the spiritual essences of the manifest world. . . . No person in these [Plains Indian] societies, it was believed, could have success in any of the activities of the culture without the special spiritual power received through the quest."[8] Among contemporary Blackfeet traditionalists, visions remain *centrally* important in receiving religious power.

George Bird Grinnell has stated that knowledge of the

future, whether valuable to oneself or to the tribe, is obtained in the solitude of "a remote region among the Rocky Mountains."[9] Wildlands or wilderness are essential for this traditional Blackfeet vision quest;[10] Clark Wissler has affirmed this *essential* requirement for retreat in wilderness solitude, declaring that dreaming at home may be abortive and fail to convey power.[11] Ake Hultkrantz also confirmed that wilderness is essential to vision quest settings: "Typically, the vision of the guardian spirit is individual, sought and obtained in solitude and isolation out in the wilderness—for example, on secluded mountains and hills."[12]

The Badger-Two Medicine wildlands are a place of profound religious significance; this conclusion can be supported by a brief overview of myths involving the area. Among Native American traditions, myth has the power of immediacy: According to Joseph Epes Brown, "cosmologies, worldviews, and religious and ritual expression" all "have their origin and reinforcement in myth."[13] Mythic themes express sacred events in the now; they are "time outside of time. . . . The recitation of a myth defining creation, for example, is not experienced in terms of an event of linear past, but rather of a happening of eternal reality, true and real now and forever, a time on the 'knife edge between the past and the future.' "[14] Myth informs and explains reality, Brown continues, not in the linear fashion of science, but in the events of ever active creation, occurring and recurring in the cycles of days or seasons and in death and rebirth. Myths respond to creation in the immediacy of process, informing of creation as it is "ever happening and observable through all the multiple forms and forces of creation."[15]

The "Backbone-of-the-World" is the name given by the Blackfeet to the Rocky Mountains; a sacred landscape, the "Backbone" is home to "powers," "spirits," or "other-than-human persons," including Thunder, Cold Maker, Wind Maker, the Medicine Elk, the Medicine Wolf, and the Medicine Grizzly. Na'pi (Old Man), the Blackfeet Creator and trickster, is a central figure in many of these myths. The following myths illustrate the "powers" and demonstrate the Creator's relationship with the Badger-Two Medicine wildlands, thereby confirming the region's sacredness.

Birch Creek and the Origin of Wind

Birch Creek forms the southern boundary of the Badger-Two Medicine area, which is the site of Na'pi's mythic encounter with the wind. In this account, a bobcat steals Na'pi's roasted prairie dogs; as a result, the bumbling trickster is angry with his nose because it failed to alert him to the thieving bobcat. Scolding his nose, he declares, "You fool, why did you not wake me?" To punish his nose, Na'pi returns to his fire and thrusts willow sticks into the hot coals. When the sticks catch fire, he burns his nose. The pain of this punishment is severe, so Na'pi declares that a cool wind may ease his suffering; whereupon he begins chanting "*Iik-so-boo-tah, Iik-so-boo-tah, Iik-so-boo-tah*" (Blow harder, Blow harder, Blow harder). As Na'pi repeats this chant, a great wind develops and blows him down to Birch Creek, where he seizes a birch tree standing firm against the wind. The tree saves Na'pi from being knocked to pieces. In gratitude, he declares that the tree deserves distinctive ornamentation. Using his stone knife, the trickster ornaments the tree with the gashes you see today.[16] The fact that Wind Maker lives in the mountains and that Birch Creek comprises the southern border of the Badger-Two Medicine area imparts an essential sacred meaning to these wildlands; clearly Na'pi was blown south to Birch Creek, which means he was blown through the Badger-Two Medicine area.

Badger and the Medicine Grizzly

According to McClintock, Badger Creek was named "on account of the many large badgers seen along its banks."[17] While draining the "Backbone," this stream originates in the home of Thunder, who is the giver of the sacred pipe. Because of the rule that "badger is substituted for bear" in the presence of the pipe, it is evident that Badger Creek is also Bear Creek. The grizzly bear has a sacred role among the traditional Blackfeet; it is one of the most powerful totems or helpers. Because of these powers and the grizzly's present endangered species status, the Badger-Two Medicine wildlands are of great importance to traditional Blackfeet religion as home to these sacred animals.

In the legend of the friendly Medicine Grizzly, the chief
bear befriends the Blackfeet cultural hero Nistae (Calf Robe),
who is saved when the Medicine Grizzly carries him north-
ward along the "Backbone" to the Blackfeet camp at Bear
(Marias) River. In gratitude, Nistae invites the bear to
live with him, but the Grizzly refuses, saying, "The moon
is now nearly past when the leaves fall off. It is time I
should find a den, for the heavy snows of winter will soon
come. The only favour I ask of you in return is, that you
will never kill a bear that has holed itself up for the winter."
Turning westward to the mountains, the Medicine Grizzly
departs for his home. As a result of his request, the Blackfeet
will not kill a hibernating bear.[18]

This myth establishes a fundamental moral relationship
between the Blackfeet and the Medicine Grizzly, who
represents all "real bears." It is significant that the Medicine
Grizzly departed westward to the mountains from the
Blackfeet camp; in following the primary fork of the Bear
(Marias) River, he eventually entered the mountains of
the Badger-Two Medicine wildlands.

Legend of the Friendly Medicine Wolf

In this story, a young mother Itsapichkaupe (Sits-by-
the-door) is made captive by the Crows and taken over
200 miles to a camp on Elk (Yellowstone) River. There
she is pitied by a kindly Crow woman who provides for
her escape. During her long journey home, Itsapichkaupe's
provisions are soon exhausted; she is deep in despair when
a large wolf approaches her. As the wolf lies at her feet,
she beseeches his aid, saying, "Pity me, brother wolf! I
am so weak for food that I must soon die. I pray for the
sake of my young children that you will help me." The
wolf responds and draws near to her; Itsapichkaupe is
able to walk by placing her hands on the wolf's back, and
the wolf seems eager to bear her weight.

Thanks to the friendly wolf, Itsapichkaupe safely reaches
the Blackfeet camp along Bear (Marias) River; the faithful
wolf retreats from the camp to the nearby mountains, but
comes every day to a hill overlooking Itsapichkaupe's
lodge. Believing the wolf and the coyote to be good medicine,
the Blackfeet never shoot them; indeed, they have a saying,
"The gun that shoots at a wolf or coyote will never again

shoot straight."[19] Like the Medicine Grizzly, the Medicine Wolf makes his home in the Badger-Two Medicine wildlands; and again like the "real bear," the wolf is protected in the moral philosophy of traditional Blackfeet.

Na'pi's Romance

In the long-ago, when Na'pi created the world, he separated the men and the women into two camps: the women living in the mellow Cutbank Valley, and the men living in the mountains along the Two Medicine River. Realizing the error of this separation, Na'pi speaks to the men: "You shall no longer live by yourselves. Come! We will go up to the camp of the women, and each of us get one of them."

All the men are most willing to meet the women, so they dress in their finery, particularly Na'pi who is the finest looking of all the men. At the camp of the women, the men all stand in a row because the women have the right of choice. Although she is poorly dressed and dirty from butchering buffalo, the Chief of the women has first choice. She walks up and down the line of men and finally returns to Na'pi and takes his hand. Na'pi notices many fine looking, well dressed women waiting their opportunity to select a mate. Intrigued by the attractive women, Na'pi rejects the Chief Woman. Angered by his rejection, the Chief Woman returns to her camp and cautions all the women against selecting Na'pi. She then cleanses herself and dresses in her finery. Returning to the hill where the men are standing, the Chief Woman appears transformed and is very fine looking; indeed, Na'pi thinks her the best looking of all the women, and he keeps stepping in front of her so that she might choose him. Ignoring Na'pi, the Chief Woman chooses another man for her mate, and all the other women follow her advice and leave Na'pi alone, unselected at the conclusion of the mating.

Na'pi becomes very angry that he has not been chosen by a woman. Because of his behavior, the Chief Woman turns Na'pi into a pine tree which stands alone at the edge of the mountains where the plains begin. It is said that Blackfeet romance endures today because of the beauty of the spot where this event took place.[20] The editors of *Historic Montana* report that the men in this myth lived in the mountains south of the Two Medicine, which means they were living in the Badger-Two Medicine wildlands.[21] It is also significant to recall that as "Keepers," the Chief Woman (Keeper of Women) and Na'pi (Keeper of Men) require an undesecrated place.[22]

Natos (Sun) and Poia (Scarface)

Affirming Hultkrantz's cosmotheistic view of nature,[23] McClintock noted that among the Blackfeet "the Great Spirit, or Great Mystery, or Good Power, is everywhere and in everything—mountains, plains, winds, waters, trees, birds, animals."[24] This *power* is an endowment from Natos, the Sun, which is acknowledged as the creative source of all power and animation. The Sun is, thus, venerated by the Blackfeet; in turn, Natos gives his blessings unto the people "for their reverence for all of Nature."[25]

The story of Poia (Scarface) explains why the Blackfeet pray to Natos; this myth is acknowledged as the most ancient tradition of their religion.[26] According to the myth, on a warm, cloudless night, Soatsaki (Feather Woman) is sleeping outside her tipi in the long grass when Morning Star, rising beautifully above the prairie, comes and makes love to her. In the autumn, she finds herself with child; yet she is a pure maiden, for none of the men have been with her. Coming to earth and making himself known to her, Morning Star invites Feather Woman to his home

Feather Woman Mountain in the Badger-Two Medicine area, Montana

in the sky, where she goes to live with him and his parents—Father Sun and Mother Moon.

In time, Feather Woman gives birth to a child, who is called Star Boy. Feather Woman and Star Boy are banished to the earth when she disobeys the command of the Sun and digs a large, sacred turnip. Going each morning before daybreak with Star Boy to the summit of a high ridge, Feather Woman mourns her banishment and pleads with Morning Star to take her back. In her grief, Feather Woman dies; Star Boy is left alone without relatives and subject to much abuse because he was born in the sky with a mysterious scar on his face. He is ridiculed because of this scar, and in derision the people call him Poia (Scarface). Poia is rejected by the maiden he loves, and in despair, he learns that only Natos, the Sun God, can remove the scar from his face.

With the help of a kindly medicine woman, Poia journeys to the mountains, following the path of the Sun. When he reaches the Sun's lodge, he is helped by his father Morning Star, and Natos agrees to remove the scar. In doing so, the Sun God appoints Poia to be his "messenger to the Blackfeet, promising, if they would give an *Okan* (Sun-dance) in his honor once a year, that he would restore their sick to health. He taught Poia the secrets of the Sun-dance, and instructed him in the prayers and songs to be used." Poia then returns to the earth and to the Blackfeet camp by the Wolf Trail (Milky Way), and there he instructs his people in the ways of the Sun-dance. Subsequently, Natos takes him and the girl he loves back to the sky, and there they become a bright star—Mistake Morning Star (Jupiter)—like Poia's father Morning Star (Venus).[27]

In his quest to remove the scar from his face, Poia travels through the sacred landscape of the Badger-Two Medicine area. First he goes to the Sweet Pine (Grass) Mountains. There he is told to "go far to the west to some very large mountains and to the highest of them all. Scarface must sleep there to seek out the spirit of that mountain, who should know the answer to Scarface's question."[28] In traveling west from the Sweet Pine Mountains, the highest peak one encounters is Morningstar Mountain (elevation 8,376 feet). It is Morning Star who helps Poia win favor with the Sun. Further in keeping with the myth, the Badger-Two Medicine landscape includes Feather Woman

Mountain, as well as Scarface Mountain and Mt. Poia. Scarface Mountain, at 8,282 feet, is only slightly smaller than Morningstar Mountain, which makes it consistent with the myth in which Morning Star is brighter than Mistake Morning Star.

Since the names of these Badger-Two Medicine peaks derive from the most important Blackfeet myth, they are seen as parts of a mythic landscape, and thereby the most sacred of lands. In the traditional naming of a thing, the name confers the essence of its meaning upon that which is named. Since the essential meaning given here is of the most sacred character, we can be assured that the landscape given these names is sacred.

Conclusion

In these mythic accounts, the Badger-Two Medicine wildlands are inextricably caught up with traditional Blackfeet cultural-religious identity; in other words, the myths confirm a sacred geography. The Badger-Two Medicine area represents Blackfeet traditional sovereignty and recalls a cherished way of life; these wildlands offer the alienated and the lost a way back into the traditional culture. This area consequently provides for the recovery of a sense of pride and honor in being Blackfeet. These sacred wildlands offer a reprieve from the demoralizing effects of alcoholism, racial abuse, and other acts of social injustice fostered by the dominant society; they have stood as a bulwark protecting traditional culture from an unsympathetic government.

Spiritually, the Badger-Two Medicine region is a source for the gathering of traditional Blackfeet "medicine power," and this quality has a significant role in restoring the moral fabric of the Blackfeet Nation. Accordingly, the Badger-Two Medicine area is not only symbolically important but essential to the recovery of traditional Blackfeet culture from decades of oppression. No monetary settlement can match the gifts of dignity, tribal identity, and the assurance of sovereignty which these wildlands hold for traditional Blackfeet culture. Nevertheless, the Badger-Two Medicine area will buttress this traditional identity only as long as: 1) the area continues to satisfy the values of the traditional religion; and 2) the values attributed to wild nature are affirmed as the essential claim of the traditional religion. Consequently, if the traditional identity is to be recovered and retained, it must include the preservation of the Badger-Two Medicine wildlands.

In a closing comment, I must stress that Blackfeet traditional religion is alive and flourishing today; it is practiced in the Badger-Two Medicine area, which is clearly a sacred landscape. The United States has recognized Native American religions via the American Indian Religious Freedom Act of 1978 (PL 95-34), and this affirmation entitles Blackfeet traditionalists to First Amendment protection as per the free exercise clause in the United States Constitution. Any development of these sacred wildlands clearly threatens this constitutional guarantee of religious liberty which is of fundamental importance to all Americans.

Notes

1. Plato. *Laws.* 5:747d-e.
2. *Indian Affairs, Laws and Treaties.* Charles J. Kappler, ed. 57th Cong., 1st Session, *S. Doc.* 452: Vol. 2, 552-55. Contains the complete text of this treaty; the original treaty is in the National Archives.
3. 29 Stat. 321, 353-354 (1896). *Agreement* with the Indians of the Blackfeet Indian Reservation in Montana.
4. Ibid.
5. Ake Hultkrantz. *Belief and Worship in Native North America*, ed. Christopher Vecsey. Syracuse, NY: Syracuse University Press, 1981: 128.
6. USDA Forest Service. *Lewis and Clark National Forest Plan— Record of Decision.* Forest Supervisor's Office, Lewis and Clark National Forest, Great Falls, MT, June 4, 1986. The Forest Service claim that the "right to cut and remove timber" denies the option of legal wilderness designation is mistaken. A careful reading of the 1964 Wilderness Act (PL 88-577) acknowledges that timber may be cut where required for beneficial mining purposes in accordance with reasonable and sound management principles [cf. sec. 4(d) (3)]. Given this model, subject to valid existing rights prior to January 1, 1984, it is possible to include the Badger-Two Medicine area in a wilderness designation while acknowledging the Blackfeet's beneficial timber privileges under the 1896 *Agreement.* Indeed, such a model was enacted when Congress returned 48,000 acres of the Carson National Forest to the people of Pueblo de Taos, New Mexico. This sacred wildland, the Blue Lake watershed,

was revested to the Taos people provided the lands "remain forever wild" and "be maintained as a wilderness as defined in section 2(c) of the Act of September 3, 1964 (78 Stat. 890)." In this same act of revestment (PL 91-550), Congress provisioned the beneficial use of wood and timber by the tribe (cf. sec. 4a), despite the official mandate of wilderness preservation cited above. Clearly then, the Forest Service statement denying potential wilderness designation on the grounds of Blackfeet timber rights is in error. Furthermore, the Forest Service apparently made no effort to protect Blackfeet reserved rights when it leased the area for oil and gas exploration and development; this point affirms the charge of hypocrisy advanced in the introductory remarks of this essay.

7. Robert J. Yetter; Keith K. Schultz; Woodrow Kipp; George G. Kipp; Galen Bullshoe, Jr.; and Steven K. Kloetsel. "Appeal of the Lewis and Clark National Forest Plan and Environmental Impact Statement." Washington, DC: Before the Chief of the United States Forest Service, USDA, June 4, 1986; and _____, et al. "Re-Appeal of the Lewis and Clark National Forest Plan," Appeal No. 1633, Washington, DC: Before the Chief of the Forest Service, USDA, January 2, 1987.

8. Joseph Epes Brown. "Modes of Contemplation Through Action: North American Indians." *Main Currents in Modern Thought,* 1973-74, vol. 30: 62.

9. George Bird Grinnell, *Blackfoot Lodge Tales: The Story of a Prairie People,* 1892, Lincoln: University of Nebraska Press, Bison Books, 1962:263.

10. Ibid., 191-192.

11. Clark Wissler. "Ceremonial Bundles of the Blackfoot Indians." *Anthropological papers,* American Museum of Natural History, 1912, vol. 7 (pt. 2): 104-105.

12. Ake Hultkrantz. *The Religions of American Indians,* translated Monica Setterwell. Berkeley: University of California Press, 1967; in translation 1970: 77.

13. Joseph Epes Brown. "The Immediacy of Mythological Message." *The Spiritual Legacy of the American Indian.* New York: Crossroad Press, 1982: 84.

14. Ibid., 84-85.

15. Ibid., 86.

16. Several accounts of Na'pi's adventure with wind along Birch Creek are available. See Grinnell, *Blackfoot Lodge Tales,* 172-173; Walter McClintock. *The Old North Trail: Life, Legends and Religion of the Blackfeet Indians.* 1910, Lincoln: University of Nebraska Press, Bison Books, 1968: 338-340, 438; J. P. B. de Josselin de Jong. *Blackfoot Texts.* Amsterdam: Johannes Muller, 1914: 10-12; Clark Wissler and D. C. Duvall, "Mythology of the Blackfoot Indians," *Anthropological Papers,* American Museum of Natural History. vol. 2 1908k: 25-27; George Bird Grinnell. *Blackfeet Indian Stories.* New York: Charles Scribner's

Sons, 1913: 184; and Percy Bullchild. *The Sun Came Down: The History of the World as My Blackfeet Elders Told It*. San Francisco: Harper & Row, 1985: 177-178, who declares that it was Na'pi's butt which committed the offence and suffered the punishment. John MacLean, "Blackfoot Mythology," *Journal of American Mythology*, 1893, vol. 7 (22): 165-172, accounts for the "origin of wind," explaining that it "is caused by a very large deer [the Medicine Elk] which dwells in the mountains" flapping its ears to create wind; or, as others claim, by "large cattle in the mountains, who roar loudly and thus cause the wind to blow; and again others [claim], that it is caused by a large bird flapping its wings in the mountains."

17. McClintock, *The Old North Trail*, 438.
18. McClintock, *The Old North Trail*, 468-473; in Grinnell, *Blackfoot Lodge Tales*, 67-69, it is Mika'pi (Red Old Man) who when injured prays to the Sun for help and a big grizzly bear who appears to inquire about Mika'pi's problems. In turn, the bear offers his help to Mika'pi by feeding him berries, by plastering his arm with mud, and by carrying him for four days to the Pikuni lodges. Upon reaching the Pikuni camp, the bear tells Mika'pi, "Get off, my brother, get off. There are your people. I must leave you." And without another word the bear turns and goes off up into the mountains. Clearly this bear is the Medicine Grizzly or Chief Bear; and in his returning home to the mountains, he is returning home to the Badger-Two Medicine area. See also Grinnell, *Blackfoot Indian Stories*, 126-127.
19. McClintock, *The Old North Trail*, 473-476.
20. James Willard Schultz *(Apikuni)*, *Blackfeet Tales of Glacier National Park*. Boston: Houghton Mifflin Co., 1916: 98-105. Other accounts of Na'pi's romance include Wissler and Duvall, "Mythology of the Blackfoot," 21-22; McClintock, *The Old North Trail*, 346-347; and Josselin de Jong, *Blackfoot Texts*, 31-32. Bullchild, *The Sun Came Down*, 222-228, also recounts this mythic courtship and places it in Alberta along the Highwood River. This location for the courtship between men and women is appropriate for the northern bands of the Blackfoot Confederacy. The apparent discrepancy of location between these two versions of the story is not an error, since the Badger-Two Medicine region of the Backbone is correct for the South Pikuni (Blackfeet).
21. *Historic Montana*, 1959, V. 9:1.
22. Schultz, *Why Gone Those Times?*, 208.
23. Hultkrantz, *Belief and Worship*, 128.
24. McClintock, *The Old North Trail*, 167.
25. Ibid., 169-170.
26. Ibid., 519.
27. McClintock, *The Old North Trail*, 491-499; Wissler & Duvall,

"Mythology of the Blackfoot," 58-65; Grinnell, *Blackfoot Lodge Tales*, 93-103; James Willard Schultz (*Apikuni*). *Blackfeet and Buffalo: Memories of Life Among the Indians*, ed. Keith C. Seele. Norman: University of Oklahoma Press, 1962: 338-343; Grinnell, *Blackfoot Indian Stories*, 87-106; Josselin de Jong, *Blackfoot Texts*, 95-97 and 80-82; Schultz (*Apikuni*) and Donaldson, *The Sun God's Children*, 71-82; Ella E. Clark. *Indian Legends from the Northern Rockies*. Norman: University of Oklahoma Press, 1966: 266-270; and Bullchild, *The Sun Came Down*, 325-390.

28. Bullchild, *The Sun Came Down*, 337.

12

Garden as Sacred Space:
Transformation of Consciousness at Tenryu Temple

NORRIS BROCK JOHNSON

An immutable aspect of religion is the idea of the sacred, and the essence of the sacred, it seems to me, is the idea of metamorphosis. Metamorphosis is not growth. Metamorphosis is transformation—transformation of form, function, and behavior.

Metamorphosis is common in the world of insects, invertebrates, and nonhuman animals and occurs among frogs, mollusks, and worms. Metamorphosis, though, does not occur among reptiles, birds, or mammals—including, of course, not among human beings. Adolph Portmann, in "Metamorphosis in Animals," accounts for this disparity by noting the morphological sameness of individual organisms among species exhibiting metamorphosis and, in contrast, the morphological variability of individual organisms among species characterized by growth rather than metamorphosis.[1] Growth without structural change in form is a biological characteristic of species emphasizing the distinctiveness of individual organisms—species such as *Homo sapiens.*

Metamorphosis is a theme in the symbolic activity of virtually every culture and society. A caterpillar transforming into a butterfly is a biological as well as symbolic experience, and for diverse sociocultural traditions is a metaphor of the true nature of life itself. Life is change, the possibility of new ways and forms of being. Human beings have compensated, I think, for a lack of structural metamorphosis as a biological characteristic of the species by generating forms and images symbolic of metamorphosis —recurrent forms and images of metamorphosis, as we will see, symbolically integrating biology and the distinctly human enterprise of culture. The manner in which we apply the idea of metamorphosis to the human experience helps define ourselves as akin to other life forms capable of transformation.

Myths of metamorphosis define this sort of transformation as sacred. Birth and rebirth to new forms and ways of being, for instance, are often depicted as miraculous events symbolically akin to the metamorphosis of a caterpillar into a butterfly—itself an event testifying to the awe-inspiring sacredness of nature. Humans, then, are sacred in a manner akin to the sacredness of nature. That humans can achieve second births to new forms and ways of being is both natural and supranatural, and invariably is deemed a profound occurrence. The metamorphosis of the individual organism *is* a quite common occurrence characteristic of our species, despite the conclusion of Adolph Portmann's comprehensive review of this matter. The metamorphosis of the individual organism symbolically occurs in the guise of panhuman myths and images of metamorphosis as spiritual growth through transformation of form, function, and behavior.

Metamorphosis and Transformation in the Garden

Thoughts about metamorphosis were a nest to which I often returned during my study at Tenryu Temple, Kyoto, Japan. I lived in Japan during 1985 and 1986, and I conducted ethnographic and ethnohistorical research while living in the temple. Tenryu is still an important *dojo* (arena) temple for training Zen Buddhist priests. The pond and garden in the temple complex are of particular interest, as temple priests say that ponds and gardens are symbolic of the *satori* transformation of consciousness important in the metaphysics of Japanese Zen Buddhism.

The History of Tenryu Temple and Garden

The present Tenryu temple complex was constructed from 1339-1345 at the order of Ashikaga Takauji (1305-1358), who had the Arashiyama site of Emperor Go-Daigo (1318-1339) redesigned into a Zen Buddhist temple.[2]

Muso Kokushi (1275-1351), a Zen Buddhist priest, suggested to Takauji that a temple be constructed on the site of the Kameyama villa to placate the possibly vengeful spirit of Emperor Go-Daigo. The pond on the site most likely had been modified earlier by Lanxi Daolong (Daikaku; Lan Chi; Rankei Doryu) (1213-1279), a Chinese Zen Master who resided at Tenryu-ji from 1261-1264. The 45x30 meter pond is an often imitated *chitei* (water and artificial mountain) garden design adapted to the practice of Zen Buddhism.[3] Muso Kokushi incorporated the grounds and buildings on the site into a Zen Buddhist temple complex. In 1345, the Tenryu-ji complex covered 10 square kilometers and comprised 150 subtemples. Tenryu is presently the administrative temple of the Tenryu school of Rinzai Zen Buddhism.

A priest at Tenryu-ji, priest Takayama, was my *sensei* (teacher) during my study of the pond garden in the temple. Takayama sensei has been a priest at Tenryu-ji for eighteen years, and he is responsible for overseeing maintenance of the temple garden.

During conversations about the temple and garden we sat, cross-legged, on the floor in the center of the veranda of the *Dai Hojo*—the traditional residence of the abbots of Tenryu-ji (Figure 1).

Figure 1. The Dai Hojo. *Note that the view from the veranda from which the* toryumon no taki *is meant to be seen shows harmonious interweaving, emphasized by the play of horizontals punctuated by circles of trees and pond stones, of building architecture and human-created landscape.*

Toryumon no Taki: The Dragon Gate Waterfall

The front of the *Dai Hojo* is laced by *shoji* screens, open to frame the pond in the garden spread before us. The eves of the *Dai Hojo* catch late afternoon light as it settles on the *tatami* mats. The leaves of maple trees, woven into the mountains in the background, slow dance in the dusk. Silence can be heard.

Priest Takayama points to one of the areas of the pond that is most important for him—a composition of stones embedded in the embankment on the far side of the pond across from the *Dai Hojo* (Figure 2).

In the 9th century, soil from digging the pond was piled up in the rear of the pond to form a *chitei* (artificial mountain). The present-day *chitei*, flattened by the weight of centuries, is a hillock forming a wide triangular backdrop for the pond. Sometime during the 13th century, an intricate arrangement of stones was placed on the hillock. Priest Takayama terms the composition in stone *toryumon no taki*—meaning to ascend up and pass through, with difficulty, the dragon gate of the dry waterfall.[4]

The toryumon no taki is composed around three massive

Figure 2. Westerly view from the Dai Hojo *looking across the pond to the* toryumon no taki *composition at center left. The stone bed in the foreground, the waterline of the pond in the midground, and the maple trees atop the* chitei *embankment in the background emphasize horizontals juxtaposed against the vertical thrusting of the* toryumon no taki.

stones set upright (*tateishi*) on the embankment. Intricately interrelated attending stones frame this triad (Figure 3).

The toryumon no taki at one time functioned as a waterfall, using water brought up from a nearby river through a channel arrangement of stones on the top of and to the rear of the hillock. The toryumon no taki, a dragon gate waterfall of stones, commands a central position in the garden when viewed from a seated position on the veranda of the *Dai Hojo*.

The toryumon no taki is an interpretation in stone of a myth originating in China. Massive waterfalls lace the upper streams of the Yellow River in Shanshi Province. Fish mass at the bottom of the waterfalls, emptying into pools from myriad rivers threaded like capillaries throughout the north China landscape. Fish leap up the falls and attempt to swim against the cascading water up to the calm waters of the spawning grounds above the falls. Fatigued by the effort, many fish are pushed back to the pools from which they emerged. A few fish, though, persist and leap into the waters above the falls. Chinese silk screen paintings depict carp twisting in the glint of moonlight, shimmering in the froth and torrent of cascading water. Hongxun Yang, in *The Classical Gardens of China*, names the legend associated with these waterfalls as "The Silver Carp Leaps Over the Dragon Gate."[5] The Chinese legend says that, ostensibly as a reward for effort and persistence, a fish reaching the top of the waterfalls does not disappear into the waiting waters but is transformed into a dragon and flies off into the western sky.

The dragons of dynastic China traditionally are associated with Emperorship. Dragon and Emperor each "give, maintain, and prolong life and guard against danger to life."[6] The dragon is one of six images traditionally depicted on the garments of Emperors—along with the sun, moon, stars, mountains, and pheasants.[7] Paintings show dragons riding the garments of the Emperor Hwang Ti, who reigned in the 27th century B.C. The Dragon King, Lung Wang, is an enduring legend according to which Chinese temples and shrines and gardens were constructed. Dragons dwelled in the garden ponds of Imperial Palaces, both in China and in Japan. The association of dragons with Emperors also occurs historically at Tenryu-ji. "When the Imperial Palace was built," says the garden historian Shigemori

Mirei, "the Ryu pond was the symbol of the garden of the Imperial Palace."[8] Dragons were believed to live in the garden pond and Imperial estate from which Tenryu-ji emerged. Muso Kokushi had a premonition of the death of Emperor Go-Daigo. On June 24, 1339, Muso Kokushi told a fellow priest that Emperor Go-Daigo, still living in Yoshino, appeared to him in a dream. Muso Kokushi saw the Emperor in the Kameyama villa, and felt that Go-Daigo longed for the place of his childhood. At about the same time, Ashikaga Takauji dreamed of a dragon rising from the nearby Oi river to enter into the Kameyama villa. On August 16, 1339, Emperor Go-Daigo died in Yoshino. Incidently, the *kanji* characters for Tenryu-ji (Temple of the Celestial Dragon) signify a dragon ascending into the sky.

The medieval period Japanese Zen Buddhist temple gardens associated with Muso Kokushi contain ponds with intricate stone waterfalls set on or in embankments— dragon gate waterfalls (*ryumonbaku*) mimetically corresponding to the Chinese Yellow River prototype. Ashikaga Yoshimitsu (1358-1409), the third *shogun*, redesigned the Kitayanma-dono villa of Saionji Kinstune into the temple of Kinkaku-ji (circa 1394). In the pond in the garden at Kinkaku-ji, "beyond the springs on this hillside is the old Dragon Gate Cascade, made for Kinstune 175 years before Yoshimitsu's day. Lying at the base of the fall is the famous carp stone, starting its ascent to dragonhood. Over the nine-foot facer rock of the cascade pours a small stream of water from an upper reservoir. It now hits the twisted carp stone, spatters in a silver shower, and then runs away to the edge of the lake. Originally this cascade must have stood almost on the lake shore, as at Tenryu-ji."[9] The garden and pond at Kinkaku-ji are modeled after the garden and pond at Saiho-ji (Koke dera, circa 1339), also designed by Muso Kokushi. There is a dragon gate waterfall at Saiho-ji. Muso Kokushi's earliest garden is in the temple of Zuisen-ji and the *toryumon no taki* at Zuisen-ji corresponds in design to dragon gate waterfalls in Saiho-ji, Tenryu-ji, and Kinkaku-ji.[10]

Muso Kokushi was aware of the dragon/carp legend ascribed, during his time, to the Tenryu-ji waterfall. A poem by Muso Kokushi, "From my Hut in Miura," metaphorically transforms him into a fish contemplating the effort of ascending the Yellow River waterfalls.

Leaving my footprints nowhere
south or north
I go into hiding here
by the bay full of moonlight
And the misty hill
I love the life that remains to me
Here out of sight in the water
My scales dimmed
I have no wish
to leap up the Dragon Gate falls
To turn into a dragon[11]

But Muso Kokushi did go through the dragon gate, to become a dragon upon his experience of satori consciousness. If the Tenryu-ji toryumon no taki was not designed and constructed by Muso Kokushi but by a Chinese priest, perhaps Lanxi Daolong, at least Muso Kokushi and successive Rinzai priests adapted the Chinese legend to Zen Buddhist pedagogy. The toryumon no taki is didactic. Priests at Tenryu-ji adapted the legend of the toryumon no taki to symbolize aspects of Zen Buddhist metaphysics. The toryumon no taki, for priests such as priest Takayama, is an interpretation in stone of the experience of satori consciousness. In Zen Buddhism experience is more important in the training of acolyte (*unsui*) priests than are discussions about satori.

In discussing the significance of the Tenryu-ji waterfall, then, I will note a correspondence between the form of the toryumon no taki, the form of the body of a priest in zazen seated meditation, and both of the preceding with attributes of satori consciousness. The correspondence illustrates the manner in which the temple and garden intentionally are implicated in metamorphosis as transformation of consciousness among priests.

Toryumon no Taki and Satori Consciousness

Daisetz Suzuki, in "The Awakening of New Consciousness in Zen," discusses satori as metamorphosis and the awakening of what he terms "original consciousness."[12] Satori is transformation of ordinary consciousness, the perception that one is separate from the Buddha, into awareness of Buddha consciousness, the perception that one is Buddha.

Priest Takayama says that transformation of the consciousness of acolyte (*unsui*) priests into the consciousness of enlightened (*roshi*) priests corresponds to the relationship between fish (carp, *coy*) and dragon (*ryu*) attributed by legend to the toryumon no taki.

The coy in the pond of the Tenryu-ji garden, the priest tells me, are the ordinary consciousness of unsui as well as the ordinary consciousness of lay people—people not yet aware of their "original face," their Buddha consciousness. People swim in illusion, dash here and there moved by desire and greed, much as coy in the pond reflexively swim to casually tossed crumbs of bread. The rigors of Zen training for priest Takayama correspond to coy attempting to swim up the waterfalls of the Yellow River in China. Only if unsui sustain their effort do they suddenly, and often spontaneously, break through ordinary consciousness to experience the Absolute Ground of Being of satori consciousness.[13]

I want to emphasize the literalness of satori consciousness, as conceptualized by priest Takayama. Satori is a literal metamorphosis of consciousness, in the Darwinian sense of the emergence of new forms and ways of being. Priest Takayama, again, conceptualizes ordinary consciousness as a fish (*coy*) and satori consciousness as a dragon (*ryu*). He made drawings to show me that, by way of analogy, if one goes up the waterfall (effort to negate ordinary consciousness) and reaches the top (satori), coy (ordinary consciousness) undergoes a metamorphosis and is transformed into ryu (Buddha consciousness), and the new form of being flies into the sky (insert, Figure 3).

Rinzai Zen Buddhism emphasizes seated meditation, *zazen*, as a necessary but not sufficient condition for metamorphosis of consciousness and the experience of satori. Zazen is a posture as well as the potential state of consciousness associated with this particular posture. Zen is zazen.

In zazen one sits cross-legged in silence, with the eyes slightly open (Figure 4). The right foot is placed on the left thigh, and the left foot is placed on the right thigh. The back and neck must be kept straight. Hands are folded on top of the legs, with the right hand under the left hand and the palms facing upward, cupped into each other with the thumbs just touching to form a circle in front of the

Figure 3. The Toryumon no Taki, *18-foot composition of stones on the embankment of the pond. The horizontal slab below, balancing the verticality of the waterfall, is an intricate bridge consisting of three stones placed on four boulders, across which priests once walked to contemplate the* toryumon no taki. *The curve of small stones leading to the tree is a channel along which water once flowed down through the upright stones. The inset figure is a sketch by priest Takayama. The priest demarcates seven stones in the* toryumon no taki *and draws a spiral line tracing the ascent of the* unsui *consciousness to the tooth-shaped* satori *(Buddha) stone on top.*

lower abdomen. "When we cross our legs like this," says the Zen priest Shunryu Suzuki, "even though we have a right leg and a left leg, they have become one. The position expresses the oneness of duality."[14]

Zazen is mimesis. Sitting meditation is adopting the posture of the Buddha. "When you sit once in meditation you are a buddha for that sitting," writes Zen Master Daikaku in a treatise on meditation. "When you sit for a day in meditation you are a buddha for a day; when you sit in meditation all your life, you are a buddha all your

Figure 4. A Zen Buddhist priest in zazen *meditation. The black robe emphasizes the isosceles triangle form of the priest's body. The priest is harmonious geometrically with the verticals of the posts and the horizontals of the veranda.*

life."[15] Satori is consciousness of inherent Buddha nature, or "original face" as it is termed by the Masters of Rinzai Zen Buddhism. ("Before your father and mother were born, what was your original face"?) Satori negates Buddha consciousness as "wholly other," to appropriate a phrase from the historian of religion Rudolf Otto. Zen Master Daikaku adds that "it takes three incalculable eons to attain buddhahood by accumulating virtue and good qualities, but if you practice the way of unity of cause and effect, you realize buddhahood in one lifetime. Someone who illumines his own mind and awakens to his real nature sees that he himself is originally Buddha."[16]

In Asia the human body is a caldron for metamorphosis as spiritual growth. The alchemists of medieval Europe, in the tradition of Hermes Trismegistos, also imaged the human body as a sacred arena for the transformation of consciousness. *Athanor*, a metaphorical image of the body,

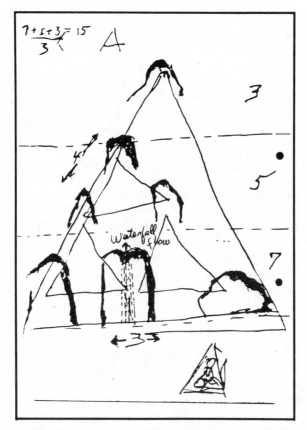

Figure 5. The Toryumon no Taki. *A drawing by priest Takayama, highlighting the manner in which seven stones in the* toryumon no taki *are isosceles triangles, in turn comprising the isosceles triangle of the waterfall. The drawing subdivides the* toryumon no taki *into* shichigosan *proportions of 7:5:3. The small figure of a priest in the position of* zazen *meditation emphasizes the isosceles triangle form.*

is the alchemist's furnace where lead is transformed into gold. The work of transforming lead into gold is the life's work of transforming consciousness. Similar to the Zen Buddhist case, athanor is embodied in "a tissue of powers of the soul which have the body as their support, and which are accessible via bodily consciousness."[17]

Toryumon no Taki: The Form of Metamorphosis

The form of the toryumon no taki concretizes the transformation of consciousness on which Rinzai Zen Buddhism is based. The form of the waterfall is isomorphic with the form of the body of a priest in zazen, as conceptualized by Priest Takayama.

Both the toryumon no taki and the body of a priest in zazen are triangular in form—specifically, both are an isosceles triangle (compare Figures 4 and 5). Priest Takayama associates the triangle with transformation of consciousness, as did Plato and Pythagoras. Metaphysically, at Tenryu-ji priest and garden are one because "the triangle symbolizes a method of organization through the joining or mediating of differences."[18] The isosceles triangle for Zen Buddhists embodies the stability of the Absolute Ground of Being of Buddha consciousness.[19] Isosceles triangles are equilateral and symmetrical when divided axially. The triangle, as such, appears more stable than other geometric forms.

And this is all quite natural. The isosceles triangle, as form, is acknowledged by a variety of sociocultural traditions as congruent with patterns of growth in nature. Plants blossom radially in a geometrically proportional manner. Pythagoras noted that the flowers of plants naturally grow from the center of the stem, to form a complement of isosceles triangles. Plato, in the *Timaeus*, argues that the elements of nature are solid bodies defined by planar surfaces, the compositional facets of which are triangular. Aristotle concluded that the isosceles triangle pattern of growth in nature is *gnomic*, meaning that "certain things suffer no alteration, save that of magnitude, when they grow."[20] As concerns human beings, Wassily Kandinsky, in *Concerning the Spiritual in Art*, feels that form itself is the outward manifestation of an inward state of being. Kandinsky suggests that the triangle, when manifest in art forms and images, is the form of spiritual consciousness.

At first gaze, the form of the toryumon no taki might appear only as an isosceles triangle. A seeming problem, though, is that Rinzai Zen Buddhism eschews the symmetry ascribed to the isosceles triangle as a form. Symmetry holds no creative tension for Zen priests. Priest Takayama resolved this problem for me by teaching me to contemplate the asymmetry *in* symmetry.

The creation of asymmetry is *hacho*—literally, the negation of symmetry. I learned to create hacho by perceiving asymmetrical proportions of 7:5:3 (*shichigosan*) in the symmetrical isosceles triangle of the form of a body in the position of zazen and in the form of the toryumon no taki. Certain forms are pleasing visually and aesthetically in large part because of their rhythmic, musical proportions. Pythagoreans conceptualized form as music, and proportion was a Divine Ratio revealing the manner in which contrasting elements interrelate to form a whole, while maintaining difference.[21] If difference does not exist, relationship is impossible.

In several drawings priest Takayama first isolated seven stones comprising, for him, the structure of significance in the toryumon no taki (see Figure 5).

The priest envisions the seven stones as isosceles triangles interlocking to comprise the large triangle of the waterfall as a whole. The Tenryu-ji waterfall initially was named *Sankyugen*, then *Ryumon Sankyu*, meaning in each case a three-tiered waterfall mimetic of the three-stepped waterfalls along the Yellow River in China. Priest Takayama then drew lines dividing the isosceles triangle of the toryumon no taki into three horizontal planes of 7:5:3 (*shichigosan*) asymmetrical proportion (see Figure 5). The arithmetic proportion 7:5:3 exhibits an equality of difference, but an inequality of ratio: 7-5 = 2 and 5-3 = 2; 7/5 = 1.4 yet 5/3 = 1.6.[22] The proportion 7:5:3 is at once similarity and difference.

In Taoism the proportion 7:5:3 is a magic square, an image of the harmony of the universe around which dynastic Chinese buildings and landscape environments were oriented. The asymmetrical triangle is pregnant geometrically, and is considered the idea of transformation of consciousness in physical form by Japanese Rinzai Zen Buddhists. Rinzai Zen Buddhist temple gardens are designed and constructed with respect to the subtle interrelationship of asymmetrical triangles in the *shichigosan* proportion of 7:5:3.[23] The hacho perception of asymmetry in an isosceles triangle defines and embraces a dynamic equilibrium "capable of endless continuation, even beyond rigid boundaries, and opens up cosmological interpretations accorded closely with both Japanese aesthetic feelings and Zen ideas."[24] Asymmetry is hacho balance—a balance defined through interrelationship more subtle than the symmetrical balance of an isosceles triangle. Asymmetry, as geometric principle and as form, is well suited to Rinzai Zen Buddhism because asymmetry encourages the apprehension of the harmony (*wa*) structuring apparent disharmony.

Priest Takayama also sees the waterfall in the pond at Tenryu-ji not simply as a composition of static stones, but as activity and motion. The triangular form of the toryumon no taki, as well as Priest Takayama's interpretation of the Chinese legend, emphasizes verticality and ascent. Coy move *up* the toryumon no taki and ryu moves *up* into the sky, as signified by the priest's penline spiraling from top to bottom along the waterfall in the insert drawing in Figure 3. The form of an isosceles triangle also suggests movement because its form is the interrelationship of height, length, and breadth. This movement is implied by perceptual awareness of decreasing mass associated with each proportional space, as is evident in considering the subdivided triangle in Figure 5. Priest Takayama envisions satori transformation of consciousness as active, vertical movement congruent with the three proportions of the triangular-shaped waterfall. It would be difficult, for example, to ascribe vertical movement to the form of a circle or a square. Satori consciousness may be existential, but it is envisioned vertically as an ascent.

The zazen of Rinzai Zen Buddhism is derived from Hinayana Indian and Mahayana Chinese meditation postures. Priest Takayama's association of the form of the toryumon no taki with vertical movement corresponds to the vertical movement associated with the metaphysics of yoga meditation and the alchemy of Taoism. The seven chakras of yoga are nodes marking movement within the body of psychic/spiritual/sexual energy from the "lower" to the "higher." Chakra nodes are spaced amid complementary opposed interlaced spirals, Ida and Pingala, comprising kundalini. Yoga enlightenment is transformation of consciousness attendant upon the movement of kundalini. Priest Takayama imaged the movement of satori consciousness as a spiral winding up the toryumon no taki (Figure 3). Spirals are images of generativity and creativity, and invariably are associated with the process of life itself.[25] The caduceus, symbolic image of healing, is two intertwined snakes rendered into a staff. Our symbolic image of the structure of life, the DNA/RNA molecule, is a double-helix spiral. Our symbolic image of infinity is a figure-eight spiral, laid horizontally. Kundalini is imaged as a dragon moving up the merudanda *axis mundi* of the spine of the body. The kundalini dragon marks transformation of consciousness as active movement, from "lower" to "higher," just as the ryu dragon in the toryumon no taki marks transformation of consciousness as active movement, from "lower" to "higher." In each case, the final plane of consciousness is apart from the body, often imaged as being above the body, symbolizing a literal new state of being. In the beginning, though, the Taoist adept through meditation nourishes an "inner embryo" preadapted to metamorphosis into a dragon.[26] Like Buddha consciousness, one already has kundalini but is not yet aware of it as a reality in one's body.

Transformation of consciousness is not just a one-time occurrence but is (or ought to be) continuous rejuvenation. A Taoist text insists that "he whose transformations are not limited by days, and whose ascending and descending are not limited by time, is called a god [*shen*]."[27] *Changsheng,* transformation, is immortality and the archetypal Chinese image of immortality is *long*—dragon. Asian dragons are not slain, as is often the case in mythologies from Europe, North Africa, and the Near East. Dragons are life, life lived as metamorphosis. Metamorphosis is life.

A Chinese silk painting, dating to the Warring States Period (475-221 B.C.), depicts people riding cloud dragons.[28] Immortals (*xian*) traveled between Paradise and Earth on dragons. The azure dragon of the Eastern Quarter, one of four numinous creatures in Chinese mythology, is a Rain King formed of water and mist of spring. The spring equinox (yang ascending) is the rising of a dragon, and the fall equinox (yang descending) is the descent of a dragon.[29] The movement of dragon (*chi*) is the hydraulic cycle of the seasons, just as chi is the movement of kundalini in human beings. Chinese and Japanese dragons are symbolic images of the interrelationship of Heaven, Earth, and Humans. The timeless, cyclical movement of ascent and descent is the form of the dragon in the myths and legends of Asia.

One conclusion here is that, for Japanese Zen Buddhists, nature (*shizen*) is implicated in human transformations of consciousness. European alchemists, also, situate the work of transformation of consciousness in a landscape of mountains, water, and trees. Transformation of consciousness is "the lonely mountain of essential Being, which is one with the world mountain, around which the heavens circle, through which the polar axis runs, and round which glide the dragons of the cosmic powers."[30] This passage occurs in a text on alchemy, dated 1330, in the Cluney Museum, and it paraphrases the meaning of the Tenryu-ji toryumon no taki as an interpretation in stone of Buddha consciousness. Medieval European alchemists, I think, would have interpreted the design form and Zen Buddhist meaning of the toryumon no taki as an ascent through the spheres. The alchemist ascent through the spheres is "an ascent through a hierarchy of spiritual degrees, by means of which the soul, which successively realizes these, gradually turns from a discursive knowledge bound to forms to an undifferentiated and immediate vision in which subject and object, knower and known, are one."[31] In Dante's *Divine Comedy*, the soul ascends to the Empyrean to participate in Christ consciousness, corresponding to the ascent of unsui consciousness (coy) up the toryumon no taki to participate in Buddha consciousness (ryu).

The elements of these cross-cultural correspondences were invented independently, compelling an image and archetypal notion of the sacred as metamorphosis via transformation of consciousness. Verticality is an *axis mundi*, in each case structuring the form and image of metamorphosis as transformation of consciousness. Metamorphosis in the spiritual realm is vigorous activity, analogous to metamorphosis in the realm of biology as vigorous activity. I have in mind the struggles of a caterpillar working its way into a butterfly. The sacred, transformation of consciousness, is experienced only with effort.

Garden as Sacred Space

The sacred is often conceptualized as a phenomenon in opposition, complementary opposition, to the profane. We "become aware of the sacred," says historian of religion Mircea Eliade, "because it manifests itself, shows itself, as something wholly different from the profane."[32] Rudolf Otto, in *The Idea of the Holy*, considers the sacred as holiness itself. But in each case the sacred is conceptualized as a phenomenon distinct from the human—a phenomenon in which humans participate, but are not structured. The holy is "wholly other," a *mysterium tremendum* inspiring awe.[33] Sacred space is a *hierophany*—a manifestation of the sacred, "a reality that does not belong to our world, in objects that are an integral part of our natural 'profane' world."[34] Mircea Eliade and Rudolf Otto imply that the sacred is preexistent, static, and that the experience of the sacred is passive apprehension rather than active construction. Hierophany, the manifestation of the sacred, dualistically occurs "out there" in Cartesian view of space and time, not phenomenologically "in here"—in what Japanese Zen Buddhists term *kokoro*, the heart of body/mind. The Tenryu-ji toryumon no taki amends these influential conceptions of the sacred, and of sacred space. If the Tenryu-ji pond and garden, dated 1339, are sacred spaces, it is owing to the embodiment of Buddha consciousness as pond and garden itself.[35]

The Tenryu-ji case in part supports the contention, by Eliade and Otto, that the sacred and the profane exist in complementary opposition. But the Tenryu-ji case also emphasizes the manner in which the sacred is embodied in the design form, experience of, and interpretation by priests of the toryumon no taki in the garden. Zen Buddhist priests, and aspects of Zen Buddhist temple gardens, are themselves a hierophany. The sacred is not theologically separate from priests, or from the temple gardens in which priests meditate. Satori is consciousness that the Buddha is Sakyamuni, a priest, and nature, each existentially participating in the other to comprise the whole. Zen Buddhism collapses Rudolf Otto's category of the sacred as "wholly other." At Tenryu-ji, the sacred is transformation of consciousness in priests as well as the design form and structure of the temple garden as a symbol of Buddha consciousness. The sacred is a construction.[36] Priests construct temple gardens and, reflexively, temple gardens are an arena for the construction of Buddha consciousness in priests.

The Tenryu-ji toryumon no taki embodies the sacred (*shinsei*) as metamorphosis through transformation (*henkei-saseru*) of consciousness. European alchemists felt that "the occurrence of spiritual transmutation is already a miracle, and is certainly no smaller a miracle than the sudden production of gold from a base metal."[37]

Norris Brock Johnson

Taoist alchemists acknowledged the "transformational process as the core of physical existence."[38] Metamorphosis in biology, and in the myths and legends of human culture, say that life itself is sacred owing to the metaphysical reality of our growth, as individual organisms and as a species, through new forms of being.

Notes

1. Portmann 1964 gives thoughtful consideration to the philosophical and religious issues raised by the fact of metamorphosis.
2. On the history of Tenryu temple and garden, see Itoh 1984: 101-110, Tatsui 1939:15-31, and Mirei 1936-1939, volume 26.
3. Types of Japanese gardens are outlined by Davidson 1982: 13-30 and Schaarschmidt-Richter 1979:20-28.
4. *Toryumon* is an opening, or gateway. The *kanji* characters for *toryumon* denote an attempt to pass through a difficult entrance. Rites and symbols of metamorphosis as a second birth often involve initiates passing through, with difficulty, womb-like passages. *Taki* is a cascading torrent of water, not merely falling water. *Taki* is the force and energy of a waterfall that, here, is symbolic of the challenges that initiates must face in order to become Zen Buddhist priests. The *toryumon no taki* is a material symbol of Zen Buddhist training as a rite of passage (cf. Eliade 1959). See also, Schaarschmidt-Richter 1979:125.
5. Yang 1982:113.
6. Smith 1919:91.
7. Visser 1919:39.
8. Mirei 1936-1939, volume 26, p. 51.
9. Kuck 1984:129.
10. Cf. Johnson 1990.
11. Merwin and Shigematsu 1989:16.
12. See Suzuki 1964.
13. See Cleary 1978:19-41, Sato 1972:143-150, Sekida 1975, and Schloegl 1976 on the meanings of *zazen* and *satori*. Traditional pedagogy for training Zen Buddhist monks is described by Nishimura 1973 and Suzuki 1959.
14. Suzuki 1985.
15. Cleary 1978:21-22.
16. Cleary 1978:24.
17. Burckhardt 1967:161.
18. Fletcher 1988:46.
19. Bring and Wayambaugh 1981 and Slawson 1987 discuss the relationship between triangles, as geometic form, and the ideology of Zen Buddhism.
20. Thompson 1961:181.

21. For neoPythagorean discussions of geometry, see Doczi 1981 and Ghyka 1977.
22. Lawlor 1982:81 defines and discusses what he terms sacred geometry. See also, Fletcher 1988 and Thompson 1961.
23. See Johnson 1989 for an illustration of the manner in which Zen Buddhist temple compounds are structured geomantically and geometrically.
24. Schaarschmidt Richter 1979:41.
25. On the symbolism of the spiral, see Cook 1979 and Purce 1975.26.
26. Morris 1983:32.
27. Visser 1919:63.
28. Little 1988:6-7.
29. I paraphrase from the Legend of Urashima (the place beneath, on the underside of, the island) which elaborates upon the *yin/yang (in/yo)* nature of the dragon. "At the time of vernal equinox, the dragon rises to the sky, and at the equinox of autumn, the dragon seeks deep waters. When big, the dragon strolls in the universe; when small, the dragon can hide in a man's fist." The dragon is the heat of rain, the snows of summer, and the sound of one hand clapping. See also, Hoult 1987 and Huxley 1979.
30. Burckhardt 1967:174.
31. Burckhardt 1967:47.
32. Eliade 1959:11.
33. Otto 1950:12-30.
34. Eliade 1959:11.
35. On gardens as sacred space, see Lau 1981.
36. See Johnson 1988 for an elaboration on the position that the sacred is a construction in which humans participate.
37. Burckhardt 1967:204.
38. Hay 1985:44.

References

Bring, Mitchell and Josse Wayemberg. 1981. *Japanese Gardens: Design and Meaning*. New York: McGraw Hill.

Burckhardt, Titus. 1967. *Alchemy*. Longmead, Shaftsbury, Dorset: Element Books.

Cleary, Thomas, ed. and trans. 1978. *The Original Face: An Anthology of Rinzai Zen*. New York: Grove Press.

Cook, Sir Theodore Andrea. 1979. *The Curves of Life: Being an Account of Spiral Formations and their Application to Growth in Nature, to Science and to Art: With Special Reference to the Manuscripts of Leonardo da Vinci*. New York: Dover.

Davidson, A. K. 1982. *Zen Gardening*. London: Rider.

Doczi, Gyorgy. 1981. *The Power of Limits: Proportional Harmonies in Nature, Art and Architecture*. Shambhala: Boulder and London.

Eliade, Mircea. 1959. *The Sacred and the Profane: The Nature of Religion*. New York: Harcourt, Brace and World.

Fletcher, Rachael. 1988. "Proportion and the Living World." *Parabola* 13:36-51.

Ghyka, Matila. 1977. *The Geometry of Art and Life*. New York: Dover.

Hay, John. 1985. *Kernels of Energy, Bones of Earth: The Rock in Chinese Art*. New York: China Institute of America.

Hoult, Janet. 1987. *Dragons: Their History & Symbolism*. Glastonbury: Gothic Image.

Huxley, Francis. 1979. *The Dragon: Nature of Spirit; Spirit of Nature*. New York: Themes and Hudson.

Itoh, Teiji. 1984. *The Gardens of Japan*. Tokyo, New York, and San Francisco: Kodansha.

Johnson, Norris Brock. 1990. "Zuisen Temple and Garden, Kamakura, Japan: Design Form and Phylogenetic Meaning." *Journal of Garden History*, (in press); 1989. "Geomancy, Sacred Geometry, and the Idea of a Garden: Tenryu Temple, Kyoto, Japan." *Journal of Garden History*, 9: 1-19; 1988. "Architecture as Construction of Consciousness: A Japanese Temple and Garden." *Architecture and Behavior*, 4: 229-249.

Kandinsky, Wassily. 1977. *Concerning the Spiritual in Art*. New York: Dover.

Kuck, Loraine. 1984. *The World of the Japanese Garden: From Chinese Origins to Modern Landscape Art*. New York & Tokyo: Weatherhill.

Lau, Susan Carol Walter. 1981. *Garden as Symbol of Sacred Space*. Ann Arbor: University Microfilms.

Lawlor, Robert. 1982. *Sacred Geometry: Philosophy and Practice*. London: Thames & Hudson.

Little, Stephen L. 1988. *Realm of the Immortals: Daoism in the Arts of China*. Bloomington: Indiana University Press.

Merwin, W. S. and Soiku Shigematsu. 1989. *Sun at Midnight, by Muso Soseki*. San Francisco: North Point Press.

Mirei, Shigemori. 1936-1939. *Nihon Teien Shi Zukan (Illustrated History of Japanese Gardens)*. Tokyo: Yokusha.

Morris, Edwin T. 1983. *The Gardens of China: History, Art, and Meanings*. New York: Charles Scribner's Sons.

Nasr, Seyyed Hussein. 1968. *The Encounter of Man and Nature: The Spiritual Crisis of Modern Man*. London: George Allen and Unwin.

Nishimura, Eshin. 1973. *Unsui: A Diary of Zen Monastic Life*. Honolulu: The University Press of Hawaii.

Otto, Rudolf. 1950. *The Idea of the Holy: An Inquiry Into the Non-Rational Factor in the Idea of the Divine and Its Relation to the Rational*. London, Oxford, and New York: Oxford University Press.

Portmann, Adolf. 1964. "Metamorphosis in Animals: The Transformation of the Individual and the Type." *Man and Transformation*. Joseph Campbell, ed. Pp. 297-325. Princeton: Princeton University Press.

Purce, Jill. 1975. *The Mystic Spiral*. London: Thames and Hudson.

Sato, Koji. 1972. *The Zen Life*. New York, Kyoto, and Tokyo: Weatherhill/Tankosha.

Schaarschmidt-Richter, Irmtraud. 1979. *Japanese Gardens*. Janet Seligman, trans. New York: William Morrow.

Schloegl, Irmgard. 1976. *The Record of Rinzai*. London: The Buddhist Society.

Sekida, Katsuki. 1975. *Zen Training, Methods and Philosophy*. New York and Tokyo: Weatherhill.

Slawson, David. 1987. *Secret Teachings in the Art of Japanese Gardens: Design Principles/Aesthetic Values*. Tokyo and New York: Kodansha.

Smith, Sir G. Eliot. 1919. *The Evolution of the Dragon*. Manchester: Manchester University Press.

Suzuki, Daisetz T. 1964. "The Awakening of a New Consciousness in Zen." *Man and Transformation*. Joseph Campbell, ed. Pp. 179-202. Princeton, N.J.: Princeton University Press; 1959. *The Training of the Zen Buddhist Monk*. New York: University Books.

Suzuki, Shunryu. 1985. *Zen Mind/Beginner's Mind: Informal Talks on Zen Meditation and Practice*. New York and Tokyo: Weatherhill.

Tatsui, Matsunoke. 1939. "Tenryu-ji no Teien (The Garden of Tenryu-ji)." *Teien (The Garden)*, 21: 15-31.

Thompson, D'Arcy Wentworth. 1961. *On Growth and Form*. Cambridge: Cambridge University Press.

Visser, Marinus William de. 1913. *The Dragon in China and Japan*. Amsterdam: J. Mhuller.

Yang, Hongxun. 1982. *The Classical Gardens of China: History and Design Techniques*. Wang Zheng Gui, trans. New York: Van Nostrand Reinhold.

III

Ancient and Modern Geomancies

Tracing something back to its origins can sometimes shed important light on the nature of its place and purpose in modern times. The work of architects, designers, landscape architects and planners has its roots in the ancient art and science of geomancy. The word "geomancy" is said to have been coined by Pliny the Elder when he met a group of Persian Magi (such as the holy men who greeted Christ at his birth) who tossed stones on the ground and then divined according to their configurations.

The art that Pliny the Elder witnessed was but one part of the work of the early designers, such as the Sufi dervish Dhul Nun the Egyptian, founder of "The Builders" sect which may have been responsible for creating King Solomon's temple and other early architectural wonders. Like the Freemasons, another early group of spiritually inspired builders, the Builders took their trade very seriously. Apprenticeships took seven years or more, and the learning process included not just mastering techniques of design and construction, but equivalent inner work, with a special emphasis upon harmony, balance and perfection through heightened perceptual awareness. The extraordinary acoustics of most modern Masonic auditoriums is ample testimony for the value of this approach to training, as well as a reminder of how mechanical we have become in educating designers today.

In agreement with the need to develop inner designers as well as perfect their skills for manipulating the outer world is the Chinese geomancer, called a Feng Shui. According to Master Thomas Yun Lin, the Grand Master of Black Sect Tantric Buddhism for the world and an expert Feng Shui, we have 100 senses by which to perceive the environment. To the five senses which we acknowledge Master Lin would add the art of dreaming, the ability to sense subtle electromagnetic fields and many para-senses.

In this section we look at some of the geomancies of the world and probe their common elements as well as examine their results. Witnessing the many outstanding cathedrals, shrines and temples which were built centuries ago guided by geomantic arts and sciences, the shortcomings of modern architecture, design and planning become more apparent. One reason these early structures captivate us so is that they are built to work with and celebrate the spirit of the place where they are built. Architecture according to this approach is like composing a musical score in physical reality—more a ritual in material form than just a building with a benefit-cost ratio.

13
Geomancy

RICHARD FEATHER ANDERSON

In this presentation, I will discuss the basic principles of western geomancy and show how they have been applied in both the ancient and modern worlds—(1) to create and enhance a community's sense of place, wholeness, and well-being; (2) to find the most appropriate place for any human activity; and (3) to heal our relationship with Mother Earth. I believe that one of the most significant implications of reviving the principles and practices of geomancy, especially for environmental planners, community leaders, and government officials, is that we must once again accept the sacred responsibility for bringing our lifestyles and the forms of our built environment into harmony with natural patterns.

What gives us a "sense of place," or a feeling of belonging in an area? What are the attributes of "placeness"? And how can we "read" the qualities or spirit of place?

One of the oldest perspectives on these questions can be found in the ancient science of geomancy. It is a multifaceted discipline and may be described in many different ways.

Geomancy is the ancient holistic science of living in harmony with the earth. It is the art of finding the right place and time for any human activity. It is an ancient form of sacred, ecological land-use planning. It originally integrated the study of ecology, geology, dowsing, earth acupuncture, architecture, sacred geometry, harmonics or music, dance, seasonal myths and rituals, astronomy, astrology, and cosmology. And so it can also be viewed as the mother of the natural sciences.

Geomancy operates within a worldview that regards the

earth as a conscious living being and regards all forms of life as interconnected. Within such a living-earth paradigm, the earth's body is perceived of as more than a hunk of inanimate matter—it is interlaced with flowing veins of biomagnetic energy. This sense is embedded in the origins of the word "geomancy," which means "to divine the Earth Spirit," i.e., the earth's energies and rhythms, since the root word for "geo" is *Gaia* or *Ge*, the Greek name for the Earth Goddess.

Geomancy's overall purpose is to maintain the web of life and keep the Earth Spirit alive and vital. Since the ancient cultures that developed geomancy lived "at one" with the land, they believed that maintaining the vitality of the Earth Spirit was synonymous with maintaining abundance and well-being, optimum health, and a fullness of life for humans as well.

The intent of geomancy is to affect how we live on the planet so that we adopt lifestyles and habitation patterns that keep us in harmony with all creation. Geomancy's unique approach to land-use planning guides us to listen humbly to the messages from Mother Earth which, in turn, guide us in finding the most appropriate ways to situate ourselves within this living planetary biosphere.

Such an interactive worldview is radically different from the deterministic and mechanistic paradigm in which all of us in modern Western societies have been raised. Therefore, to study or practice geomancy in ways that preserve the essence of its principles, we need to go through a radical reorientation in our view of reality and of our place in the world. We need to shift our position from one of living *on* the planet as the dominant species, to one of living *within* an organism interconnected with all life forms. Fortunately, this conference and the preceding Gaia Conferences are contributing to such a reorientation.

In its broadest sense, geomancy is best described as an ancient, holistic, integrated system of natural science and philosophy, which was used to keep all human activity in harmony with natural patterns—from seasonal cycles, to the processes that maintain the balance of nature, to the universal geometrical proportions found in the way all organisms grow.

The Sense of Place

One of the most important uses of geomancy has been the enhancement of our sense of place—or sense of belonging to a place. Basically, a sense of belonging to a place is generated when an individual or community consciously makes a relationship with its environs. This process involves placing ourselves physically and psychologically within ever-expanding circles of relationship—with the place we call home, with the people, plants and animals with whom we share the land, and with the cycles of the weather, the days, lunar months and seasons. In this way geomancy fulfills its mission of creating places of wholeness, by integrating all the relationships necessary for a complete ecosystem and social system.

Understanding the nature and origin of the human sense of place is useful in the practice of enhancing that sense in any given area. Our sense of place is an emotional response to our environment. It is an innate sense that has evolved and been developed as we adapted to living on this planet. It probably came originally from noticing which places gave us a feeling of comfort, safety, wonder, or "being part of." By remembering the characteristics of the places evoking the strongest sense of place, humans accumulated an understanding of the elements of placeness.

Using wilderness areas as a model of the original untamed state of the earth in which humans must have evolved their sense of place, we find the spots we are most often drawn to have the following elements: 1) There is enclosure—a sense of being held by the landscape. Valleys (contained by hills) and meadows (surrounded by trees) evoke this feeling. The more the landscape cradles us the greater is the sense of placeness. 2) These places also feel complete. There is water, sun, shade, wind, i.e., all the basic elements of air, fire, water, and earth. Chinese geomancy is called *feng-shui* (fung-shway′), or wind-water. The name refers to the auspiciousness of places with a moderate, smooth flow of wind and water, lush vegetation, and moderate sunlight.

In feng-shui traditions, the most auspicious site is the "armchair position," a valley cradled by a large windbreaking mountain at its head and flanked by two ridges which encompass the site like two arms bent at the elbows. The heads of the ridges should create a sense of enclosure but not constrict views or the gentle flow of wind and water.

As our predecessors developed ways of creating a sense of place in the human-altered environment, I think they most likely attempted to mimic nature and to recreate the same kinds of places that gave people a sense of place in the wilderness. The underlying pattern here is of boundaries to enclose and contain, gateways to provide a transition into an area and give us a sense of arriving somewhere, and a center within which to come to rest and focus our attention, and from which to view the place and orient ourselves within the place.

The geomantic process for enhancing a community's sense of place begins by finding the most appropriate center, boundaries, and gateways for each human settlement. It continues by orienting ourselves within the natural boundaries of the region. When we define a center and boundary, we create a specific domain, and when we leave openings in that perimeter, we provide ways to enter and depart from the domain. The cross-cultural symbol of a circle around a cross represents these three elements of placeness. It is the astrological symbol for the earth, the Celtic cross, and the Hopi symbol for life in balance.

Village greens, market squares, town wells and fountains, sacred trees, and omphalos (navel) stones have all been used to establish a community's center and focus of activity. City walls and towers, moats, "no-man's lands," and green belts have provided clearly identifiable boundaries. The traditional center of a home has been the hearth.

A geomantic center is a unifying place, a place of connection. At the public common, plaza, or town hall, the diverse constituencies of an area can come together to make decisions for their mutual benefit or to share common unifying experiences, like town fairs and other celebrations. Clearly identifiable boundaries like medieval town walls or the Great Wall of China obviously function to repel marauders. But on a more subtle level, the town walls contain the industrious energy of the inhabitants, preventing its dissipation across the surrounding landscape.

Creating gateways along a boundary is essential for the exchange between the worlds within and without. Portals provide for the proper entry of strangers, initiating them into the customs of the place. Whenever the Romans established a town, temple, or fort, they divined a center, then enacted a ritual called "cutting the first furrow," by plowing around the perimeter three times, sunwise. When they came to the beginning of each of the four quarters, they lifted the plow to avoid severing the breast of the earth at that point. This created a passageway for the entrance of telluric energies from the surrounding countryside.

It makes good sense to provide these gateways, to allow people, goods, and earth energies to flow in and out of the town center, ensuring the continual revitalization of the people and the land. Modern society has abandoned the practice—our inner cities are decaying, literally cut off from the rejuvenating power of nature.

The lack of a well-defined center, boundaries, and gateways can lead to the feeling that there is "no there" there, as with suburbia, the commercial "strip," and other forms of urban sprawl. If there are no centers and boundaries, it is difficult to know who you are and where you are.

These same principles can be applied just as easily to creating a sense of community or group identity. Geomantically speaking, to become a community, i.e., to create "common-unity," everyone needs to agree on the focus and purpose (center) and the extent or limits (boundaries) of their common activities, as well as the procedure for joining or leaving the group (gateways).

Geomancy further posits that a healthy sense of identity is inseparable from a sense of place—a sense of being part of the region's ecological processes, weather patterns, and the native cultural customs generated through adaptation to the local ecosystem. To apply this principle today, we need to develop better ways of becoming related to where we are.

We should realign our arbitrary county and state boundaries with natural watershed boundaries, so we can make land-use decisions with whole ecosystems in mind. We should accentuate the unique characteristics of each region, using local building materials and indigenous styles, to reverse the anonymity of identical suburbs and Manhattans. To counter the confusion of urban sprawl, we need to give each city its own place-identity, by clearly defining it with a center, boundaries, and gateways. We need to plan the size of our cities to fit what the surrounding landscape can support. As our sprawling cities deplete the natural resources of the rest of the world, we are actually borrowing from the future, reducing the ability of the land to support life. If we had a clearer sense of town and regional boundaries, it might also affect our habits and attitudes of living beyond the means of the land to support us. We could learn from the traditions of earth-centered cultures, whose elders made decisions considering the effects of changes on seven generations into the future.

Finding the Right Place

Geomancy is commonly known as the "art of harmonious placement," for it has been used to find the right time and place for all human activities. Since the beginning of human society, people have sought the best places to dwell, dig wells, commune with the Great Spirit, bury and honor their ancestors, and the right time to hunt, plant seeds, or come together as a community. Indigenous cultures around the world developed their own flavor of geomancy in direct response to the geography and ecology of the region. So when we borrow geomantic practices from other lands, whether it be Europe, China, India, or elsewhere, it is important to import only the underlying universal principles and adapt them to our specific situation, rather than follow another culture's model like a recipe.

For example, in China the armchair layout of a valley is usually most auspicious when the large mountain at the head of the valley is to the north, to protect the site from the cold prevailing north winds. However, in coastal California this same principle would direct us to look for an east-west valley with a mountain to the west or northwest to block the strong winds, fog, and storms coming off the ocean.

In finding the right place, it is essential to use a holistic approach. For instance, a primary source of our current ecological crisis is our exclusive focus on short-term, materialistic considerations in land-use decisions. In contrast, geomancers determine the subtler, invisible characteristics of the land by reading their effects on plants, animals, and land forms, or more directly through dowsing and psychic skills. Most people are familiar with dowsing or divining only as a technique to locate well sites; but it is well suited to geomancy because it draws upon both the spatial/intuitive and linear/analytical ways of perceiving reality, in the two hemispheres of the brain. Dowsing stretches our awareness beyond the five senses, enabling us to tune into the spirit of place and discover Mother Earth's intent for the use of each place. Thus, it is an appropriate "magical technology" for a holistic science like geomancy.

One of the qualities geomancers look for when divining the most appropriate place for everyday living and working is a moderate flow of energy. If you live in a canyon by a rushing river, you are likely to be swept away by frequent flash floods. If the water is stagnant, it becomes a breeding ground for mosquitoes and malaria, and you are likely to become lazy there. If the wind is always raging, it can dry out the soil and make you irritable. Again, the notion of good feng-shui points to the auspiciousness of places with a moderate, smooth flow of wind and water, lush vegetation, and moderate sunlight.

In Irish folk tradition, the procedure for picking the proper location for a house includes placing four sticks in the ground to mark the corners of the proposed building. If the sticks are knocked over during the night, it is regarded as an indication that the place is on a "fairy path," and so not suitable for human habitation. Earth mysteries research in the last two decades has put forth some interesting correlations with this lore. Sheep and other cloven-hoofed animals prefer to walk along these "nature spirit" paths. The larger of the "spirit holes," or openings in fences, walls, and hedgerows all over the British Isles left for the fairies' perambulations, are also used by sheep. Dowsers have discovered that sheep, deer, bees, ants, cats, and burrowing animals put their homes and trails above particular veins of underground water. German medical and geomantic researchers have documented that the occurrence of a variety of human illnesses (cancer, arthritis, rheumatism, and multiple sclerosis) correlates strongly with places that possess a crossing of underground water flowing in constricted veins. One of the current theories is that this water-flow creates a turbulent frequency detrimental to human health, but beneficial to the animals mentioned. So it seems that the consideration of avoiding fairy paths also locates houses in areas free from detrimental water veins. Similar customs exist among northeastern Native Americans and were adopted by the early colonists.

Caring for the Spirit of Place

Until recent times every structure was situated with regard for the patterns of biomagnetic energy within the earth's body. Geomancers were employed to maintain the most beneficial flow of ch'i within the veins of the earth's body, variously known as dragon paths or energy ley-lines. It was taboo in earth-centered cultures to sever these vital channels, for the same reason that it is suicidal to cut our own arteries. Where the flow of earth ch'i has stagnated, "earth acupuncture" procedures can be used to stimulate the ch'i. Some earth mysteries researchers believe that the megalithic standing stones of Europe may have functioned as acupuncture needles for the planet.

In one of its best-known applications, geomancy was utilized to site and construct the pyramids, Gothic cathedrals, and megalithic stone circles and passage mounds at sacred sites worldwide—in ways that amplified place-specific patterns of earth energies to stimulate human well-being and states of expanded awareness. Aura expansion, the slowing down of the frantic mind, and the stimulation of right-hemisphere brain activity are so common that they have become hallmark ways of recognizing sacred places among many earth mysteries researchers. Exactly at the spots where human auras expand severalfold (at church altars, the central area of stone circles, and passage mounds), dowsers have found a crossing of yang cosmic "energy leys" and yin, telluric veins of "primary water." Apparently this combination of yin and yang energies makes us balanced and whole.

In other words, a place possessing a balance of yin-yang, cosmic-telluric energies expands our auras and awareness, sometimes to such an extent that we approach deep states of universal consciousness. It balances our rational and intuitive ways of perceiving, making us whole. It is no mere coincidence that these places are also called "holy ground"—places of wholeness and healing. Most of us today think it is primarily the rituals at the inner sanctum that connect us with the Creator. However, we now know that the earth energies play a major role in stimulating the spiritual experiences that cathedrals and megalithic sites are known to produce.

Living in Harmony with Natural Patterns

All of these ancient structures on sacred sites were built according to sacred geometry, a system of proportions based on the universal ratios found in the growth patterns of all organisms; in the energy structure of the human body and the cosmos; and in the harmonic intervals of the musical scale. We are most familiar with these "golden proportions" from Leonardo da Vinci's famous drawing of the man proscribing a circle and square, which illustrates the canon known as the "golden section" or "golden mean."

Humans are the only creatures that build things out of harmony with these universal patterns. When art and architecture were practiced as sacred disciplines, it was the artist's responsibility to create a material culture that keeps us in harmony with these patterns and proportions.

The shape and proportions of buildings have a great effect on the qualities of a space. Every enclosed space resonates at a particular frequency, depending on its proportions, and it appears that the master builders knew how to create a place with particular frequencies of sound and light to tone our nervous and endocrine systems and tune our brainwaves to the earth's frequency (the Schumann resonance, 7.8 Hz.). The ancient way of building utilized the ratios of sacred geometry. So when you were in a building, you were within a model of the universe, which mimicked the proportions of your own body and everything else in the universe, thus bringing you into harmony with the spirit of that place.

To create more harmonious, healthy environments, environmental designers need to pay attention to the wishes of the land itself. This mandate also requires architects to live in their own "houses," i.e., to know their own souls, before designing houses for others, so as not to project their egos onto the clients' living and working spaces, or onto the earth. They should lay out activities directly on the site, so they can be influenced by the feel (the energies) of the place, rather than just by the way it looks on the site plan on the drawing board. They should dowse for the most appropriate boundaries, gateways, and center of each project or activity. We must all learn the techniques that increase sensitivity to subtle energies so we can hear the intent of Mother Earth for the appropriate use of each place—for the most harmonious relationship with Gaia, the living earth.

To live as a culture in harmony with the earth, we need to develop a modern form of geomancy that combines appropriate technologies with an intuitive sense of what is in harmony with the natural history and patterns of each place. A number of contemporary environmental movements—among them bioregionalism, Green politics, deep ecology, and sustainable agriculture—have been reviving age-old geomantic principles and methods. We need to re-member the common roots of such disciplines as architecture, ecology, geology, astronomy, astrology, sacred geometry, music, dance, ritual, and cosmology. And we need to reweave the connections between them, recreating a unified body of knowledge that will once again allow us to live in harmony with Mother Earth.

14

Befriending the Dragon:
The Art of Feng Shui Geomancy

Interview with Master Thomas Lin Yun

JAMES A. SWAN

Until the early 1970s modern Western psychology paid little attention to the influence of the environment on health and behavior, unless there were obviously intrusive conditions like run-down housing, extremely confined living conditions, or extreme crowding. There wasn't even a division of environmental psychology in the American Psychological Association until after Earth Day 1970. This attitude is in sharp contrast to ancient traditions around the world, which assert that people are the product of their surroundings and that understanding the interplay between people and the world around them is the key to health and happiness.

One of the earliest recorded environmental psychologies came from China, where according to oral history, Fu Hsi, the first Emperor, looked upwards and identified the images and symbols in the skies created by planets and stars and looked downwards and observed the patterns in nature and in landforms of the earth. From these initial observations came the Chinese book of wisdom, the *I Ching*, which describes the patterns of nature and prescribes appropriate methods to deal with each type of earthly situation.

Chinese culture is a creative mixture of many religions, traditions, and cultures, many of which are contrary to modern scientific theories. Although acupuncture is now recognized, licensed, and practiced in the United States, for example, Western science cannot explain why and how it works because there is no scientific validation for the Chinese concept of a life force energy, *chi.*

Another ancient Chinese practice finding increasing

201

acceptance in the West is Feng Shui, the original Chinese art and science of design. The words "Feng Shui" translate literally as "wind and water," a name which conveys the spirit of this centuries-old paradigm for ordering human affairs to increase health, prosperity, and good fortune.

While many in academic circles are skeptical of Eastern solutions to human problems and needs, there are signs everywhere of growing acceptance of the idea that East and West may be able to help each other. Each year in San Francisco, a massive exposition called Workspace is held to showcase the latest in office furniture and interior design techniques and technologies. In addition to a collage of floor exhibits in the exhibition space of the Mosconi Center, Workspace 1988 offered a full program of lectures and workshops by architects, designers, and business people. While there were many internationally-known experts presenting, the most popular workshop presenter at the 1988 show was Master Thomas Lin Yun, a world-renowned expert on Feng Shui.

In 1986, Master Lin Yun moved to Berkeley, California, to establish a temple, and to teach at San Francisco State and the University of California at Berkeley. To find out more about Feng Shui, I interviewed Master Lin Yun at his temple on Russell Street, a tree-lined artery which climbs from San Francisco Bay to the crest of the Berkeley Hills.

From the outside the temple looks like the home of a corporate banker, I discovered. It's a four-story gray mansion sitting atop one of the hills at the east end of the street. As I pass through the iron gate and proceed up the steep brick stairs, I notice that the place feels very peaceful. In the yard there is a sense of orderliness, but not of control. The first hint that something special is about to happen is the front door, which is bright red.

I'm greeted at the door by Crystal Chu, Master Lin's secretary. Stepping inside, I expect to see a conventional living room and dining room. Instead, my senses are startled since the entire first floor has been converted into a meditation hall, with massive altars holding statues, burning candles, pictures, and ikons, surrounded by clouds of incense.

Crystal now leads me up three flights of stairs. The stairwell is bathed in warm sunlight, which is in sharp contrast to the darkened first floor shrine we have just passed through. Above us a skylight pours down light, which is caught and reflected by mirrors covering the walls. Here and there are statues of holy figures and symbols.

On the third floor I'm led into a sunlight-filled dining room, with a rich light-brown teak table sitting in the middle, and colorful tapestries and pictures of spiritual leaders on the walls. As I sit down, I notice immediately behind me three pictures of Master Lin greeting the Dalai Lama, the head of the Tibetan Bon religion, and Pope John Paul.

Soon Master Lin enters the room. He is a short gentle bear of a man with a large radiant smile, who wears a black silk suit, with a single string of white beads around his neck. Today he is accompanied by Professor Jagchid, an expert on Mongolian history from Brigham Young University, who will act as his translator. The following interview is distilled from several hours of lively interchange, periodically refreshed with tasty food and lots of tea.

* * * * * *

JAMES A. SWAN: Master Lin, when I attended your appearance at the Workspace Exposition, at the very beginning someone handed you a red envelope. You opened the envelope, which contained some money, and gave the money back, but kept the envelope. Why did you do this?

PROFESSOR JAGCHID: Let me explain this tradition, which arises from Master Lin Yun's lineage, for he is the Grand Master of Tibetan Black Sect Tantric Buddhism. Because of the sacred nature of what Professor Lin Yun is supposed to share with seekers, it is believed the gift will protect the teacher from being punished, although he is revealing sacred information, and it represents a sincere intention on the part of the questioner, which will insure the best outcome for the information which is given. Incidentally, Master Lin has never accepted money when he has shared transcendental knowledge. Due to his high level of attainment, he can only accept the red envelope and not the money.

J.A.S.: Master Lin, would you please explain what is unique about the Black Sect of Tantric Buddhism which you head?

LIN YUN: To answer this question, you must first go

back to the source, which is the enlightened mind of Buddha, and its original state in India. This is the root of Buddhism. Then when Buddhism spread to Tibet, different sects developed according to different interpretations of the seed: the White Sect, the Red Sect, the Yellow Sect, and the Black Sect.

When Buddhism, primarily Tantric Buddhism, arrived in Tibet in the seventh century, it was met with strong resistance by the native religion, called Bon, which is animistic and shamanistic. As the two religions merged, a new Bon religion, which has since been regarded as the Black Sect of Tibetan Tantric Buddhism, emerged, characterized by many elements of Tibetan ancient traditions as well as Buddhist teachings.

From Tibet the Black Sect then traveled to China where it again changed as it merged with Sutra Buddhism, Confucianism, Taoism, Yin Yang Theory, and various other native beliefs. Each sect has its own unique focus, and we deal a lot with material world conditions but with a spiritual philosophy.

J.A.S.: Feng Shui is usually seen as Chinese geomancy. How does this tie in with Buddhism?

LIN YUN: Feng Shui can be seen as being the harmonizing of human life with the universe and nature to obtain health and prosperity. Good Feng Shui contains many different elements, both spiritual and material to help us attain and maintain harmony and balance.

There are many different approaches to Feng Shui. The Black Sect approach is especially interested in working with the life force energy, chi. There are three kinds of chi: one that circulates in the earth, a kind that circulates in the atmosphere, and a third which moves in our bodies. We work with all three to align our lives with the Tao, the life force which ultimately moves all things and arises from the interplay of the opposing forces of yin and yang.

J.A.S.: In the *I Ching*, there is a passage which says, "Heaven and earth determine the places. The holy sages fulfill the possibilities of the places. Through the thoughts of men and the thoughts of spirits, the people are enabled to participate in these possibilities." Does this describe the essence of Feng Shui?

LIN YUN: The *I Ching* is a very wise book. Our actions don't just happen. Many seemingly unrelated events and conditions may lead to something happening. We each have a destiny, but this can be changed. There is a Chinese saying which goes:

Born with good looks is not as important as being
  born with a good fate or destiny;
Born with a good fate or destiny is not as important
  as having a kind heart;
Having a kind heart is not as important as having a
  positive state of chi.

In Feng Shui we seek to maximize good or positive chi which brings good fortune and health. There are two major ways of doing this. One is called *sying*, which is the art of forms, and is like what you call interior design and landscape architecture. A steep-rising hill has a certain kind of chi, just as a dismal swamp has a negative feeling, and certain rooms in a house or business may feel good or bad. Traditional Feng Shui works a lot with the shapes of things, as well as the directions of the compass, which is a very old Chinese instrument for divining as well as telling which way is north or south. Traditional Chinese buildings often have special shapes to invite in good spiritual forces, and they are placed in various ways to honor the powers of various landforms, which are often animals like dragons, elephants, snakes, phoenixes, tigers, and people. Aligning these forms on earth with astrology in the heavens is part of Feng Shui.

The Black Sect doesn't reject these views. They are helpful to blend with nature, but there is something else at work, *yi*, which means will, wish or intention. Yi is a blessing and state of mind. It includes prayers, gestures or *mudra*, and visualizing certain things, often as part of a ritual. We say the art and science of working with sying is *ru-shr*, which is the art of placement. Inside a building, it might call for mirrors, crystal balls, or wind chimes to help chi flow. This all helps, but ru-shr alone is only 10-20 percent effective to solve our problems. The art of working with the "transcendental cure" is *chu-shr*, and this mystical method is able to achieve over 100 percent positive results in most cases.

An example of how this works might be found in an office which has many conflicts between people who work

there. The ru-shr solution might be to sit down and talk
about problems and maybe rearrange the furniture or
walls. This can help, but often more is involved. The chu-shr
solution would be to place mirrors in places, hang wind
chimes, maybe build an altar, and then conduct a ritual,
possibly with no talking about the problems.

J.A.S.: Do Westerners accept this? Don't they say you
are just playing with foolish superstitions?

LIN YUN: Some people say Feng Shui is superstition,
perhaps because modern science cannot explain why
Feng Shui works; but it does work, and has been working
very effectively for centuries. Part of the difficulty with
understanding Feng Shui is that modern science says
we have five senses, but actually we have at least a hundred
senses.

J.A.S.: Our school books say we have five senses, and
maybe then mention a sixth sense. Can you explain what
some of these other senses are?

LIN YUN: We all have insights. When we go places, we
pick up feelings. These feelings can come from many
sources, the earth, the furniture, the neighbors, atmospheric
energy, maybe the people who used to live or work there.
We dream too. That is a sense. Other times we sense things
that are about to come.

J.A.S.: How can events in previous times in a place influence what happens today?

LIN YUN: We call this the "predecessor factor." Suppose
the people who own a home become ill, meet misfortune,
or even die violent deaths there. These thoughts and actions
leave memories. They can be changed, but we need to
acknowledge that places have memories like people or
animals.

J.A.S.: Recently you were hired by Creative Artists Agency,
Inc., in Hollywood to conduct a blessing ceremony for
opening a new building of theirs. We can fathom good
design sense, but why is it necessary to use rice, high-proof
rum, cinnabar, flutes, and red cloth to bless a building?

LIN YUN: Places have memories, people have thoughts,
and there is a spirit world which affects our life very much.
All these things affect our chi, not just the chi around you,
but the chi in you which makes you healthy or not, influences
your interactions with other people, and even can affect
the way you think. If I place a crystal ball in your home
and your married life improves, or hang a mirror in another

corner and your income suddenly jumps, these are results. Just because modern science cannot explain why these things happen doesn't mean that they don't happen.

J.A.S.: How do you know where to do what you do to make the fortunes of a place change?

LIN YUN: First you must understand that there are forms and forces in the world which cannot be seen, but they are there at work all the time. Centuries ago Chinese scholars and sages learned this by studying nature, asking how does it work. This is what the *I Ching* talks about, the patterns of life. Then to help determine what to do to be in accord with universal harmonies, they also created an eight-sided wheel called the *ba-gua*. When the ba-gua was first invented, it linked all important powers to directions like north as the direction of career, the southwest as the direction of marriage, the southeast as the direction of wealth, and so forth. Black Sect Feng Shui says these factors may work outside, but for inside a room, what is more important is the "mouth of the chi," which is the door. To understand the forces of the universe at work in a room, take the door as signifying the north on the ba-gua, regardless of what the actual direction may be. Then you can see the positions in the rest of the room or house according to the ba-gua. This is the pattern which comes to us from the unseen world. I don't know why. But I know it works.

J.A.S.: How would you use this pattern of the ba-gua?

LIN YUN: You can use it to determine the "nine basic cures," and where to place them (Figure 1). But to get more value, you use the "Tracing the Nine Stars" ceremony. In this ceremony you walk through the house, visiting the eight points of the ba-gua and the center in order (family, wealth, center, helpful people, children, knowledge, fame, career, and marriage). At each place, you talk about what these things mean, and bless the place with prayers, gestures, and thoughts. This activates the chi and drives away bad luck, allowing good chi to come in.

J.A.S.: How do you know what to say and think?

PROFESSOR JAGGHID: In the two books by Sarah Rossbach about the work of Master Thomas Lin Yun, [*Feng Shui: The Chinese Art of Placement,* 1983, and *Interior Design with Feng Shui,* 1987] there are suggestions based upon Black Sect philosophy.

LIN YUN: You must understand that people cultivate their

Direction	Element	Color	Influence
1. north	water	black	career
2. nw			helpful people
3. west	metal	white	children
4. sw			marriage
5. south	fire	red	fame
6. se			wealth
7. east	wood	green	family
8. ne			knowledge

To apply the ba-gua to a room, the North direction is always the door, which is called "the mouth of the chi" according to Black Sect Tantric Buddhism. Interior design actions in each of the positions of the room then relate to the specific qualities of the ba-gua.

the mouth of the chi

The Ba-Gua and its application to interior design, according to Black Sect Tantric Buddhism

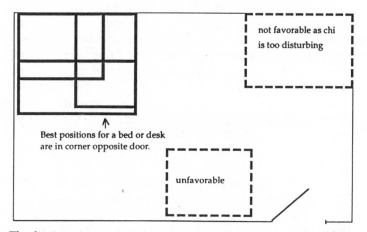

The dominant or commanding position for a room, according to Black Sect Tantric Buddhism

chi and their minds. Chu-shr takes a long time to develop. When I go to a place, I always pray to ask for guidance. Often I may use forms like in the book, because it is the spirit of Buddha which comes to me. But not always. We must always honor the spirit of a place, too, which is why the Black Sect has changed so much. In each new land we come to, we must meet and make friends with the religions which already exist there. I have recently met with the Pope, and I hope to meet and work with American Indian leaders too.

J.A.S.: In this country American Indian people are especially concerned about their sacred places being destroyed. What does Feng Shui say about sacred places?

LIN YUN: These places exist and are best known by people who have recognized their value for so many years. We say that if a sacred place is defiled, those who destroy it will experience bad omens and misfortunes, like a curse has been placed on them. Accidents and bad luck can arise from mistreating a sacred place. You talk about lawsuits to settle such matters. If people understood Feng Shui, this would not be necessary. Consulting a Feng Shui practitioner would settle the matter.

J.A.S.: One of the big problems with preserving sacred places is determining where they are, since people do not understand Feng Shui. What can we look for to help determine the specialness of places?

LIN YUN: You learn to sense the chi of a place, to see it, feel it, notice how it works on your body, and other ways. Then pay attention to the animals, the trees, the fish, etc. There is more beneficial chi, uplifting your spirits, at a sacred place. This influences your mind, your body, and can make the spirit world and this world closer to each other.

J.A.S.: Can you change the chi of a place, like an acupuncturist adjusts the chi in your body?

LIN YUN: Oh, yes. Not so much with big needles, but by working with nature. You can plant trees in places to change the chi of a place, as trees help direct chi upward. Each tree does this in its own special way. You can also make hills, level areas, move earth around to change chi. Dowsers know this. Underground streams of water are related to chi surface flow. Placing a flag pole or a light can also help elevate chi, as can shrubbery, fountains, and fish ponds. Computers and electrical machines can change chi too, for good or bad, depending on how they are made and where they are placed, as well as how they are used.

J.A.S.: Have you done anything to change the chi of this house?

LIN YUN: First of all, please understand that this house is sited in a good place. As you drove up the street, you rose up from San Francisco Bay. A dragon lives along this street. His tail is down by the water. His head is right here on top of this hill. Being at the head of the dragon helps our chi come up, which aids our spiritual connection.

Then you see how the plants around the house are placed to catch chi, groves of shrubs, bamboo, etc. The bird bath helps too. Birds are good fortune, as are fish in ponds.

Then the downstairs rooms as altars help establish this as a temple, and focus the chi on spiritual matters. The mirrors on the stairwell reflect light, and uplift your spirits too. These are important ru-shr things. We have done ceremonies here, too.

J.A.S.: Is there anything bad about this place?

LIN YUN: (smiles) Yes. I did not build the house, and the kitchen is right beside the stairs. It attracts people to go and eat too easily. Hard to keep down your weight!

J.A.S.: Peace is an issue which deserves a lot of attention, in these times. What can Feng Shui do for peace?

LIN YUN: First, let me again refer to the "Multi-Causes Theory." Peace is the result of many things: your state of mind, the place where you live, your neighborhood, prosperity, and international relations. We must make peace with the place where we live and ourselves to begin.

The leaders of world government would benefit greatly from practicing good Feng Shui, especially through designing their offices so that they all have some common elements. This would help develop understanding, which is aided by sympathy and is the result of similar attitudes and forms in building design and decoration.

The White House in Washington, D.C., is now situated at the end of 16th Street. This long arrow-like road rushes toward the White House, carrying far too much agitated "killing chi." This does not help presidents to have peace of mind, and it also lends itself to creating national problems. Trees could be used to shield the White House from this negative chi, but better strategies would be placing a large fountain outside, a weather vane on the roof to help direct chi upwards, and mirrors inside which would help redirect this unwanted chi back into the street. These are design solutions which would help, but the best thing of all would be for the leaders to pay attention to the spiritual dimensions of life, and practice wisdom based on transcendental states of mind.

J.A.S.: What is "killing chi," and where does it originate?

LIN YUN: Chi is the force that makes all things alive and moves the many cycles of nature. Without chi, nothing would be alive. In Chinese, the character for chi has two meanings: one is cosmic or universal; the other is human. Chi spirals around the earth, constantly moving, ever-changing, following the patterns of the Tao. That is to say, it expands and contracts, just as when we breathe we inhale and exhale. The chi of people is strongly influenced by both the chi of heaven and the chi of earth. Chi is what moves us to paint, dance, work, and love.

Chi must flow smoothly. Too little chi makes people, animals, plants, and places weak, and people are likely to get sick. A "killing chi" is one that races along, sometimes violently, and without the smooth, water-like quality of good flow. Yin and Yang, the yielding and the asserting principles, naturally strike a balance when healthy chi flows. The "killing chi" I speak of is a force of chi moved by traffic, congestion, maybe pollution, and many people. It is directed like an arrow toward the White House with nothing to break this flow and cause it to return to its natural water-course manner. Chi propels us through life and unites mind and body. We need to cultivate healthy chi in all things to bring about peace.

J.A.S.: Most people are familiar with the practice of acupuncture, in which a healer directs chi through the body with the help of needles, massage, or *moxa* [a burning herb held over acupuncture points]. Aside from practicing the art of placement according to Feng Shui, what else can be done to cultivate good chi in us?

LIN YUN: The chi around us shapes our destinies, but we can actively cultivate inner chi through meditation, tai chi, spiritual practice with sincerity, and right exercise. Try this. Stand up, raise your hands, reaching upward. Now move your feet so they are shoulder-width apart. Now direct your mind to the palms of your hands and the center of your forehead. As you inhale, imagine that sunlight is streaming down through your hands and forehead into your body, filling it up. Now as you exhale, see this sunlight swirling around, bathing all your cells. Try this nine times. It is important that you visualize this chi in you moving upward with the heat of the sun. This is called the "Sunshine Buddha" exercise.

(I rise to my feet and try this. A warm glow seems to permeate me as I repeat the exercise, and my body feels more relaxed.)

LIN YUN: People can take chi into them, and they can project it outward onto people and places. When a person with strong chi comes into a room, you know they are there. You feel their presence.

CRYSTAL CHU: Master Lin also has demonstrated how he can help a person at a distance. He demonstrated out-of-body healing several years ago for the American Society for Psychical Research.

J.A.S.: Master Lin, how can you heal at a distance with chi?

LIN YUN: The mind and spirit can do many things. Things like this are developed through years of study and spiritual practice.

J.A.S.: Just how did you come to your calling for the work you do with people and places?

LIN YUN: There are two sources. One is my family, which has a long history of spiritual practice (smiling). The second is that when I was six or seven and was living in Beijing, I was playing with a group of older boys who were sometimes rowdy. One day they began throwing stones at some monks, and I followed their actions. The monks began to chase this group of naughty boys. I was the smallest, and they caught me. To atone for what I had done, they instructed me to pray in front of a statue of Buddha. I took this very seriously, and did so all day. The monks saw me, and at the end of the day they told me to come back. I did. Soon, I became a student of Grand Master Ta Teh at the Yung Ho Temple in Beijing. For the next ten years I received individualized instruction in Black Sect mystical arts, including Feng Shui theory and practice.

* * * * * *

At this time one of Master Lin Yun's students reminds him that he must catch a plane for Taiwan in a short time.

As a gesture of goodwill, Master Lin gives me copies of the two books written about him and Feng Shui by Sarah Rossbach. He then asks if he could take my picture as he gives me the books. We stand and take our poses. A camera is brought out, but each time the photographer takes the picture, the flash doesn't work. Suddenly Master Lin turns and looks behind him. There is a picture of him and Pope John Paul standing in the same positions. Master Lin says, "Oh, I think he does not like this," at which point the flash on the camera suddenly goes off. We sit down at the table for the book-passing picture, and the camera and flash work perfectly.

As I am leaving the temple, Crystal Chu points to the two large pine trees in the front yard, one on each side of the entrance. She says the trees were an important reason why Master Lin chose this house. The reason, she says, is that "Lin" in Chinese means "two trees become a forest." "Yun," Crystal adds, means "reach to the clouds." The trees are a living statement of Lin Yun's name, she says.

As I walk down the path, a bird is splashing in one of the bird baths. Another in the bushes begins to sing. Peace. It lives here. One wonders how many of the world's problems could be helped or solved by Feng Shui.

Across the street, I turn and take a picture of the trees. Suddenly I think of the Sunshine Buddha exercise, and then it dawns on me that the house itself is designed as if it were the image of the exercise, with the sunlight pouring down through the central staircase, just as you would visualize the same light streaming down through your forehead. Feng Shui—lots of lessons to be learned for a culture which practices cash and carry architecture and then wonders why there is so much tension and anxiety in the world.

*   *   *   *   *   *

The Nine Basic Cures of Feng Shui

According to the wisdom of Feng Shui as practiced by Master Lin Yun, you can adjust the chi around your home to improve good fortune and health by performing simple practical acts, especially when these are in relation to the "mouth of the chi" or doorway entrance, and the pattern of the Ba-Gua, which is an ancient eight-sided chart of the forces of the universe and how they balance each other. Here are some simple practical acts:

1. Install bright objects, mirrors, or crystal balls. Mirrors reflect away bad chi and brighten up spaces. The general rule of thumb is the bigger the better. Lights can also help.

2. Install bells or wind chimes which make pleasant sounds. These dispel negative chi and summon positive chi.

3. Cultivate living objects in and around your home—plants, fishbowls, flowers, bird feeders, or birdbaths.

4. Place heavy objects like stones in places to help stabilize energy.

5. Install moving objects—mobiles, windmills, and fountains, all of which stimulate chi flow.

6. Place machines powered by electricity in special places in accord with the Ba-Gua design.

7. Bamboo flutes can be played or used for decoration. They symbolize spiritual swords, and tying red ribbons around them and pointing them upward helps chi flow. Shaking flutes helps drive away bad spirits.

8. Choose colors to increase beneficial chi. Yellow is the color of longevity, red is an auspicious color, and green is a color of spring and growth.

9. Red ribbons can be placed on doors with knocking knobs. Fringe can be used to hide slanted beams.

The Yun Lin Temple is located at 2959 Russell Street, Berkeley, California, 94705. They publish an informative quarterly newsletter, *Yun Lin Temple News*, as a way to answer the many letters which come to Master Lin. They ask that a donation of $20 be made for a one-year subscription.

15

Feng-shui as Terrestrial Astrology in Traditional China and Korea

DAVID J. NEMETH

The question of questions for mankind—the problem which underlies all others, and which is more deeply interesting than any other—is the ascertainment of the place which Man occupies in nature and of his relations to the universe of things.

—Thomas Huxley

When in early antiquity [Fu Hsi] ruled the world, he looked upward and contemplated the images in the heavens; he looked downward and contemplated the markings of birds and beasts and their adaptations to the regions. He proceeded directly from himself and indirectly from objects. Thus he invented the eight trigrams in order to enter into connections with the virtues of the light of the gods and to regulate the conditions of all beings.

—*I Ching*

Introduction

During the early Chinese Han dynasty (B.C. 206-220 A.D.) there emerged an imperial cult of "centrality," and its sacred number "5." Chinese emperors and elites became preoccupied with systematically finding and keeping themselves "at the center of the universe, where cosmic forces were strongest" (Cammann 1961:49). They believed that occupying the sacred center inspired their ability to "regulate conditions" in their realms.[1]

Although the comprehensive quest for centrality on the terrestrial surface was an early pursuit of Chinese emperors,[2] centerquest eventually became a popular obsession of all Chinese and Koreans under medieval Neo-Confucian administrations (circa 12th-18th centuries A.D.). Tradition-minded East Asians, for example in China,

215

South Korea, Taiwan, and Hong Kong, continue to pursue centerquest.

Centerquest throughout the traditional Chinese cultural realm was and is characterized by its unique system of divination through skilled surveying and interpretation of landform. It is this surveying system and its underlying theory that Western writers often refer to as *"feng-shui,"* or "Chinese geomancy." "Topomancy" and "terrestrial astrology" are less commonly encountered English-language terms for *feng-shui*.[3] Geomantic surveyors in China and Korea, ideally scholar-technicians educated in the Confucian classics,[4] are termed "geomancers" by Western writers.

Chatley's (1917:175) succinct and accurate definition for Chinese geomancy is: "The art of adapting the residences of the living and the dead so as to co-operate and harmonize with the local currents of the cosmic breath." In practice, geomantic surveying attempts to "center" human residences exactly where "cosmic breath" concentrates. For this reason, geomancy is regarded here as "centerquest."

Centerquest by Chinese and Korean imperial cults early on resulted in identifying many sacred places throughout East Asia, where temples, shrines, palaces, and royal tombs were subsequently built to access "cosmic breath." Centerquest as a mass pursuit in medieval China and Korea resulted in creating a more popular, secular and profane kind of geomantic landscape; one filled with what were perceived by many common folk to be propitious or lucky places for their own residences and tombs.

The deep roots of the cult of centrality and geomancy in ancient China entwine also the hoary beginnings of numerology there, which in one manifestation became a "magic" square of three (Figure 1). This square of three was used as a numerical "proof" that nature intended humankind to pursue centerquest through geomantic surveys. The magic square of three appears to have elaborated on two other ancient Chinese inventions. One was the "eight trigrams" of the *I Ching*, symbols used in many forms of Chinese divination, including geomancy. The other was the "well-field," a diagram or pattern that embodied an idealized system of arranging agricultural settlement. The systematic arrangement of human settlement, in turn, relates directly to geomantic theory and practices.

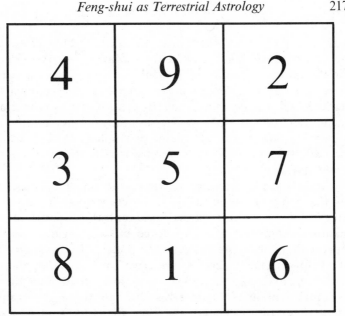

Figure 1. The Chinese "magic square of three" has peculiar numerological qualities that supposedly validate many ancient Chinese ideas about nature's "law" or "ethic" governing self-organizing principles in physical space: centrality, periodicity, connectivity, hierarchy, similarity at different scale, and completeness.

Neo-Confucianism and the Well-Field System

During the Sung dynasty (A.D. 1227-1379), classical Confucianism in China underwent extensive transformation to become a highly sophisticated, abstract and political mode of Confucian philosophy (Yang and Henderson 1958; Henthorn 1971:170). The resulting ideology was termed "Neo-Confucian" by Western observers who "noticed new developments in Sung Neo-Confucian thought which were not simply reducible to their classical antecedents" (DeBary 1981:xiv). Chen (1972:239) maintains that these "new developments" were more Taoist than Confucian. They also incorporated some of the abstract cosmological speculations of the Buddhists. Geomancy and other occult sciences (for example, alchemy and astrology) became part of medieval Neo-Confucian everyday life.

What became known as the Chu Hsi School of Neo-Confucianism eventually prevailed in medieval China

and spread to Korea where it became state orthodoxy under
the Yi dynasty (A.D. 1392-1910). Many Chu-Hsi Neo-
Confucians in Korea, as in China, were obsessed with
the quest for the center as a means for achieving a productive
agricultural society according to nature's self-organizing
principles in physical space, as they perceived them.
Centrality was one of these principles. Others were:
periodicity, connectivity, hierarchy, similarity at different
scale, and completeness.

Chu Hsi's philosophical commentary on "the Diagram
of the Supreme Pole" (Figure 2) elaborated on how a
creative force (*chi*) occupied the central place/origin in
nature's plan, and how this force moved, organized and
operated, as principle, process and pattern. In the diagram,
the central "One" becomes the "Two" of a complementary
Yin (negative) and Yang (positive) force field, and these
eventually manifest themselves through the Five Agents
(sometimes translated as "the Five Elements") as myriad
things in the living environment.[5] The entire living environment was therefore shaped by this One principle/process/
pattern. If observing their environment had revealed nature's
own principles of self-organization to the Chinese, how
could they benefit from this knowledge? By participating
in nature's plan, through centerquest.

Chinese Geomancy

The Diagram of the Supreme Pole as interpreted by
Chu Hsi provided the philosophical underpinnings of
the popular quest for the center, for the One, by medieval
Chinese, who strived to obey nature's principle, to follow
its process and to fit into its pattern. To gain prosperity
as earthly inhabitants, Chinese believed they must be
principled (virtuous), meanwhile occupying the place
of the central One, according to nature's plan.[6] Discovering
this place was the task of geomantic surveying. Once
geomantically sited, or centered, a person had "entered
into connections with the virtues of the light of the gods."
Prosperity would follow.

Geomantic surveying in China probably predates the
Han dynasty. Its age and origins are unknown. If one
speculates on the etymology of the term *feng-shui* (wind

Figure 2. The "Diagram of the Supreme Pole," sometimes called the "Diagram of the Great Ultimate." The Central One of the pole becomes Two, and the Two become Myriad Things. This is according to the speculations of the medieval Chinese philosopher Chu Hsi (1131-1200 A.D.). The illustration is from Kupter (1906:335).

and water), it seems reasonable that at a very early date Taoist naturalists in a blossoming agricultural society might have invented a location theory and surveying system that identified and glorified as sacred centers those places where wind (*feng*) and water (*shui*) gathered naturally, as springs or pools beneath the terrestrial surface that could be tapped by wells. But this is just speculation. What is certain is that geomancy long predates Chu Hsi Neo-Confucians in China and Korea, who eventually popularized it and used it as an effective means of spatial organization and social control. As they did so, they wrote often of an ancient "well-field" system in China, an institution that may have also influenced the development of geomantic theories and practices there.

The Well-Field System

Sometime prior to the Han dynasty a "well-field" system of agricultural organization and settlement was invented. The well-field system is thought to have been an ideal plan for human settlement.[7] The system is an idea embedded in a simple, ancient ideogram, or character, representing a water "well" (Figure 3). This ideogram consists of two pairs of intersecting parallel lines creating nine squares of equal size. At one time this character included a dot in its central square, suggesting the location of a well: The water "well" ideogram probably represents two wooden crossbeams centering on a wellhead, but suggests further a centralized system of a productive agricultural society where well-irrigated agricultural land is divided into nine fields of equal size, with eight of them surrounding a well-field. Farmers were drawn to the center by the water source for their survival. In an idealized interpretation, the centripetal force of the well's location generated communalism, cooperation and self-sufficiency in agricultural productivity, social and political stability, and peace.

Whether or not this well-field system was actually a workable system of land management for the ancient Chinese state was of secondary importance to the medieval Neo-Confucians, who promoted the well-field ideal primarily as a plan for maintaining a productive and prosperous

Figure 3. The "well" ideogram, representing two wooden crossbeams centering on a wellhead. Imbedded in the ideogram is an idea for arranging a productive and peaceful agricultural settlement, which the Neo-Confucian Chinese called the "well-field" system.

Chinese civilization. They tried to recreate the spatial and social organization of the earlier successful Han dynasty, which appeared also to be based on the well-field model.

For example, during the Han dynasty the Middle Kingdom of China was perceived by its rulers and philosophers as the center of the inhabited world, consisting of nine provinces "of which the central one contained the capital with the residence of the supreme ruler" (Cammann 1961:41). They held also that "China was one of the Nine Territories comprising a continent, and that there were nine such continents that together made up the world, the central one containing the great mountain that formed [centered] the cosmic axis (Ibid:42). This mountain was named Kunlun.

The Well-field and the Magic Square of Three

As idealized, the well-field system works because of the organizational potential of the well itself, the central One. An impressive numerical "proof" that the well-field pattern was inspired by nature's own principles of self-organization (centrality, periodicity, connectivity, hierarchy, similarity at different scale, and completeness) is found by super-imposing it over the magic square of three.

Note that the configuration of the well-field pattern is such that if the magic square of three were superimposed upon it, the number 5 takes the position of the well. Since all numbers of whatever magnitude in ancient China were represented by the digits 1 through 9, the 5 was medial to their extremes (halfway between 1 and 9) and balanced between them, and it was therefore "special" in an abstract sense to the ancient Chinese.

When Chinese numerologists first experimented, for whatever reason, with assigning these nine digits to the nine spaces of the well-field, the central square was probably allocated to the special digit 5. Assuming that the eight remaining digits were assigned randomly to the remaining eight spaces of the well-field, one configuration (Figure 1) resulted in peculiar if not amazing qualities: A) The sum of the digits in every direction is 15. B) If one multiplies the central 5 by 3 (which happens to be the base number of the square) the result is 15. C) When the square of the base number 3 is multiplied by the central 5 the sum is

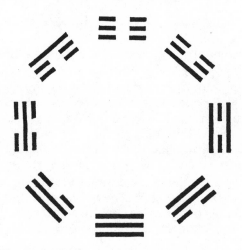

Figure 4. The Eight Trigrams of the I Ching *classic. The circular arrangement implies a centripetal force at the center.*

45, which happens to be the total sum of all the numbers in the square. D) The central 5 happens to be the physical (contrasted to the "abstract") mean of all opposing numbers. E) The central 5 is the mathematical mean of each opposing pair of numbers, whose sums are 10. F) Odd and even digits surrounding the central 5 alternate in space, creating perfect balance about it. (Cammann 1961)

Other seemingly "magical" properties of this square of three are equally esoteric, yet highly significant within the context of ancient Chinese thought. Not least of these was the happy coincidence of the eight digits surrounding the central 5 and the circular configuration of the Eight Trigrams of the *I Ching* classic (Figure 4). The Eight Trigrams are among the most important symbols in geomantic theory and appear prominently among the many symbols surrounding the center ("heaven pool") of the geomantic compass (Figure 5).

The River Lo Diagram

The special numerical properties of the ancient Chinese magic square remained a state secret for thousands of years, hidden from the public. During the Neo-Confucian era the magic square pattern became widely disseminated. The *I Ching* classic was revised by the Neo-Confucians

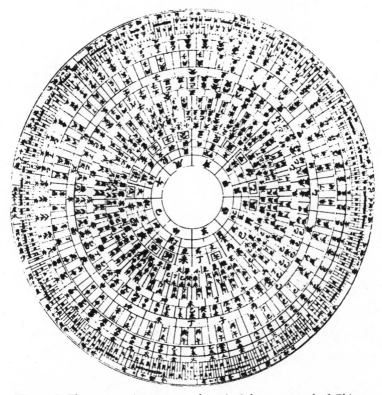

Figure 5. The geomantic compass, the principle survey tool of Chinese and Korean centerquest. The illustration is from DeGroot (1897:280).

to include a "diagram of the River Lo" (Figure 6). The revised *I Ching* attributes this diagram to the legendary emperor Yu, who mastered hydraulic engineering and tamed China's turbulent rivers. His engineering feats permitted a productive agricultural system based on flood control, canals and irrigation. Yu, claims the revised classic, discovered the diagram on the back of a large turtle as it rose up from the waters of the River Lo. The diagram is in fact the nine digit arrangement of the ancient magic square of three.

Geomancy as Terrestrial Astrology

Verification of nature's self-organizing principles in physical space was not limited to Taoist esoteric applications of numerology to the ancient well-field ideogram, which

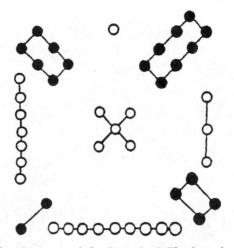

Figure 6. The "Diagram of the River Lo." The legendary Emperor/ hydraulic engineer Yu observed this diagram on the back of a turtle as it rose from the River Lo (a tributary of the Hwang or Yellow River). It is the digits 1 through 9 arranged as a magic square of three.

seems to have resulted in the discovery of the magic square of three. The development of geomancy as a sophisticated system of centerquest by a Chinese imperial cult still might never have occurred but for one outstanding mani-festation of nature's principles of centrality and hierarchy that was impossible to ignore. This was the north pole star configuration at the time of the Han dynasty.

That configuration, slightly idealized, is shown in Figure 7. It resembled the well-field pattern insofar as it appeared to be a circle (the pole star) enclosed in a square, an en-closure formed by an imaginary line connecting four surrounding stars. Extending these lines created a well-field pattern that divided the heavens into nine divisions and nine directions. The plane formed by eight directions surrounding the pole star is intersected by the ninth direction (the polar axis) as it reached the terrestrial surface.

Heaven itself appeared to be organized according to nature's principles of self-organization in physical space. In China the apparent centrality of the One pole star in the heavens, as well as its supreme rank in a heavenly hierarchy of stars, had important social consequences on earth. The pole star, perceived as the "Emperor star" by Han dynasty Chinese, appeared to reside at the center of heaven. All other stars circled about it. Nearby, the slow, circular movement of the Great Bear or Big Dipper star formation appeared to direct the heavens during the course of the year on behalf of the "Emperor star," pointing east, south, west, and north, in endless sequence, year after year. The cyclic stability of the heavens seemed due to the force of the pole star at its center, and the organized celestial bureaucracy empowered therefrom. Here, writ large in the night sky, impossible to ignore and inviting to contemplate, was something of a prototype organizational pattern for a productive human society. This prototype inspired Chinese social, economic and political organization on earth, especially through the long and pervasive influences of geomantic theory and surveying. Eitel (1873:10) has captured the deterministic relationship perceived by traditional Chinese between heaven on the one hand, and themselves and the earth on the other: "Everything terrestrial has its prototype, its primordial cause, and its ruling agency in heaven." Feuchtwang (1974:84) makes it clear that it is "the influence of the stars and cosmic

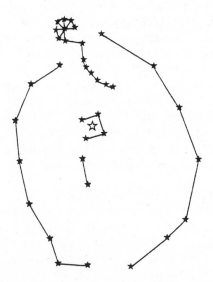

Figure 7. A modified diagram of the north pole star configuration observed during the early Han dynasty (206 B.C. - 220 A.D.). Extension of the lines connecting the four stars surrounding the pole star results in a "well" pattern. The pole star occupies its center. The illustration is revised from Rufus and Tien (1945; see also Needham 1959:260).

processes on earth" that is geomancy's main concern. For this reason it is best to think of Chinese geomancy as terrestrial astrology.

The Imperial Cult of the Center

The Chinese emperor gained authority by claiming heavenly inspiration and influence by virtue of his central position on earth, a position that mirrored and was influenced by the central position of the pole star in the sky. Paul Wheatley (1971:430) has quoted Confucius, who made an analogy between the mechanisms of state control and celestial patterns and motion: "He who exercises government by means of his moral force may be compared to the Pole Star, which keeps its [central] position while all the [other] stars do homage to [that is, revolve about] it."

The centralized position from which the Middle Kingdom of China has been ruled and regulated was sacred space inhabited by the One earthly emperor. The location of the emperor's residence in the Middle Kingdom was divined by means of terrestrial astrology. The heavenly mandate for the emperor's rule on earth came in large part from the emperor's occupying what was perceived to be the sacred center of the terrestrial surface, corresponding to the pole star inhabiting the sacred center of the heavens. At this position the emperor, aided by his bureaucracy, was inspired to make those timely decisions about agricultural productivity and family life that was given to the farmers in the yearly almanac. In return for this inspired advice, part of the productivity of the realm was returned to the emperor and his bureaucrats, as taxes, labor and loyalty.[8]

According to geomantic theory, the energy to rule successfully—the source of the emperor's divine inspiration—was supplied from heaven through an earthly conduit. That conduit was identified as Kunlun Mountain, the source of the Huang (Yellow) River. It was near the confluence of the Lo and Huang Rivers that the Emperor Yu found his inspiration to tame China's rivers and build a powerful and productive agricultural civilization. Kunlun was once perceived as the highest mountain on earth, and medieval Chinese and Korean maps show it as the center

Figure 8. A medieval Korean map of the world. Kunlun Mountain occupies the center, where according to geomantic theory, it "rules the hills and the pole Star rules the stars" (Edkins 1872:293). The illustration is from Hulbert (1904:600, facing page).

of the terrestrial surface, at the center of the Middle Kingdom (Figure 8). According to geomantic theory Kunlun reached to heaven. Moreover, as Edkins (1872:293) reports:

> It is the backbone from which the other mountain chains proceed, and they form together a kind of terrestrial skeleton. The rivers form the veins and arteries, and the mountains the bones of a living earth. The whole is imagined to be so like the heavens that certain stars correspond to certain terrestrial spaces, and exercise rule over them. [Kunlun] rules the hills as the Pole star rules the stars.

The "life blood" of this terrestrial organism is the heaven-sent *chi* or "cosmic breath," sought by geomancers over the centuries in the employ of both emperors and commoners.

Centerquest and the Ming Tang, or Sacred Place

Centerquest is accomplished by surveying for "cosmic breath," using landforms as indicators as well as consulting a specialized hand-held compass. The center of the compass is a small housing for a magnetic needle. This part of the compass is called the "Heaven Pool." Concentric circles of cosmic symbolism surround the needle.[9] The geomancers accomplished centerquest by knowledgeably superimposing the compass device over the terrestrial surface, and by systematically moving over that surface and being naturally "drawn to the cosmic well."[10] Success for both geomancer and client is a blending of technique and humility for, "It is the boast of [geomancy] that it teaches man how to rule nature and his own destiny by showing him how heaven and earth rule him" (Eitel 1873:60).

Chinese geomancy is a system of divination because it reveals hidden knowledge about the location of the cosmic breath, which flows through the mountain "dragons" from Kunlun until it collects in "yellow springs" here and there beneath the terrestrial surface. Earth surface features are "indicators," their shapes and positions in-fluenced by heavenly prototypes, including stars, planets, sun and moon, that direct geomancers to the yellow springs. This indirect divination of heavenly phenomena through terrestrial indicators characterizes Chinese geomancy as terrestrial astrology, that is, astrology using a terrestrial medium.

Since centerquest applies nature's own self-organizing principles in physical space to locate sites for human residences on the terrestrial surface, the result is the birth of a place organism at that site. This is obvious when one inspects a geomancer's diagram of the ideal configuration of topographical features—mountains and rivers—around a site representing the central One (Figure 9). It resembles the human female anatomy in the vicinity of the birth canal. If the site is indeed appropriate to nature's plan, the One will become the Two and lead to myriad pro-ductive things.

At the dedication of the site Korean geomancers have been observed to fix the cardinal directions there with a special device called the "golden well," which is a "frame composed of two transverse and two lateral rods in the

Figure 9. The ideal configuration of topographic features—mountains and streams—around a geomantic site, or Central One.

shape of the Chinese character for well" (Hulbert 1896). The geomancer also draws a topo-cosmo-graphic map of the site, accompanied by poetic marginalia (Figure 10). The difficulty of accessing highest quality "yellow springs" beneath the terrestrial surface is revealed by contrasting the geomantic diagram of an ideal configuration of topographical features around a "best" site (Figure 9) with the configuration around the site described in Figure 10.

One of nature's basic principles of spatial organization is similarity at different scale. Therefore, it would be surprising if residences constructed above yellow springs were not also manifestations of the ancient well-field pattern. Figure 11 represents the actual layout of a rural farm compound in South Korea, with structures occupying some of the eight compartments of the well-field pattern surrounding a central courtyard. Knapp (1986:19) writes that the courtyard in medieval China was called a "sky well."

A third dimension also existed, called a Ming Tang.[11] As manifested in Chinese imperial palaces, it was a towering construction rising along a vertical axis above the yellow springs.[12] It reached to heaven as brick and stone and,

Figure 10. A topo-cosmographic map of terrain surrounding a geo-mantic site in South Korea. The illustration is from an unauthored eighteenth-century (?) atlas of Cheju Island geomantic sites.

by extension, to the stars above, for astronomical instru-ments were placed upon it. As manifested in the everyday constructions of farm households, the Ming Tang was the ridgepole above the head of household, in the room where the ancestral tablets also resided. Into this ridgepole, on the ritual day of house construction, a diagram of the Big Dipper or the Diagram of the Supreme Pole was usually inscribed (Cammann 1985:253).[13]

Concluding Comments

Imperial Ming Tang towers no longer exist in China or South Korea. In South Korea the term *myongdang* (Ming Tang) *chari* survives to signify in the vernacular any propitious or lucky (but not necessarily sacred) place. However, centerquest continues in both China and Korea, where geomancers continue to find some clients, but

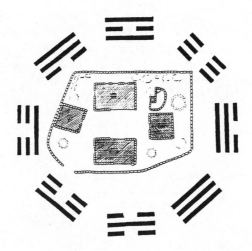

Figure 11. The layout of a farm compound in South Korea, surrounded by the Eight Trigrams from the I Ching.

where Neo-Confucianism has been in rapid decline for over a century.

Throughout East Asia, wherever the modern, urban-industrial age has penetrated, the value of cosmic symbolism rooted in ancient Chinese agricultural civilization retains little or no currency. Even where geomancy still claims adherents, their centerquest is often motivated by personal gain rather than by a desire to cooperate and harmonize with "the local currents of the cosmic breath."

It is ironic, though not surprising, that nature's ethic or law governing the self-organizing principles of physical space applies also to economic centerquest: centrality, in particular, is a guiding principle of modern economic location theory. Nature's principle, in this case, is now being corrupted for profit. No one can claim that the economic centerquest that results in another hamburger franchise creates sacred space, or that the local environment is more harmonious because of an economically central, convenient location. Competition is rapidly replacing cooperation as the prevailing ethic worldwide. If this development is truly contrary to nature's law, the outcome may be disastrous for humankind.

A logical response to this threat would be to begin to search now for a comprehensive environmental ethic

appropriate to a 21st-century post-industrial world system.
Perhaps the search could begin by examining successful
pre-industrial ethical systems worldwide. Certainly the
positive aspects of agrarian Neo-Confucian ideology and
its use of *feng-shui* practices in establishing and maintaining a stable and productive social order should not
be overlooked.

Notes

1. The desire to occupy a sacred center is one response to the
   universal human notion that "being in the right place at the
   right time" is beneficial, and can be achieved by observing
   nature and learning natural "laws" or "ethics" governing
   time and space.
2. The layout of early Chou dynasty (1050-256 B.C.) cities
   demonstrates that the imperial cult of centrality is extremely
   old in China.
3. What Western writers call "Chinese geomancy" is *feng-shui*
   (various spellings) to Chinese and *p'ung-su* to Koreans. The
   qualifier "Chinese" is necessary to distinguish this tradition
   of "geomancy" from Arab, African and European geomantic
   traditions. Feuchtwang (1974:4, 224) suggests "topomancy"
   as more descriptive of *feng-shui* practices than the term
   "geomancy." He elaborates that "it is divination based on
   topographical and architectural features" or "the divination
   of earthly signs," and that it is "a science of surveying in
   which symbols are used." Many of these symbols represent
   celestial objects and patterns and their influences in earth
   surface formations, so "terrestrial astrology" may be an even
   more revealing English-language term for describing *feng-
   shui* practices.
4. The *I Ching* [Book of Changes] and *Li Chi* [Book of Rites],
   for example.
5. The number 5 has much significance to Chinese and Koreans,
   as is indicated in the discussion of the magic square. In the
   West, too, the central 5 is perceived as "special" by the masses.
   This is illustrated by public three-digit lotteries in the United
   States, where 555 is so popular a choice that lottery operators
   lose millions each time these digits are drawn.
6. Kim Hei-chu (1973:114) writes, "The Confucian gentleman was
   enjoined to orient his behavior according to propriety rules
   in every social situation. By observing propriety rules, it was
   believed, the individual could be fitted into the cosmic and
   social order, thereby facilitating adaptation of the individual
   to the given world." To properly orient oneself—to "be fitted
   into"—physical space required the advice of the geomancer.

7. Some scholars argue that the well-field was more symbolic than of practical utility in traditional China (DeBary and Haboush 1985:32).

8. The emperor's claim for heaven's mandate to rule on earth, as nature intended, is revealed in the diagrammatic organization of a typical Sung dynasty farmers' calendar. The calendar includes the emperor's timely instructions for planting, harvesting, marriage, burial and so on, arranged for the year, in a cyclic pattern. At the center are depicted the directing "stars" of the emperor's earthly imperial bureaucracy.

9. To paraphrase Eitel (1873:43), the geomancy compass is a clever contrivance, making the most of a very rudimentary knowledge of astronomy, for it comprises in one perspicuous arrangement all the different principles of Chinese physical science: the male and female principles, the 8 diagrams, the 64 diagrams, the solar orbit, the lunal ecliptic, the 360 degrees of longitude, the days of the year, the 5 planets, the 5 elements, the 28 constellations, the 12 zodiacal signs, the 9 stems of the bushel, the 24 seasons, and the 12 parts of the compass.

10. In medieval times the geomancer walked, rode horseback or was carried over hill, dale and stream in a litter. At present, leading geomancers in South Korea may prospect even by helicopter.

11. The meaning of *ming tang* in the technical vocabulary of geomancy is "threshold to the One, rather than the One itself."

12. In A.D. 688 the Empress Wu of China ordered a 300 foot high Ming Tang constructed within her palace (Soothill 1951: 107-108).

13. The geomancer consulted the almanac to determine when to raise the ridgepole (Knez 1960:156; Knapp 1986:115).

References

Cammann, Schuyler. "The Magic Square of Three in Old Chinese Philosophy and Religion," *History of Religions* 1 (1961), 37-80.

Cammann, Schuyler. "Some Early Chinese Symbols of Duality." *History of Religions* 24, 2 (February 1985), 215-254.

Chatley, H. "Feng-Shui." In *Encyclopaedia Sinica* (ed. Samuel Couling), p. 175. Shanghai: Kelly and Walsh, 1917.

Chen, Shih-chuan. "How to Form a Hexagram and Consult the I Ching," *Journal of the American Oriental Society,* 92, 2 (April-June 1972), 237-249.

DeBary, William Theodore. *Neo-Confucian Orthodoxy and the Learning of the Mind-and-Heart.* New York: Columbia University Press, 1981.

DeBary, William Theodore and Jahyun Kim Haboush (eds.). *The Rise of Neo-Confucianism in Korea.* New York: Columbia University Press, 1985.

DeGroot, J. J. M. *The Religious System of China,* 5 vols. Leyden: E. J. Brill, 1892-1910.

Edkins, J. (Rev.). "On the Chinese Geomancy Known as Feng-shui." *The Chinese Recorder and Missionary Journal* 1872: March, 274-277: April, 291-298; May, 316-321.

Eitel, Ernest J. *Feng-Shui, or the Rudiments of Natural Science in China.* Hong Kong: Lane, Crawford, 1873.

Feuchtwang, Stephan D. R. *An Anthropological Analysis of Chinese Geomancy.* Vientiane: Editions Vithagna, 1974.

Henthorn, William E. *A History of Korea.* New York: Free Press, 1971.

Hulbert, Homer B. "The Geomancer." *Korean Repository,* 3 (January-December 1896), 387-391.

Hulbert, Homer B. "An Ancient Map of the World," *Bulletin of the American Geographical Society,* 36 (1904), 600-605.

I Ching [Book of Changes]. Translated by Richard Wilhelm and rendered into English by Cary F. Baynes. Third edition. Princeton, N.J.: Princeton University Press, 1967.

Kim Hei-chu. "The Role of Religious Belief and Social Structure in Korea's Breakthrough into Modernity." Ph.D. dissertation in Sociology, New School for Applied Research, New York, 1973.

Knapp, Ronald G. *China's Traditional Rural Architecture.* Honolulu: The University of Hawaii Press, 1986.

Knez, Eugene Irving. *Sam Jong Dong: A South Korean Village.* Ann Arbor, University Microfilms, 1960.

Kupter, Carl F. "The Mandarin's Grave." *East of Asia Magazine,* 5 (1906), 335-342.

Needham, Joseph. *Science and Civilisation in China.* Vol. 3 of 7 volumes. Cambridge, England: Cambridge University Press, 1959.

Nemeth, David J. *The Architecture of Ideology: Neo-Confucian Imprinting on Cheju Island, Korea.* Berkeley: University of California Press, Special Publications in Geography 26, 1987.

Rufus, W. Carl, and Tien Hsing-chih. *The Soochow Astronomical Chart.* Ann Arbor: University of Michigan Press, 1945.

Soothill, William Edward. *The Hall of Light: A Study of Early Chinese Kingship.* London: Lutterworth Press, 1951.

Wheatley, Paul. *The Pivot of the Four Quarters.* Chicago: Aldine, 1971.

Yang, Key P., and Gregory Henderson. "An Outline History of Korean Confucianism, Part 1: The Early Yi Period and Yi Factionalism," *Journal of Asian Studies,* vol. 18, no. 1 (November 1958), 81-101.

16

Your House Cares About You

PETER C. HJERSMAN

Your first step in a design project is to define the Intent.
The project is being undertaken for what purpose? What
is the conscious Intent, what is the expected result? Is the
primary Intent for beneficial profit? Is it to provide a space
that will stimulate the well-being and success of the occupants? If the foundation of the Intent is a positive, beneficial
energy, the entire process will give a new name to our
structures and the process of building them. As the Intent
is clarified, defined clearly, written down, and agreed upon
with all involved, many of the hitches in construction will
not appear. Definition of Intent takes time, patience, and
a willing team. Also, with the added installation of care,
the investment will be returned many times over. Your
house cares about you—give it the chance to prove it.

The Intent of this presentation is to give you something
to use. Hopefully, this will be a way to expand your awareness of your spaces and the interaction with them. After
a brief introduction, I will share with you several ways
to use in your own house and workspace.

The best case scenario is something we all strive to
achieve. As I put together a scenario from living examples,
this scene starts with a master builder. With the Intent
in hand, the master builder will seek the ideal site; the
right building begins on the right land. This involves a
quiet listening to the land, honed with your needs (Intent)
and allowing your mind to open to the voice of the land
energies. The same attitude is used to arrange the rooms.
This is the design stage. Construction documents are the

end result. This step also involves listening to the land, at a more local level than used in choosing the site.

After the site is chosen, the entry is determined, and the room arrangement is designed, the next step is to choose the materials. For a wood structure, the master builder will go to the forest and pick the trees most appropriate for the specific requirements of the structural members. This takes into account the Intent, the site-specific climate and ecology, and occupant use.

For example, in Japan, a master builder (miya daiku') was chosen to rebuild a temple that recently burned down. He wanted the temple to last a thousand years. To do this, he sought for trees that were at least a thousand years old. He could not find trees of this age in Japan, so after searching, he found them in Taiwan. The cutting time and method of the selected trees were indicated, the milling was directed, the drying time and method were related to the lumber-smiths. During milling this builder had the outer twenty years of growth removed from the trees so the lumber would last longer. During the drying time (which was five years), the carpenters were interviewed and hired. This was done with the same listening by the master builder. Since we are products of the land and the carpenters are daily working with the land, then their hearts can be assayed with the same listening as can the land itself.

The master builder oversees construction as one member of the team working together to create a structure that will bring well-being and success to the future users. This is the basic Intent the master builder uses not only with the buildings, but as a way of living—living with the land, with the buildings, with the people.

Before I teach a session, I come into the classroom to sense its qualities. First I walk the space to "feel" the room, then sit and "listen" to the energy in it. I ask permission to give the presentation in this space. Then I voice aloud the Intent of the presentation, and begin the energy-analysis of the room. I sometimes start with a magnetic compass to locate electromagnetic anomalies. Those I observed in a room where a "Spirit of Place" symposium was held are noted in Figure 1 (floorplan).

I measured and sketched the room. With a pendulum, I indicated and marked the beneficial and detrimental zones. These are energies inherent in the ground that tell

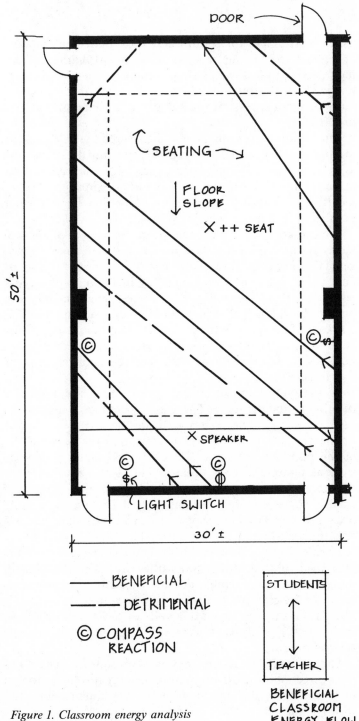

Figure 1. Classroom energy analysis

us the best places for certain activities. Beneficial energies are those that bring positive benefits to humans. This includes happiness, well-being, content, success in ventures undertaken. Detrimental energies are those that can lower our energy, depress us, bring us to a state of physical disharmony.

After finding these energies, I discovered the best location for the speaker, and I marked the spot on the floor with tape. I noticed that one speaker in particular spent a lot of time standing on the tape, with no knowledge of its location or marking. I began to worry that he was stuck to the tape, but his vivacious explanations proved otherwise.

Feeling complete in this short analysis, I ask if there is more to know. The response for the room in Figure 1 was yes. I followed the lead of the pendulum on the floorplan, and it indicated a very beneficial location in the seats. Using my hand for dowsing, I walked the area indicated on the floorplan and located the "lucky seat," number 7F. I asked, "Is there anything else to know about this space at this time?" The response indicated a completeness for now. I gave thanks for the data received, and the drawing was finished.

In the floorplan, several diagonal lines are indicated running across the room. These are sometimes called energy lines or energy zones. They indicate the energies inherent in the site. Overall, they existed prior to the construction of the building, just as would other geographical features such as mountains and streams. The dotted lines indicate locations that are detrimental to human well-being and usually to be avoided for any length of time. The solid lines are beneficial to people and can stimulate positive growth, well-being, and wealth. The lines indicate the "center" of the zone area. The actual shape is more that of a river in three-dimensions plus time. For the limit of the analysis a river can be defined by using any two points along its length and connecting them with a straight line. This is the same as using the walls of the room for the set limits of the analysis. It is a convenient way to indicate general areas.

The difficulty with the lines in the room in Figure 1 is their direction. The direction of the energy flow is a stronger influence than the energy level of the lines themselves. Ideally, the classroom energy will travel between the speaker and the audience, simultaneously in both directions. Here the lines under the seats stifle a smooth and clear flow of energy between the speaker and the listeners. The location of the lines divides and separates the people in the room.

Now, with this background, you may be wondering what you can do to express your care for your own building. The first thing is to listen. Listen to yourself, listen to the building and what it has to offer. Just sit in the room and let data and ideas come into you. Verbally, tell the room why you are sitting there, what your Intent is, and what you hope to accomplish. The response will come, but often slowly and in its own way (often from a source you could never have guessed, let alone planned for).

For example, one person was creating a quiet place in her backyard. She was having trouble keeping the foliage in it healthy and lush. While sitting at the site, she told the place of her opinion and her desire for healthy greenery. A few days later, while walking down the street, she felt the urge to walk in a different direction. Along this route, she found a plant for sale that felt just right for her quiet garden. It must have felt right to the yard and to the plant itself, for it continues to grow and prosper.

To listen takes time. You have to put yourself in a receiving state of mind, receive, and allow the response to emerge. The more you think and concentrate on the task, the longer it will take. Once the Intent is stated, let it go, "hang up the phone," and shift your energy and attention elsewhere.

Listening includes listening to yourself, to the land, to the built structures, and to the site-specific climatic conditions. Any preconceptions and expectations you lug around bog down the process.

Another way is to meditate in and with space. By clearing the mind, a place is created for the room to speak to. Clients who spend time listening to their rooms are bringing significant qualities into the design process.

A simple way is to sleep in all the rooms of your residence. I find that my mind while I sleep is very receptive. When I move into a new dwelling, I give a night to each of the spaces—a small effort considering the information that can be gained about the space this way. Even if no cognitive sparks jump out immediately, the building recognizes your effort. It is heard and will have beneficial results.

Another simple way to further your observance of the spaces is to walk around with a compass. Electromagnetic anomalies will be observed. Sometimes the needle moves sharply, and at other times only a few degrees will be indicated. Often these reactions can be traced to sources such as pipes or electrical boxes. To find the source does not reduce the relevance of anomalies, for they still influence the space and therefore the occupant. Some reactions will not be traceable, and in such cases dowsing can be of assistance.

Dowsing is a method of asking questions of a location. Most often we hear of people asking for water locations. Yet in antiquity people who built monuments (and houses) used dowsing to ask for the best location for the building, for the entrance, and for the room arrangement. We can do the same.

One method of introducing dowsing into our lives is to practice the "silent clap." Hold your arms apart as if preparing to clap. Slowly bring them together. At some point one hand will sense the other hand before they touch. If no response occurs, shake the hands, stretch the arms and back, reach outward, and try it again. Once you feel a response, you will know that you have the capability for dowsing. To learn more you can find books about the subject, or better yet, contact the local chapter of the American Society of Dowsers, Inc., Danville, Vermont 05828-0024, phone (802) 684-3417.

The purpose, the Intent of dowsing is to put us in touch with ourselves, with our environment, and with the interaction between the two. Often certain implements—L-rods, pendulums, bobbers, Y-rods—are useful, for they can stimulate our awareness of ourselves, our capabilities.

In our work, we aim to help draw the design response from the client, the occupant of the land. We are not trying to impose our wills or egos or personal goals on the client, the site, the existing building. "Ego-design" is rarely beneficial for the occupants.

One client spent an hour or more just sitting in the rooms of her house. Doing this, with no particular method, she was able to allow the energy of the house to provide harmonious design ideas. Not only have outstanding designs emerged in this way, but with this active statement of responding with the building, other benefits have emerged. For example, this client's awareness of spaces has expanded. Her ability has gone beyond her own residence into her office and any spaces she interacts with. She even found that with the expansion of her spatial awareness came expansion of awareness in general, including a deeper understanding of herself, her family, and her office staff. The last time we discussed the design for her house, she began talking about herself (which naturally followed the design awareness)—the insights she was gaining and the beneficial changes in her life. After a while, she stopped and really looked at me, and thanked me for the psychological "counseling." We both laughed with delight and went our ways. This is the type of response we hope for, since no longer can we separate people from buildings.

One alternative to "ego-design" is "source design." The client listening to her rooms was practicing source design—allowing her mind to be receptive, giving the time to listen and the willingness to be open, letting the response come into her conscious mind and move into physical production. The only people I have met who do not have the capability for this are those who do not want to learn it. The source is where geomancy came from eons ago. Our procedure is to be aware of the standard textbook methods, the "data knowledge," as a basis for understanding the source. Listening to the source is "direct knowledge"—from the land directly through you (not *to* you) into awareness and production.

One way I learned about this was by participating in sweat lodge ceremonies with a Native American sacred pipe holder. I followed him around, asking endless questions, taking photos, making pages of notes. At first, I could not get the answers I wanted. No, he had not heard of geomancy or Feng-shui or of siting structures by dowsing. Well, without a common vocabulary, how could we communicate? I read and reread my notes, studied the photos, thought about and felt about the ceremonies. If the geomancy is of the land, then it must be available everywhere, not only in some other country. After the next sweat lodge ceremony, I dowsed the sweat lodge and, sure enough, two water lines crossed in the very center of the lodge. I asked the Native American how he had found the location for the lodge. He said, "It felt right. . . ." Direct from the source.

A project is frequently begun with an energy-analysis, as was done with the classroom described earlier, only usually with more detail. The analysis is then used as one of the design resources, like a soils report.

The methods indicated can put us in touch with the source, the approach from which the beneficial designs come, from which geomancy was born. By listening to the land, our ancestors could respond with a design which came directly from the land. Over time, certain attitudes and approaches were found to be consistent for a specific geography, climate, culture, life-style, and building material. Then "data knowledge" was developed, the standard, textbook approach. The Intent has remained, but it becomes a bit foggy at times. If we listen to the land and have some practical, professional training and education, the source will be more ready to respond with us.

One use of the source is "map dowsing," dowsing a site remotely, one that we may never go to. When I was living in Japan, people would send their floorplans and site plans from the United States. I would do the analyses and send them back. When I have visited and dowsed sites after having dowsed them remotely, I get the same results as I did with remote dowsing. Normally, we use this method for site energy-analyses; it is easier, sometimes safer, and frequently faster and more complete. Analyzing the current energy condition of existing buildings as well as unbuilt sites is done this way.

To conclude, I would like to share our design objective. People often ask, "What can I do? What can one person do?" Starting with a positive, beneficial Intent is the basis for each project. This stays foremost through every step of the process. In this way, a small bit of peace is instilled into the project, into a small corner of the universe, whatever the size and type of project. Yes, as one person, you or I *can* do something.

IV

Modern Science and Ancient Wisdom

Science came to the forefront of human thinking when the claims of many early mystics were found to be invalid. Casting out theories like the flat earth and the sun revolving around the earth, the application of the scientific method to meeting human needs has resulted in many of the wonders around us today, as well as most of our environmental problems. Science has a Dr. Jekyll and Mr. Hyde identity because of its insistence on trying to explain everything according to known laws of chemistry and physics, which arise from a mechanical model of reality.

Today it seems more and more evident that promoting a closed mind may be the biggest danger of science. A reconsideration of ancient wisdom shows that in many cases we may have thrown away too much just because our theories could not explain certain phenomena. Acupuncture is a good example. Officially for many years it was considered a foolish superstitious practice. Today we have licensed acupuncturists and ample evidence that it does work for many uses, even though modern science still cannot accept that acupuncture works by manipulating a subtle life force energy called chi. *Geomancers insist that their practice, too, works by manipulation of this life force energy. Will science seek to block geomancy from being popularly used, or have we learned our lesson from the success of acupuncture?*

In this section we explore the work of several scientists who are bold enough to ask if geomancy can have any scientifically supportable aspects. It is now known that everything gives off certain types of energies, and that the entire earth has an electromagnetic field with variations from place to place which are significant enough to influence the health and behavior of living things. These conditions have existed for as long as life has existed. They undoubtedly have been sensed and recognized by sensitive people as well. The breakthrough today is that we now have instruments which can begin to measure subtle fields, giving us an objective check on the claims of sensitives about the specialness of places.

What we create is a reflection of who we are. In human growth, we now know that the key to successful development is increased awareness. In a similar fashion, the key to the future success of science and technology to serve humankind and not kill us off may be in the area of inventing and using a technology of ever-increasing awareness.

17

The Ley Hunters

RICHARD LEVITON

Since June 20, 1921, when the mysterious and controversial earth energy lines known as ley lines were rediscovered for our epoch by the British photographer Alfred Watkins, speculation hasn't ceased as to their origin, purpose, and significance. With Watkins's twentieth-century revelation came the implicit consideration that the earth holds far more secrets than we have suspected, that it is a more subtle, intricately complex, and living organism than our technologized culture presently appreciates.

Official academic opposition to ley lines has been formidable, too. The archeological establishment, when not maintaining a stony silence, puts forth sarcastic, dismissive comments, but this is understandable. The implication of ley lines is staggering and calls for a complete reassessment of the foundations of archeological interpretation and all its tidy schema. But even with the force of scholarly officialdom and its war of silence against them, Earth Mysteries (the whole field of study that includes ley lines, stone circles, and megaliths) advocates have persevered, if in small disputatious cadres, and today, at least in England, a large body of published thought has emerged about ley lines (something like twenty books and a half-dozen tiny magazines) such that if ley lines are not well understood, the term itself certainly teeters on household-word status.

Contemporary writers like Doris Lessing in *Shikasta* and Carlos Castaneda in *The Eagle's Gift* speak in fictional or

---

Reprinted with permission from *East West: The Journal of Natural Health and Living*, P. O. Box 1200, 17 Station St., Brookline, MA 02147, subscription $24/yr.

philosophical terms of ley line phenomena, while well-
known spiritual figures like Peter Caddy, founder of the
Findhorn community in Scotland, speak of "centers of light"
occupied by deliberate human communities linked together
with other light centers, by telepathic and oral means, or
"lines of light." Ley lines as a concept, then, has already
entered our written culture, yet the reality of the phenomena
is still obscure.

The primary difficulty in understanding, verifying,
and accepting ley lines is simple. They are not physical
but subtle. They are less quantifiable than experiential.
Their perception requires some measure of heightened
sensitivity, through dowsing or clairvoyant means. Their
existence challenges many of our cherished views of material
reality, cause-and-effect, and the nature of the earth. Yet
the same could be said, if one were a conventional Western
physician, of the fourteen subtle energy meridians of the
human body described in the classical Chinese medicine of
acupuncture. These subtle meridians have had an effect on
the body and human consciousness, and their energy
flows of chi are mapped, understood, and can be manipulated. This biological, anthropomorphic model has great
relevance in appreciating the similar organization of the
earth's energy fields typified by the phenomenon called
ley lines.

On that solstitial day in 1921, Alfred Watkins stood
on a hilltop in Herefordshire and suddenly perceived
the beautiful English landscape before him as newly laid
out in a web of lines linking together all the holy sites of
antiquity. Watkins called these invisible straight lines
"the Old Straight Track," which he likened to "a fairy
chain stretched from mountain peak to mountain peak."
Sited at intervals along these delicate, intangible connecting
tracklines were numerous "markpoints": stone circles,
single stones, wells, old churches, castles, beacons, notches,
track junctions, camps, crosses, old crossroads, ditches,
moats, even legendary trees. These were the telltale markers
placed in the pathway of the old straight tracks almost as
guideposts, Watkins believed, for the pre-Roman traders
moving across the difficult terrain. Watkins published his
vision, expanded and extrapolated, though conservatively,
in various books (*The Old Straight Track; Archaic Trackways
Around Cambridge; British Trackways*) and founded The

Old Straight Track Club which flourished between 1926 and 1935, visiting sites, hunting leys, and having lovely outings in the ley-rich countryside.

To Watkins old straight tracks remained simply that— convenient transport routes marked in straight lines over the terrain. He managed to overlook the problem that often the lines followed entirely inconvenient routes, straight over difficult mountains or through bogs, routes certainly not practical for traders.

After Watkins it was the Germans, curiously, in between the two wars, who advanced ley line theorizing. They focused on site alignment patterns formed by the ley lines. In 1939 Josef Heinsch reported on the geometrical arrangement of ancient sites in Germany, disclosing unsuspected metrological laws which he claimed had been once used to measure and divide large land tracts, grouping them into harmonious geometrical patterns. Heinsch had stumbled upon another ancient science, once widespread in preChristian Britain and Western Europe: *geomancy*, which means "the sacred layout of the landscape" or "the divination of the Earth" (from its Greek roots *Ge* for Gaia, or earth, and *mantos*, for divination).

This kind of large-scale, landscape-systems approach continues into our own time with the work of Cambridge, England, mathematician Michael Behrend, who in the 1970s began detecting vast networks of alignments across southern Britain. He plotted the topographical location of churches and megalithic sites and found they were disposed according to multiples of fixed distances, forming geometrical figures like the heptagon overlapped by a decagon. Yet another, and more radical, extrapolation of the concept of regular geometric alignment of landscape features is what is called by some researchers the planetary grid system. This involves a planetary mapping system, based on mathematics, Platonic solids, and Pythagorean geometry, and is being promoted by William Becker and Bethe Hagens, of Governor's State University in Illinois, and others.*

Geomancy, landscape geometry, and planetary grids are all part of the ley line interpretive model that sees them as straight alignments of ancient sites in the physical

---

*See Becker and Hagen's "The Rings of Gaia" p. 257

landscape. Even today, as in Watkins's day, mainline ley hunters maintain Watkins's original topology for ley lines, namely, that they consist of five aligned sites in a ten-mile stretch. Ley hunting with close-detail Ordnance Survey maps is practiced studiously by ley afficionados who continually discover new ley lines on their maps. The ease of such ley line discovery, of course, only adds fuel to the critical fires of the archeological denigrators of the whole proposition.

Paul Devereux and Ian Thomson demonstrate the technique of ley hunting and summarize the most widely acknowledged ley alignments in Britain in their useful *The Ley Hunter's Companion* (Thames and Hudson, 1979). They rank numerous markpoints for importance in determining map-leys, while documenting forty ley lines in Britain, covering 411 miles, with a range of two to twenty-two miles. One of the more famous ley lines is the St. Michael Ley, which runs for hundreds of miles across the southern chin of Britain. A key premise in the standard ley hunters' approach is site continuity, or the evolution of a site whereby, over the millennia, different cultural groups have recognized the sanctity of a place and erected in commemoration or for geometric/templic uses, various structures, first the stone circle or tumulus, later the imposing Christian church. The typical pattern is for a church to succeed a megalithic structure, maintaining in its central axis the original alignment.

The popular interest in ley-hunting waned after Watkins's death in 1935 until the mid-1960s when it sprang into life again, also in Britain. One of the prime impetuses was the linking of purported UFO sightings with ley lines, thus introducing the next key ley hunting concept that regards ley lines as energy pathways between holy sites. It was an American named Tony Webb who proposed the theory whereby the frequency of UFO sightings was linked with landscape ley pathways which might have served as navigation routes for low-flying spaceships. This approach, whether it is ultimately shown to be bogus or valid, was immediately fruitful, for it inspired the two principal works of the doyen of Earth Mysteries, John Michell, who summarized and greatly expanded current ley line thinking in his *The View Over Atlantis* (1969) and the role of leys and geomancy in *City of Revelation* (1973).

Michell, following in the footsteps of other sympathetic researchers like Guy Underwood and T. C. Lethbridge, introduced the energetic concept of leys, seeing them as pathways carrying an etheric but detectable current of unusual, subtle energy, "a mysterious stream of terrestrial magnetism." He stressed that these energy lines had been recognized and utilized by ancient humans for positive uses in their landscape temples, themselves situated strategically at points along the ley pathways.

The reaction to Michell's more subtle rendering of ley lines and Earth Mysteries was inevitable: raves from the ley hunters, and rotten tomatoes from the academics. The critics, raised and nurtured in a materialist culture, were unable to see or feel these energies, nor could scientific instrumentation at the time measure them. Therefore, such leys as Michell envisioned did not exist—and shouldn't— and such daft ley hunters who believed in leys were promptly relegated by the establishment to the familiar "lunatic fringe."

Another subtle explanation was elaborated by William Bloom and Marko Pogacnik recently in their booklet, *Ley-lines and Ecology* (Gothic Images Books, 1985). "Ley lines are the essential structure of the etheric body of the Earth Spirit," they write evocatively. They propose that we imagine the Earth "as having no dense physical existence, but being a globe of interconnected lines of electric energy, a sphere made up of webs of energy." The "life-enhancing radiation" of ley lines is best understood by experiencing them, they stress, by feeling them as energy fields that affect "the whole electric human being." Such human expressions of consciousness as meditation, contemplation, prayer, worship, ritual, ceremony, and folk dance are recommended for ley line centers. "Each of these methods involves raising and peaking human awareness so as to reach and draw in new energy fields," they say. Powerful ley centers can enhance human consciousness by revelation; because at such places, both dense and etheric matter vibrate at higher, therefore more conscious, frequencies, contend Bloom and Pogacnik. For people who visit such ley centers with calm, open minds, the effects on consciousness can be powerful, positive, and transformative.

In recent years a discipline existing on the fringe of the magical/materialist cultures has been successfully employed to measure and substantiate leys. This is dowsing,

and experts in this field often speak of "dowsing leys."
Tom Graves, a well-known British exponent of ley dowsing,
in his *Needles of Stone* (Turnstone Books, 1978) presented
evidence highly supportive of these nebulous energy flows.
He called them "overgrounds" and dowsed their effects
on standing stones and stone circles in England. Graves
experienced these overgrounds as energy pathways "living,
breathing, pulsing," and circulating through ancient stone
sites. He developed a conceptual model whereby such
megalithic sites acted as "telephone exchanges" that moved
along energy messages through the overgrounds linking
the sites. The large stones, inserted into the earth's skin,
were seen as earth acupuncture needles, knowingly placed
at key landscape nodes (variously called sluice gates, valves,
or ley centers). Such stone needles could change, redirect,
or even purify the energy flow and have marked effects
on the landscape and meteorological environment.

Graves followed both Michell's concepts and the ancient
Chinese classifications of human energy, and talked of leys
in terms of the "two breaths of chi." The Chinese called
their ley lines *lung mei*, the paths of the dragon current,
which flowed as a white yang tiger in the high mountains
and as a yin blue dragon in the low hills and valleys. Where
the two *lung mei* met, where the two breaths became one,
was a node or power point, full of chi. British geomancy,
says Graves, was once a complex system of earth acupuncture
whereby the earth was regarded as homologous to the
human body. Ley lines formed "the focal points in a vast
multilayered cobweb . . . somewhat reminiscent of a micro-
graph of nerve cells and their ganglia . . . the circulation
and nervous system of the body of earth." In Graves's view,
then, ley lines were alive, interactive, capable of transformation and pollution, and were properly dealt with only by
trained geomancers.

Dowsing for leys in Britain has gained some measure
of acceptability, in part due to the efforts of J. Havelock
Fidler (author of *Ley Lines: Their Nature and Properties*,
Turnstone Books, 1983) to substantiate leys with precisely
reported dowsing. Fidler went to great lengths to develop
a scientific, even mathematical, technique (using a hand-
held pendulum, and having its own energy vocabulary)
for dowsing energy charges at stones, in churches, and at
other landscape nodes. "Using statistical techniques of

this type," Fidler comments, "I found it was quite possible to use the 'unreliable' art of dowsing to make repeatable measurements to a degree of probability that would have been quite acceptable to an agricultural scientist." Fidler observed that humans could impart an energy charge to stones and that, over time, the stone could retain this charge. His subsequent speculation was that "Megalithic man could have set up his grid of ley lines simply by charging stones . . . and placing them in straight lines or circles."

Fidler's notion of energy originating by acts of human consciousness imparted to resonating stones, which then established a linking current among similarly charged and strategically placed stones, is intriguing. Michell had been moving somewhat in this same direction when he noted the anomaly that ley lines, as experienced in China, for example, were not naturally straight, but "spiral and undulate like surface rivers or currents of air." Therefore the existence of very straight landscape ley lines must indicate that the lines were "of human construction rather than the work of nature" and that "the present pattern of the earth currents in Britain must be of artificial origin."

One of the brightest and most sensible Earth Mysteries advocates today is a Vermont native, now living in Glastonbury, England, named Sig Lonegren. Lonegren has been writing informative articles for the *New England Antiquities Research Journal* and leading tours in America and Britain for several years. He's gathered his thoughts on ley hunting together in a most useful booklet called "Earth Mysteries Handbook: Wholistic, Non-Intrusive Data Gathering Techniques" (1985), which unifies the differing descriptions of leys as aligned sites and leys as energy pathways.

Lonegren speaks of the "energy ley" which, he says, is "usually a six-to-eight-foot-wide beam of yang energy," whose width varies with time of day, year, and lunar phase, but whose length is always straight. Wherever energy leys begin, cross each other, or terminate, there is a body of "primary water" underneath. Energy leys have a direction of flow which usually moves right through the central axis of megalithic and Christian sites. They have a beginning and end, coming in vertically to the earth's surface at places called "downshoots." "Turning ninety degrees, they then travel across the surface of the earth as an energy ley crossing other energy leys as they go. Finally they once again turn ninety degrees and go to earth at what is called an earthing point," he says. Now ley lines, in the classical Watkinsian sense of five aligned sites in ten miles, don't always carry a dowsable energy charge, and some may in fact be randomly generated map-leys, pieces of real energetic leys heading in different directions.

Other ley line writers have written about the role of water in ley systems, calling their patterns variously aquastats, water tracks, and blind springs. For Lonegren, it is primary water, the yin underground element balancing off the yang overground energy beams. Under great internal pressure in the earth, water at faults was originally forced upwards, condensing into fractures as it neared the surface and forming water domes with numerous exiting veins. A water dome is like "a vertical chimney of water," says Lonegren, which ascends towards the earth's surface "until it is stopped by an impermeable layer like clay, then moving out laterally through the veins or fractures." A power center or holy site is found "at any point on the earth's surface where one or more energy leys and primary water converge." Hence we have energy flowing over the ground, water undulating underneath, meeting with great chi at the power centers.

While some ley theorists are coming up with innovative, often hard-to-document ideas, other ley hunters like Paul Devereux of Wales are busy conducting scientific experiments to measure and analyze these subtle energy leys. Devereux in 1977 launched the Dragon Project as an attempt to document, using scientifically accredited instrumentation and methodology, energy or radiation anomalies at a single potent stone circle, the Rollright Stones in Oxfordshire. Devereux was already busy with his *The Ley Hunter* journal, the leading Earth Mysteries publication in Britain, when he undertook the Dragon project, but the results (and publicity) have been impressive.

The Dragon Project assembled the various skills of dowsers, psychics, electronics engineers, a chemist, even a daring archeologist, for a strong cross-disciplinary team. Since 1977 Devereux and team have visited various stone circles and noted astronomical, astrological, and meteorological factors. Their instrumentation was formidable. They have used a "wide-band ultrasonic detector" (dog-whistle frequency), employed at dawn. They noted cyclical patterns of "anomalous radio emissions," strongest at the equinoxes, at twenty-five minutes before dawn during the new moon, and eight minutes before dawn during the full moon. Geiger counter readings were made using a "robust portable rate-meter in a round-the-clock, month-long monitoring effort." Geiger flares were observed, which were unusually high in periods of two to three minutes. The use of a sensitive Scintillometer indicated that high spots among the Rollright stones "gave a strong emission of beta-radiation over and above the background radiation," while readings seemed higher inside the circle than out. The Dragon Project recorded several thousands of averaged radiation readings, all of which indicated definite energy circuits within and around the stones, much more pronounced than the "background" energy fields. These higher energy anomalies varied with circadian, lunar, and season progressions.

Despite the admirable attempts by field researchers like Devereux and his fellow Dragons, the archeologists refuse to come to the discussion table. The recent *Ley Lines in Question* (Tom Williamson, Liz Bellamy, Worlds Work, 1983) is the first book to appear from within the archeological aegis that discusses the claims of ley hunters with more than a pithy dismissive barb. Even so, Williamson and Bellamy do dismiss leys.

The focus of *Ley Lines in Question* is conservative, limited to only the classical ley line formulations of Watkins, namely, of intentionally aligned sites in straight lines over the countryside. "It therefore seems fairly unlikely that the lines drawn by ley hunters represent intentional prehistoric alignments. . . . The case for ley lines appears to be hopeless, for there does not seem to be any evidence for their existence." The authors disparage what they brand "ley eclecticism" and its uncouth, nonacademic methodologies. They reject as evidence the concept of site continuity and site evolution, stating instead that most of the sites chosen as corroborative material by ley hunters aren't ancient at all, but medieval, even modern in terms of their structure and habitation. Truly straight lines dotted with deliberate alignments do not exist in Britain, stress Williamson and Bellamy, and statistical computerized analyses indicate that many of the proposed topographical leys are randomly generated and not true purposeful alignments. We have instead a pattern of "coincidental alignments of otherwise unrelated features." Ley hunters, in stressing a gloriously sophisticated ancient past when the ley network was engineered, are only propagating a false Golden Age which never happened, "a vision of the past that's nothing but a false dream. . . . Ley-hunting is an ideological non-starter." Of the more bold speculations of Graves, Michell, Bloom and Pogacnik, and others about the subtle energy components of ley lines, the authors are silent, other than to say these approaches belong to "the lunatic fringe of the lunatic fringe."

The ley hunting cadre, not surprisingly, comes across in its publications as beleaguered and belligerent, like a gang of tough street kids battling the wealthy, well-groomed older boys from the suburbs. The pages of *The Ley Hunter* are hoarse with challenges, threats, and name-calling. The academics remain smug and unassailed in their safe ivory towers, yet many critics believe the archeologists are by their provincialism committing the ultimate apostasy to their own scientific credos. Little money is generated for genuine ley research.

However, many ley enthusiasts believe that the debate is the preliminary confused reaction to a gradually emerging new view of the earth and human consciousness that is radically different from anything our materialist society has prepared us for. Yet it is also an understanding that resonates deeply because we once knew and worked with the subtle earth energies. The emergence of the perception of ley lines as light or energy pathways arranged in a purposeful, geometrical order over the surface of the planet is part of a larger perception of the earth herself as a living, evolving, conscious, and sacred being—Gaia. Thus, geomancy, when comprehended and practiced correctly, becomes *the divinization of earth*. The debate over ley lines, as alignments or energy meridians, is only a portion of a larger conflict currently working through the Western psyche.

From my own research in geomantically charged Somerset, from numerous conversations with dowsers, ley hunters, and clairvoyants, I think that the truth of ley lines will not be decreed by the smug archeological establishment, nor by the bombastic Earth Mysteries street gangs, but quietly, by independent, detached, observant visionaries like Alfred Watkins. The theory which appeals to me now, as it is being developed by a number of people, is in the non-materialist tradition. This theory brings together nearly all the scattered threads of ley hunting activity by supposing a planetary system of dome centers, consisting of etheric canopies or domes occupying the space over sacred enclosures (creating them in fact), from which numerous short-distance straight-running and spiralling dome lines of light radiate outwards over the land. The dome lines link dome centers with each other, in a kind of subtle communications grid.

The number of domes on the planet is a fixed and symbolic one, but each one is thought to be capable of sending out up to forty-eight curving lines of light terminating in what can be called dome caps. The picture that emerges from this new theory is one that reconciles the Chinese *lung ta*, or curving ley lines (for these are the dome cap lines), and the British straight ley lines (for these connect the primary domes). Another theory states that there are a number of planetary ley lines which are like broad avenues encircling the globe, of which the St. Michael ley is one.

The subtle landscape is thus characterized as an intricate pattern of spirals, straight lines, and pulsing circles of light, sequentially marked first by stone circles and tumuli, then second by churches. The straight dome lines came first, laid out over the subtle landscape in a regular geometric, purposeful pattern. Later religious structures (tumuli, stone circles, churches) were sited at the various dome centers along the lines and at their beginnings and ends. What map-ley hunters often find as long-running leys, alignments linking eight to twelve sites, may in fact be technically several independent dome lines involving several dome centers—but this descriptive difference, though real, is not of any functional importance. The important point is that certain dome centers have a pronounced and positive (even transformative) effect on human consciousness, a quality much appreciated in earlier days. And these outdoor meditation halls can even today be used again for those who want to "tune into" them. Remembered vaguely in myth, folklore, and local custom, these landscape temples, animated by dome lines, may be forgotten, but they haven't been closed down.

The rediscovery of ley lines is only a fragment of the eventual unveiling of the secrets of nature. Ley lines are the luminous strands that many are pulling at today, hardly suspecting what riches lie at the end of these subtle light lines. When dome lines and dome centers are perceived as sensitive energy/consciousness points on the earth's living body, when Gaia is appreciated as a sentient, coherent being, when we have attained awareness of what Teilhard de Chardin calls the "noosphere" and "planetary Omega point," or what José Arguelles terms "the planetization of consciousness," then we will awake in horror at the scope of the injuries we have inflicted upon Gaia.

18
The Rings of Gaia

WILLIAM S. BECKER
BETHE HAGENS

Since 1983, and the beginning of our research on the planetary grid, we have encountered an ever-widening circle of colleagues and co-researchers whom we identify as "new" or "holistic" scientists. Beyond their usual commitment to scientific Truth, this growing worldwide network of theoretical and empirical researchers supports as a common goal the sustaining of all life (in both the individual and planetary sense). What distinguishes this group of "scientists" from those in the conventional orthodoxy is their shared belief that only through the development of a truly comprehensive scientific tradition, one that unites transphysical knowledge with current mechanical and solely materialistic laws, can humanity evolve to its next stage. Now globally based (and gaining experience in both eco-politics and expanding political/economic debates with an increasingly defensive techno-science orthodoxy) this new culture of researchers and seekers is becoming more and more aware of the dawning of a new multicultural, multidisciplined, pluralistic, scientific paradigm. This worldview increasingly draws on discoveries in archeology, biophysics, and the revolutionary psychology of consciousness which no longer can exclude any category of knowledge (i.e., the paranormal, anomalous phenomena, or the occult) from the now global libraries of science.

Within the hardening orthodoxy of modern science, words like "intuitive," "serendipitous," and "visionary" have almost lapsed into adjectives of derision when linked to the work of contemporary researchers. This, ironically and even predictably, comes at a time when fundamental and revolutionary discoveries are being made in mathematics (chaos and string theory), quantum physics (unified field theory), biophysics (self-organizing systems), and astronomy (black holes and galactic bubbles). Orthodox scientists often forget that 16th century pioneers like Sir Francis Bacon and René Descartes based their faith in science on their visions. Bacon had "seen" a future utopia supported by mechanized vehicles. Descartes had been visited by an "angel" who had revealed to him his revolutionary mathematics. Sadly, neither of them could qualify today for publication in a modern journal of orthodox science.

Consciously or unconsciously, these two great philosophers were perhaps equally inspired by the visions of artists of the 15th century Renaissance. Artist/alchemists like Leonardo da Vinci and Albrecht Durer had seized upon the legacy of the East—the lost knowledge from the Alexandrian Library that had slowly been reintroduced to the West as centuries passed. They had translated that hoary information into a new world view. This radically new world view rested directly upon the invention of linear perspective which for the first time (since the Alexandrian Library) placed the human individual at the center of the cosmos. Without this artistic paradigm shift which brought new importance to the individual's viewpoint, perspective, and personal point of view, René Descartes might never have dared defy traditional Christendom by asserting, "I think, therefore I am!"

Only 500 years have elapsed since linear perspective first truly elevated the individual consciousness above that of tribal tradition. Already we may have become too individualized in the cultures of the West. Other cultural traditions from around the world have begun to reveal to us our implicit alienation and over-detachment from nature, our habituation to a view that equates technical progress with spiritual evolution, and our deep cultural fear of death. The vast majority of informed planetary citizens know we must change but are unsure of the real options we have to consider.

Just as the perspective pictorial systems of the Renaissance first established, and then brought into focus, a new individualistic mythos—we feel that the current network of "Gaian" planetary ecologists (of which we are a part) may be on a similar path toward developing the next unifying symbol of a new cosmos and a new earth. What makes this proposition fascinating is a parallel analogy: just as the rediscovery of ancient knowledge from the Alexandrian Library opened the creative enterprise of the

Renaissance, so now the re-evaluation of that same knowledge is setting the stage for an unprecedented shift in global scientific consciousness. Basic to this shift is the rediscovery of the language and deep syntactical structure of what we now call geometry. Its power is most concisely and eloquently summarized in a statement attributed to the great shaman-geometer Pythagoras:

> The experience of life in a finite, limited body is specifically for the purpose of discovering and manifesting supernatural existence within the finite!

The bold intuitive quantum theories from computer-assisted researchers in the areas of physics, math, biology, and astronomy are a part of this rediscovery—which is nothing less than a totally new approach to the way we relate to planet Earth.

We believe that the planetary grid[1] is a new model for Gaia. It reveals not only an ancient global mapping system but a universal energy code that will help transform our culture's vision of a dying, entropic, material, mostly empty cosmos into one bursting with an unending froth of full bubbles of living energy. Because this grid is comprised entirely of great circles on the sphere of earth, we have come to think of it as the Rings of Gaia. This holistic global model may be part of a vital informational bridge needed to link Renaissance individualism to a vision of community that is at least planetary in scope—and soon to be interplanetary with the additions of the moon and Mars in the early 21st century.

"Rings of Gaia" Researchers— Ice Age to the Present

The oldest evidence of an ancient "geometric worldview" rests in the Ashmolean Museum of Oxford, England, and in archeological collections held privately and publicly in Great Britain and Italy. On exhibit at the Ashmolean are several hand-sized stones of such true geometric proportion and precise carving that they startle the casual viewer (Illustration 1). It is equally startling to hear them conventionally explained away as hunting bolas.

In his book *Time Stands Still: New Light on Megalithic Science*, Keith Critchlow convincingly links these leather-thong-wrapped stone models (and thousands of very similar

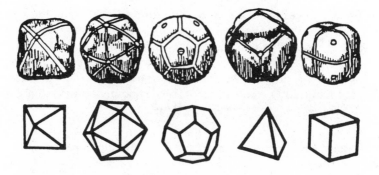

Illustration 1. These 3500-year-old carved stones are each about 2½ inches in diameter. Thousands have been found through Britain— some carved, others apparently modeled in clay and then fired. Because they have been found near stone circles, it has been argued that the stones are simple (yet extremely accurate) astrolabe-compasses used by megalithic builders. In fact, the geometries represented in the stones are not only precise, but were known by the Greeks and the Egyptians to have been suitable for astronomical observation.

others found all over northern Scotland) to the Neolithic peoples who were living in Britain approximately 3500 years ago. The painstaking attention to symmetry and detail immediately evident in these carved stones indicates the presence of a culture intent upon the refinement of a very sophisticated spherical geometry. Critchlow believes the stones were specifically employed in the design of "astronomical" stone circles such as Maes Howe, Stonehenge, and others throughout Great Britain.[2] A. M. Davie, a Scottish historian and archeological researcher, dates similar stone polyhedra even earlier, to approximately 12,000 years B.C.—and relates their origin to the ancient craft of "finishing the form" of crystalline volcanic rocks which exhibit (to a craftsman) an inherent geometric symmetry.

Either date is paradigm-shattering. Among the stones are exact representations of five classic geometric figures, arrayed for comparison and analysis, many still bearing fragments of leather thongs used to mark out various measurements and proportions. These figures, the so-called 5 Platonic solids (the 8-faced octahedron, the 20-faced icosahedron, the 12-faced dodecahedron, the 4-faced tetrahedron, and the 6-faced cube) were not even recognized in the West until Plato's *Timaeus* of the 5th century B.C.![3]

It is exciting to learn that the stones were not unique to Britain, even in antiquity. We recently discovered in the writings of the 19th century German geometer/mathematician F. Lindemann an account of his decade-long search throughout Europe and the Middle East for ancient examples of these classic polyhedra. So prodigious were his discoveries, numbering in the hundreds, that he became convinced that the "ancient" mind was truly that of a master mathematician.[4]

Of particular importance is his discovery of a Neolithic (possibly Etruscan) dodecahedron unearthed by Italian archaeologists at Mt. Loffa near Padua. A numbering system of "conic" dots and linear grooves seems to have been etched into the 12 pentagonal faces of its ceramic body—before it was fired to well over 2000 degrees Fahrenheit!

To Plato, and all who preceded him, the 5 (and *only* 5) equal-sided, equal-angled polyhedral (many-sided) volumes were sacred "libraries." In the hands of those who had been orally instructed in the secret sciences of antiquity, they could reveal all truths regarding humanity, the Earth, and the cosmos. The dodecahedron (middle figure in Illustration 1) was always most important, however, along with its close companion, the sphere. The dodecahedron was so important to Plato that he never described it directly in any of his writings, and mentioned it only cryptically in contexts which, we believe, serve to confirm its power and unique status.

With its 12 pentagonal (5-sided) faces, the dodecahedron stands in fairly clear symbolic relation to the 12 zodiacal signs. But what if what we now call the zodiac was originally derived from the dodecahedron? What if the special distinction the Greeks granted to the dodecahedron was based not only on its being the largest among "The Five" (given a standard edge length), but also on its close and clear resemblance to that most important of all shapes, the sphere?

The Greeks themselves knew they did not have the answers and appear to have craved the "wisdom of the ancients" that might be gleaned from their kin, the Egyptians.[5] Both cultures used the sphere ubiquitously in their cosmogony. Among the Greeks, it organized physical atoms, bubbles, planets, and stars, and was central to their religion which involved geometry. It defined the metaphysical structure of the cosmos and housed what Plato and others called "ideas," upon which all realities were based.

Orthodox historians, of course, reject most of the above, attributing solely to Plato and other Caucasian Greeks the discovery of these invaluable spatial tool/concepts. However, one modern Danish scholar, Tons Brunes, disagrees persuasively with this orthodoxy after nearly 20 years of exhaustive study in which he collected and analyzed not only conventional historic records, but also source material from the archives of the Freemasons. His 600-page 2-volume work, *The Secrets of Ancient Geometry*, traces the lineage of the so-called Platonic solids first to Pythagoras (with Plato writing as a Pythagorian initiate), and then to the Egyptian priests who for 22 years taught Pythagoras their secrets in the temples at Memphis and Thebes.[6]

In addition, Brunes makes the case that Moses and his Egyptian teachers did not arbitrarily designate the sphere as the sacred form of the cosmos, but rather had grasped the profound importance of the fact that "The Five" polyhedra are "perfectly inscribable" in a sphere. (That is, if a sphere were made to contain tightly any one of the five figures, *all* of that figure's corners would precisely touch the sphere's surface.) This powerful cosmology sidestepped the hard science *or* mythology dichotomy which entraps much contemporary Western thought. It combined a satisfying spiritual imagery with sophisticated principles of geodesic architecture only recently rediscovered by R. Buckminster Fuller.

It is through the ancient sacred form of the cosmos, the sphere, that Gaia, the beautiful mythos of a living Earth, connects with the biophysical structure of geometry. Surprisingly, the relation between the two is quickly revealed in their common word histories. "Geometry" is easily separable into its classic Greek roots: *Geo* is "earth," and *metry* is "measure." Earth measuring. Both *ge* and *gaia* mean "Earth."

All along in this research, we have been greatly inspired by the ancient linguistic connections that bind the *ge* in geometry, geology, generate, gene, Genesis, to Gaia, the Greek goddess of Earth and mother/consort of Uranus. As with the origin of the Ashmolean polyhedra, most orthodox linguists believe that the root word *ge* (*gaia*) is solely of Greek origin with no known antecedents. In fact, connections abound. As far away as the isolated interior mountain wall of New Guinea is a creator named Geb. In ancient Egypt, Geb is god of flora, fauna, and the underworld (possibly meaning *this* world). In early Scotch-Irish Gaelic, *Gael* is "love."

In the Gaelic, we also find *guaigean*, "a thick, little, and round object." Is this the indigenous name for the stone polyhedra of Britain? Further etymological analysis makes this a strong possibility, and even hints at ancient usage of the guaigean as a hand-held map of the cosmos.

The paths by which words and meanings twist from one language to another are by no means agreed upon, guaigean being a clear case in point. Linguists have tended to agree that thousands of years ago a language existed in India and Europe to which most historical languages in these areas can be connected. The word "polyhedron," for example, is Greek and means "many seats." *Hedron* is derived from a proto-Indo-European root *sed*. Many contemporary words that imply sitting down or settling come from *sed*: e.g., sedentary and soot (that which settles). *Sed* also means "to go," however, and words such as "episode" and "exodus" are derived from it. "Cathedral" is derived from *sed* and is, therefore, both a seat (or place) *and* a way or journey. "Polyhedron" can be "many places" and "many ways"!

Guaigean is all the more fascinating in this light. In Gaelic (an Indo-European language) *gu* means "go, to"; *aig* is "egg"; *aigean* is "sea, an abyss"; and *gean* is "keenness, good humor." What ancient journeys "to the sea" were made using the "thick, little, round object" as a guide? Is guaigean the cosmic egg, a reminder of our original descent to Earth? Is the Aegean Sea of ancient mythology a metaphor much diminished in translation? From such tentative beginnings as these, we may be able to establish a new, warmer relation with geometry—not as a cold, inhuman series of abstract proofs, but as a body of ancient symbolic wisdom humans have almost instinctively drawn upon to better know themselves, the planet, and the outlines of our finite yet infinite cosmos.

Imagine, for example, a Neolithic artisan who had decided to create the ultimate guaigean (or polyhedron)—one that would display on the surface of a *single* small sphere the corners and thong-wrappings of *all five* of the figures shown in Illustration 1. This task is easier than might be imagined. It would have been immediately obvious that the 12 icosahedron "corners" would fit precisely into the centers of the 12 faces of the dodecahedron. (Note in Illustration 2 that those center spots are clearly marked.) And of course, the 20 corners of the dodecahedron would fit perfectly into the centers of the 20 faces of the icosahedron. At places where the edges of these two figures cross, and only at these places, corners of the octahedron would fall. Imagine the artisan's delight to discover that, were one corner of either the tetrahedron or the cube placed at a corner of the dodecahedron, every other corner would also fall at another dodecahedron corner. This is the essence of the knowledge Brunes attributes to Moses and the Egyptian priesthood—that the figures are "perfectly in-scribable" on a sphere.

The cumulative result of nestings and wrappings just described is a set of fifteen rings symmetrically circling the sphere, each of which divides it in half (Illustration 2). These are the Rings of Gaia which create the 62 inter-sections and 120 identical scalene triangles of the planetary grid. Modern mathematicians know this figure well as a kind of Mother Sphere, for all regular polyhedra can be placed within its net of 62 intersections. It is also the prodigious structural framework that underpins the archi-tecture of geodesic domes.

In the *Timaeus*, Plato seems to be describing this same structure in his discourse on the Creator of the Universe:

> For the original of the universe contains in itself all intelligible beings, just as this world comprehends us and all other visible creatures. . . . And he gave to the world the figure which was suitable and also natural. Now to the animal [the living Earth/Gaia?] which was to comprehend all animals, *that figure was suitable which comprehends within itself all other figures* (emphasis ours). Wherefore he made the world in the form of a globe.

We have variously called this figure the Mother Sphere, UVG (United Vector Geometry) 120 Polyhedron, or most recently the Rings of Gaia—depending upon the context in which we were speaking.

The 120 identical scalene right triangles of the Mother Sphere created by the 15 equators or rings are exactly those described by Plato in the latter half of the *Timaeus* as "the triangle upon which all polyhedra are based." We believe

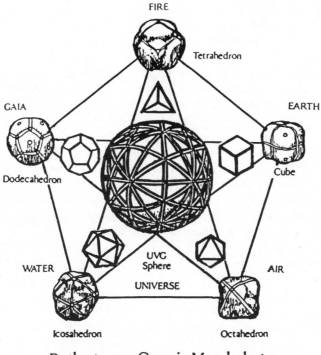

FIRE

Tetrahedron

GAIA

EARTH

Dodecahedron

Cube

UVG
Sphere

UNIVERSE

WATER

AIR

Icosahedron

Octahedron

Pythagorean Cosmic Morphology

Illustration 2. In the "ultimate polyhedron," the five figures are arranged as shown in the order of increasing geometric complexity (from tetrahedron to cube to octahedron to icosahedron to dodecahedron). The meanings roughly chart the progress of planetary development as it is explained today by geologists (barysphere [fire ball] to lithosphere to atmosphere to hydrosphere to biosphere).

this same triangle was described in the ancient cosmologies of Egypt as the MR Triangle, and that it contains not only the advanced knowledge of Thoth (known to the Greeks as Hermes Trismegistus), but also reveals the archetype of the Trinity upon which the mysteries of both Hinduism and Christianity rest (Illustration 3).

The ancient Egyptians referred to their country as the "Land of MR" (in hieroglyphics symbolized by a stylized triangular hoe), with MR meaning cultivate, love, hack up, or Meridian Triangle. The right-angled scalene MR Triangle, with its smallest angle at 36°, is exactly the one most important to Plato. On ancient maps, 4 of these triangles joined together at their right-angled bases defined the boundaries of Imperial Egypt—that land Arab nations still refer to as "the country built according to a geometric plan." Eight of these same triangles, joined structurally at their 36° vertices, create a proportionally exact replica of the Great Pyramid at Giza. Twenty-eight MR triangles cluster to form a squared circle with twelve "corners." The "four corners of the Earth" are represented on ancient maps of the traditional known world of Mediterranean cultures in just this way—with 12 geometrically derived nodes creating a squared circle. And of course, 120 MR Triangles are arranged to match the structure created by the 15 Rings of Gaia, and the base for a global mapping system we believe is well suited to represent our contemporary knowledge of Earth's biosphere (Illustration 3).

Once we accepted the possibility that deeply embedded structures of geometry had shaped both ancient artifacts and philosophies, we made enormous strides with our theory that the Rings of Gaia had been the basis for a comprehensive world mapping system. Plato, for example, could not have been more clear when describing, in *Phaedo*, the organization of Earth as a spherical dodecahedron:

> But if I must tell you a story, Simmias, it is worth hearing what things really are like on the earth under the heavens....

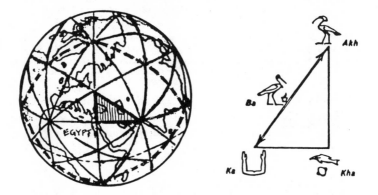

Illustration 3. The 120 identical right triangles formed by the fifteen rings of the planetary grid (one is shown highlighted) were known to the Egyptians and given the name MR. The triangle was used in Egyptian funerary texts to illustrate the relationship of the mortal body (kha) to three more subtle and divine essences—akh, ba, and ka—of which humans are composed.

It is said then, my comrade, that first of all *the Earth itself looks from above, if you could see it, like those "twelve-patch leather balls"* (emphasis ours).[8]

We are far from the only contemporary researchers to have explored the ramifications of this image. In 1866, Leonce Elie de Beaumont, one of the founders of the modern science of geology, published a geological map of France centered on Paris and based on a pentagon format. Predictably, orthodox cartographers today (who are untrained in three-dimensional geometry) dismiss de Beaumont's work as arcane; in fact, his Paris-centered pentagon is exactly 1/12 of Earth's surface—a perfect "patch" of the spherical dodecahedron. In his own time, however, Elie de Beaumont was well on his way to convincing the austere French Academy that the ancient tradition of geometry would ultimately overcome the apparent disorder of geology. Had it not been for his involvement in a scandalous court case in 1867, he almost certainly would have secured Academy endorsement of the spherical dodecahedron (our Mother Sphere) as the preferred mapping format on which to base the science of geology.[9] His dream may yet be realized in the 21st century.

Probably the most important source for arguing not only the existence of ancient maps based on the Mother Sphere, but also for affirming the possibility that these maps originated prior to 3000 B.C., is the revolutionary book by Charles H. Hapgood, *Maps of the Ancient Sea Kings: Evidence of Advanced Civilization in the Ice Age.* Using exhaustive cartographic, geological, archaeological, and ultimately mathematical methodologies, Hapgood (until his death, Professor of History of Science at the Keene State College of the University of New Hampshire) was able to muster overwhelming evidence that ancient cultures possessed a sophisticated global world view technically equivalent to our own.[10]

The maps Hapgood studied were largely sea charts, maps made or copied by sailors whose lives depended upon their accuracy. Since the maps were not produced within the land-bound halls of "the academy," they have commonly been dismissed as items unworthy of serious inquiry. Hapgood was fascinated by the tortuous process of copying by which the maps reached present times at all. Seen in the light of a seafaring as opposed to land-based tradition, they reveal to the modern navigator a well-developed knowledge of spherical coordinates needed to sail (or fly) efficiently around the globe. In turn, an open-minded scholar is hard-put to deny the presence on these charts of detailed information about Earth's geology and history not available to science until the first International Geophysical Year (IGY) in 1958. Despite scholarly protest that these maps are clever fakes, most of the charts Hapgood studied were documented into "official existence" prior to the turn of the century. The latest map he cites was discovered and officially recorded in 1931.

Of all the maps Hapgood reintroduced to the light of day, the most interesting to us is the di Canestris Map of 1335-37, a degenerated (copy of a copy of a copy...) medieval rendering of what must have been a sophisticated chart of the Mediterranean world. It is centered precisely on the Library at Alexandria. This map has not received the kind of attention it should, owing to its "fantasy" aspect: North Africa and Europe are anthropomorphized as a king and queen. Yet the primary lines of the map are oriented to true north/south and east/west, and reveal the pattern of the 4 MR Triangles which defined Imperial Egypt.

Hapgood was able to place this chart within the twelve wind system of map organization, the oldest and most accurate true geometry underlying his most ancient maps. This system establishes what we have previously referred

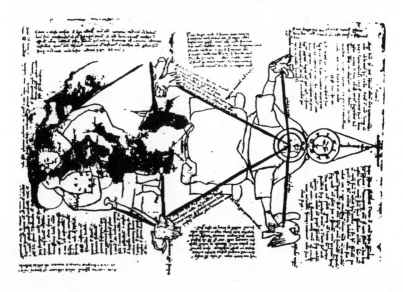

to as a twelve-node-perimeter (the 28-triangle "squared circle"), and thus exactly corresponds to the Rings of Gaia.

Because of its uncanny accuracy, the most controversial of the maps in Hapgood's collection is a chart dated 1513 A.D. and attributed to one Piri Re'is, a known 16th century admiral in the Turkish/Ottoman Navy (Illustration 5). Along with several other charts "copied" from pre-Alexandrian sources and discussed at length in his book, Hapgood's Piri Re'is map reveals clear details of the twelve-node or twelve-wind cartography pattern, which naturally extends from a cluster of 28 scalene MR Triangles. This is the four corners orientation visible in later, considerably less sophisticated Roman sea charts of the Mediterranean world. The Piri Re'is map also reveals sections of the coast of Antarctica and clear renditions of the Atlantic sea bottom, which could only have been visible during the last ice age.

EarthStar

By early 1984, our inventory of evidence supporting the theory that a geodesic model of the Earth had been

Illustration 4. The di Canestris map of 1335-37 (left) reveals the outlines of four MR triangles centered upon the Library of Alexandria. The seated fantasy figure to the east retains vestiges of five-fold symmetry that characterizes this type of intersection on the planetary grid. The map is almost certainly the result of hundreds (if not thousands) of years of copying—with resultant loss of knowledge of the sophisticated context within which the map was originally developed. The figure on the right shows how the map of Europe can be superimposed on the di Canestris map.

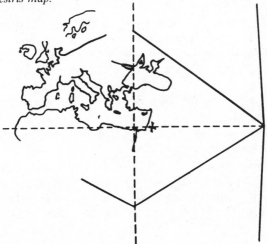

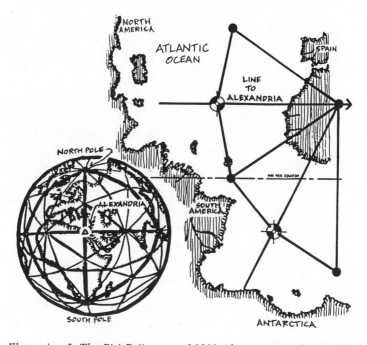

Illustration 5. The Piri Re'is map of 1513 (shown in greatly simplified form) reveals details of the coast of South America and Africa—also of Antarctica—years before this knowledge was theoretically available. This map is believed to have been sourced from charts as old as the last ice age. Because of its astonishing accuracy when projected to planetary scale (left), some have labeled it a hoax. We were intrigued by three factors: first, the map is composed of MR triangles; second, the "turning points" in the Atlantic Ocean correspond with intersections of the 15 planetary grid rings; and third, four MR triangles meet at Alexandria.

available to pre-Egyptian peoples had grown to a point where we (as with those preceding us) desperately needed some method to begin to organize and catalog the mountains of evidence we were finding. Our evidence came from disciplines as diverse as the synergetic geometry of Buckminster Fuller and the anthropology of the world's creation myths. We also came to recognize that neither of us was going to be able to organize all this alone, that it would have to be as.a team or not at all.

The task of analysis at hand seemed to require combined backgrounds (such as ours) in anthropology, geometry, archaeology, history, geography, cartography, linguistics, and even music. We also found that we relied heavily upon written correspondence with other "new science" researchers around the world, and we longed to meet them. We had our first opportunity in 1985 at a conference organized by Jim Swan at the University of Massachusetts entitled "Is the Earth a Living Organism?" Later, in 1987, we received a travel grant to the British Isles from Governors State University to meet firsthand with A. M. Davie, John Michell, Paul Devereux, and James S. Brooks, whom we found to be as deeply enmeshed in related puzzles of the new paradigm as we have been. It was at the Amherst conference, however, that we formally introduced EarthStar, our foldable globe/map that incorporates the insights of Plato with the geometry of Buckminster Fuller and contemporary earth-modeling theories compiled by Christopher Bird.

Christopher Bird, along with Peter Tompkins, has produced and/or disseminated some of the most fertile and controversial research regarding the life of planet Earth that is currently available.[9] His work on how to *cultivate* energies of the soil (MR, it will be remembered, also means "to cultivate") is really an extension of ideas he developed in the early 1970s that describe the planetary grid as "a network, lattice or matrix of cosmic energy the study of which will give us more understanding of [Gaia's] structure than we have heretofore possessed."[10]

We were fascinated by the fact that his matrix was exactly compatible with dome frameworks developed by Buckminster Fuller. We extended Bird's original lattice into the ring structure—and tied it to the planet with latitude and longitude coordinates to see if a pattern of cosmic energy could indeed be mapped.

Because of the historical importance of Alexandria in human history, and the geophysical evidence supporting Cairo/Egypt's established location in the center of the world's continental land masses,[11] we oriented EarthStar's 120-triangled mapping pattern to a meridian of longitude running through the axial North and South poles and through the pyramid complex at Giza, just east of the estimated location of the Library of Alexandria and just west of Cairo. This "Orienting Ring" is crossed by another ring just north of the Nile Delta at a point called Behdet. We designated this as point #1 on EarthStar. The fifteen Rings of Gaia intersect each other 62 times to form the 120

MR triangles of the Mother Sphere. Beginning with #1 at Behdet, we numbered the remaining 61 intersections according to a convention established by Bird in his original article (Illustration 6).

We based EarthStar—our flat projection of the Mother Sphere's round geometry—on a polyhedron known as the rhombic triacontahedron. Each of the triacontahedron's 30 diamond faces is made up of 4 MR Triangles. Each of its edges is the *ba* (the first incarnating principle) edge of the MR Triangle. The figure is closer to the sphere than even the dodecahedron and, unlike other geodesic maps, it is easy to read and equator-based when displayed flat.

We were truly surprised to discover a mathematical oddity of EarthStar's 120 MR Triangles when we had charted them out on a world globe: the ratio of each triangle's side lengths was virtually 7:11:13. We assigned mile distances of 1400 miles, 2200 miles, and 2600 miles to the sides of the MR Triangles, and found that one Ring of Gaia (the Earth's circumference) would measure 24,800 miles. This accords well with the standard geophysical calculation of 24,885 miles.[12]

The significance of EarthStar's planetary grid intersections and triangles is both scientific and mythological,

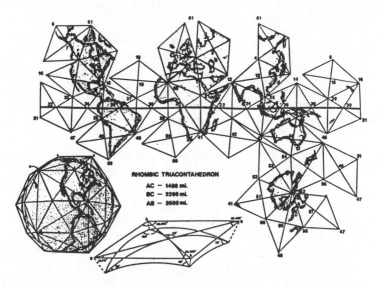

Illustration 6. EarthStar is our foldable planetary grid globe/map. An advantage of this mapping system is the ease with which distances can be calculated.

intriguing and elusive. It is an inescapable conclusion that any satisfying description of what it is will be not only multidisciplinary, but multicultural. It will echo the timeless wisdom "as above, so below." Clues are everywhere. At the microscale, scientists now know the 30-sided rhombic triacontahedron to be the structure of the living virus. In the Hebrew *Kaballah, lamed* (the 30th letter, which is also the number 30) symbolizes the metabolism and manifestations of Gaia at the planetary scale. Echoing ancient theories of the music of the spheres, harmonic proportions between tones of the classic scale are mirrored in proportional distances between intersections of the Rings of Gaia. In a Brule Sioux creation story, the Sun empowers the Earth by calling the orbits, planets and stars to "come to the sixteen hoops!" While there are 15 theoretical Rings of Gaia, once the planet is set in place in the solar system, it acquires a 16th—the Equator.

We have included, as an appendix, a very condensed summary of our map of cosmic energies as we can currently describe them. (Illustration 5 provides a visual guide to our numbering system.) If, as the MR Triangle suggests, the Earth's body is analogous to a human body, the intersections of the planetary grid rings may mark planetary chakras. Perhaps the general health of the Earth's body is reflected and magnified at these locations. By our very long-standing and ancient attention to the *map* of the Rings of Gaia, we may have actually imprinted it upon our collective species memory—and thus created enduring geographical patterns of human energy and emotion. Because of its resonance with the molecular carbon and cellular structures that compose our physical bodies, it is completely predictable that the mnemonic of the Rings of Gaia should be powerful within us. We may simply *see* this way.

We continue to think of the Rings of Gaia as a web of life, especially when the full array of rings shines forth from the planet in a pattern that Buckminster Fuller predicted (Illustration 7). Bringing the web into creation is Spider Woman:[13]

> When she [Spider Woman] awoke to life and received her name, she asked, "Why am I here?"
> "Look about you," answered Sotuknang, "Here is the earth we have created. It has shape and substance, direction and time, a beginning and an end. But there is no life upon it.

What is life without sound and movement? So you have
been given the power to help us create this life. You have
been given the knowledge, wisdom, and love to bless all
the beings you create. That is why you are here."

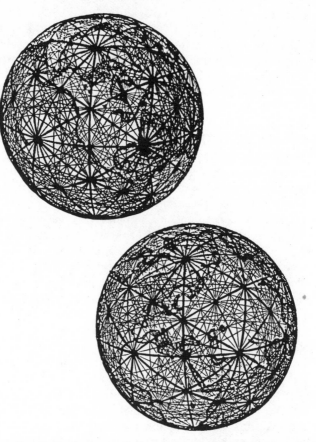

*Illustration 7. Buckminster Fuller spent his life exploring spherical
geometry. In one experiment, he used microphotographic techniques
to chart energetic stresses and reactions on the surface of a round
balloon. The result turned out to be an elaborated form of the Rings
of Gaia. In our research, we have discovered startling coincidences
between this more complex ring structure and the patterns of ley lines,
dragon lines, and songlines that recur again and again in world cultures.*

Notes

1. William Becker and Bethe Hagens, "The Planetary Grid: A
   New Synthesis," *Pursuit*, Vol. 17, No. 2, 1984.
2. Keith Critchlow, *Time Stands Still: New Light on Megalithic
   Science*. St. Martin's Press: New York, 1982.

3. Raphael Demos, ed., *Plato Selections*. Charles Scribner's Sons: New York, 1927.
4. F. Lindemann, "Zur Geschichte der Polyeder und der Zahl-zeichen," *Sitzungberichte der Mathematisch-Physikalischen Klasse der Koenighlich. Bayerischen Akademie der Wissenschaften 26*, pp. 625-783 (1897).
5. Martin Bernal, *Black Athena*. Rutgers University Press: New Brunswick, 1987.
6. Tons Brunes, *The Secrets of Ancient Geometry*. Copenhagen: Chronos, 1967.
7. Raphael Demos, ed., *Plato Selections*. Charles Scribner's Sons: New York, 1927.
8. L. Elie de Beaumont, "Note sur la correlation des directions des different systemes de montagnes," *C. R. Acad. Sci. Paris*, Vol. 31, 325-338, 1850.
9. Peter Tompkins and Christopher Bird, *Secrets of the Soil*. Harper and Row: New York, 1989. Peter Tompkins and Christopher Bird, *The Secret Life of Plants*. Harper and Row: New York, 1973.
10. Christopher Bird, "The Planetary Grid," *New Age Journal*, May 1975.
11. Peter Tompkins, *Secrets of the Great Pyramid*. Harper and Row: New York, 1971.
12. *Rand McNally World Atlas*, Rand McNally and Company: Chicago, 1975.
13. Frank Waters, *Book of the Hopi*, Penguin Books: New York, 1963.

Appendix

Some Major Intersections

ORIENTING RING. The "great circle" (equator) beginning at Point 1 and running completely around the Earth through the axial north and south poles and back again to Point 1. It is the most important of the fifteen rings that make up the most basic planetary grid system.

Point 1. The longitude meridian running through this point has traditionally marked the division between the East and the West. Many ancient mapmakers used it as the orienting line for their charts (see Charles Hapgood's *Maps of the Ancient Sea Kings*). Folklore has it that this meridian crosses more land than any other line of longitude.

Contemporary salting of the Nile Delta is a serious ecological disaster. Cairo is one of the fastest growing cities in the world.

Archaeological points of interest include (within the nearby vicinity) the Great Pyramid at Giza, the ancient Library of Alexandria, King Herod's fortified palace, the Dome of the Rock, and the Temple of Solomon.

The point is 2160 miles from the Equator, precisely the diameter of the moon. In the Ruwenzori range at the Equator (and also on the Orienting Ring) is a sacred Mountain of the Moon of the Pygmies. The ancient Egyptians revered the Pygmies as both their ancestors and as holy people.

Moving south, the Orienting Ring roughly maps the path of the Nile and passes through the ancient territory of the Nubians. It touches the modern city of Khartoum, site of unprecedented drought, famine, incidence of AIDS, political turmoil, and refugee settlements. There are literally millions of orphaned refugee children in the city. It is also reputed to be the center through which plutonium is being sold underground to Middle East nations.

Point 2. Site of the Chernobyl nuclear plant disaster. Kiev has historically been the most beloved and perhaps most politically important city in the Ukraine. Because of the extraordinary number of rivers (Dneper, Volga, Dvina) which flow through the area, the city has always been an important trading center. The area immediately around the point is of predominant importance to the U.S.S.R. in terms of food production, coal, iron ore, manganese, and natural gas.

Moscow, with its current political upheavals, is nearby to the northeast. (Point 2 may come to represent the collapse of communism.)

Point 4. Lake Baikal is the planet's oldest, deepest, and largest lake. It is about the size of Belgium and accounts for 1/5th of the Earth's freshwater reserves. The threat of pollution to this unique ecosystem, home to more than 1000 species of plants and animals unknown anywhere else, has stimulated an activist environmental movement within the Soviet Union. It has been called the "symbol of the nation."

Point 6. A significant U.S. military base exists here. World War II veterans have referred to Attu as "one of the most beautiful spots in the world." The world's largest concentration of marine animals is found here: vast colonies of sea lions, seals, sea otters. Plankton, tiny marine plants and animals that are the basis of the ocean's food chain, thrive in record numbers. The ring connecting it to Point 7 marks a unique volcanic zone as well as a wildlife refuge protected by the U.S. government since the early 1900s. Birds such as puffins, cormorants, and kittiwakes mass in these islands in the hundreds of millions.

Point 7. Most recently, this pristine Aleut environment was the site of the Exxon Valdez oil spill, which has catalyzed world environmental thought and action. Several years ago, two days after nuclear testing in Nevada, an immense volcanic eruption occurred near the point. A number of geographers believe the events were related.

North on the Orienting Ring are Mount Denali (McKinley), the Alaska pipeline, and the massive Prudhoe Bay oil deposits. Also to be found are some of the most ancient Siberia/New World migration sites, such as Chugwater.

Point 8. This portion of central Alberta is the site of Canada's most prolific oil and gas reserves. It is also its richest wheat-producing area. It may well become a center of massive world environmentalist action if Mitsubishi is allowed to build the world's largest pulp mill nearby on the Athabaska River. (Pulp mills are first-class polluters of water resources.)

Archaeologically, the area is notable for its 5000-year-old Majorville "medicine wheel," a structure somewhat like Stonehenge, presumably constructed by Paleo-Indians.

Points 10, 19, 37, 38, 39, 50, and 60. These roughly mark the outline of the Mid-Atlantic Ridge. Associated with this spreading of the sea floor are not only unique hot spots but clusters of bacteria which appear to be kept alive on inorganic chemicals. Creatures known as tube worms eat the bacteria. This has prompted a re-evaluation of our entire theory of how evolution happens. The older "warm sunlight and gentle tide pools" theory is virtually being abandoned by scientists everywhere.

Point 11. This part of the world is the subject of countless books, ranging from the mystical legends of King Arthur to contemporary stories of giant cabbages grown at the community of Findhorn. It is home to Loch Ness; the Giant's Causeway in County Antrim, Ireland (sometimes referred to as the eighth wonder of the world); numerous ancient stone circles and cairns (somewhat similar to Stonehenge and constructed thousands of years ago). The point also precisely marks the location where the last battle between Protestants and Catholics took place on the island of Great Britain.

A curious and unique species of hallucinogenic mushrooms grows for some miles around the point, and sheep are known to become totally intoxicated by eating them!

Point 12. Here at the mouth of the Indus River is the 6000-year-old origin spot of all Hindu culture and the site of archaeologically significant ruins such as Mohenjo Daro, Harappa, and the "Mound of the Dead." It is not far from contemporary Karachi and has always been a communications center and home to royalty. The infamous Bhopal disaster occurred on the ring connecting Point 12 to Point 25.

Point 13. This spot, near Chengdu, is known in China as Little Beijing. It is most noted as a communications center, but also as the site of the most massive irrigation project in the entirety of China. More than 3000 years old, the Du Jiang Dam system is still keeping the vast plain fertile and is considered a markedly superior engineering feat, in comparison to the Great Wall. The same area is also the natural home of the panda. Slightly north of the point on the ring connecting it to Point 4 is a concentration of Xia dynasty pyramids.

Point 17. Near here are Organ Pipe National Monument; an enormous communications dish array; small pyramids; and Mt. Pinacate. The Hohokum people of ancient times built immense irrigation canals here, and their civilization lasted some 9000 years. They made a ceremonial wine of the cactus we call "organ pipe." In general, this area marks the most sacred territory of the oldest native peoples in North America. The area is currently one of the most intense drug trafficking.

Point 18. Here is probably the most alluring mythological site for the American popular culture—the Bermuda Triangle. A number of people believe Atlantis is rising here, for the sandy undersea floor occasionally reveals what appear to be walls and pyramids. Nearby is Cape Canaveral. The shuttle Challenger disaster, which caused such a dramatic re-evaluation of the real priorities in the space industry, occurred here.

Point 21. Farther south, near the headwaters of the White Nile and an ancient Bedouin watering hole, is Point 21, site of the largest concentration of sickle-cell anemia in Africa. It also marks the heart of the breeding ground for the locust, currently causing widespread devastation that may eventually extend as far as the Atlantic and Pakistan. The United Nations refers to this as "the beginning of a true plague."

Oddly, this same area (slightly southeast of the point) has yielded some of the most crucially important finds in the human evolutionary record (e.g., Olduvai Gorge, the Serengeti Plain, Laetoli, Lake Victoria). Finds by Donald Johannsen and the Leakey family were all made in this general region of east Africa.

Point 25. This area has been crucially important in terms of the future of the United States as a world moral symbol. It marks the focal point of the Vietnam War. Geographically, the Mekong Delta was once (prior to bombing and defoliation) one of the world's most prolific rice-producing regions. It also marks the site of some of the most prominent 'Hindu shrines, including Angkor Wat and the temples of the Khmer kings.

Point 35. This is another area that is the subject of a raft of archaeological and speculative research—everything from Van Daniken's "landing strip for the chariots of the Gods" on the Nazca Plains, to an enormous ancient pyramid complex discovered and described in a *U.S. News and World Report* story of April 30, 1990. Nearby are the very ancient sites of Machu Picchu, the huge unexplained megalithic walls of Sacsayhuaman, and numerous pyramids and stone circles.

Ironically, this is the most prolific coca producing region in the entire world. (Coca is the source of cocaine.) It marks the headwaters of the Amazon River. Just off the coast from Point 35 was once the most prolific anchoveta fishery in the world. The catch went into sharp decline in 1972 with the advent of El Nino, a mass of warm water that intruded upon the nutrient-rich Peru current underpinning the fishing industry.

Point 41. Continuing south, just north of Point 41, is Great Zimbabwe, often referred to as "Africa's Stonehenge." This massive structure is unprecedented in African history and is of such importance to Africans that its name was adopted when Rhodesia became the independent nation of Zimbabwe. Not far from this site, the first hominid fossils (the australopithecines) were found early in this century by Raymond Dart.

Point 41 is in Swaziland and marks the Ngwenya iron ore mine—one of the oldest, if not the oldest, in the world. It is also the site of the second largest rock in the world (Sibebe Rock, 10 km. outside Mban). In general, South Africa and nearby Johannesburg mark not only modern extremes in racial tension and the political legacies of apartheid—but also some of the most substantial deposits of gold, diamonds, chromium, and other essential minerals in the world.

Point 44. This is the site of Wilpena Pound, an enormous meteor crater in the Flinders Range that is also the most popular vacation spot in Australia. There are numerous sacred aboriginal sites here. A unique environmental preserve is maintained at Chinamen's Creek, just south of Port Augusta. The same area is currently slated as a toxic chemical waste storage zone—one of Australia's most controversial proposals.

Geophysicists have discovered a huge natural underground electrical circuit in nearby Broken Hill, which contains electrical currents of more than a million amps. The circuit was found using a sensor which detects fluctuating fields in the Earth's crust. They are created in response to electrical events such as thunderstorms and the movement of dissolved salts in artesian water.

Point 61. An ozone hole over the North Pole was discovered in 1986.

Point 62. Most obvious, at present, is the ozone hole over the South Pole. It is interesting historically that the first landing at the pole by Admiral Byrd was made on the Orienting Ring in an area now known as the Rockefeller Plateau. On his visit to the South Pole, Admiral Byrd had a number of visions involving alien landscapes and spacecraft. He had similar visions, yet to be explained or really accounted for, during his North Pole journey.

19

Earth's Environmental Fields and Human Health

JAMES B. BEAL

Travelers to the Midwestern states in the summer who venture into prairie areas may chance to find a colorful wild sunflower, the "compass plant" (*Silphium laciniatum*), which can grow to ten feet in height. Aside from its height and colorful yellow and brown flowers, the compass plant is unique in that in open sunny areas its lower leaves align with the north-south magnetic axis, just like a compass.

Orienting to the earth's electromagnetic field, "magnetotropism," is found among many plants, bacteria and animals. Researchers now believe that homing pigeons, when released on cloudy days, return home because they have tiny compasses built into their brains. Dissecting a pigeon's brain reveals tiny deposits of magnetite, which seems to be the natural built-in compass. Similar magnetic sensors have now been proven to exist in nearly thirty species of creatures as diverse as salmon, sharks, bees, oysters, and primates, including Homo sapiens.

From the moment we take physical form, our bodies are immersed in subtle environmental fields, and held together by others. Life as we know it is a matter of "fields within fields," as Julius Stulman has pointed out. In the distant past, free from the burden of making so many decisions and being flooded in a world of words, neon signs, concrete and electricity, tribal shamans felt in their bones that some places were special. They did not understand that certain places are situated at dipoles—nodes in the earth's magnetic fields. They did not fathom that under their feet deep within the earth the circuits of subterranean streams had formed a pattern which in turn generated changes in the earth's local magnetic field, and are associated with improvements in positive electrostatic field strength and negative ion concentration. Nor could they say that waterfalls, crashing ocean breakers, mountain locations with many electrical storms and many pine trees have additional beneficial electrical effects.

Shamans did not know these things—they could not know them. But they sensed them in the excited electrochemical processes at work in their own nervous systems, which in turn triggered inspired firing of neurons and synapses in the circuits of their own brains. Instead, to tribal seers, the place felt special and magical, spiritual, and in their trained minds they understood that this is a place for intercourse between humans and the gods. And so at the holy mountains, springs and caves, rituals were conducted and temples erected to create physical ritual forms, many of which honored the four directions . . . which brings us to the story of one of the earliest scientific instruments, the compass.

The Compass

There is debate as to whether the compass originated in Persia or China, but one of the earliest written references to it can be found in the *Ku Chin Chu*, a Chinese dictionary of the fourth century, which reads:

'Hsia-ma' (the tadpole) is also called 'hsuan chen' (the mysterious needle), or 'hsuan yu' (the mysterious fish), and another name for it is 'kho tou' (the spoon-shaped beastie), its shape is round and it has a long tail.

This "spoon" was carved from a lodestone, or filled with pieces of lodestone to make it into a bar magnet oriented along its length to the north-south axis. In this first compass, however, the handle always swung toward the south, a yang direction. It would have been just as easy to make it point to the north, but the south was chosen instead because the north was seen as being dark, evil and female.

From very early times, compasses were used to guide travelers. They also were inserted in the middle of a magical divining wheel used by Chinese geomancers to discern the right acts for each given place. In those days magic was prevalent and freely mixed with science. The "spoon-shaped beastie" was probably as closely guarded a secret then as the atomic bomb is for us.

The compass first appeared in western Europe late in the twelfth century. Some say it was brought to the West by Marco Polo. Initially, the magic stone that pointed north was suspected of being black magic, but soon its use spread widely, particularly among the Mediterranean seafaring nations. Incidentally, Christopher Columbus is credited with being the first to realize that the magnetic compass did not point exactly north and south.

With all our sophisticated knowledge of magnetic materials today, our understanding of the earth's magnetism is still spotty. Note the surprise occasioned by the discovery in early 1958 of the Van Allen Belts, two belts of intense radiation surrounding the earth beginning at 800 kilometers altitude. Or, note the discovery in the last two decades of widespread magnetropism among animals.

In some respects the ancients' wisdom may still exceed our own. The Chinese very early understood that some kind of current in the earth was responsible for their south-oriented needle being such a dependable direction guide. They reasoned that if it is natural for the lodestone to align itself with the north-south axis, much as a moored boat aligns itself with current flow of a stream, it must also be important for humans beings and their homes and gardens to be aligned with the cosmic current. This reasoning no doubt was instrumental in the development of Chinese Feng Shui geomancy, which places great significance in the powers of each direction. The ancient wisdom of geomancy "adapts the residences of the living and the tombs of the dead so as to cooperate and harmonize with the local currents of the cosmic breath." This explains the extraordinary loveliness of the Chinese countryside and the mystical beauty of the temples, shrines and landscaping, designs which make modern architecture seem so simple and mechanical. City planners take note: Though in the modern world, we may scoff at geomancy, investigators are finding more and more evidence that human happiness does depend on harmony with the earth's magnetic field.[1] More and more, geomancy seems worthy of serious consideration.

Effects of Electromagnetic Fields

A clearer understanding of how electrical earth currents modify the positive and negative ionization of the atmosphere is an absolute necessity to avoid reaching unsubstantiated conclusions. By and large, our democratic institutions are based on the faith that we control our destiny through human-made political, scientific, technological, religious and other institutions. The hard evidence, however, shows that we are products of the environment—sustained, nourished and influenced by the electromagnetic gravitational-tidal system of the earth-sun-moon group.[2]

As more and more data become available, it is increasingly clear that, to maximize human potentiality and preserve ecological quality, we must develop a new perspective or paradigm which can embrace the broadest possible view of 1) our effects on the environment; 2) the environmental effects on us; and 3) the mental/physical results of these interactions. We are a product of nature and "tuned in" in subtle ways not explained as yet.

The earth's natural electrical field is normally of positive polarity, ranging from zero to many thousands of volts per meter in a thunderstorm, depending on altitude, humidity, temperature, and geographical location. Weather conditions, such as hot dry winds, cold wet fronts or other storm conditions, cause rapid, significant electrical changes beyond visible lightning bolts. The electrical field gradient (sometimes called the "electrostatic field") changes cyclically over twenty-four hours—highest in the early morning and lowest in the afternoon—and has other cycles of lunar, yearly and sunspot duration (11.6-year average).

Inside metal-frame buildings, automobiles, airplanes or any structures surrounded by metal, the normally changing earth electrical field is zero polarity; a shielded room or "Faraday cage" is produced. The extensive use of plastics (almost all of which have a high negative electrical field) for clothing, and inside buildings and vehicles can provide a strong negative field condition, which may augment fatigue, irritability and allergies,[3] and natural apathy and extra stress in sensitive individuals. This statement, based on the overwhelming evidence available today, raises an intriguing question: Are we polluting our environment *electrically*, as well as chemically? Data increasingly support this position. Robert Becker, M.D., formerly an orthopedic surgeon at a Syracuse, New York, VA hospital, found that exposure of laboratory rats to the 60 cycle, 15,000 volts per meter electrical field (100 times earth's normal field), which would be generated at ground level by 750,000 to

1,000,000 volt power lines proposed by the New York State Power Commission, caused *50 percent mortality* in the second generation of rats.[4] Becker found that some blood factors changed in the exposed adults, but the main thing to consider here is the impact on subsequent generations. Other data has suggested that people living near high voltage electrical power lines may also be adversely effected, not to mention other members of the web of life similarly exposed.[5]

A recent study by C. W. Smith, from the Department of Electronic and Electrical Engineering at the University of Salford in England, discusses in detail how biosensors react with weak environmental electromagnetic stimuli at the quantum level.[6] Smith uses frequencies of very weak field strength to induce or suppress allergic reactions, which he finds is possible in both cell cultures and humans. He shows that nature has clearly evolved sensitive detectors in living structures, right down to the quantum level. Smith's research has great significance for human vision and hearing, both of which are very sensitive to electromagnetic conditions. Biological sensitivity to extremely small magnetic and electrical fields is present in certain discrete frequency bands associated with commonly found geomagnetic fields. These findings now shed light on the potency of extremely dilute solutions (way beyond Avogadro's number) used in homeopathic treatments, for they now can be explained in terms of electromagnetic quantum detection effects.

Our minds and bodies are made up of fields, as is the world around us. The two worlds, internal and external, are constantly interacting. When a strong external electromagnetic field (EMF) is encountered, it may influence weaker internal field conditions, moving them toward the same frequency, called "biological entrainment," or it may affect normal sensory systems of hearing or vision. The possibilities for enhancement, training or suppression of some mental, physical or psychical ability (or of driving someone crazy!) with bioentrainment or EMF sensor effects are now with us. Electrical stimulation of hearing, first reported by Volta in 1800,[7] is an example. Since the mid-1960s devices have been available to electrically induce sound by EMF into the cochlea. Those in the vicinity hear nothing, but the subject receiving the exposure perceives the experience as though hearing through ear phones.[8]

Many people living in cities today encounter this phenomenon when they pick up their telephones and hear background music playing or voices speaking, one example of EMF induction causing confusion and pollution. In the Los Angeles area one rock rap station has such a strong signal that some people have reported its music coming out of chain-link fences and even bathroom plumbing!

The ability of some people to "hear" radar microwaves as a sound like "bees buzzing" is well documented,[9] as are sporadic reports of people "hearing" aurora borealis displays (northern lights) and meteors passing overhead. As one might expect, these reports have until recently been dismissed as unfounded—after all, the effects were subjective and not heard by others present. Nurses in mental hospitals describe patients who are always trying to get the "terrible noise" turned off. Certain rooms or areas seem to be quieter for them. Are these electrical field null points? How many people now in mental institutions or psychologically afflicted are there because of hypersensitivity to electrical fields? Russian investigators report that changes in hypothalamus activity can increase sensitivity to electromagnetic fields many times.

Some persons, most often women and young children, are very sensitive to sound frequencies above the range of hearing for the general population. Some large department stores, many jewelry stores and many government buildings use ultrasonic burglar alarms. During normal business hours, the alarm response is cut off, but sometimes its high frequency speaker (about 20,000 cycles per second) is not. The effects which have been reported to me are headaches, heavy oppressive "gotta get out of here" feelings, nausea and disorientation. Just how many stores have lost business or employee efficiency from this condition is not known. But when these fields are added to other electromagnetic field pollution and an environment filled with plastics, the chances for any sensitive person not being affected are slim. The data collectively show that we are building far too many environments which may look modern and chic, but which are not beneficial for many people.

Electrical fields can influence the rate of spontaneous electrical impulse generation by the nerves, thus affecting visual brightness discrimination, alertness and reaction time during stress situations.[10,11] The earth's electrical field reaches its maximum between the third quarter and the full of the moon; the oxygen metabolism rate in living systems also rises then, thus causing more plant and animal activity at that time.[12]

The term "lunacy" arises from the belief that mental disturbances or crazy behavior increases during the full of the moon. In a study of aggravated assault cases in Dade County, Florida—11,613 incidents over a 5-year period—there was a statistically significant clustering of cases around the full moon.[13] Due to changes in the earth's field around that time, the viscosity index of blood and lymph fluid declines. This suggests that it is wise to avoid surgery during the fullness of the moon to prevent excessive bleeding. This would seem to be especially advisable for outpatient situations such as dental surgery and tonsillectomies. Veterinarians consistently report that the best time for operations on livestock is at the new moon, when oxygen metabolism is at its lowest point.

Positive and Negative Air Ions

Air ions are oxygen molecules with a temporarily unstable electron balance. Negative air ions, such as created by lightning, waterfalls, crashing ocean waves and pine forests, have an extra electron, which gives them a negative charge. Positive air ions, with a positive charge and fewer electrons than normal, are created by winds, fires and concrete and asphalt surfaces which air rushes over. On the average, the ratio of positive to negative air ions in the air is 1.2 to 1.

Negative air ions can penetrate our body via the respiratory system when inhaled. They are then able to transfer their electrical charges over to the platelets in the blood, thus providing extra energy for electrochemical interactions. They also interact with the electrochemistry in process on the surface of the skin. In the respiratory system, especially the trachea, negative ions work directly on the tissues, improving the protective, filtering function which helps prevent illness.

Positive air ions, on the other hand, impair the working of the trachea surface, weakening the system so that illness and infection can occur more easily. Animals exposed to positive-ion-rich air in laboratory experiments develop diarrhea and muscle spasms and have difficulty breathing. It is now believed that positive air ions create these effects by stimulating the production of serotonin in the brain, a chemical associated with mental dis-ease. Negative air ions, in contrast, increase the oxidation of serotonin, speeding its removal from the blood.

Other studies have shown that negative air ions inhibit the growth of airborne micro-organisms. Positive ion-rich air seems to encourage some kinds of bacterial growth.

The research on air ionization has many implications for interior design and for people living in urban areas, where air pollution particulate matter becomes another force to strip negative ions from the atmosphere. Since many sacred places in nature have water, *part* of their pleasant feel may be related to negative air ionization. It is also important to note that naturally occurring uranium ore creates negative air ions through the natural decay process which activates geiger counters. Since some sacred places, such as the Black Hills of South Dakota and places in Australia, have uranium ore deposits, it seems likely that the inspirational feelings of people at these places are partially linked with negative air ion abundance.

Effects of Electrical Fields on Living Organisms

Living organisms, devoid of interference from modern society, have evolved in harmony with nature over millions of years. As a result, they have become very aware of the fields inside of them as well as those around them. In China, "barefoot seismologists" roam the countryside looking for unusual animal behavior and other geological signs to help forecast earthquakes. Science has shown geological signs do foretell quakes by buildups of pressure in the rock strata surrounding fault lines. If a lot of quartz is present in these rocks, tremendous electrical energy (piezoelectricity) is stored, which may occasionally be released before a quake occurs. Some of the resulting electrical phenomena which can occur under these conditions include "earthquake lightning," auroral "skyglows" like the northern lights, and visible electrical discharges called "Saint Elmo's fire," which has a bluish-white color.[14-16]

The enormous electrical changes in earthquakes travel at the speed of light, but earthquakes can travel physically only as fast as the speed of sound. Nearby animals sense the sudden shift in the usually stable, slowly varying environmental background frequency and radiation level which occurs before the actual quake. They head for safety, often coming out in the open and acting nervously before a quake strikes. Animals also pick up the electrical and microwave energy given off by hurricanes and tornadoes and seek hiding places before danger strikes. These are the kinds of unusual behavioral changes which Chinese earthquake predictors look for.[17] It has also been recently discovered that animals higher on the evolutionary scale, such as sharks and the duck-billed platypuses, have an extremely sensitive electrical sensing system in their snouts.[18,19]

There is some speculation that earthquake field effects can cause visual hallucinations (or visual symbolic archetypes of geometric shapes) by electromagnetic induction into the brain's visual center. These patterns, spirals, squares, triangles and other geometric shapes, are often observed in laboratory conditions. We also see them in the pictographs and sacred meditation art of many cultures around the world where meditational disciplines are practiced. These perceptual patterns can be induced by exposure to certain electrical frequencies, ingesting psychoactive chemicals, fasting, meditation and sleep deprivation, with each individual having specific factors which seem most easily to trigger this imaging. This explains why some in a group of people exposed to the same conditions "see" things that others may not.

In a recent paper,[20] Michael Persinger discusses the possibility of perceptual anomalies in areas where electrical fields are strong due to subsurface geological stresses which are not yet sufficient to result in quakes. Persinger states that if the fields are sufficient to ionize the air, then luminous stimuli might be perceived—or "mis-perceived." If the human observer is nearby during a release of energy, then stimulation of one of the most electrically unstable portions of the brain, the hippocampus, would allow imagery to be experienced. More subtle biophysiological responses could also be evoked by stimulation of this area by geophysical phenomena. These responses include sleep difficulties, autonomic instabilities, arthritic complaints and unusual experiences such as UFO sightings. These effects would be short-lived, their duration depending on the subsurface stresses and the electrical sensitivity of the persons involved. Individuals vary greatly in response to electrical factors in the environment; hormone level, attention level and environmental factors affect sensitivity. Therefore, in a group some could "witness" an unusual phenomenon while others would not ("Did you see that weird light?" "Of course not!").

There seem to be parallels here with certain types of psychic phenomena, such as apparitions, mind-to-mind visual imagery induction (whether expected by the receiver or not) and at least some UFO sightings. Quite a number of UFOs appear to be seen traveling along earthquake fault zones and high tension electrical power lines. It does not seem too far-fetched now to imagine that one mind, or some electrical equipment, could induce imagery in the mind of another—for good or ill! The 1983 movie *Brainstorm*, starring Natalie Wood, describes just such a thing happening. Perhaps this sort of "projection" has been around for centuries and practiced by shamans, yogis and dervishes who are said to be able to trigger visions in people by transferring their energy to another through *shaktipat*.

Of great interest is Persinger's discovery of a helmet, which he has manufactured, that elicits transcendental experiences in the wearer.[21] He feels that these experiences are most common during times of stress, when neural firings can become more intense along the sides of the brain and at its base, because stress causes a number of chemical changes in the brain. These results suggest the reason why certain mystics undergo self-induced hardships and stressful "purification rituals," for hopefully the experiences will trigger states with significant imagery and other perceptual anomalies.

Persinger terms his results the "magnetic phosphene effect." Aside from its usefulness in gaining insights into mental imagery, the magnetic phosphene effect has been investigated for several years as a possible aid to the blind. Some success has been obtained by implanting wires directly through the skull into the visual cortex in the back of the brain. With the electronic marvels of large scale integrated circuits, charge-coupled devices and microelectronics developed for various space programs and satellites, it will not be too many years before a crudely functional, implantable electric eyeball will be available!

Desert Winds

Of particular interest to those in the Middle East is the research on the desert winds, called the *Khamsin* or *Sharav*, which move out of the desert each spring and fall. These warm winds, like the Santa Ana of Southern California or the Chinook of the Pacific Northwest, pick up hot air and dust as they sweep across Africa and the Sinai Peninsula. The moistureless air causes feet to swell painfully, noses and eyes to itch and asthmatics to gasp for breath. As the winds blow into urban areas, automobile accidents, crime rates and mental problems increase. Young people become tense, irritable and occasionally violent. Older persons become fatigued, apathetic, depressed and sometimes faint when the desert winds are strong. Professor F. G. Sulman of the Hebrew University in Jerusalem has recently completed a study[22] of 500 "weather sensitive" women ("weather sensitive" people normally compose about 30 percent of the population), who react to either hot, dry heat or cold, rainy weather with an increase in the neuro-hormone serotonin, with adrenal deficiency or with hyper-thyroidism. This reduces breathing capacity by about 30 percent, and causes headaches or dizziness, sore throats and nasal obstructions. The monoamine oxidase inhibitor (MAO) drugs and negative ion generators prevented serotonin reactions to the weather fronts in 75 percent of the 215 cases treated. Hyperthyroidism was also prevented in 45 percent of the 65 subjects treated. The late Dr. Albert Kruger of the University of California at Berkeley replicated Sulman's studies and conducted numerous other studies which support the relationship between "witches' winds" and dis-ease.

These studies have significant importance for both medicine and planning. In the fifth century B.C. Hippocrates, the father of modern medicine, wrote that "northern winds occasion disorder and sickness." The *foehn* of Germany, the *mistral* of France, the *sirocco* of Italy and other high positive air ion winds with disruptive electrical field effects do influence behavior and impair health. In Israel, in some civil court cases, a plea of guilty because influenced by the *Sharav* will get a lighter sentence. The tension of the Middle East, long a hotbed of political unrest, is certainly fueled by its weather, at least in part. As the Foehn blows through Geneva, Switzerland, one must wonder how it influences decision-making and diplomacy at the United Nations. What effects are we creating in urban environments by constructing buildings with totally enclosed air systems?

Negative ion generators have been used for decades in Europe. They have been shown to successfully combat fatigue and decrease allergic reactions. Some studies show that they also help healing and prevent infections to a certain extent.

Meditation, biofeedback and other mind control techniques also have proven useful to help people assume greater control over their personal energy fields. It does not seem impossible that many of these techniques have been developed in countries subject to warm desert winds, as a way to attempt to counteract the influence of the winds. Meditation also has been shown to increase sensitivity.[23] With sensitivity comes increased awareness of the environment.

During the week of December 8, 1988, a violent earthquake shook Armenia, causing widespread damage. Many people saw damage on television and perhaps were moved by the immensity of destruction. Many other people, however, who knew little or nothing about the Armenian quake, may also have been influenced. During an earthquake, the most visible effects are right along the shifting fault line. Aside from the actual physical action at the quake, waves of electromagnetic energy radiate outward, ultimately spreading over the entire earth. Based on my observations and those of my wife, it seems that many more people sense these fluctuations than we might think. At a psychiatric hospital where my wife works, all the patients started drawing pictures of death and destruction around the time of the quake. Two drew pictures about wanting to escape from the earth into space.

We personally experienced sleeplessness and irritability for several days during that period. We began to wonder if this had any relationship to the earthquake's geomagnetic aftereffects. A poll of peers at a meeting of the Louisiana Art Therapy Association showed similar experiences

during that time. Calls to friends in California, Texas
and Canada revealed similar experiences. The earth has
an electromagnetic rhythm, which has twenty-four hour,
monthly and annual patterns. When a big earthquake
strikes, waves of energy are generated outward, upsetting
these natural rhythms. Since we have evolved in this unique
set of fields, it is understandable that changes in them
would cause changes inside us. When people talk about a
"sixth sense," they usually refer to parapsychology. It now
seems that psychic phenomena should be the "seventh
sense," and electromagnetic field sensitivity should be
the sixth sense.

Looking to the Future

Current work with biomolecular electronics, the study
of biosensory systems, and the developing energy medicine
areas of electrical and magnetic field therapies should
in the long run provide the biggest breakthroughs in the
field of medicine. Rapid healing of wounds and injuries,
and even the regeneration of limbs and organs, have been
achieved with biological electrical stimulation, which
causes cell growth according to genetic coding.[24] Work
in France[25] seems to indicate that microwave fields, combined with low frequency, intense magnetic fields, are
very effective in the treatment of cancer, sleeping sickness
and arteriosclerosis. These fields activate or stimulate
the body's defense mechanism, the immune system, so that
the body can cure itself, which is ultimately the true healing
mechanism. There is also evidence that ion and field effects
are acting through the acupuncture electrical system of
the body's surface to affect the central nervous system.
Already we see small hand-held electrical acupuncture
stimulators being used by sports teams to relieve cramps
and spasms of muscles. In some experimental cases,
healing of acute burns has been helped by exposure to
artificially generated fields of positive electrical charge
with negative-ion-rich air. In the not so distant future,
it is quite likely that hospitals may have special environments set up to facilitate healing.

Advances in sophisticated environmental monitoring
equipment will also help us gain a better understanding
of low level fields and how they influence our lives. In

addition to studying color, texture and lighting, more and more people will be looking at environmental fields and how they affect our lives, both positively and negatively. In time we may find that data from satellites about the earth's fields will provide important new guidance about what is best done in each place; a scientific approach to geomancy in fact seems very possible in the not too distant future. And such an approach will be essential, for as we enter an age of increasing scientific sophistication, without a growing precision in our definition of the quality of life to guide our actions, we run the risk of damaging life on earth even more seriously by electromagnetic pollution. As a product of the cosmos, we are all tuned in to earth's fields, and our biorhythms react accordingly (though with subtle effects) to electromagnetic and electrostatic fields, low frequency radiation, ions and perhaps other un-known factors.[26]

One of the most energetic minds of recent times, perhaps ever, is Buckminster Fuller, who taught us to look for the great unifying principles of life to use as a basis for sound thought and action. Fuller leaves us with the following guidance:

> We used to say that the scientist brought order out of chaos. The scientists are about to discover that all that was chaotic was in our illiterate and bewildered imagination and fearful ignorance. Our knowledge of the universe, at the present, is only measurable in dimensional units of energy, time and space. These are mostly above or below the narrow dimensions which we are accustomed to detecting by direct sensing and by conscious awareness. Recent extension of our perceptions to other areas such as radio, microwave, x-ray and beyond has shown that new information is gained whenever we examine the patterns of nature *with* imagination and *without* bias.[27]

Notes

1. F. B. Jueneman. "Interesting to Note," *Product Engineering*, April 1, 1963.
2. J. F. Goodavage, "Skyquakes, Earthlights, and Electromagnetic Fields," *Analog Science Fiction/Science Fact*, Sept. 1978.
3. C. W. Smith, et. al. "Preliminary Investigations into Accept-ability of Fabrics by Allergy Patients." *Clinical Ecology*, Vol IV, No. 1, pp. 7-10 (1985 or 1986).

4. Prepared Testimony of R. O. Becker & A. A. Marino. Cases 26529 & 26559, "*Common Record Hearings on Health & Safety of 765 KV Transmission Lines.*" State of New York Public Service Commission. Test Results, equipment description, 150 pgs testimony, 74 refs.

5. Paul Brodeur. *The Zapping of America.* New York: W. W. Norton and Company, Inc., 1977.

6. C. W. Smith. "High-Sensitivity Biosensors and Weak Environment Stimuli," *International Industrial Biotechnology*, April/May 1986, Vol. 6, Issue 3. Contact Smith at Dept. of Electronic & Electrical Engineering, Univ. of Salford, Salford M5 4WT, England.

7. A. Volta. Roy Soc, trans (London) 90, 402 (1800).

8. C. W. Wieske. "*Human Sensitivity to Electric Fields,*" Lab for the Study of Sensory Systems, 4242 E. Speedway, Tucson, AZ. 1963.

9. J. C. Lin. *Microwave: Auditory Effects and Applications*, Springfield, IL: Charles C. Thomas. ISBN 0-398-03704-3, 1978.

10. K. Mizusawa. "The Effects of Atmospheric Ions on Visual Parameters," *Proceedings of Space-Optics Seminar.* Santa Barbara: Univ. of California, Sept., 1969.

11. S. Sugiyama. "Control of Visual Fatigue by Means of DC & AC Electric Fields," Chapter XV in *Biologic & Clinical Effects of Low-Frequency Magnetic & Electric Fields*, by J. G. Llaurado, et.al. Springfield, IL: Charles C. Thomas, 1974.

12. F. A. Brown. "Living Clocks," *Science*, Vol. 130, No. 3388, p. 1535. 4 Dec. 1959.

13. A. L. Leiber. *Human Aggression & the Lunar Synodic Cycle.* 7th Int. Biometeor. Congress, College Park, MD, Aug., 1975.

14. "Sky Glow Can Herald Quake." *Huntsville Alabama Times*, 16 Jan. 1973.

15. "Tangshan Quake: Portrait of a Catastrophe." *Science News*, Vol. 111, 18 June 1977.

16. B. Webster. "Earthquake Lights Sky," *New Orleans States-Item*, NY Times News Service, 29 July 1977.

17. J. Loewe. "Lowly Cockroach May Predict Quakes," *The New Orleans States-Item*, Knight News Wire, 19 Feb. 1977.

18. S. Begley, "A Plugged-in Platypus," *Newsweek*, Feb. 17, 1986, p. 78.

19. P. Redgrove. *The Black Goddess and the Unseen Real.* New York: Grove Press, 1988.

20. M. A. Persinger. "Comments on Transient Seismo-Electric/Magnetic Fields & Proximal Human Behavior," 7th Int. Biometeor. Congress, College Park, MD, Aug. 1975. Dr. Persinger is associated with the Dept. of Psychology of Laurentian Univ. in Sudbury, Ontario, Canada. Also see Persinger, M. A., *ELF & VLF Electromagnetic Field Effects*, New York: Plenum Press, 1974.

21. "Visionary Helmet," *The Kansas City Star*, Jan. 11, 1987.

22. F. G. Sulman, et al. "Effects of the Sharav & Bora (wind) on Urinary Neurohormone Excretion in 500 Weather-Sensitive Females," *Int. J. Biometeor.*, Vol. 19, No. 3, pp. 202-209, 1975. Also see Sulman, F. G., *Health, Weather & Climate*, Perspectives in Medicine #7, S. Karger: Basel, Munchen, Paris, London, New York, Sydney, 1976.

23. Michael Murphy and Steven Donovan. *The Physical and Psychological Effects of Meditation.* San Rafael, CA: Esalen Institute Study of Exceptional Functioning, 1988.

24. R. O. Becker. "The Basic Biological Data Transmission & Control System Influenced by Electrical Forces," in *Electrically Mediated Growth Mechanisms in Living Systems*, Annals of the New York Academy of Sciences, Vol. 238, 11 Oct. 1974, pp. 241-263. Also see: Becker, R. & Selden, G., *The Body Electric: Electromagnetism and the Foundation of Life*, William Morrow & Co., Inc., New York, ISBN 0-688-00123-8, 1985.

25. D. M. Rorvik. "Do the French Have a Cure for Cancer?" *Esquire*, July 1975.

26. G. G. Luce. *Biological Rhythms in Psychiatry and Medicine*, NIMH Public Health Service Publication 2088, 1970.

27. R. B. Fuller. *No More Second-Hand God*. Carbondale, IL: Southern IL Univ. Press, 1963.

20

Working with the Earth's Electromagnetic Fields

ELIZABETH RAUSCHER

If you were a spirit floating in space and came upon this planet we call the Earth, it would be a striking sight. We have been able to actually see this image recently with the aid of space photography, and what is very clear is that we are living on a glowing ball of life. But from the air it also strikes one that there is almost no place left on the face of the earth which humans have not disturbed. There is virtually no untouched virgin earth left, and in the sky we see smog showing that the air is also affected. These impacts point out only too clearly how we must learn to live in harmony with nature. Essential to living synergistically with the earth is coming to a better understanding of what life is and what is life-enhancing.

Technology has come out of the scientific endeavor, but the background notions about what life is and how technology works are also science. Too often we have tended to avoid looking at the basics in favor of getting results. I believe there is an important and potentially very happy marriage between the spiritual, the mystical and the scientific world views, because they are all methods for looking at the nature of reality. Today it is essential to look at reality and know it well in order to live successfully for very long on planet Earth. The environmental problems result from people living out of harmony with nature.

In our work in measuring and researching the magnetic pulsations of the earth, we have found that there are certain magnetic signatures which occur before volcanism and seismic activity. Certain specific frequencies of magnetic pulsations appear before the event. Some of these frequencies associated with the earth are quite similar to human brain wave frequencies. Indeed we have found certain changes in brain wave activity correlate with occurrences of local seismic and solar wind activity. So when people say they "feel" an impending quake or weather change, they may at least in part be reacting to real physical signals, as opposed to parapsychological perception alone. This does not mean that the scientific method downgrades personal experience and perception. Years ago comets were thought to be the hand of God. Scientists said they were balls of rock with gas around them, but that does not negate the first idea. Rather it is just another perception. Holding both of these views helps us enjoy nature.

If you were to look at the Earth from space, you would find our sun to be an average star on one of the spiral arms of the Milky Way Galaxy. You would also find that we see the large universe of astronomy with our largest instruments, but that with instruments to examine the small we might see the smallest thing, which physicists now refer to as a quantum. We exist halfway between these two extremes, with consciousness as a way to relate to all these dimensions, as well as their parts.

According to modern "mechanical" physics, we want to know the set of simple principles from which the properties of particles, and hence everything else, can be deduced. I believe this approach has value, but I think we can obtain other information and answers, sometimes much more useful, from other views. It seems useful, for example, to think of all life on earth as arising from the earth—that is, out of a common set of forces, fields, and experiences: the strength of the gravitational field, the pulsation of the magnetic field, the electric fields, the electromagnetic spectrum, etc., that have evolved all life. Since we too come from this same origin, it is not hard to imagine that some of our properties are not unlike the earth itself. At a recent conference on the "Gaia Hypothesis," there was a statement quoted in a newspaper saying, "This is clearly an untenable hypothesis because we are so out of touch with nature and cause so much pollution." Anyone who has tuned a musical instrument will understand that harmony takes work. If we try to avoid keeping ever in tune with nature, we may make short-run advances, but we will find that the feedback from them outweighs their long-term consequences.

One of the things we must address is how to enhance our quality of life and become more in tune with our environment, and yet use the benefits of technology. This issue shows that we must face the fact that we ultimately create from values. I want to suggest that at least some of our values have a relationship to actual conditions to which science may speak.

Since 1973 I have been looking at the measurement of electromagnetic fields, their effects on biological systems, and recently a set of experiments examining the effects of low intensity electromagnetic fields on humans, administered to enhance healing processes. This has necessitated developing instrumentation that did not exist, such as a magnetic field detector, which we recently patented. It is a little device, weighing about five pounds, that has an antenna coil with about seventeen miles of wire wound on it to detect pure magnetic fields. The Squid Magnetometer is also a device to measure fields, but such devices cost about half a million dollars including ancillary equipment and are not very portable. We needed something we could afford and that we could take into the field. Our device came about in part because one of the Hopi elders said to me, "I know there are magnetic anomalies at sacred places. Can you go measure these?" I began to think about how to go out in the field to do this by charging devices with liquid nitrogen or liquid helium, as required by the Squid Magnetometer. I decided that we needed to develop a new instrument which was more portable and economical, yet still accurate. My coinventor was William Van Bise.

One of the first experiments I did along this line with my recorder, in 1980, was to examine magnetic pulsations associated with Mount Saint Helens. We began to measure unusual large oscillations in the earth's electromagnetic field, and we did not know what the source was. In fact, at first we thought there was something wrong with the electronic equipment. Very large fluctuations continued for about five months, off and on, within the range of .01 to 300 Hertz. This range includes most of human brain wave activity as well. Particularly prominent was a signal of 3.2 Hertz/cycles/per second. Then we heard about Mount Saint Helens developing a bulge on its side. Indeed, we began to observe certain very indicative precursors of volcanic activity. In fact, when the first eruption took place, the signature of about 3.2 Hz went away and then slowly came back before the next eruption. Thus we could use this observation to predict future eruptions.

Based on this, we began to feel that maybe we could start predicting seismic activity by monitoring pulsed magnetic fields. Then we successfully predicted two eruptions of Mount Saint Helens on the radio. We saw a buildup for a third eruption, which was actually much smaller than we predicted, so we realized that the method needed further refinements. But then over the next year and a half we had an 84 percent success rate predicting seismic activity within 100 square miles of our area. Our predictions were accurate to plus or minus 1½ on the Richter scale.

Here we are looking at the non-ionizing, extremely long wave, low frequency radiation (ELF) used to make these predictions. To give an example, one ELF signal is the 60 and 50 Hertz power line frequencies in the United States and Europe. The area of electromagnetic radiation in the ELF region has not been researched much, and that is one reason we began to look at it. Also, this region is where human brain wave frequencies lie.

When you gather data in this area, you need to look at both the signatures of different frequencies and the time domain—how the fields change in time. The low frequency associated with seismic activity is about 1.6 Hertz, and is what we call the "rotational vector of the earth"—it oscillates between 1.2 and 1.8 Hertz. Once you find a fluctuation, such as 1.56, then you can direction-find by triangulation with magnetic detectors to locate its origin. There is about a 3 Hertz signature right before the quake; then it disappears when the quake occurs. We registered these data with the Library of Congress Project Migraine, as they relate to a series of quakes we predicted.

When we attempt to examine natural field conditions, it is extremely important to understand the origins of the fields we measure. For example, one strong reading proved to be an air conditioner in the building in which we were collecting data. Air conditioners and space heaters run from 15 to 19 Hertz. Also, we start to get into military sources, such as Project ELF (formerly called "Project Sanguine"), which is a submarine communications system located near Clam Lake in Wisconsin. It utilizes miles and miles of antennas. It produces a spurious side band which is near to the earth's resonant frequency of 31.5 Hertz; you usually see it at about 30.4 to 30.6 Hertz. These frequencies are not natural. In 1905 Nicolas Tesla patented a system which was to utilize frequencies near 31.5 Hertz as an information and energy transmission system.

The set of frequencies from .01 to 10 Hertz falls within the range of human brain waves associated with relaxation, creativity and sleep. We found an onset of volcanism with a signal of 2.8 to 4.2 Hertz. I like to think of a 3.2 Hertz reading right before a quake or volcano as a little like a heart arrhythmia, following the Hopi idea of the "heart of the Earth Mother" as being a viable model of reality.

The earth's steady state magnetic field is about 0.5 Gauss along the 40th parallel, which runs through San Francisco. Interacting with the earth's field is a spectrum of pulsations, which we are just beginning to understand. Some of these fields arise in the earth and some arise externally to the earth in the ionosphere and magnetosphere. "Father Sun," which produces solar flare activity, appearing as electromagnetic radiation of about 7-10 Hertz (about the alpha brain wave frequency) interacts with the earth's field. Then there are interactions with the magnetosphere and the ionosphere of the earth also. It is as if the sun's fields "tweak" the system of the earth and life on it to make it work. In the cardiac system of a human being, there is an electromagnetic cycle which sets off the actual muscle contractile cells of the heart itself. It seems almost like Father Sun and Mother Earth are interacting, using these complex fields to communicate with each other. I think this is very important to life. It makes me wonder about the idea of settling on another planet; the subtle wave patterns seem to be so important to life here and would be so different there. We are looking at this question in the space program, by the way, because the solar winds and electromagnetic fields would be very different on Venus or some other planet.

When one examines these fields, too, one finds some strange things. For example, while working on the space shuttle, we came upon a 5.6 to 11 Hertz signal, which is the excitation of the D and E layers of the ionosphere from outer space. We named this the UFO signal, because we did not know what it was. Later, we found it originated from the shuttle itself during re-entry. But the electrical and magnetic conditions of the ionosphere can be quite complex. This is also true for volcanoes. The movement of liquid rock and the heat, for example, can generate many different things.

We have found that, at least in some cases, the brain waves of people seem to lock to the electromagnetic waves generated by the earth's ionosphere system which drives our "inner electricity," so to speak. For example, one subject who was quite tense generated primarily beta waves. When a 10 Hertz wave-generating machine was activated, her brain waves changed as they locked into the external signal, and she generated a normal alpha wave pattern. She did not know when the generator was turned on, as it was out of her view. When we turned it off, her brain wave activity went back to her normal beta pattern. This effect was consistent in 26 cases we studied. It is amazing how externally generated fields can influence brain waves and hence states of consciousness. Some of the frequencies and wave forms we generated are similar to those we measure in the natural environment.

I believe that ionic changes are induced by these fields in the charged layers of the earth and in the atmosphere. These changes induce a current which produces a magnetic field effect, and this couples with the earth's steady state magnetic field. If there is a strong enough influence, then field changes trigger and produce energetic conditions. It seems plausible that in this manner the earth may store incoming energy arising from space as well as from the Coriolis Force of the earth, and then periodically release it in the form of seismic and volcanic activity, just as we release stress. There are many small quakes occurring all the time.

We are just beginning to really appreciate how the fields of life may interact with each other, especially how external fields affect consciousness. It may well be that the feeling state reality of Hopis and other traditional people may be like the proverbial canaries in the coal mine, that their perceptions of the earth and different places on earth can tell us when something very important happens somewhere. Science certainly does now support the premise that everything is interconnected.

A more detailed treatment of the research reported here can be found in a research document, "Fundamental Excitatory Modes of the Earth and Earth-Ionosphere Resonant Cavity," Tecnic Research Laboratories, P. O. Box 60788, Reno, Nevada, 89506 (formerly in San Leandro, California).

V

The Spirit of Place
in Modern Times

"I want to be a part of a culture where the spirit of place is a part of everyone's language, experience and practice," asserted former California State Architect Sim Van der Ryn, as he showed us his designs for new spiritual and healing centers. Like psychologist Robert Sommer, Van der Ryn went on to agree that his best work seems to come from an intuitive understanding of place, which he often cannot express well in words because we do not have a good language to describe our experience of place.

In this final section we see examples of the spirit of place sense at work in art and design, as well as research. Embracing this point of view does not mean dropping science, we find, but rather surrendering to our own senses and allowing them to become voices for places. Listening to these voices, we can use our modern skills and work with a fresh passion to create, knowing that our works can become expressions of harmony and beauty only if we first recognize these feelings within. Moving toward an expanded perceptual awareness of place and nature will cause some conflicts, because we all experience the world uniquely and translate these impressions according to our values. But consider the future of a surely self-destructive world run only according to mechanical paradigms.

The Huron Indians say that the spirit of Lake Ontario is a serpent. Once the serpent spirit tried to leave the lake, but the Creator said no and struck the serpent for trying to abandon its proper place in keeping ecological balance. Even today the serpent roars at the memory of this blow. His voice is loudest at the place modern people call Niagara Falls, which is known to the Hurons as "the place where Thunder strikes." The spirit of Lake Erie, which is a panther, is no doubt thankful for this spiritual enforcement of boundaries.

The work of mythologist Joseph Campbell made us all more aware of the importance of myth and symbols in our lives. We can debate the existence of spirits long into the night, but the pull of Niagara Falls on honeymooners remains strong for reasons they best understand. Apparently in his 1990 visit to the United States, African civil rights activist Nelson Mandela agreed that Niagara Falls is a place of great power.

Psychiatrist Carl Jung said that the people of the United States would never find true peace until they could come into a harmonious relationship with the land where they live. Learning to engage, harmonize with and perhaps even converse with the spirit of each place may be an essential survival skill to create a future world of peace where people live an ecologically sustainable lifestyle. "Sustainability was the original economy of our species," observes William Ruckelshaus, former Director of U.S. Environmental Protection Agency. The challenge for the future clearly seems to be for us to rediscover our roots and then apply the primal wisdom of our senses to making science and technology work in harmony with nature and place. And when we seek that spark of inspiration which can help us undertake such transformation, being at the right place at the right time seems essential. No doubt that site will be a place of true power.

21

Design with Spirit

Interview with Lawrence Halprin

JAMES A. SWAN

Lawrence Halprin is the most widely recognized practicing landscape architect today. He is author of seven books and two films, and the recipient of countless awards including the Gold Medal for Distinguished Achievement from the American Society of Landscape Architects. *Time* magazine recognized Halprin as one of the "Leaders of Tomorrow." Some of his best-known projects are Freeway Park in Seattle, Levi-Strauss Plaza and Ghirardelli Square in San Francisco, Sea Ranch in northern California, Franklin Delano Roosevelt Memorial in Washington, D.C., Nicollet Mall in Minneapolis, and large areas of Jerusalem.

As I walked into Halprin's modest office in a renovated warehouse in San Francisco for this interview, Lawrence was putting the finishing touches on a sketch of the Grand Canyon to give to some friends.

JAMES A. SWAN: Lawrence, your drawings of places and people express an extraordinary liveliness. You're known as a landscape designer. Just how does your skill as an artist influence your work, if at all?

LAWRENCE HALPRIN: Over the years I've made ninety notebooks of places I've been and impressions I've gathered. Ever since I can remember, I wanted to be an artist, even as a little kid. When I was twelve, my parents took me abroad for a year, all across Europe, ending in Jerusalem. There was something about the architecture which touched me, but I could never articulate it. When we came back, I went to prep school, and after I finished, I went back to Jerusalem because it had so affected me. I lived on a kibbutz for three years, from sixteen and a half to nineteen.

The social qualities of this utopian ideal were important to me. Most of the kinds of utopian thinking that have come out of the United States have never continued, but the kibbutzim have. I still go back to that kibbutz when I'm in Israel. I have a special attachment to that stony, barren ground, where we planted trees and made the social qualities of a utopian ideal come to life. This kibbutz is still a thriving community today. My tent mates at that time are still there.

When I came back to go to college, I wanted to do something that would be valuable in a kibbutz at that time. The fact that I was an artist was interesting, but at that time had no immediate value in a kibbutz. Now they have some wonderful artists there, but at that time everyone had to work with agriculture.

I went to Cornell, and although I was painting, I majored in agriculture with the intention of going back to Israel. Then the war started, and I couldn't go back, and so I went to Wisconsin, and studied with Frank Lloyd Wright. That helped me see that the best thing that I could do was to combine my interest in art with botany and ecology, and so I developed my own profession. By that I mean that I had never heard of landscape architecture until then. But, I was fortunate, and they sent me to Harvard on a scholarship, where I did all my graduate work in architecture and landscape architecture. I came into this field from this variety of backgrounds, which I think is very important in most professions. It's good to come into your work from a variety of backgrounds like art, architecture, agriculture, botany, ecology, design. Then I married Anna, who is a dancer, and she's had a strong influence on my work, too.

J.A.S.: You seem to have an ability to make magic happen at a place. Something special is there; you can feel it. Can you describe how you call upon all these fields to create a single design?

L.H.: I think it's wonderful that you use those terms, because it's true that most design training doesn't talk a great deal about magic, poetry or the effect of places on people. It focuses on design and how you put pieces together, special relationships and all that, but it leaves out a lot of what you just said. This is true of a lot of professions, like medicine and engineering, as well as design. They teach you the tools and don't try to get at the magic, which is what I consider to be the essence of it. With the Olympics going on now, what comes to mind is that whether you win a race or not has a lot to do with how highly motivated you are, not necessarily whether you are the best natural runner.

The same thing I think is true of the form of art which I'm in. It looks for a motivation which goes way below the surface of the technique, the program, or the money, and finds out what the real intention is which will bring magic into people's lives. The magic has to be functional in my field. You've got to get the drains to work and make sure the cars don't run people down, etc., but that's assumed. But the real issue is what kind of things can bring magic to design, to people, to ideas, to communities—that makes their lives more important to them.

J.A.S.: This is the kind of discussion which people don't seem to ever have in natural resources, planning or architecture school. They don't talk about magic there. Most educational programs in these areas are very technique oriented. Why do you think that's so?

L.H.: I know why. I think I became aware of it from my friendship with Ansel Adams, which dates back to when we worked together on saving Big Sur. We were fairly good friends, and people always asked me what Ansel and I talked about. The answer to that is very simple. All we talked about was how we make a living. He was talking about how he liked some photos, but he couldn't sell them. Then we got into why he was working for such and such a corporation, and he said, "Well Larry, I've got to feed the kids."

I've known a lot of great artists and creative people, and they all have to pay the bills, deal with family problems, etc. We have to live in an economic reality, and that shapes what we do for a living, at least for most of us. You have to set up situations to avoid getting trapped by the pulls of the world we live in.

J.A.S.: It sounds like your own orientation to landscape architecture has been a very organic process.

L.H.: That's right, and for me, Jerusalem has been an important source of my personal growth. I'm Jewish, and for the Jewish people, there is a saying that goes "If I forget thee, Jerusalem, may my right hand forget its ability." It literally means that if I forget Jerusalem, then I am nothing.

I don't want to say this only about Jerusalem, because you get the same feeling up on the high mesas of the Four

Old City, Jerusalem

Corners area with the Hopi Indians. The Hopis and the pueblos have the same experience as the Jews and Jerusalem, the same kind of relationship between a place and the people who have learned to live there. The people and the land seem to develop the same image which represents them; the people and the land are inextricably intertwined. The "I" and "Thou" of Martin Buber reaches out and becomes a oneness between people and land.

J.A.S.: You're describing something that people like Carl Jung and Franz Boaz talked about. They called it "physiographic determinism." And I clearly agree with you and them that it exists, but now I'm going to ask you a harder question. Why does this occur?

L.H.: A good deal of this has to deal with history, that is, what happened to the people, and how it happened. As information is passed down over the years, say that Jerusalem is the center for the temple, for your faith, the place where the ark finally stopped wandering around, it becomes the center of the world.

Jews were wanderers, and, while we don't have a central synagogue, we have a Torah, and it talks about the ark coming to rest at Jerusalem, which gives you a center point, a kind of cultural anchor. The "book" and the historical significance of the place then focus attention on Jerusalem and make it the source of our identity.

The city also has gone through all kinds of experiences like being attacked. Then there are some kinds of anthropomorphic things, like starting the city down in the valley and then going up on the hill when they could find a spring there. On all the holidays they talk about "going up to Jerusalem," which designates it as a high, holy, spiritual place.

You might ask about other people coming there. What do they feel? That's a good question, but what I'm saying here is that any Jew coming to Jerusalem comes with a lot of baggage. There is a quality to the place itself, though. Jerusalem is built of the stone on which it sits. All the buildings are built from this stone, and it has a kind of ineffable quality or color to it. It's pink. It glows. That's why it's called "the City of Gold." It's on the edge of the desert and the Mediterranean, the dividing line. Many, many religious experiences occur in the desert.

J.A.S.: Why do you think that's so?

L.H.: I think it's because everything else is pared away. There's nothing between you and it; spirituality is pure there. Like the Navaho Indians, Jews don't believe in an afterlife, but that doesn't mean there isn't spirituality.

J.A.S.: You talk about the kibbutz and its success as an enduring utopian community. What makes a kibbutz work? Is it the common shared religion that makes it work?

L.H.: No. Most of the kibbutz people are non-religious.

J.A.S.: Then what makes it work?

L.H.: In the beginning the kibbutz was a socialist ideal. The common ownership of land, with everyone equal and everyone working, made it work. The collective community sense, as opposed to the individual, makes it hang together and work, especially in a somewhat harsh environment.

Monte Reggone, Florence, Italy

In the beginning there was a high motivation to make these places in difficult surroundings.

J.A.S.: That's a fascinating point, as the Hopi Indians also speak in terms of their choice of the high mesas as linked to their being somewhat harsh places. They say that they could live there only if they maintained their ceremonies, because their ceremonies helped keep things in balance, such as enabling favorable rains to fall, etc.

L.H.: That may also speak to what happens in some of the kibbutzim. It seems as though they keep together as long as there is something to overcome, and then as they start succeeding, they start falling apart.

J.A.S.: This issue of the spirit of place is really a sort of intangible thing, at least in terms of modern psychology. You can't see it, taste it, or touch it, but it's there. I think what's so important about your work is that you know how to create it.

L.H.: I try to. In the best things that I do, I accomplish this. That's why they are good. Where I've been most successful, it's often not so much that I alone create the design, but that it arises from a group effort, involving other people in the decision-making. But I also acknowledge that my own interest in art helps. This work that I do, I think, is the highest art. It's the connectiveness to a community of people which helps them to function in a certain way that makes this work so special. The reason that some of the greatest works of art are linked to places, I think, like Florence, Venice, Jerusalem, the Four Corners, is that the making of place includes dance, theater, ritual, costumes, and architecture, beautifully sited, all of which links to nature. When you put all those things together, then you have what opera tries to do, but really doesn't.

J.A.S.: But the real key is attunement to nature.

L.H.: Yes. The thing about the Southwest, which I think is the most brilliant example of this, particularly the pueblos

HOPI - 1st mesa
Walpi pueblo - recall of the
race at dawn up from the valley
to the mesa - men on mesa call down
encouragement & directions to the runners below
who call back to them -- spectacular evocative relation both
to environment & religion -- on mesa women wait with
corn plants as part of the festive blessing...

Walpi Pueblo

where the Tewas are, is that the architecture is the location where the art takes place. The Navaho healing ceremonies work best where they are linked to the places around them.

J.A.S.: You seem to be implying that life itself is a ritual form which reflects the art?

L.H.: Yes. It's different from saying that this person's life was an art. That's shallow. In these places, when people bring all these elements together, then they no longer are seen as works of art, but they become the most significant thing in life.

J.A.S.: Yes, this is true, but what you are saying now points to great problems for modern society, for the places you've been talking about are all inhabited by more or less indigenous tribes or groups. What do we modern people do? If we rely only on people of the past to tell us what the sacred places are, then what happens if they are extinct, or they don't like us? Doesn't everyone need to have sacred places in their lives?

L.H.: I think there are many places which have a transcultural value—not all, but many. Some places start out with it, like Machu Picchu. Geomancy can help here, and I agree with geomancy on a mystical, non-scientific basis. I don't agree with the idea of ley lines and all that, but I do agree that there are mystical qualities to places which exist whether people have done anything there or not. Some places have this even though people haven't done anything, but there are other places that are great because people have done things there. These interest me more. Take Florence. Look at all the great things that people did there in the Renaissance. Physically, the place is not that beautiful or majestic. You wouldn't select it as a great mystical place by the obvious criteria. Machu Picchu is different. Most of the great religious places tend to have mystical qualities existing by the landforms and other forces.

J.A.S.: Several years ago I had a conversation with Joseph Campbell about sacred places, and I asked him what were his favorite places. He replied that Palenque, Delphi and the caves at Lascaux were his most favorite places. Then I asked him why. He sat there for a minute and then said that it was because "I, Joseph Campbell, feel most powerful there, and I haven't the damnedest idea why."

L.H.: I'm glad to hear that. I think that too many people try to mystify it too much. If you try to mystify things too much, they become cliches. Delphi is special; I agree with him there. The landform and the views are spectacular there.

And there are special kinds of experiences you have at a place like Delphi. When you're on the summit of certain peaks, you get on the top, and you feel a sense of power for yourself, and you feel closer to the world above. You can see and know where you are. Trees also give a special feeling, especially tall trees. There are still religions which worship trees. I think that most of the great religious movements have a sense of spirituality connected to place.

J.A.S.: Carl Jung had a belief that places influence the unconscious in certain predictable ways. He called this "psychic localization." No one has really researched this, but we seem to make reference to it and acknowledge it when we talk about the "sense" of a place. Suppose we brought people from a wide variety of backgrounds to a certain place which may not be as well known as Delphi, like where Esalen is at Big Sur. Do you think they could agree that the place is special or not? What I'm getting at is, can a sacred place exist if there isn't a powerfully evocative landform there?

L.H.: I don't think it has to be powerful. It can be, for example, poetic. I think there are biological responses that you can call mystical which arise from being at places. They don't have to be powerful, but they are there. You can't confuse this with what people have done there. A place like Lourdes or Jerusalem is very heavily overlaid with history now. People go there, and they expect something to happen. When you go to the Wailing Wall, you have so much baggage. You're very vulnerable, and you fall prey to the suggestiveness of the experience.

I think there is no question that some places exist which have a greater spiritual or mystical value than others. It's like saying that some people are more talented than others.

J.A.S.: I agree, but the words you're using here are artistic ones. I wonder if we can go beyond this. The National Academy of Sciences has suggested that Four Corners be designated a "National Sacrifice Area," where environmental quality standards should be lowered, in this case to mine for coal and uranium. Yet this is the area where the pueblos and Navahos are. Do you think we can ever arrive at a common language which people can use to communicate their feelings about the specialness of place? Not everyone has the eyes of an artist.

L.H.: Quantification of aesthetics is a rough issue. When

I was brought into a national study of freeways by the President, it was very clear that they used cost-benefit analysis based on economics to do the siting. It was starting to destroy the countryside. What we tried to do was to think about how to inject subjective values into their decision-making process. Some people tried having people evaluate places on, say, a 1 to 10 scale, and quantify people's impressions. I think this approach misses too much.

J.A.S.: What does it miss?

L.H.: If you have the home range of an endangered species sitting on top of an oil deposit which we need desperately, and then you try to weigh the two, you get into trouble. The same thing with places. If a tribe of 5000 people have a cemetery, and someone wants to run a freeway through there, you have to look at all sides. It's not that easy to assign numbers to such things.

What you can and should do, I think, is to identify all the values and put them out there for discussion. Then develop some criteria which we can use to talk about things. You can generate numbers here, but not a simple 1 to 10 for a lot of things. That's why I developed the "RSVP Process,"* which is a way to look at all these things and take them into consideration for a humane design solution. This kind of process allows for issues to float to the surface, and encourages people to articulate values which go far beyond dollars and cents. That's how the Sea Ranch design was created. The place isn't really mystical, but it has a quality. When we could get people to come together and work as a group to report on how it felt to them, we came up with a design which has worked and has inspired other people all around the world to try this kind of approach. This is the kind of design which generates a spirit all its own, which encourages the human spirit to soar. That's when real magic starts to happen.

---

*The value of Halprin's RSVP Cycles approach is supported by former Secretary of Interior Stewart Udall, who says of Halprin's book *RSVP Cycles: Creative Processes In The Human Environment:* "This is an original work of striking clarity and force; it should become a handbook for the environmentalists of tomorrow."

22

Circle the Earth:
A World Peace Dance

ANNA HALPRIN

I want to frame my presentation by putting the idea of places of spirit or spirit of places in three different perspectives. I am always aware of these when I'm doing my work in an environmental setting.

One perspective is that to me places of spirit have an almost generic idea behind them. There are certain elements in nature which seem to draw us to them, such as caves or rocks like Ayres Rock in Australia or Stonehenge. There are rocks and then there are *rocks*. I'm interested in *rocks* which have drawn people into making a personal investment to get to them. Much the same is true for caves, like those where beautiful rock art graces the walls. Such caves are very special. They have been selected to portray those graphics to communicate a very special meaning.

There are special lakes too, like Blue Lake which the Taos Pueblo Indians finally have been able to save for their own ceremonial and mythical uses. The lake in Scotland with the magical monster, Loch Ness, is also a special place.

There are special trees. The Balinese wrap their trees with special cloth. American Indians have sacred trees which they worship, like the cedar.

Then of course there are special mountains—Mount Fuji, the Himalayas, Mount Shasta, San Francisco Peaks which are important to the Hopi. There are sacred rocks too. The Hopi Indians chose the place where they live because of the placement of a rock; a rock made known where to site their homes.

The second perspective is a theory I have about these special trees, lakes, mountains and caves. I believe we have an inner geometry in our bodies and an inner biology which becomes an extension of our planet/world, and our bodies and the planet are interchangeable. We reflect what's out there because it's in us, and because it's in us, we see it out there. Our spinal column is like the mountain. It is the vertical. Our legs are the base and our head the peak.

We also have a connection to the four directions. We have a front, a back, and two sides. In addition, we also have an up and a down. The seventh place is the center, inside of us. We have caves, wombs, that which is contained within. We have rocks, the solidity of our bodies, which is a masculine quality, and water, the flow in us, which is a feminine quality. Nature is deeply ingrained in the biology and geometry of our bodies. As we begin to connect with the places of spirit in our environment, we also through awareness can begin to connect with places of spirit in our bodies. The two must go hand in hand; they cannot be separated. This is very important to me in my work.

What makes a place of spirit is not just physical appearance. Mount Tamalpais in Marin County, California, is not as spectacular as other mountains in the world. But many people have invested into that mountain, walking her trails, holding events there, telling legends that have been built about the mountain. It is the investment people bring that makes a difference—the reverence, the aspirations, and the vision.

The third perspective I am interested in concerns those ordinary places that become places of spirit because of some unique way we connect with them. Recently my husband and I joined with people all over the world in a planetary dance, and we heard about it from people of many countries. One man from Japan said, "We did our planetary dance in our backyard. My son and I did this." He sent a picture of four spirals he had made in his backyard. One represented fire, one earth, one wind and one air. Then he drew a picture of himself and his son spiraling in all four. That backyard will never be the same. The love and the sharing and the vision which was passed on from father to son that day made it a place of spirit.

In a sense Mount Tamalpais is my backyard. It has been for the past forty years. Mount Tamalpais covers all perspectives I have mentioned. It is probably the most popular mountain in the country because it is so accessible and so many people go there. For that reason, it was shocking to a whole community when the mountain became inaccessible to us. In 1979 a series of murders occurred. Three women on the mountain and two others close by were killed. It created such a sense of intimidation and terror that no one walked the mountain for two years. Warning signs were posted on the trails. If you dared to go on a trail, they confronted you. One night an alarm went off in my home because I had forgotten to turn it off. I had gone to bed and didn't know the alarm had gone off. In minutes police were swarming around my home with guns drawn. They walked into my unlocked house and put terror into me, as they reminded me of the trailside killer. The mountain had become our shadow side.

About the same time this was occurring on and around Mount Tamalpais, my husband (architect Lawrence Halprin) and I were leading some workshops in the community. We were looking for a contemporary myth that would be meaningful to us and help bring our community together so that we could have some voice in the direction that Marin County was going. This program was called "A Search for Living Myths and Rituals through Dance and the Environment."

The mountain is a beautiful and romantic place and has many legends. Mount Tamalpais is named from a Miwok Indian story that the mountain is a sleeping princess, Tamalpais. You can see her long hair sweeping down the slope, her breasts, her nipples, her body. A long line traces her belly and legs. She went to sleep, the old legend says, because her mother, who was a shaman, learned that Princess Tamalpias had fallen in love with a young brave from the tribe that was at war with her tribe. The mother was very protective of her daughter, as in *Romeo and Juliet*. So the princess went to sleep and said she would not wake up until the two warring tribes made peace. For me, she has become a peace symbol.*

Another legend of Mount Tamalpais is that chief Marin showed his bravery by climbing the mountain and planting a stick on which he placed his shirt. He did this because some Indians believed that on the mountain was a spirit so dark and strong that no one who went to the top would ever come down again alive.

---

*We named our dance institute after her—Tamalpa Institute.

These kinds of stories and legends do not seem to mean much until one experiences something of the mountain. As our urban sprawl comes into this area and crowds around the mountain, it seems to cut us off from contact with it. In our workshops, my husband wanted to help people become aware of what was happening to the environment. I wanted them to become aware of how their responses could become a dance. So we did the workshops as a community event to develop environmental awareness of the world around us as well as within us.

We began to make pictures of what we were noticing as we walked streets, getting in touch with our feelings. We had sharing sessions after exploring our sensorial impressions of the place, and sometimes we would dance our responses to the environment. We would tap into ourselves through movement and then express outwardly what we felt about ourselves and the place, and then explore how this connected with the place. We began to construct a fantasy world, and in it we kept finding a center pole that we wanted to plant there. Around this pole we brought our sensations of touch, taste, sight and sound, weaving them into a community creation, always with the mountain in the background.

Sharing as a group for over nine months, we sought a project to take on together. We were not trying to talk about the mountain or the killings; in fact it was almost a taboo subject. But one day there was an explosion of feelings. Everyone began to talk about their rage and their sense of helplessness and hopelessness over the killings on the mountain. Out of this groundswell came the idea of a dance to create a new legend with which we would reclaim the mountain.

We developed a dance score "In and On the Mountain" that enacted our own myth of the mountain, the killings and our response to this. The parents of the murdered women were there as we danced, and it was very real. The next day we invited the community to climb the mountain. Eighty people appeared. We were scared, afraid that the killer would come and shoot at us. There were police cars on guard and helicopters overhead.

We began the dance with some people running up the mountain, led by Walt Stack, an eighty-year-old runner, a symbol of strength, endurance and commitment. This was

Anna Halprin's dancers become Mt. Tamalpais.

in keeping with the tradition of the coastal Indians to walk or run on the mountain to give energy back to it. We ran up the mountain in four directions. Some people were chanting. Some were in groups, large and small, young and old. People streamed the mountain, climbing its rocks, reclaiming it.

At the top we invited spiritual leaders to make blessings and ceremonies for us. They led songs, said prayers, recited poems and told stories. An Indian planted corn between a male and a female rock. Rabbis and priests delivered blessings. A genuine outpouring of love and concern brought us all together. Then we walked back down. Some were afraid of the killer. The police told us to stay together in groups for safety. We danced, chanted, meditated and made offerings along the way.

We were investing energy back into the mountain, driving off the veil of fear that infected this sacred place. Individually and as a group, we helped bring the mountain back to life, back to its place of spirit.

Two weeks after our ceremony a man was arrested who since has been convicted of the killings. He was found through an anonymous tip. I believe we cared so much for our mountain that our collective spirit brought the mountain back to us cleansed and healed.

A Mexican shaman, don Jose Matsuwa, a Huichol Indian, came to visit us a few months later. He was over 100 years old. No one had invited him, but he said that he felt pulled to the mountain. We took him up to the top and told him what had happened. He planted a feather on the mountaintop, and then began to cry. He said that this was a holy mountain which he had seen in a dream many years ago. He told us that we should keep doing the ceremony for the next five years for its healing.

So every spring we performed what we now call "Circle the Earth." Different religious leaders came to join us, Aztecs, Shintos, Jews, Baptists, Catholics, Indian medicine men and sufis. Each year our ceremony is slightly different. The mountain became peaceful. No more killings took place. On the eve of the fifth annual cycle of the ceremony, the man accused of being the killer was finally convicted.

As we invested more and more energy into that mountain it seemed to become more sacred. I wondered what this means for the entire earth. If we could effect peace on one mountain through our process, could the same dance create peace in other parts of the world? What started as "Circle the Mountain" became a peace dance which now is performed around the world in more than thirty countries. The circle of peace we created at Mount Tamalpais is now circling the planet. Each community finds its own sacred place to dance prayers for peace and healing of the earth.

(For guidance in participating in "Circle the Earth" ceremonies in your community, write:
Anna Halprin,
Tamalpa Institute,
P. O. Box 794,
Kentfield, CA 94914

23
Making Places Sacred

THOMAS BENDER

I. Do We Need Sacred Places?

Sacred places seem alien to our culture. Yet in an important sense, we very much need to hold all our places sacred. The places we make act as mirrors to our lives. They reflect the good or ill, passion or indifference, with which we hold them back onto the people whose lives they touch. Places, as well as people, draw sustenance from how they are held in our hearts. How we feel towards them does strongly affect our lives.

A friend once commented how tourism was destroying the cathedrals of Europe. "Each person came," he said, "and took away a little of the cathedrals—in their cameras, in their mind, or in their conversation—and now nothing remains."

As I thought about that, I realized that all places live through the reverence with which we hold them. Without that reverence, they crumble to pieces unloved, unmaintained, abandoned, and destroyed. That reverence is the glue that in reality binds the stones, the blood that sustains the life of a place, and the power that raises the funds for its upkeep. And it is that reverence first which is taken away, piece by piece, flashbulb by flashbulb, tour bus by tour bus. Without it, a place has nothing to give to those whose lives it must sustain, and they in turn fall into the same dereliction.

Far different is the visit of a pilgrim. A pilgrim brings love and reverence, and the visit of pilgrims leaves behind a gift of their reverence for others to share.

We lessen the soul of all places, and ourselves as well,

when we take without giving and come to them without
reverence to life and to land, to people and to place, to
ourselves and to the creation of which we are part. This
is the root of the destruction of tourism, and also where
we can find a healing power for our land and our lives.

II. What Kinds of Places Are "Sacred"?

Places which are held sacred vary immensely in their
nature and their reasons for being valued:

Physically special places with unusually powerful patterns
of nature draw us apart from our everyday lives and into
awareness of primal forces. Sacred mountains, lakes, the
redwoods, Glacier or Yosemite rarely fail to make a powerful impact on us.

Places where our actions don't dominate, such as national
parks or wilderness areas, allow us to shed the self-centered-
ness and self-importance of our actions and dreams and
become aware of the greater context within which we
are embedded.

Special places enhanced by enlightened building have in
rare cases been able to embody particularly powerful visions
of our universe and our place in it. The palace and gardens
of Louis XIV at Versailles give an unmatched expression
of "power over nature." The layout of the temples, lakes
and waterways of Angkor Wat in Cambodia embody without
parallel their society's vision of the sacred act of distributing
the waters and prana of life throughout the land.

The chess pavilion on Hua shan in China conveys a
unique sense of "life among the gods." Zen gardens in
Japan convey a depth of action attainable only by individual
experience of the depths of knowing. The feng-shui of
Chinese pagodas or Alpine village churches communicate
a powerful sense of balance and peace with nature. The
Kailasa Temple at Ellora, carved out of living rock, conveys
an unmatched intimacy with our planet, economy of means,
and sure and living sense of the power of sacred imagery.
Together, these suggest the special power which can, on
occasion, be evoked through our building.

"No" places, by merely placing some limit on our actions,
remind us in unequivocal terms of the necessity to limit
our dreams and use of power. The sacred cows of India
and the Ise Shrine in Japan show the flip sides of this

Vision questing site in Rocky Mountains

powerful kind of statement. By saying no to access or to denying access, they convey the significance of limits—of not letting anything become all-powerful.

Places of important history/context, such as the Dome of the Rock, the Lincoln Memorial, or the Agora of Athens, hold before us events, actions, lives, and places which have stood witness to values we hold high.

Places with special electromagnetic conditions have long been held sacred. Hawaiian birth centers, favorable Chinese feng-shui locations, English cathedrals, vision-quest sites, and Serpent Mound all give documentary evidence of the proven ability of places with unusual electromagnetic field conditions to influence human activities favorably, either materially or through our belief systems.

All this suggests how varied and powerful sacred places can be, but also that their real significance may not lie in the places themselves.

III. Making Places Sacred

What is significant about sacred places turns out not *to be the places themselves.*

Their power lies within their role in marshalling our inner resources and binding us to our beliefs.

*Our act of "holding sacred" is the root, not the place where
we choose to carry out that act.*

It is in that act that we give places power to affect our lives.

*In holding a place sacred, we grant power to a place and
acknowledge that power of the place. As an ikon or through
its own inherent patterns, we acknowledge its ability to impact
our awareness of certain relationships and their value to us.*

*Sacred places thus forge and strengthen bonds between us
and the universe in which we believe.*

*They empower us by affirming the wholeness of the universe
we see revealed about us, and by reflecting our chosen place
and role in that universe.*

*The inviolability of sacred places is essential. Through
making them inviolable, we affirm the primacy in our beliefs
of the values which they embody.*

IV. Making Our Places Sacred

Great achievements, such as Angkor Wat or Chartes
Cathedral, give us a sense of the possible.

Equally important, however, is to know that the same
possibilities lie within the scope of our own actions. Few
of us has the power of a Khmer king, the real estate of
Yosemite, or the honed skills of a Zen master. Yet what
each of us has is enough. There is opportunity in every
action to show what we love and hold sacred.

Making Our Places at Home in the Universe

A city is more than a place to work, and a home is more
than a place to lay our heads. We reflect in our building
the harmony we see in our universe. Doing so, we strengthen
our confidence in sensing the underlying power and nature
of the universe, and in our ability to fit within its flow and
marshal it to our needs.

The order of a Chinese city or Renaissance palace, the
symbolism permeating a Navajo hogan or Plains tipi, the
spiritual directness of a Shinto sacred spring or Shaker
furniture, the sacred geometries of Islamic ornament or
Gothic cathedrals, or the bold power of a 20th century
skyscraper all give voice to a particular universe felt and
inhabited by their makers. In doing so, our architecture
renews and strengthens that universe and those who inhabit

it. The sense of order with which we organize our places expresses our own sense of order and creation in our universe. Immutable Euclidian geometry, topological organization, fractal growth rhythms all offer vastly different opportunities.

Feng-shui presents another way to connect with our universe. The Chinese feng-shui tradition, and the divination used in siting temples and cathedrals in other countries, locates and designs homes, cities, and tombs in alignment with energy currents in the earth, creating a subtle harmony between buildings and their landscape. Aspects of the practice echo good ecology, good design, and good psychology, as well as good "energy." Equally important, they ensure that we bring our buildings, our beliefs, and our understandings of the cosmos into alignment with one another.

Ornament gives us a particular opportunity, free of the functional constraints of building, to infuse a building with our sense of cosmic order. The delicate interlacing geometries of Islamic ornament reflect the unfolding of the limitless forms of creation from a single source, as well as the eternally transforming relationships that tie together all of creation. The sculpture of a Scandinavian stave church or a French Gothic cathedral reflects their

Buddhist Temple on Oahu, Hawaii

society's view of their universe as purely and powerfully as does the spareness of Shaker or Japanese design.

Ornament is important even in the austere beauty of Japanese temple design. The temples have long been cited as a prime example of the beauty of "pure unadorned structure." Yet on closer examination, the temples turn out to have layer upon layer of "ornamental" structure overlaying the actual structural members, to give a coherent sense of the beauty sought by the builders.

On a community meeting hall and tourist information center in Cannon Beach, Oregon, we are trying to infuse this sense of cosmic order through a major crafts component in the building. Our sense of our universe is undergoing dramatic new unfoldings, and little of this heretofore invisible universe has yet found expression in our building.

Aligning our buildings with our sense of our universe gives us the opportunity to affirm and clarify our beliefs. It strengthens those beliefs and our resolve to keep our actions in positive concert with them. And it renews within us the wonder and joy of being part of an awesome and incredible creation.

Making Our Places at Home with their Surroundings.

Powerful meaning is found, too, in how architecture ties us to the specialness of a place. No two places on our planet are entirely alike, and the communities of life that each brings forth are as unique as the patterns of its weather, terrain, geology, and its own surroundings. Each place has unique powers to stir our hearts and minds, and brings into being a human community as uniquely molded to the potentials and limitations of that place as are its communities of plants, birds, animals, and insects. In becoming at home in these places and responding to the special kinds of comfort, challenge, and sustenance we find in each, we become a different people. Whether Californian, New Englander, Southerner, or People of the Plains, we come to have special qualities of our own to give to the tapestry of human society.

When we live close to these natural surroundings, we come to know and love them deeply, and to build in ways which reflect our joy in being a part of them. Our buildings come to connect us to, rather than isolate us from, the natural forces of the place and they take form from the special spirit of the place. Such buildings vent or hoard heat as needed. They shade from or welcome the sun and wind, depending on the season and place. Their palette of colors is attuned to the space-filling white light of snow country, the pastels of fog country, the green light of the forest, or the golden sunsets of the tropics. They know their world, and are fully a part of it.

There are buildings that do fit their region and evoke the poetic power of the region in our lives. Paolo Soleri's Cosanti residence in the Arizona desert fits into the desert itself. Earth-covered concrete domes and vaults nestle into the desert, tempering the heat of the day and cold of the night, giving shade or sun when needed, while blocking the piercing desert winds. Cape Hattaras beach houses become unique mesh-enclosed spider webs on stilts—open to summer breezes, but protected from sun, bugs, and storms. Northwest homes of log and cedar nestle their wide rain-sheltering roofs among the lush vegetation. Persian dwellings grow from a garden, not a building—a cool and verdant oasis in the desert.

Spurred by the Canadian architect Arni Fullerton, an interesting movement has developed concerned with "winter cities." Bringing people together from Japan, China, Scandinavia, and North America, the movement has made considerable advancement in dealing with the problems of winter living. Most significantly, though, it has focused on making winter a positive thing in people's minds, rather than a burden. Winter tourism brochures, winter festivals, snow gardens, skylights on homes to see the winter sky and the aurora borealis are a few of the outcomes that are developing a dramatic excitement and enthusiasm for winter.

Following their lead, we have been working in the Pacific Northwest on "rain gardens" to celebrate our endless rains. Such things as slug races and mud and mushroom festivals take advantage of the unique features of our region. In buildings in process, we have designed star rooms—sleeping rooms under wall-to-wall skylights—so we can stay close to the stars. In every house design, where possible, we place morning rooms, moonrise rooms, and sitting places to follow the rising and setting of the sun and moon and the cartwheels of the stars across our skies.

Mt. Burdell, site above Miwok village of Olompali in Marin County, California

Doing so, we stay aware of how the moon moves the tides of our feelings in harmony with those of the ocean. Being in touch with the sunrise and sunset, we stay in touch with the rhythms of work and rest in nature—rhythms of giving and absorbing that are important to acknowledge for our own health. With window seats, doorsteps, verandas, porches, and outdoor rooms, we can create places to live and work that nestle between protection and contact with our surroundings.

The Sounds of Silence

Late one night at the Taj Mahal, I discovered that silence can be a vital tool of design. Alone inside the dome room, I felt the quiet swell to fill the majestic space. Even the sound of my breathing echoed. As it settled into silence, it drew me deeper and deeper into stillness. The silence was as eloquent as the finest music I have ever heard, and it penetrated into the core of my being. All the richness and beauty of the Taj was nothing compared to the power of its eloquent silence.

I learned by that to listen to our surroundings. Half-ignored music, unheard mechanical noises, and other unwanted sound often dominate our places. In our own home we replaced a noisy refrigerator with a passive cooler. We eliminated noisy heating systems and use a wood stove and passive solar heating. We isolated laundry equipment and got earphones for listening to audio equipment. We planted shrubs where birds can feed and nest. We decided against dogs when we discovered that few things are more wonderful than looking up from your dinner to see elk emerge silently from the fog a few feet from your window.

Eliminating unwanted "music" and making space for welcome sounds of life can be one of the most important contributors to the peacefulness of our buildings.

Honoring Others

A tree root once opened my eyes to the many ways our buildings deny the seamless web of love, awe, and respect that is part of the sacredness of our world. I found the old, twisted spruce root on the beach after a storm. I dragged it home, and eventually made it into the handrail of our stair. Its gnarled shape silhouetted against the soft light from inside nudged my mind every night as I came in from the dark.

Part of the root's specialness, I discovered, was that it still held the history of its past life. Most building materials have had their history trimmed, sanded, and varnished away. The contortions of an old tree, like the wrinkles and stoops of an old person, tell of the adventures and struggles of its life. This is worth sharing. There is a beauty in that history and those shapes and a value in honoring those lives that have been given up into the making of our buildings.

Honoring others goes far beyond the use of materials. We can honor the self-worth of carpenters and masons by giving them latitude to do their best rather than their least. We can honor our guests as the English do with a parlor or the Japanese with art and flowers in a *tokonoma*.

By using the traditional design wisdom of a region, we can honor the work, insights, and hard lessons of the past. By planting trees, we can honor a will to have a future. Providing opportunity for birds to nest, wildflowers to grow, and squirrels to play, we can honor the other lives with which we share our world. Whatever we honor—a television, children, a good cook—shows in how we design and use our buildings. Our buildings speak clearly of where we place our values.

The Art of Saying No

In an age of plenty, restraint (or learning to say "NO!") can be one of the most important means of giving value. What we leave out of a building can be as important as what we put into it. The trappings of comfort, convenience, and luxury often stand in the way of simplicity, peacefulness, and harmony. Richness, expense, and obvious beauty are not necessarily the best and deepest ways to move our hearts. Learning to let go of our limitless desires is as essential in our building as in our lives. Lao Tzu long ago reminded us that emptiness is the essence of a teacup, and that the shaping and forming of empty space is the essence of making both a room and a window.

Some opportunities to say no can unfold new potentials for wholeness. Saying no to a noisy automatic dishwasher releases funds for other uses in a building. It enhances the peaceful quietness of our homes, and opens opportunity for quiet meditation or talkative sharing while doing dishes. Taken farther, it leads to "Zen dishwashing"—using a single bowl and chopsticks, rinsing the bowl with tea, and drinking it, thus eliminating the need for others to wash our dishes.

Looking at the handling of human and household wastes leads to compost toilets or other ways to recycle our wastes to the fields and gardens, to ways of eliminating packaging, and maximizing recycling materials. All these leave indelible marks on our living patterns and the nature of our buildings.

The stark simplicity of the Ise Shrine of Japan stands as a dramatic example of the power of saying no—of setting a place apart from our actions and honing simplicity to an ethereal power.

Some things need to be discovered, not pointed to. A special view may be less to us if we find a bench pointing it out than if we discover it ourselves and come across a convenient wall to sit on while we enjoy it. A building that shouts for attention soon becomes tiresome. We need to put ourselves actively into discovering, absorbing and finding meaning in things, for any depth of experience or usable understanding to emerge. Unobtrusive surroundings provide the quietude to absorb, digest, and embrace the world with our deeper mental processes. Shadows are as important as sunlight.

A famous Japanese tea master was once given a piece of land with an outstanding view of the Inland Sea. When his teahouse was finished, his first guests arrived, eagerly awaiting the view. They were shocked to find that he had planted a hedge that totally blocked out the sea. Then as each bent to drink a dipperful of water before entering, a hidden opening in the hedge exposed a view of the waves breaking on the rocks below. The water in the dipper touched their lips as they saw the breakers below. Inside, when the master had finished the tea ceremony, he quietly slid aside the shoji screens, and the sense of water that still lingered on their lips (and in their hearts) was brought together with a vista of the sea below.

Cliff Palace, Mesa Verde National Park, Colorado

Love, Energy, and Giving

Every building that truly moves our hearts conveys one message above all. That message turns out to be of unhindered pouring forth of love and energy into its making.

This is the boundless energy of a universe that creates, in exquisite detail and variety, even its smallest and least significant elements. It is the love and perfection, as Wendell Berry notes, that an old woman pours into an intricate piece of crochet work she knows she will never live to finish. This unstinted giving is found in the hidden parts of Gothic cathedrals—work whose perfection is visible "only to the eyes of God" and to the heart of the builder. It spills forth in the exuberant carving of Indian temples or the intricate design of Persian carpets. It lies like a blinding white light within the spareness and purity of a Shinto shrine or Shaker chair, or in the embracing warm glow of a country hearth.

In some cultures this attitude of giving has been developed to great heights. Many temples of India are scarcely more than a spiritually centered framework to fill with sculpture. The temple construction is made possible through the giving of donors, and the sculpture itself is created as an act of devotion, offering, and spiritual growth by the worker.

Such an act of love or giving is the single most powerful act in making or using a place. The extra touch put into a door by its builder, the love with which a new marriage bed is built, the window added to see a favorite tree outside— all echo that love long beyond the lives of the makers. The most mundane building can be transformed through the spirit with which it is used, expressed in the flowers in the window, the well-scrubbed doorstep, or the smell of freshly baked bread. What counts is that someone has done the best, not the least, they could. And that comes not from necessity, but only from love.

Reflections in an Open Window

Giving our full attention to details in designing our places can uncover unexpected potentials. Mirrors, for example, may seem an inconsequential part of our homes. Yet getting rid of mirrors can do wonders for our spirits. We stop seeing and thinking about ourselves, stop being so concerned with the outside packaging of people and things, and become more attuned and responsive to important inner qualities.

Relocating a mirror inside a closet or medicine cabinet door or on the back of a bathroom door can make it available when needed, but out of sight and out of mind when not wanted. A mirror we cannot move can be covered with fabric when not in use, or we can tape pictures on it to cover it up. What would we really like to look at standing at the bathroom sink? An American bathroom with wall-to-wall mirrors looks into a very different world from that of a Japanese bath with a window open to a garden.

Giving our full attention to details, we begin to find where we have lost some of the richness of meaning we recognize in buildings of other ages. We see that Japanese architecture does not "flow" from inside to outside, but very specifically and carefully recognizes and creates places for being "in between." We discover that windows and entrances unfold into special places for joining the inside and the outside, the public and the private, places for the ceremonies of greeting and saying goodbye. We rediscover the specialness and infinite variety of window seats and doorsteps that occur when the two different worlds touch.

The Four Elements

A fireplace is an archetypal image of home, comfort, and security. It is so familiar we hardly pay attention to it. Experiencing fire, water, earth, or air intimately yet freshly, can add new vitality and meaning to our places. New feelings are awakened by curling up on a granite boulder still sun-warmed from the day, or napping on a rock nestled in an imprint made by a life form a hundred million years ago. Bathing outside in a tub with the snow falling around you, or inside with a fire or the moon reflected on the water; watching a butterfly wander in one open window and out another—things like this make new connections with the world around us.

In the end, all that really matters is that we approach wherever we live with full attention and an open heart. We must let our hearts guide us in deciding how we will inhabit that place. An open heart will embrace any new place and bring to it what is needed for a good life. It will find and make in it the "wholiness" that brings us to hold our places sacred. A bouquet of flowers, a song, the smell of freshly baked bread, an affectionate embrace, such things can transform any place into a happy, heart-warming abode.

24

Spirit of Place: The Modern *Relevance of an Ancient Concept*

KAZUO MATSUBAYASHI

*The seat of the soul is where the inner world
and the outer world meet. Where they overlap,
it is in every point of the overlap.*

Novalis[1]

Barry Lopez, in his book *Arctic Dreams*, tells the following story:

> A Chippewayan guide named Saltatha once asked a French priest what lay beyond the present life. "You have told me heaven is very beautiful," he said. "Now tell me one more thing. Is it more beautiful than the country of the musk-oxen in the summer, when sometimes the mist blows over the lakes, and sometimes the water is blue, and the loons cry very often? That is beautiful. If heaven is still more beautiful, I will be glad. I will be content to rest there until I am very old."[2]

In conventional Newtonian physics and mathematics, which are the foundations of modern positivism, space and time are uniformly distributed, neutral, and therefore, universal. These qualities constitute the Cartesian view, in which space is defined by x, y, and z coordinates, and time is measured by a universal clock. This spatial-temporal system is effective in formulating an intellectual explanation of the physical world. In this world, the position of matter can be precisely located and predicted, and yet every point is essentially the same as every other point on the grid. In other words, there is no "spirit of place," and we are attached neither to place nor to time.

Cultural expressions, on the other hand, are based on entirely different kinds of spatial-temporal systems. Their phenomena are existential, unique, and different at each

---

1. Robert Bly, *News of the Universe—Poems of Twofold Consciousness*, translated by Charles E. Passage (San Francisco: Sierra Club Books, 1980), p. 1.
2. Barry Lopez, *Arctic Dreams—Imagination and Desire in a Northern Landscape* (Toronto, New York, London, Sydney, Auckland: Bantam Books, 1987), p. 66.

moment and location. Cultural expressions show universality only at a structural level. Human beings have created various cultural space and time systems in order to maintain their spiritual relationship with the universe.

What is spirit of place?

Certain landscapes stir a sense of awe and admiration in people by their sheer presence. These landscapes have clearly visible and distinct shapes, sizes, and characteristics. They are like "landmarks," according to Kevin Lynch's term, and are "figures" according to Gestalt psychology. For example, the Japanese believe Mt. Fuji to be the most beautiful mountain in the world. It rises from sea level to nearly 13,000 feet and dominates its surroundings. It has been depicted in paintings, prints, poems, and literature from earliest times. The military regime of the Second World War claimed that Mt. Fuji symbolized the "true Japanese national character." Of course, many volcanic mountains around the world are spectacular. They have symmetrical, conical shapes with dramatic curb lines, resulting from the uplifting and the settling forces of explosion and gravity. Waterfalls, likewise, impress people and have been sites of worship in many cultures. Volcanic mountains and waterfalls are examples of landscapes whose unique physical features induce spirit of place.

The Chippewa scout mentioned in the story told by Barry Lopez, however, lived on the vast, barren, and featureless Arctic tundra. How do we discover spirit of place in ordinary environments?

Shinto mythology tells us that Japan is filled with 8 million *kami*—spirits or gods. Kami reside in rocks, trees, grasses, small hills, caves, tiny islands, rivers, oceans, and mountains; and in every snake, fox, and deer—literally everywhere and anywhere. The word for "spirit" in Japanese is *ki* (in Chinese *chi*) which means "air," "breath," "atmosphere," "source of vitality," or "life." The translation of ki as breath or air suggests that kami are invisible sources of life surrounding us all the time. To mark their presence, Japanese people attach simple, white paper ornaments or tie ropes around things where kami are supposed to reside. Sometimes a small area of forest is cleared and paved with gravel. These places, called *shiki*, are areas where kami will appear to communicate with humans. To awaken the spirits, one

claps hands twice or rattles a bell hanging at the entry
of the shrine. (Levi-Strauss noted that in almost all societies,
sounds are used to bring out spirits.)

The most unique aspects of Shintoism are the ideas of
kiyome, harai, or *misogi* (cleansing and purification), and
kegare (polluting or defiling). Shinto monks perform rituals
to cleanse and purify polluted air and to dispel evil spirits.
As Shinto's kami are air-like entities, maintaining clean
air is essential. Throwing a handful of salt purifies defiled
air. In fact, the Japanese word *sumu* which means "dwell,"
originated from the homophonic word *sumu* which means
"clear water" and "air." The human body, as the receptor
of spirits, must be washed thoroughly before any rituals
are conducted. Many shrines and temples were built on
spring sites. Before entering shrines, visitors wash their
hands and rinse their mouths with clean spring water from
stone basins. The Christian baptism ceremony and the
Hindu custom of bathing in the Ganges are similar. For
Japanese people bathing is more than a simple, daily
hygienic activity; it is a ritual. On New Year's Day, people
plunge into or swim in cold rivers to cleanse themselves
for the year. Many make pilgrimages to holy waterfalls
and sit under pounding water to dispel evil spirits. Going
to a hot springs resort with family and friends is more
than leisure; it is an opportunity to cleanse body and soul.
Bathing naked together with others is a symbolic gesture
which signifies becoming a family member.

Because Japan is mountainous country, mountains play
a vital role in shaping people's living environments. The
world *oyama* sometimes means "shrine." The word was
derived from *yama,* meaning "mountain." Mountains
themselves were considered to be shrines which connect
the earth and the sky. Tadahiko Higuchi, in his article
"The Visual and the Spatial Structure of Landscape,"
describes seven prototype configurations for shrine and
temple complexes. They are: 1) "Water-Distributing" type;
2) "Bowl" type; 3) "Lotus Flower Calyx" type; 4) "Wind
and Water" type; 5) "Valley" type; 6) "Thickly-Forested,
Small Mountain Located Near Plain" type, and 7) "Country-
Viewing Mountain" type.[3] Each prototype served a unique
purpose:

---

3. Tadahiko Higuchi, *The Visual and the Spatial Structure of Landscape*
(Tokyo: Gihodo, 1975), pp. 166-168. Descriptions of these types have been
edited and translated by this author.

1. Water-Distributing: In rice farming, water irrigation is vital, therefore, shrines were often built at the first intake of water flowing from a mountain, at the head of slightly inclined basins. The god always looked down at the rice paddies, while farmers looked up at the god. The stream flowing from the up-paddies to the down-paddies was regarded as the god's road.

2. Bowl: According to legend, the first Emperor, Jimmu, founded his capital in Akitsushima-Yamato, a small, peaceful plain surrounded on all sides by green mountains, which served as boundaries, separating the place from the external world. The fact that Akitsu-Yamato was small coincides with one of the important conditions identified for an intimate place by E. Minkowski, author of *Espace, intime, habitat*. This layout was popular because tree-covered mountains were at a short distance, and the changes of seasons could be felt intimately through colors of the leaves.

3. Lotus Flower Calyx: Kukai (774-835 A.D.), one of the great Buddhist monks, built an esoteric temple on Mt. Koya. The mountain temple, surrounded by eight other mountains, was thought to look like the calyx of a lotus flower, the symbol of the Buddha's Pure Land. Again, a feeling of sacredness was created by the surrounding mountains.

4. Wind and Water: The idea of *fusui* (wind and water) is based on the view that the land contains a vital force. Terrain where this force cannot be blown away by winds and is secured by water is an ideal place to build a city, house, or tomb. Such terrain normally has mountains to the north, hills to the east and west, and a sea or river to the south. Sites chosen for the old capitals, like Nara, Kyoto, and Kamakura, as well as many palaces and temples, belong to this type.

5. Valley: A canyon is a narrow, dark, and quiet space enclosed on both sides by mountains and reached by going up a stream. The ancient people believed canyons to be places where the spirits of the dead hid themselves.

6. Thickly-Forested, small mountain located near Plain: Located near a settlement on the plain, this type of temple site has a low mountain or hill covered by thick foliage. The shape of the site is in sharp contrast to the surrounding plains. Not only was this site believed to be a sacred place where the god dwelt, but it also served as the focus of a village. Even today, there are many sacred places of this type which one is forbidden to enter.

7. Country-viewing Mountain: Like the previous type, this type has a low mountain or hill located near a plain or standing in the middle of a plain. The site commands a good view of the surrounding area. On such spots,

farmers and rulers held agricultural rites every spring,
praising the good spirit of the earth and praying for a
rich harvest. The difference between this and the previous
type is that people can enter into these areas to perform
rites while looking down at their own villages.

Shrine and temple compounds often have an ecological
aspect as well. Temple sites often occupy large pieces of
land, densely filled with large trees and other plants. Birds
and animals often find refuge there. During the time of
the Meiji Reformation, the government tried to combine
smaller shrines and temples so that each village had only
one shrine or temple. The Meiji government's goal was
to save money and to free up land for development, a very
rational policy indeed. Kumagusu Minakata, a natural
historian of the Meiji period, vigorously opposed the
proposed regulation (1911). He pointed out that shrines
serve as escape areas in case of disasters such as earthquakes
and fires, and as economically viable, outdoor market
places during festival times.[4] According to Shinto belief,
disturbing the spirits brings calamity to society. Today
shrines and temples are the last buffers in the city against
commercial and industrial encroachment. They are no longer
just religious sanctuaries, but also act as communal,
ecological assets.

Zen Buddhism has had a profound influence on the
Japanese attitude toward nature and the arts. Depending on
one's tradition, the essential goal of Buddhism is either
the attainment of nirvana or satori, which means freedom
from the sufferings of this life, or the attainment of complete
enlightenment, called Buddhahood. Zen appealed to the
Japanese sensitivity because it shares some Shinto ideals, i.e.,
simplicity and a close relationship to nature. Like Shintoism,
Zen Buddhism holds that every thing has life. Zen values
action rather than words. This attitude led Zen to embrace
the arts and the martial arts. Arts are intuitive, disciplined
actions, not intellectual speculations or arguments. To
practice art is to practice Buddhism. Through art, one
grasps the meanings of life and attains nirvana; therefore,
art becomes a matter of daily activity. Tea, flower arrangement, calligraphy, pottery, *sumie* (brush painting), poetry,
architecture, garden design, archery, swordsmanship, and,

---

4. Yoshio Nakamura, *Fukeigaku* (Tokyo: Chuokoron Publishing, 1981), p.
22.

in fact, almost every activity becomes art. As one tea master said, "All these years I thought I was pursuing the way of tea, but indeed, it was the way of Buddha."[5] Zen's view of the arts is associated with the Taoist ideal of living, in which one is connected with the spirit of the universe.

Attachment and Caring

An acquaintance of mine, a visiting professor from Japan, once told me, "I have heard much Western music, including Beethoven and Mozart, but I honestly believe Japanese Koto music is the most beautiful of all music." Japanese people often have an equally difficult time appreciating the American landscape. For visitors from Japan, Utah's desert landscapes are spectacular, but not necessarily beautiful. One visitor even remarked, "It reminded me of Hell." My mother-in-law, looking at the Grand Canyon, said, "Well, this is certainly out of this world. But I really don't know whether I should say this is beautiful; it is almost scary. This is so different from the landscape I am used to." Another young woman musician, after living in Salt Lake City for six months, told me that the brown, bare mountains appeared so foreign to her that she could not feel at home here.

In my case, five years passed before I began to perceive the beauty of the barren western deserts. This revelation came to me while I was driving through northern Nevada on my way home to Salt Lake City from San Francisco. I had driven the route along U.S. I-80 many times before and always thought the landscape boring, featureless, and desolate. This time, however, as the sun was setting, I suddenly found myself in this glowing reddish-brown desert like in a dream, and was awe-struck by its beauty. In 1976, my family and I spent a year in Japan for my sabbatical. Returning to Salt Lake City, we all felt like we were coming home. It had taken us seven years to feel the sense of home in a foreign land. Attachment to a place is a prerequisite for developing a sense of the spirit of the place. Caring evolves through attachment to a place. As one puts down roots in a certain location and becomes familiar with the surroundings, one begins to distinguish

5. Hiroshi Hara, *Space—From Function to Modality* (Iwanami Publishing, 1987), p. 119.

subtle differences in even the most ordinary landscapes.

A detailed understanding of the workings of nature was a matter of survival for primitives and early settlers. Findings about the environment became communal information; then the memories of these findings were transferred to the next generation. Attachment results when people perceive the order of nature, feel its regularity and rhythm, and identify its spatial-temporal reference points. Beyond the intellectual matter of obtaining knowledge for survival, attachment provides emotional and spiritual stability to both individuals and the community.

Attachment is both a physiological and a psychological interaction with the environment. Gaston Bachelard's phenomenological study of the house, *The Poetics of Space*, describes how the physical house and our inner psyche become inseparable.[6] Frank Lloyd Wright understood the idea of a house as a home—that is, the spirit of place. International-style architecture ignored it, as rational functionalism tended to emphasize detachment from nature. Attachment is an existential and phenomenological experience. Our body and physiology become attuned to temperature, humidity, rain, snow, changes of season, sound, smell, and other sensations, and we grow accustomed to certain local crops, foods, ways of cooking, and to the local water. We adjust, plant roots, and grow in the environment; and we are shaped by it. The idea of caring was important to Zen artists, who paid particular attention to craftsmanship, material quality, and details. Caring is not only for survival, but for maintaining spiritual relationships with people, things, and the environment. A simple routine of backyard gardening begins to change one's attitude toward nature and things. Taking care of things is satisfying.

As one settles and becomes attached to a location, one activates space and time, and turns them into places and events which become meaningful in our daily lives. We mark a space with signs and decorations to distinguish it from other places, and we punctuate time with rites of transition. Spirit of place exists in this interactive zone where nature and human interaction shape each other. Kukai, the esoteric monk who shared the Zen view of nature, said, "Landscape changes as one's soul changes." However,

---

6. Bachelard.

some cautions must be made in this context about attachment and religion. Sometimes attachment to place combined with religion leads to the creation of a self-centered culture, as was the case with the nationalist fascist regime in Japan during the Second World War, with its fanatic devotion to Shinto purity. Each culture is a unique center, but a culture also needs to accept that it is only one part of a world in which many cultures coexist.

Shikake

We also reshape environment according to our needs and desires. It is in this relationship with nature that civilization since the Renaissance has made a drastic reversal: humans became the center of the universe. Every society and civilization seems to develop a peculiar way of seeing the universe. For example, in modern times, our views have been dominated by rational functionalism. In architecture, "form follows function" has become a dictum. For example, each machine has a specific task or function to perform. For a machine to be effective, its variables must be limited, the fewer the better, therefore, most machines are single-task oriented. Reducing variables is really preselecting a problem and ignoring others, or, at best, attacking one problem at a time. Modern people, with powerful technology, have drastically altered nature to suit their needs, mostly for materialistic, economic gains.

There is a Japanese term *shikake* which reflects a different human attitude toward nature and society. *Shikake* means "a plot," "a clever plan," and "a trick." It is an artful, intelligent, shrewd, and creative device which can be used in either a physical or a non-physical situation. It is a multilayered, paradoxical mechanism with an equivocal character. Shikake is fictional as well as real; and, above all, it deals with meanings. In architecture, for example, a gas furnace is simply a heating machine—a very efficient, technological, single-function element, normally hidden away in the basement. A fireplace, on the other hand, is not only for heating; it is a sort of central and formal element of a house—a hearth around which a family gathers for special occasions. The mantlepiece acts as a picture or trophy shelf, a place of memories. A furnace does not add meaning to a house, but a fireplace, as shikake, activates space.

Another example of shikake is the *torii*, or Japanese shrine gate. A torii is not really a functional structure; it demarcates the entry into a Shinto compound. The great red torii at Miyajima Shrine, for example, stands in the inland sea. This shrine is dedicated to the sea god protecting fishermen and vessels. In mid-July, a sea festival takes place there on the day of the full moon, when the biggest tidal height occurs. In the morning, when the tide is still high, hundreds of boats sail through the torii. As the tide recedes in the afternoon, the boats go aground, and the fishermen and other boaters eat, drink, and sing. With nightfall, the full moon rises, and the tide returns again. With the colorfully decorated shrine boat at the head, all the boats leave the shrine area through the torii. Thus at Miyajima once a year, the natural phenomenon of the full moon, the human desire for celebration, and religion are all brought together.

Perhaps this Japanese custom could be adapted to the American landscape. There could be festivals for rivers, mountains, lakes, waterfalls, deserts, canyons, islands, and seas; and for corn, potatoes, lobsters, crabs, salmon, whales, and giant redwoods. People could create art works, poems and songs, stories and markers to celebrate natural phenomena, showing where our livelihoods come from, how we are related to nature, and how to preserve it. For example, there could be a festival for the Mississippi River, with participants from towns all the way from Minneapolis to New Orleans.

American artist Nancy Holt has created another kind of artistic celebration of nature with her sculpture titled "Sun Tunnels," located in the remote northwestern Utah desert. It takes nearly three hours of driving from Salt Lake City through desolate landscape to get to the sculpture. It consists of four concrete cylinders, eight feet in inside diameter, each eighteen feet long. The four tunnels are aligned with the angles of the rising and the setting of the sun on the days of the solstices, forming an X-configuration. In the upper half of the cylinders, small holes are punctured which correspond to four constellations—Draco, Perseus, Columba, and Capricorn. Nancy Holt describes her impressions of camping alone there: "I had a strong sense that I was linked, through thousands of years of human time, with the people who had lived in the caves around there for so long. I was sharing the same landscape with them.">[8] When my wife and I visited there, a dust storm swept across the desert, blowing tumble weeds; and we could not observe the summer solstice sunset. Nature has her own way. The wind reminded us that people like the Navajo rejected the idea of leaving marks or scars on the earth's face; like the wind, the Navajo erased all traces when they left a place.

In the Japanese tea ceremony, an ordinary daily routine is elevated to an art form. Having a cup of tea in a quiet moment cleanses the mind and body. A tea room is as small as six feet by six feet, barely large enough for two persons. Tea is meditative; in silence our body and soul become fully alert, sensing the slightest stir of sound, the scent of flowers, the aroma of tea, and the changes of light quality. In a small space, we become attentive. Through gentle conversation, we renew friendship and activate spirit of place. The tea ceremony is shikake, or a performance to create a moment of spiritual experience. Someone said the tea house is the smallest architecture which expresses the ideals of reduction. Teiji Itoh says, "A tea garden is as a passage to a house deep in the mountain."[9]

All-Things-In-All-Things

We feel the spirituality of our existence when we have a sense of connection to other things and to the universe. This view is reflected in the idea of "all-things-in-all-things." Anaxagoras, the Greek naturalist, proposed a theory about the physical world which states: "There is a portion of every thing, i.e., of every stuff, in every thing, but each is and was most manifestly those things of which there is most in it."[10] The Neoplatonist philosophers postulated that "The levels of being, though distinct, are not separate, but are all intimately present everywhere and in everyone. Each sphere of being is an image or expression of a lower level of the sphere above it."[11] These philosophers remind us that even in the most minute things, the universe is revealed. Macrocosm is reflected in microcosm. The notion

---

8. Nancy Holt, "Sun Tunnels," *Artforum*, April 1977, pp. 32-37.

9. *The Japan Architect*, 8409, p. 64.

10. Helen Heminway Benton, "Anaxagoras," *Encyclopaedia Britannica*, 1978, I, 345.

11. Helen Hemingway Benton, "Platonism and Neoplatonism," *Encyclopaedia Brittanica*, 1978, XIV, 541.

of the universe as the projection of our own bodies was prevalent in many early cultures; and, at the same time, the universe was often thought to be inside of the body. A small tea house is the universe itself. The world is contained even in a tiny cup, as in the following poem:

> Inside this clay jug there are canyons and pine
> mountains, and the makers of canyons and pine
> mountains! All seven oceans are inside, and
> hundreds of millions of stars. The acid that
> tests gold is there, and the one who judges
> jewels. And the music from the strings that no
> one touches, and the source of all water.
> "The Clay Jug," Kabir[12]

The photograph of the Earth taken from the Moon gave us a sense of spirituality, largely due to this sense of all-things-in-all-things. The Earth appeared like a giant molecule, and humans like subatomic particles within it. Indeed, the whole Earth is a garden requiring constant care. The Earth emanates spirit of place in the darkness of the universe.

Story Telling

Story telling preserves spirit of place. Mythology is a form of story telling, a non-physical shikake. Childhood memories stay with us most of our lives and often shape our view of nature. Shintoism was really a collection of stories.

Terry Tempest Williams has most vividly written about story telling. Here I would like to quote from her book *Pieces of White Shells.*[13]

> I can look for my own stories embedded in the landscapes I travel through. A story allows us to envision the possibility of things. It draws on the powers of memory and imagination. (p. 3)
> Story telling is the oldest form of education. (p. 4)
> We must create and find our own stories, our own myths, with symbols that will bind us to the world as we see it today. In so doing, we will better know how to live our lives in the midst of change. (p. 5)
> To tell a story you must travel inward. We have all been

---

12. Bly.
13. Terry Tempest Williams, *Pieces of White Shells—a Journey to Navajoland* (Albuquerque: Univ. of New Mexico Press, 1983).

nurtured on stories. Story is the umbilical cord that connects us to the past, present, and future. Family. Story is a relationship between the teller and the listener, a responsibility. After the listening you become accountable for the sacred knowledge that has been shared. Shared knowledge equals power. Energy. Strength. Story is an affirmation of our ties to one another. (p. 129-30)
The Kalahari Bushmen have said, "A story is like the wind. It comes from a far-off place, and we feel it." Those things that are most personal, are most general, and are, in turn, most trusted. Stories bind. They are connective tissues. They are basic to who we are. A story has a composite personality which grows out of its community. It maintains a stability within that community, providing common knowledge as to how things are, how things should be— knowledge based in experience. These stories become the conscience of the group. They belong to every one. (p. 135)

When Japanese visit famous landscapes, what they see are composites of nature superimposed with images created by artists, such as the poetry of Manyoshu, Basho's haiku, Hokusai and Hiroshige's prints. The landscapes are full of stories. In fact, for the Japanese, nature is created by the arts, or as Oscar Wilde said, "Nature copies art."

The Newtonian system is useful in making maps, such as road and contour maps, land use maps, forestry and other natural resource maps, weather maps, etc. Through a universal language, maps illustrate factual information necessary to solve our pressing ecological problems. But can they really? Aren't maps more likely to be used to exploit nature? Maps are scientific, intellectual views of the physical world seen from outside. What is critically necessary is a phenomenological understanding of nature from the inside. The views of phenomenology and Zen are very sympathetic in this respect.

Today, a global society is emerging in which technology, international economics and law, and instant electronic information (all universal and neutral) eliminate differences and create a sense of identity between various points of the world. The end result is homogenous space, as described by the architect Hiroshi Hara.[14] Concurrently, the same forces are reducing varieties in nature, causing the most critical problem of all—namely, ecological crisis. Japan,

---

14. Hiroshi Hara, *Space—From Function to Modality* (Iwanami Publishing, 1987), pp. 23-83.

probably more than any other nation, has experienced a drastic change in its physical environmental conditions. The Japanese have paid dearly in trying to Westernize and industrialize the country. Philosophers, anthropologists, artists, designers, and writers are all searching for ways to restore the once beautiful nature which surrounded their daily life. Could it be that the ideals of rational positivism and functionalism are the cause of these problems? Globalization and industrialization are inevitable, but in order to get out of this vicious cycle, we need to make a fundamental shift in our attitude toward nature. The notions of Shikake and of all-things-in-all-things must replace functionalism and rational positivism. We need to turn neutral space and time into meaningful places and events. In order to navigate in the world of spirits, we need new maps—mental, psychic, metaphysical, maps by artists, and even invisible maps—which reflect our inner worlds.

25

People-Environment Relations: Instrumental and Spiritual Views

DANIEL STOKOLS

Philosophical Foundations of People-Environment Research

The study of people-environment relations emerged as a distinctive scientific field during the last two decades, marked by the establishment of new journals, monograph series, handbooks, professional societies, and both regional and international conferences. Yet, the philosophical roots of people-environment studies span several centuries and cultural contexts. Examples of these early precedents include the religious traditions of Shinto and Buddhism and the more recent writings of 19th and 20th Century scientists and philosophers.

The present discussion is not intended to provide an historical overview of these philosophical and scientific traditions. Excellent analyses of these developments are available elsewhere. Rather, I will focus on three distinctive views of people-environment relations that I believe are reflected in the contemporary scientific literature: namely, the minimalist, instrumental, and spiritual perspectives. Having contrasted the key assumptions underlying these orientations, I will discuss some important tensions between the instrumental and spiritual perspectives and the challenges that they pose for future research.

The Minimalist View

This perspective assumes that physical environments exert minimal or negligible influence on the behavior, health, and well-being of their users. This assumption was prevalent among designers and behavioral scientists prior to the mid-1960s. Aside from meeting people's needs for safe and comfortable shelter, designers felt free to indulge their own aesthetic whims without concern for the occupants' environmental preferences. Similarly, researchers all but ignored the links between physical environmental conditions, human health, and behavior.

An example of the minimalist perspective is Herzberg's (1966) characterization of the physical environment at work as a "hygiene factor"—something that detracts from job satisfaction when its quality is very low but cannot improve employee morale at moderate or even high levels of quality. According to Herzberg, employee motivation and morale depend primarily on economic and social incentives at work, but are minimally related to the physical quality of the workplace. Maslow's (1962) theory of psychological health and "self-actualization" also reflects a minimalist stance toward the environment. While recognizing that the physical and social environment serves basic human needs for shelter and security, Maslow contends that the environment ultimately impedes psychological growth and autonomy and, therefore, must be "transcended." In his words, "I feel we must leap . . . to the clear recognition of transcendence of the environment, independence of it, ability to stand against it, to fight it, to neglect it, or to turn one's back on it (p. 180)."

The minimalist view of people-environment relations was abruptly challenged by the global dilemmas of the 1960s, including the foreboding "silent spring" of environmental pollution (Carson, 1962), the "population bomb" (Ehrlich, 1968), and the "tragedy of the commons" (Hardin, 1968). Suddenly, the world was awakened to the very real and immediate impacts of the physical environment on human health and behavior. The emergence of people-environment studies during the late 1960s reflected widespread rejection of the minimalist perspective. The rapid growth of this field over the past two decades has been fueled by efforts to replace minimalist thinking with alternative conceptions of environment and behavior in which the strategic design of physical settings is seen as a vehicle for promoting human effectiveness and well-being.

The Instrumental View

The instrumental perspective views the physical environment as a means for achieving important behavioral and economic goals. This "means-ends" orientation is clearly reflected in the functionalist or Modern movement in architecture and in the positivist tradition of behavioral science. The instrumental view pervades much of the recent research on strategic facilities planning. As noted by Becker and Sims (1986, p. 68), "corporations have begun to realize that their facilities can have a substantial effect on organizational and individual performance and productivity." Similarly, Brill, Margulis, and Konar (1984, p. 27) state that "we can reconceptualize the office as a tool and not just as a place to house tools. It is not such a conceptual leap, for Webster defines a tool as 'something that serves as a means to an end; an instrument by which something is effected or accomplished.' "

Instrumental analyses of people-environment relations measure the quality of environments by their capacity to promote not only behavioral and economic efficiency, but also enhanced levels of occupants' comfort, safety, and well-being. For example, architecture has been described as an instrument for promoting public health and for enhancing the therapeutic effectiveness of health care facilities. Increasingly, empirical evidence for the health and behavioral effects of the physical environment is being used as the basis for revising existing building codes and for developing new design standards and guidelines.

From an instrumental perspective, research is viewed as an objective process by which knowledge is discovered and used to achieve technological solutions to environmental problems. Research activities are assumed to be value-neutral and as separate from the social dynamics observed and recorded within particular settings. Emphasis is placed on the refinement of standardized research tools for gathering reliable and valid data. Generally, quantitative methods are emphasized over qualitative techniques.

The Spiritual View

A third philosophical orientation that has received increasing attention in recent years is the spiritual view of people-environment relations. This perspective stands in contrast to instrumentalist views of the environment in several respects. First, spiritually-oriented analyses construe the sociophysical environment as an end in itself rather than as a tool—as a context in which fundamental human values can be cultivated and the human spirit can be enriched. Environmental settings are designed not only to facilitate the smooth performance of everyday activities but also to provide places to which people are drawn by virtue of their symbolic and affective qualities. The overall quality of environments is measured in terms of the richness of their psychological and sociocultural meanings, as well as in relation to physical comfort, safety, and performance criteria. Moreover, rather than encouraging the development of standardized, technical solutions to environmental problems, the spiritual view of environment and behavior assigns greater value to customized, indigenous design strategies that give expression to the unique needs and identities of particular user groups. These and other differences between the instrumental and spiritual perspectives are summarized in Table 1.

An emphasis on the spiritual dimensions of environment and behavior is evident in numerous religious, architectural, and social-scientific works. According to the religious precepts of Shintoism, for example, physical settings are designed to invoke sacred spirits and to foster a deep reverence for nature. Recent architectural and social science theories also highlight the symbolic and spiritual facets of environmental design. Franck (1987, p. 65), in her review of developments in architectural theory, observes that designers are turning away from positivism and functionalism and "are becoming increasingly interested in history, culture, myth, and meaning." For instance, Jencks (1985) calls for a symbolic architecture in which clients and designers develop "iconographic programs"—written statements of symbolic design intentions—that are as explicit as their economic contracts. Similarly, Perez-Gomez (1983) emphasizes the poetic aspects of architecture while Alexander, Anninou, Black, and Rheinfrank (1987, p. 129) advocate a "new sensibility" in design, "in which human activity, human feeling, color, and light together create an ordinary human sweetness, something almost entirely missing from the works of this century."

Much of the recent work in environmental psychology, sociology, geography, and anthropology has addressed the issue of environmental symbolism, suggesting that physical objects and places gradually acquire social meaning through their association over time with group activities and experiences. This symbolically-oriented research distinguishes organized social settings from unoccupied or sporadically occupied places, in the sense that the physical milieu of the former has acquired "social image-ability"—the capacity to evoke vivid and widely-held social meanings among their occupants. Once established, the symbolic qualities of the physical environment become a "surrogate" source of social influence—their impact on individuals' emotions and behavior can occur even in the absence of direct interpersonal contact.

Studies of the symbolic and spiritual dimensions of environments generally use qualitative methods to assess occupants' perceptions of environmental meanings. Such research often establishes a communication process for sensitizing occupants to alternative environmental meanings and for articulating and strengthening their values. Thus, rather than remaining aloof and objectively neutral, the research team becomes an active part of the observed setting, thereby exerting a transformative influence on the social organization and physical form of the environment (see my *Handbook of Environmental Psychology*, 1987).

Table I

Differences Between Instrumental and Spiritual Views of People-Environment Relations

Instrumental	*Spiritual*
• environment viewed as a "tool," as a means for achieving behavioral and economic goals	• environment viewed as an end in itself, as a context in which human values can be cultivated
• emphasis on material features of the environment	• emphasis on symbolic and affective features of the environment
• environmental quality defined primarily in terms of	• quality of environments measured in terms of the

Instrumental	*Spiritual*
behavioral, comfort, and health criteria	richness of their psychological and sociocultural meanings, as well as their comfort, healthfulness, and behavioral supports

- emphasis on the development of design standards and environmental prototypes in accord with the activity requirements of general user-group categories (reliance on exogenous design guidelines)
- emphasis on the distinctness and separation of key functions associated with public and private life domains

- designed environments viewed as relatively stable and inanimate; little attention given to the generative and regenerative qualities of environmental settings

- research viewed as the discovery and application of generalizable knowledge; research activities assumed to be value-neutral and as separate from the social dynamics observed and recorded within particular settings; greater emphasis on quantitative than on qualitative methods

- emphasis on customized design in keeping with the unique needs of specific individuals and groups (development of indigenous design guidelines that are suited to specific contexts)
- emphasis on the integration of public and private domains, and the increasingly multifunctional nature of environmental settings

- designed environments viewed as dynamic and organic extensions of individuals and groups, and as capable of serving as "social surrogates" (e.g., through symbolic communication of social support)

- research viewed as a communication process that can enhance the awareness, participation, and cohesion of environmental users; as a process for articulating and strengthening the values of participants; equal emphasis given to qualitative and quantitative methods

Current Tensions Posed by the Instrumental and Spiritual Perspectives

The preceding discussion outlines some of the contrasting assumptions associated with minimalist, instrumental, and spiritual views of people-environment relations. This brief sketch reveals certain philosophical tensions, especially between the instrumental and spiritual views of environment and behavior.

One source of tension is the potential contradictions that can arise between the instrumental and symbolic meanings of physical objects and places. For example, the incorporation of new technologies and efficient furnishings within an office may convey managerial commitment to improving employee productivity and morale. However, if the newly-installed equipment is unequally distributed among high- and low-status workers, then these physical objects can become a symbol of alienation and deprivation for many members of the setting. In Merton's (1957) terminology, the manifest instrumental meanings of the environment can be at odds with its latent symbolism. The material elements of the office are configured to maximize efficiency and cost-effectiveness. But at a symbolic level, the organization of the setting sorely lacks what Mannheim (1940) referred to as "substantial rationality," or intelligent insight into the interrelations among participants and events within a given situation.

The inherent tensions between instrumental and spiritual views of environment and behavior may be intensified incoming years by society's growing reliance on high technology and increasing emphasis on the regulatory and public health implications of environmental design. From an instrumental perspective, design technology is seen as a powerful tool for enhancing human health and productivity. As scientific evidence for the health and behavioral effects of the environment continues to mount, there will be greater pressure to apply that information toward the development of design standards and prototypes which can be incorporated within a wide variety of settings.

While a considerable body of scientific evidence already exists for the behavioral and health impacts of the physical environment, the links between environmental design and spiritual enrichment are less well understood. Therein lies the potential contradiction between the pursuit of technological innovation and questions of human value. On the one hand, the search for prototypical design solutions gives priority to the goals of standardization and cost-effectiveness. On the other hand, prototypical and technically-based design strategies are often at odds with occupants' desire for personalized, customized, and socially distinctive surroundings. For example, the "new sensibility" in architecture espoused by Alexander et al. (1987, p. 140) is ". . . by its nature, personal and unique. It is non-mechanistic, concerned with feeling and life. It creates deep feeling because it relies on deep feeling during the process of creation."

Technologically-oriented approaches to environmental design are based on additional assumptions that downplay the symbolic and spiritual dimensions of environments. For example, technical analyses often view the physical components of settings as independent "levers" for achieving desired effects on occupants' behavior and well-being. Also, environmental settings are grouped according to certain key functions (e.g., residential, employment, school, and public recreational settings) and design solutions are developed to support those functions. Alternatively, spiritual views of people-environment relations emphasize the close interdependence between physical and social aspects of the environment and the fact that organized settings often incorporate multiple functions and user groups. These latter assumptions suggest that especially within complex, multi-functional settings, it will be extremely difficult if not impossible to leverage human performance and morale through technological interventions alone, which focus almost entirely on physical features of the environment. Instead, efforts to enhance environmental quality and human well-being may rely increasingly on more integrative analyses of the links between physical, social, and organizational structure, which recognize the diverse needs and interests of multiple groups.

Interestingly, "multifunctional" settings may become more and more prevalent in future years. Brill (1987) has suggested that the distinction between public and private domains has undergone considerable blurring in recent years. Others have noted trends toward "telecommuting" between home and the workplace via computers (Galitz, 1984), job-sharing and diversified household structures (Michelson, 1985), and mixed land-use planning that combines commercial, residential, and recreational functions within the same geographical area (Francis, 1987). If these trends continue, environmental settings will be expected to accommodate increasingly disparate instrumental and spiritual functions. Already, residential and work settings are being modified to support many of the same kinds of activities and experiences. This increasing fusion of environmental functions suggests important challenges for future theorizing and research on people-environment relations. A key challenge is to develop new concepts and research methods that foster greater coordination, rather than polarization, between instrumental and spiritual views of environment and behavior.

Challenges and Future Prospects for Environmental Design Research

The tensions between instrumental and spiritual views of environment and behavior, noted earlier, suggest several conceptual, methodological, and professional challenges that remain to be addressed in environmental design research. For example, the contradictions that sometimes arise between instrumental and symbolic aspects of environments suggest the importance of distinguishing among settings in terms of their degree of "multifunctionality." Some recreational, domestic, and work settings may be associated with highly compartmentalized functions while others incorporate a wide range of individual and group activities, and a correspondingly diverse set of instrumental and symbolic meanings.

The greater complexity of multifunctional settings raises some important issues for future research. First, to the extent that settings are associated with multiple functions and user groups, the potential for "counter-productive programming" (Mazumdar, 1984) may increase due to the diverse and sometimes competing interests among activities and occupants. In such situations, sophisticated programming and assessment techniques are required to identify the unique preferences of different user groups and the multiple symbolic meanings conveyed by the physical environment. A related task is the development of qualitative and quantitative techniques for assessing the clarity, complexity, and compatibility of symbolic meanings conveyed by a particular environment. Such methods could be used to identify settings in which the instrumental and spiritual needs of occupants are coordinated and consistent, or disjointed and contradictory.

An additional direction for future research is to examine the spiritual qualities of environments in greater detail, and to identify the physical and social attributes of settings that contribute to individuals' experiences of spiritual enrichment. More specifically, what environmental and social arrangements are most closely associated with feelings of esteem, autonomy, insight, competence, coherence, tranquility, restoration, social acceptance and belongingness; or, in the words of René Dubos (1965, p. 279), with a "reverence for the past, love for the present, and hope for the future"? The potential links between these basic human values and experiences, and alternative environmental arrangements, have scarcely been addressed in environmental design research.

Previous studies suggest that physical elements such as artwork, music, color, fragrances, graphic symbols, interior plantscaping, natural lighting and views of verdant parks may function as "environmental associators"—as elements that can enhance the attractiveness and emotional appeal of interior and outdoor settings. At the same time, however, the question remains as to how effectively these design elements can enhance occupants' sense of attachment to the setting and the quality of their spiritual experiences, in the absence of sustained organizational and social supports. Along these lines, some theorists suggest that the symbolic meaning and spiritual quality of environments must be cultivated or "choreographed" over time through repeated rituals and group activities.

Turning from these conceptual and methodological issues, I want to mention some more general issues, concerning professional training and research collaboration, that are raised by instrumental and spiritual views of environment and behavior. First, the spiritual perspective with its emphasis on human values and enrichment moves ethical concerns from the background to the forefront of environmental design research and training. Within minimalist and instrumental analyses, planning decisions are based on the aesthetic whims of the designer or on managerial concerns about organizational cost-effectiveness. From a spiritual perspective, however, design decisions are explicitly guided by considerations of occupants' emotional and physical well-being, and by consultative and participatory processes that reveal the diverse interests and environmental preferences of setting members.

The complexities of ethical decision-making are most pronounced within functionally-diverse settings that are comprised of multiple user groups. It is in such situations that the adjudication of competing interests and environmental preferences becomes most challenging. Assuming that multifunctional settings will become increasingly prevalent in the future, ethical dilemmas are likely to become more salient within the arena of environmental planning and design. Thus, as Tzamir and Churchman (1984) observed earlier, it is essential that ethical issues and participatory processes be incorporated into the core curricula of environmental design and research training programs.

Clearly, one of the most pressing ethical issues of the 1990s is the achievement of world peace and international cooperation. The quest for personalized environments and the strengthening of local culture must be balanced by the realization that global stability is vitally dependent on cross-regional collaboration and understanding. As researchers, we can make greater collaborative efforts to integrate the concepts and findings from our respective regions. Eventually, we may even develop a system of "global icons"—pictorial and graphic symbols of human fellowship that can be displayed within public and private settings to remind us of our common global interests and responsibilities. Ultimately, we must find ways to promote a better balance between the instrumental objectives of high technology and the spiritual dimensions of environmental design.

Notes

1. For discussions of these historical developments and philosophical traditions, see Altman & Rogoff (1987); Canter and

Donald (1987); Hagino, Mochizuki, and Yamamoto (1987); Jodelet (1987); Kruse and Graumann (1987); Kuller (1987); Moore (1987); Niit, Heidmets, and Kruusvall (1987); Sanchez, Wiesenfeld, and Cronick (1987); Stringer & Kremer (1987); Thorne and Hall (1987); Wapner (1987); and Wicker (1987).

References

Alexander, C., Anninou, A., & Black, G., & Rheinfrank, J. (1987). Toward a personal workplace. *Architectural Record Interiors*, 129-141.

Altman, I., & Rogoff, B. (1987). World views in psychology: Trait, interactional, organismic, and transactional perspectives. In D. Stokols & I. Altman (eds.), *Handbook of Environmental Psychology,* Volume 1. New York: Wiley & Sons, 7-40.

Becker, F. D., & Sims, W. (February, 1986). Mastering the baffling art of long-range strategic planning. *Facilities Design and Management*, 68-73.

Brill, M. (1987). Transformation, nostalgia, and illusion about public life and public environments. Keynote address presented at the 18th Annual Conference of the Environmental Design Association, Ottawa, Canada.

Brill, M., Margulis, S., & Konar, E. (1984). *Using office design to increase productivity, Volume 1*. Buffalo, New York: Workplace Design and Productivity, Inc.

Canter, D., & Donald, I. (1987). Environmental psychology in the United Kingdom. In D. Stokols & I. Altman (eds.), *Handbook of Environmental Psychology, Volume 2*. New York: Wiley & Sons, 1281-1310.

Carson, R. (1962). *Silent spring*. Boston: Houghton Mifflin.

Dubos, R. (1965). *Man adapting*. New Haven, CT: Yale University Press.

Ehrlich, P. (1968). *The population bomb*. New York: Ballantine Books.

Francis, M. (1987). Urban open spaces. In E. Zube & G. T. Moore (eds.), *Advances in environment, behavior, and design, Volume 1*. New York: Plenum Press, 71-106.

Franck, K. (1987). Phenomenology, positivism, and empiricism as research strategies in environment-behavior research and in design. In E. Zube & G. T. Moore (eds.), *Advances in environment, behavior, and design, Volume 1*. New York: Plenum Press, 59-67.

Galitz, W. O. (1984). *The office environment: Automation's impact on tomorrow's workplace*. Willow Grove, PA: Administrative Management Society Foundation.

Hardin, G. (1968). The tragedy of the commons. *Science*, 162, 1243-1248.

Hagino, G., Mochizuki, M., & Yamamoto, T. (1987). Environmental psychology in Japan. In D. Stokols & I. Altman (eds.), *Handbook of Environmental Psychology, Volume 2*. New York: Wiley & Sons, 1155-1170.

Herzberg, F. (1966). *Work and the nature of man.* Cleveland, OH: World Publishing.

Jencks, C. (1985). *Towards a symbolic architecture.* New York: Rizzoli International Publications.

Jodelet, D. (1987). The study of people-environment relations in France. In D. Stokols & I. Altman (eds.), *Handbook of Environmental Psychology, Volume 2.* New York: Wiley & Sons, 1171-1193.

Kruse, L., & Graumann, C. F. (1987). Environmental psychology in Germany. In D. Stokols & I. Altman (eds.), *Handbook of Environmental Psychology, Volume 2.* New York: Wiley & Sons, 1195-1225.

Kuller, R. (1987). Environmental psychology from a Swedish perspective. In D. Stokols & I. Altman (eds.), *Handbook of Environmental Psychology, Volume 2.* New York: Wiley & Sons, 1243-1279.

Mannheim, K. (1940). *Man and society in an age of reconstruction.* New York: Harcourt Brace & Company.

Maslow, A. (1962). *Toward a psychology of being.* New York: Van Nostrand.

Mazumdar, S. (1984). Can programming be counter-productive? In *Proceedings of the Fifteenth Annual Conference of the Environmental Design Research Association,* California Polytechnic State University, San Luis Obispo, CA.

Merton, R. K. (1957). *Social theory and social structure.* New York: Free Press.

Michelson, W. (1985). *From sun to sun: Daily obligations and community structure in the lives of employed women and their families.* Totowa, NJ: Rowman & Allanheld.

Moore, G. T. (1987). Environment and behavior research in North America: History, developments, and unresolved issues. In D. Stokols & I. Altman (eds.), *Handbook of Environmental Psychology, Volume 2.* New York: Wiley & Sons, 1359-1410.

Niit, T., Heidmets, M., & Kruusvall, J. (1987). Environmental psychology in the Soviet Union. In D. Stokols & I. Altman (eds.), *Handbook of Environmental Psychology, Volume 2.* New York: Wiley & Sons, 1311-35.

Perez-Gomez, A. (1983). *Architecture and the crisis of modern science.* Cambridge, MA: MIT Press.

Sanchez, E., Wiesenfeld, E., & Cronick, K. (1987). Environmental psychology from a Latin American perspective. In D. Stokols & I. Altman (eds.), *Handbook of Environmental Psychology, Volume 2.* New York: Wiley & Sons, 1337-1357.

Stokols, D. (1981). Group x place transactions: Some neglected issues in psychological research on settings. In D. Magnusson (ed.), *Toward a psychology of situations: An interactional perspective.* Hillsdale, NJ: Lawrence Erlbaum Associates, 441-488.

Stokols, D. (1988). Transformational processes in people-environment relations. In J. McGrath (ed.), *The social psychology of time: New perspectives.* Newbury Park, CA: Sage Publications.

Stokols, D., & Altman, I. (1987). *Handbook of environmental psychology, Volumes 1 & 2*. New York: John Wiley & Sons.

Stringer, P., & Kremer, A. (1987). Environmental psychology in the Netherlands. In D. Stokols & I. Altman (eds.), *Handbook of Environmental Psychology, Volume 2*. New York: Wiley & Sons, 1227-1241.

Thorne, R, & Hall, R. (1987). Environmental psychology in Australia. In D. Stokols & I. Altman (eds.), *Handbook of Environmental Psychology, Volume 2*. New York: Wiley & Sons, 1137-1153.

Tzamir, Y., & Churchman, A. (1984). Knowledge, ethics, and environment: Behavior studies in architectural education. *Environment and Behavior*, 16, 111-126.

Wapner, S. (1987). A holistic, developmental, systems-oriented environmental psychology: Some beginnings. In D. Stokols & I. Altman (eds.), *Handbook of Environmental Psychology, Volume 2*. New York: Wiley & Sons, 1433-1465.

Wicker, A. W. (1987). Behavior settings reconsidered: Temporal stages, resources, internal dynamics, context. In D. Stokols & I. Altman (eds.), *Handbook of Environmental Psychology, Volume 1*. New York: Wiley & Sons, 613-653.

Picture Credits

p. 265   Original illustration by William Becker, including Rod Bull-inspired renderings of carved stones

p. 266   Drawing of the gridded earth by William Becker

p. 269   Adapted by William Becker from a photograph of the original in Charles Hapgood, *Maps of the Ancient Kings*, E. P. Dutton, New York, 1966.

p. 270   Map by Bethe Hagens (left); Piri Re'is fragment adapted from Charles Hapgood, *Maps of the Ancient Sea Kings,* E. P. Dutton, New York, 1966 (right)

p. 272   Map by Bethe Hagens. Rhombic triacontahedron mathematical angle renderings adapted from R. Buckminster Fuller, *Synergetics 2*

p. 274   Map by William Becker. Spherical geometric pattern adapted from R. Buckminster Fuller, *Synergetics 2*

Chapter 21
pp. 308, 310, 311   Drawings by Lawrence Halprin

Chapter 22
p. 319   Photo by Jay Graham

Chapter 23
pp. 323, 325, 328,   Photos by James Swan
331

Index